# THE OLD FARMER'S ALMANAC

CALCULATED ON A NEW AND IMPROVED PLAN FOR THE YEAR OF OUR LORD

Being the 3rd after Leap Year and (until July 4) 247th year of American Independence

FITTED FOR BOSTON AND THE NEW ENGLAND STATES, WITH SPECIAL CORRECTIONS AND CALCULATIONS TO ANSWER FOR ALL THE UNITED STATES.

Containing, besides the large number of Astronomical Calculations and the Farmer's Calendar for every month in the year, a variety of NEW, USEFUL, & ENTERTAINING MATTER.

**ESTABLISHED IN 1792
BY ROBERT B. THOMAS (1766–1846)**

*The moments fly—a minute's gone;
The minutes fly—an hour is run;
The day is fled—the night is here;
Thus flies a week, a month, a year!*

–Author unknown

*Cover illustration by Steven Noble • Original wood engravi...*

The Old Farmer's Almanac • Alm...
P.O. Box 520, Dublin, NH 03444 • 60...

D0032619

# CONTENTS

## 2023 TRENDS
Facts to Ponder and Forecasts to Watch For   6

# "SOMETIMES DRY, SOMETIMES WETTLED"

**H**ello, friends! For the past year or so, we have been doggedly attentive to the mission set forth by our founder, Robert B. Thomas (pictured on the cover): to make this edition, like every previous one, "useful, with a pleasant degree of humor." Indeed, although putting together each Almanac is serious business, if truth be told, we do have a lot of laughs throughout the process—in meetings, in discussions about articles, even when titling stories—and a theme of humor and good cheer has always been present in this book.

Consider, for instance, our Essay Contest. We choose topics that we hope will inspire you to submit your most entertaining tales. Winning entries are often sentimental, but sometimes they are silly—and that's okay. We all need a lift.

Our Anecdotes & Pleasantries are intended to bring smiles or, at least, a good-spirited groan.

Even weather forecasts can have a humorous aspect. *What?* Well, certainly not our state-of-the-art, science-based predictions for the various regions of the continent— these are no laughing matter.

I refer you instead to the other weather predictions, the ones that appear in italic type, vertically, on the Right-Hand Calendar Pages.

These whimsical verses—formulated with as few syllables as possible—contain a modicum of truth: Each month's rhyme is loosely based on our data-driven prognostications, playfully interpreted to capture the character of the season, occasionally with invented words. (What rhymes with "wettled"? See page 139.)

The literary form—called "doggerel"—is considered by many to be low art, but creating it demands a high degree of verbal dexterity and a vivid imagination. Our late colleague, Tim Clark—a wit in his own right—employed both of these memorably across his 42 years of doggereling. (See page 101 for more about Tim.)

"Well-versed" in all things Almanac, Managing Editor Jack Burnett will now be writing this time-honored part of the book with what no doubt will continue to be "a pleasant degree of humor" for long into the future, we hope.

–J. S., June 2022

*However, it is by our works and not our words that we would be judged. These, we hope, will sustain us in the humble though proud station we have so long held in the name of*

*Your obedient servant,*

# 2023 TRENDS

## ON THE FARM

Higher fertilizer costs are spurring more farmers to invest in conservation and soil health practices to get more yield with less cost.

*–Stefan Gailans, research and field crops director, Practical Farmers of Iowa*

### CROPLAND COSTS
*Average rental cost per acre (2021):*
- $35 in Oklahoma
- $331 in California

*Average value per acre (2021):*
- $1,050 in Montana
- $14,800 in New Jersey

### GROWING, ORGANICALLY
- **16,585:** organic farms in the U.S.
- **5.5 million:** acres in use for organic production in the U.S.

**BUZZWORD**
**Grow-cers:** grocery stores that sell produce from on-site indoor farms

- **60,611:** acres on conventional farms in the U.S. that are going organic
*–Organic Survey, 2020*

### FIELD NOTES
- Nonfamily transitions are becoming common, as retiring farmers without a family successor want to ensure that their land goes to a farmer.
*–Darcy Smith, B.C. land-matching program manager, Young Agrarians*

### FARMERS ARE . . .
- selling beef direct-to-consumer and "meat box" subscriptions
*–Caitlyn Lamm, spokesperson, Iowa Farm Bureau Federation*

- offering shares for flours, dry beans, and grains

FOLLOW US: 🇫 ⓟ 🐦 ⓘ

## BY THE NUMBERS

**8.4%** of Canadian farmers have a written succession plan.

**182:** matches made between beginner farmers and farmers with land to spare, under Young Agrarians' British Columbia land-matching program

**$2.8 billion:** value of direct-to-consumer sales for U.S. farms

**1,798,439:** number of small family farms in the U.S. (with gross cash farm income of less than $350,000)

■ joining with other farmers to obtain and distribute larger orders

## FARM TECH IN USE

■ devices that detect emissions from tomato plants indicating whitefly infestations

■ nanoscale sensors inside plant leaves that detect water needs

■ autonomous tractors that take readings of soil quality

## COMING SOON

■ specially bred honeybees that thrive on select diets— artificial nutrition or plants that are prevalent in the region

■ signaling devices that disrupt mating calls of glassy-winged sharpshooters (large leafhopper insects) to keep them from spreading disease in grape vineyards

## ECO-CONSCIOUS FARMERS . . .

■ surround fields with early- and late-blooming flowers to help beneficial insects

■ "potty-train" cows to go in designated areas to control ammonia waste (one farmed cow produces 8 gallons of urine daily)

## PEOPLE ARE TALKING ABOUT . . .

■ milk produced by heritage-breed Guernseys that's high in beta-carotene

■ urban farmers cultivating people's backyards and giving owners produce as rent

## THEY'RE HIRING . . .

■ staff for indoor aeroponic (soilless) farms at public housing developments, where produce is grown year-round for residents

■ urban vertical gardeners who can rappel up tall buildings to tend plants on the buildings' exterior

*(continued)*

'GALA' APPLES

# IN THE GARDEN

We are witnessing the end of the long reign of 'Red Delicious'.
There is a welcome acceptance of apples that are not
solid red, with different flavor profiles, and dwarf varieties.

–*Bob Osborne, author,* Hardy Apples: Growing Apples in Cold Climates *(Firefly Books, 2022)*

### GOOD APPLES
*In-demand varieties:*
- 'Gala' and 'Ambrosia'
- historical apples
- disease-resistant cultivars

### WE'RE FOCUSED ON . . .
- pollinator-friendly, water-wise gardens with plants that are different from our neighbors'.

*–Kathleen Hennessy, chief marketing officer, Axiom*

- feeding the soil microbial life with compost, compost tea, and worm castings.

*–Christy Wilhelmi, author,* Garden Variety *(William Morrow, 2022)*

- turning yards into self-sustaining ecosystems so that there's less work,

### BY THE NUMBERS
**54%** of young adults (ages 18 to 34) would rather go to a garden center than a nightclub.

**48%** of gardeners are planning to start seeds indoors for the first time.

**$2.6 billion:** expected U.S. sales of bird feeders and feed by 2026

more productivity, and more resistance to diseases and pests.

*–Stephanie Rose, founder, Gardentherapy.ca*

- plants that do more: pollinator-friendly, ornamental, and edible, with higher yields.

*–Diane Blazek, executive director, All-America Selections, National Garden Bureau*

- creating greenspace courtyards to connect with nature through garden sanctuaries outdoors or lush, vibrant foliage indoors.

*–Egypt Sherrod, real estate broker and star of HGTV's* Married to Real Estate

*(continued)*

Photo: Eric Yuen/Free Range Stock

FOLLOW US:

# Best Natural Fertilizer On Earth

"Chicken Soup for the Soil® improves your soil by feeding the microbes and supplying all the nutrients most fertilizers neglect."

- Grow higher quality fruits and vegetables with more color, better taste, less bug infestations, and disease
- Contains all the elements in the periodic table (sea nutrients, amino acids, humic, fulvic, and other herbal extracts).
- All natural, toxin free, and bioavailable
- Non-leaching formula/ingredients accumulate over time
- Perfect for gardeners, growers, and farmers

## 64 oz Jug
## 34⁹⁵*
+Free Shipping in USA

*Makes up to 128 gallons with 1 tablespoon per gallon.

*Commercial quantities also available.
Works on pastures and farm. Prices are subject to change.

## 888-394-4454

### SEE ALL OUR PRODUCTS AT:
# www.DrJimZ.com

9

## U.S. GARDENERS' GROWING PASSIONS

- **72%:** flowers
- **66%:** vegetables
- **41%:** houseplants
- **26%:** fruit trees
- **19%:** berries

*–Axiom*

## TOPS IN CROPS

- For Millennials: organic vegetables, herbs, fruit
- For baby boomers: vegetables (not necessarily organic), flowers
- For all gardeners: tomatoes, pumpkins, garlic, squashes, herbs

*–W. Atlee Burpee & Co.*

## TOP INTERESTS WORLDWIDE

- container gardens
- vertical gardens
- composting

## NEW VEGGIE VARIETIES

- 'Armenian Pale' green cucumber, 'Rainbow Candy Crush' hybrid kale, 'Taboo' lettuce, 'Ketchup 'n' Fries' cherry tomato and yellow potato, Fiesta Blend radish

*–Jung Seed Company*

- 'Twister' cauliflower, 'Merlin' hybrid crispy

'MOCHA SWIRL' PEPPERS

cucumber, 'Mocha Swirl' and 'Nibbler Red' sweet peppers, 'Honeoye' strawberry

*–W. Atlee Burpee & Co.*

- 'Prospera' mildew-resistant basil, 'Starstuck' crunchy lettuce blend, 'Enroza' beefsteak tomato

*–Johnny's Selected Seeds*

- 'Berlin Berlicum' carrot, 'Mini-Me' cucumber, 'Bauer' oakleaf lettuce, 'Gum Drop Black' hybrid cherry tomato

*–Park Seed*

## CONTAINMENT TRENDS

- plant containers of different sizes, side-by-

'GUM DROP BLACK' TOMATOES

side, to suggest a wild meadow on balconies, sidewalks, or rooftops

- pairing naturally incompatible plants in nearby containers

## HERE, HERE, HERBALS!

We're growing ingredients for home and body care use . . .

- *For cleaning products:* sage, with infusions of orange peels in vinegar; rosemary, with lemons in alcohol
- *For lotions, salves, lip balms:* lavender, calendula, and rose (with grapeseed or olive oil and melted beeswax)

*–Stephanie Rose*

## MILLENNIALS' #1 GARDENING OBSTACLES

- *For men:* lack of time
- *For women:* lack of money

## HOW'S IT GROWING?

- **16%** of U.S. gardens weren't as successful as growers had hoped.
- **38%** of gardens were very successful.
- **20%** of gardeners do so to lower stress.

*–Axiom*

*(continued)*

FOLLOW US:

> **BUZZWORD**
> **Climatarians:** folks who eat local foods that are in season and avoid plastic packaging

## GOOD EATS

In-store meal advisors are helping shoppers by suggesting plant-based or gluten-free diet-friendly meals.

*–Jo-Ann McArthur, president, Nourish Food Marketing*

### PEOPLE ARE TALKING ABOUT . . .

■ food labels that develop bumps when the food is no longer safe to eat

■ restaurants using robots to prepare food, serve diners, and clean floors and equipment

■ bars serving low- or no alcohol or low-sugar libations

■ ordering "surprise" bags of leftover (usually expensive)

### BY THE NUMBERS

**48%** of Canadians don't buy groceries online because they want to select their own produce.

**63%** of Canadians cook dinner from scratch most days.

**58%** of U.S. consumers would buy imperfect produce for a discount.

food from restaurants and groceries at less than menu/store prices

### FOOD FADS
*Earth-friendly options:*

■ seaweed burgers that sequester carbon

■ vodka made by capturing $CO_2$ from the air

■ skincare goods made from food waste: skin cream from coffee; eye care products from avocado and citrus peels; shower gel from misshapen cucumbers

### MOUTHFULS

■ *U.S. flavor of choice:* **salt**—in sauces, seaweeds, and cocktails; on fries seasoned with furikake (a Japanese condiment)

■ *Canada flavor of choice:* **butter**—on burgers, in kombu (edible kelp); yeast butters; herbal or browned butters in cocktails; buttermilk; butterscotch; nut butters
*–Technomic*

■ *Global food favorite:* egg sandwiches, with homemade sauces

*(continued)*

FOLLOW US:

# YOUR HEALTH OUTLOOK

More people are actively managing their cognitive health.
*–The Hartman Group*

## WE'RE SEEING . . .

■ greater availability of primary care providers such as nurse practitioners, osteopaths, and integrative doctors

■ easier access to health information to share as we choose

*–Raquel Garzon, M.D., president/founder, Revitalize Project*

■ more food-as-medicine treatment plans: "prescriptions" for beans/legumes, whole grains, fruit, vegetables, herbs/spices, and water

*–Kristi Artz, M.D., medical director, Spectrum Health Lifestyle Medicine*

### BY THE NUMBERS

**48%** of U.S. adults say that access to walking, hiking, and biking trails is "very" or "extremely" important.

**58%** of U.S. adults spend more than 30 minutes a day outside.

*–National Recreation and Park Association*

## OUTDOORS IS "IN"

■ We're hiking into forests to work on tree-mounted desks.

■ We're analyzing recordings from wilderness areas to identify Earth's quietest places (those with no more than one human-source sound every 15 minutes).

■ Therapists are booking sessions on nature trails.

■ Doctors will check our time indoors and prescribe time in nature accordingly.

## HEALTHY AT HOME

"Hospitals without walls" will blend inpatient care with community- and home-based care.

*–Tina Wheeler, health care sector leader, Deloitte, LLP*

*(continued)*

**FOLLOW US:**

**gdefy** by Gravity Defyer

# LIVE LIFE PAIN-FREE

**FREE ($50 Value)**
**Corrective Fit Orthotics**
with every shoe purchase
*Excludes sandals.*

## PATENTED VERSOSHOCK® SOLE
### SHOCK ABSORPTION SYSTEM

**85%** LESS KNEE PAIN

**91%** LESS BACK PAIN

**92%** LESS ANKLE PAIN

**75%** LESS FOOT PAIN

In a 2017 double-blind study by Olive View UCLA Medical Center.

## Enjoy the benefits of exercise with GDEFY

✓ Ultimate Comfort
✓ Renewed Energy
✓ Maximum Protection
✓ Improved Posture

---

**gdefy MIGHTY WALK** *$145*

X-WIDE WIDTH AVAILABLE

This product is not intended to treat, cure or prevent any disease.

**Men Sizes** 7.5-15 M/W/XW

- TB9024MGS   Gray
- TB9024MLU   Blue/Black
- TB9024MBL   Black

**Women Sizes** 6-11 M/W/XW

- TB9024FGS   Gray
- TB9024FGP   Salmon/Gray
- TB9024FLP   Black

# $20 OFF
## YOUR ORDER
**Promo Code ND9AQS3**
www.gdefy.com
**Expires January 31, 2024**

Free Exchanges • Free Returns
**60-Day Home Try-on**
Call 1(800) 429-0039

Gravity Defyer Medical Technology Corp.
10643 Glenoaks Blvd. Pacoima, CA 91331

**BBB** ACCREDITED BUSINESS
BBB Rating: A+

VersoShock® U.S Patent #US8,555,526 B2. May be eligible for Medicare reimbursement. $20 off applies to orders of $100 or more for a limited time. Cannot be combined with other offers. 9% CA sales tax applies to orders in California. Shoes must be returned within 60 days in like-new condition for full refund or exchange. Credit card authorization required. See website for complete details.

15

## PEOPLE ARE TALKING ABOUT . . .

■ saunas that collapse to the size of a bookcase or are mobile chair/desk units for working on laptops

■ bedside devices that play soothing sounds when they detect that we're restless

## TAKE A BREATHER

Doctors will recognize lung capacity as a vital sign.

*–Cindy Conlon, J.D., Ph.D., breathing instructor, Northwestern University*

## MOODS, WELL-MANAGED

*People are happier when:*

■ in parks

■ near bodies of water

■ hiking or walking with friends

*–World Happiness Report*

# MONEY MATTERS

People are renegotiating salaries and changing jobs—or even careers.

*–Lisa Hannam, executive editor,* MoneySense

## CUSTOMER RECOGNITION

In the future, stores will be identifying the customer at check-in rather than checkout.

*–Euromonitor International's webinar "Commerce 2040: The Future of the Store in a Digital World"*

## SMART MONEY MOVES

■ downloading data that Web sites have about you, then uploading it to sell elsewhere

■ buying REITs (real estate investment trusts) with properties in your neighborhood

## WORKERS WANT MORE

■ Companies will be competing on who can offer the best lifestyle, not pay alone.

*–Jason Feifer, editor in chief,* Entrepreneur

*In demand:*

■ flexible hours

■ free childcare and education

■ remote work

## REPAIR IS ALL THE RAGE

Planned obsolescence is losing traction, and repair is climbing

*(continued)*

FOLLOW US:

**Struck in 99.9% Fine Silver!**
For the First Time EVER!

**First Legal-Tender Morgans in a Century!**

**VERY LIMITED!**
Sold Out at the Mint!

O PRIVY MARK

*Actual size is 38.1 mm*

# The U.S. Mint Just Struck Morgan Silver Dollars for the First Time in 100 Years!

One of the most revered, most-collected, vintage U.S. Silver Dollars ever, the last Morgan Silver Dollar was last struck for circulation in 1921. Morgans, struck in 90% silver, were the preferred currency of cowboys, ranchers and outlaws and earned a reputation as the coin that built the Wild West.

## Celebrating the 100th Anniversary with Legal-Tender Morgans

Honoring the 100th Anniversary of the last year they were minted, the U.S. Mint struck five different versions of Morgan Silver Dollars in 2021, paying tribute to each of the mints that struck the coin. The coins here honor the historic New Orleans Mint and feature an "O" privy mark, a small differentiating mark. They were minted at the Philadelphia Mint because the New Orleans Mint no longer exists. These beautiful coins are different than the originals because they're struck in 99.9%

fine silver instead of 90% silver, and they were struck using modern technology that enhances the details of the iconic design.

## Very Limited. Sold Out at the Mint!

Production of these gorgeous coins was limited to just 175,000, a ridiculously low number. Not surprisingly, they sold out almost instantly! That means you need to hurry to add these bright, shiny, new legal-tender Morgan Silver Dollars with the New Orleans privy mark, struck in 99.9% PURE Silver, to your collection. Call 1-888-395-3219 to secure yours now. PLUS, you'll receive a BONUS American Collectors Pack, valued at $25, FREE with your order. Call now. These will not last!

**To learn more, call now. First call, first served!**

## FREE SHIPPING!

Limited time only.
Standard domestic shipping only.
Not valid on previous purchases.

the list of consumer priorities.

*–WGSN (formerly Worth Global Style Network)*

■ Companies will be required to rate their products on repairability.

■ Subscription services will offer ongoing appliance repairs for a set fee.

■ Speakers and phones will have modular designs so that separate parts can be replaced.

### TOMORROW'S ECONOMY

■ Companies are realizing that the future of our economy lives in rural America.

*–Rebekah Collinsworth, spokesperson, Center on Rural Innovation*

#### BY THE NUMBERS

**19%** of U.S. adults have made financial decisions based on horoscopes.

**53%** aren't sure how much is in their bank account because they're afraid to check.

**$400:** median amount that people are owed by friends or family

## AROUND THE HOUSE

Architects are building homes with accessible design features—zero-step entry points, full bathrooms on the main floor, and wider doorways—to avoid renovations later.

*–Kelly Martin, M.S., interior design lecturer, Auburn University*

### FUTURE HOMES

■ "iceberg" houses with multilevel basements

■ houses that rotate, for varying views

■ removable roofs on houses (for adding floors later)

### LET THE SUN SHINE IN

We want natural light in skylights, domes, peekaboo doors—for health and wellness and to seem spacious.

*–Egypt Sherrod*

*Popular features . . .*

■ floor-to-ceiling windows

■ oculus (round) windows in hallways

■ patio doors that fold to open an entire wall

■ glass wall dividers

■ walls of windows in kitchens

### TO MAKE AGING EASIER:

■ Houses are being designed for three generations.

*(continued)*

FOLLOW US:

19

- Communities are hiring staff to introduce multi-generational residents to one another.

- Folks are helping older neighbors with chores and errands for reduced rent, while seniors, in turn, help with child care.

## COMING OR HERE . . .
- electric trucks that power owners' homes during outages
- toilets that offer recipes based on an analysis of the user's diet

## THE VALUE OF OLD
- We'll see second-hand furniture tagged with previous owners' stories: how they used pieces and why they gave them up.
- Bathrooms are going really retro, with authentic vintage toilet seats, tanks, and lids.

- Frayed rugs and old couches are being repaired (not replaced).

## STYLE-SETTERS
*In the kitchen . . .*
- mismatched china patterns bought used
- mixed metal faucets, hardware, and light fixtures

*In the bath . . .*
- sound and light systems

### BY THE NUMBERS
**74%** of Americans worry about the smell of their homes.

**76%** of renters would rather own homes.

**2%** of homeowners would rather rent.

**1,000:** minimum number of books for a "home library"

**8 degrees F:** difference in temperature between surrounding air and a roof painted ultra-white (the paint absorbs almost no sunlight)

- voice-operated tubs (you direct the water's depth and temperature)

*In the bedroom . . .*
- wallpapered closets

*In the backyard . . .*
- woodburning "smokeless" fire pits (that double as grills)
- vine-covered pergolas for privacy

## OPEN HOUSES ARE BEING DIVIDED
Open floor plans have fallen out of favor; we are closing off with . . .

- curtains on ceiling tracks
- back-to-back book-shelves or a bookcase backed up to a dresser
- old doors, cut to fit floor-to-ceiling, as partitions
- barn doors in large rooms

*–Anna Ruth Gatlin, Ph.D., interior design assistant professor, Auburn University*

*(continued)*

Photo: denisik11/Getty Images

# 5th Generation Nitric Oxide Breakthrough

# Proven in Studies to Restore Maximum Blood Flow in Minutes

## A newly improved version of America's best-selling male supplement gives older guys the results they enjoyed in their youth

America's best-selling male performance enhancer just got a lot better.

It's the latest breakthrough for nitric oxide – the molecule that makes pleasure possible by increasing blood flow where you need it most.

Nitric oxide (NO) won the Nobel Prize in 1998 for heart health, although it soon became clear NO was the key to satisfying sexual health for men.

And this new discovery increases nitric oxide availability resulting in even quicker, stronger and longer-lasting pleasure.

One double-blind, placebo-controlled study (the "gold-standard" of medical research) involved a group of 60-year-old men. Within minutes of their first dose, their blood flow measurably increased.

"It's amazing," remarks nitric oxide expert and regenerative medicine MD, Dr. Al Sears. "And it's encouraging for millions of men who are looking for support in the bedroom."

### WHY SO MUCH EXCITEMENT?

Despite the staggering amount of money men spend annually on older nitric oxide therapies, there's one well-known problem with them.

They don't always work for everyone. Because if they're not bioavailable, your body can't absorb the nutrients that relax your blood vessels. And that can lead to disappointment and failed intimacy.

Until now, there's never been a reliable solution. But with over two decades of helping men with nitric oxide boosters, Dr. Al Sears discovered that a precise combination of nutrients and amino ac-

ids fix this "glitch," resulting in significantly stronger blood flow.

This led to his NEW "5th Generation" formula called **Primal Max Red**. Taken as a powder mixed in water or juice, **Primal Max Red** contains a huge 9,000 mg per serving. Far more than most other options. It's becoming so popular, it often goes on backorder.

Everyone who takes it reports a big difference. "I have the energy to perform three times in one day, WOW! That has not happened in years. Oh, by the way I am 62," says Jonathan K. from Birmingham, AL.

### HOW IT WORKS

Loss of staying power starts with your blood vessels. Specifically, the inside layer called the endothelium where nitric oxide is made. Nitric oxide is required to expand the blood vessels when the opportunity strikes... This releases a potent rush of blood for satisfying nights and enhanced pleasure.

Here's the bad news. Nitric oxide levels start declining in your 30s. And by age 70, nitric oxide production can drop by as much as 75 percent. This makes supplementing with a reliable nitric oxide booster like **Primal Max Red** essential for every man, regardless of their current age.

There's not enough space here to fully explain how it works, so Dr. Sears will send anyone who orders **Primal Max Red** a free special report that provides all the details, plus tips on how to get the best results.

### FREE BONUS TESTOSTERONE BOOSTER

Every order also gets Dr. Sears'

*A new discovery that increases nitric oxide availability resulting in quicker, stronger and longer-lasting performance.*

testosterone boosting formula **Primal Max Black** for free.

"If you want passionate pleasure, nitric oxide lets you rise to the occasion, and testosterone gives you the drive and stamina," says Dr. Sears. "You get both with **Primal Max Red** and **Primal Max Black**."

### HOW TO GET PRIMAL MAX

To secure free bottles of **Primal Max Black** and get the hot, new **Primal Max Red** formula, buyers should contact the Sears Health Hotline at **1-800-906-4782 TODAY**. "It's not available in retail stores yet," says Dr. Sears. "The Hotline allows us to ship directly to the customer." Dr. Sears feels so strongly about **Primal Max**, all orders are backed by a 100% money-back guarantee. "Just send me back the bottle and any unused product within 90 days from purchase date, and I'll send you all your money back."

Call NOW at **1-800-906-4782** to secure your supply of **Primal Max Red** and free bottles of **Primal Max Black**. Use Promo Code **OFAPMX0822** when you call. Lines are frequently busy, but all calls will be answered!

# OUR ANIMAL FRIENDS

As regional pet specialty stores expand rapidly, big box stores are losing customers, often because of subpar customer service.

*–Phillip Cooper, president, PetIndustryExpert.com*

## PEOPLE ARE TALKING ABOUT . . .

■ insulated homes made from rubber tires for stray city cats

■ pet food refill stations in stores: Shoppers bring reusable containers.

■ canine treats that modify oral bacteria and combat bad breath with a minty smell for hours

■ plant-based dog treats that taste and smell like real meat

## BY THE NUMBERS

**62%** of pet owners say that a pet helps them to exercise.

**83%** of dogs and **17%** of cats have health insurance.

## PET INDUSTRY UPDATE

■ More pet firms are selling to consumers on their Web sites to increase profits and customer loyalty.

## ALL IN THE FAMILY

■ People want portable, adaptable, low-maintenance dog breeds.

*–Brandi Munden, vice president of communications and public relations, American Kennel Club*

■ The American public will be going outside the dog and cat category when selecting a companion animal.

*–Glenn A. Polyn, editor in chief, Pet Age*

*(continued)*

Photo: XiXinXing/Getty Images

FOLLOW US:

# Choose Life
# Grow Young with HGH

From the landmark book Grow Young with HGH comes the most powerful, over-the-counter health supplement in the history of man. Human growth hormone was first discovered in 1920 and has long been thought by the medical community to be necessary only to stimulate the body to full adult size and therefore unnecessary past the age of 20. Recent studies, however, have overturned this notion completely, discovering instead that the natural decline of Human Growth Hormone (HGH), from ages 21 to 61 (the average age at which there is only a trace left in the body) and is the main reason why the body ages and fails to regenerate itself to its 25 year-old biological age.

Like a picked flower cut from the source, we gradually wilt physically and mentally and become vulnerable to a host of degenerative diseases, that we simply weren't susceptible to in our early adult years.

Modern medical science now regards aging as a disease that is treatable and preventable and that "aging", the disease, is actually a compilation of various diseases and pathologies, from everything, like a rise in blood glucose and pressure to diabetes, skin wrinkling and so on. All of these aging symptoms can be stopped and rolled back by maintaining Growth Hormone levels in the blood at the same levels HGH existed in the blood when we were 25 years old.

There is a receptor site in almost every

cell in the human body for HGH, so its regenerative and healing effects are very comprehensive.

Growth Hormone, first synthesized in 1985 under the Reagan Orphan drug act, to treat dwarfism, was quickly recognized to stop aging in its tracks and reverse it to a remarkable degree. Since then, only the lucky and the rich have had access to it at the cost of $10,000 US per year.

The next big breakthrough was to come in 1997 when a group of doctors and scientists, developed an all-natural source product which would cause your own natural HGH to be released again and do all the remarkable things it did for you in your 20's. Now available to every adult for about the price of a coffee and donut a day.

GHR is now available in America, just in time for the aging Baby Boomers and everyone else from age 30 to 90 who doesn't want to age rapidly but would rather stay young, beautiful and healthy all of the time.

The new HGH releasers are winning converts from the synthetic HGH users as well, since GHR is just as effective, is oral instead of self-injectable and is very affordable.

GHR is a natural releaser, has no known side effects, unlike the synthetic version and has no known drug interactions. Progressive doctors admit that this is the direction medicine is seeking to go, to get the body to heal itself instead of employing drugs. GHR is truly a revolutionary paradigm shift in medicine and, like any modern leap frog advance, many others will be left in the dust holding their limited, or useless drugs and remedies.

It is now thought that HGH is so comprehensive in its healing and regenerative powers that it is today, where the computer industry was twenty years ago, that it will displace so many prescription and non-prescription drugs and health remedies that it is staggering to think of.

The president of BIE Health Products stated in a recent interview, "I've been waiting for these products since the 70's. We knew they would come, if only we could stay healthy and live long enough to see them! If you want to stay on top of your game, physically and mentally as you age, this product is a boon, especially for the highly skilled professionals who have made large investments in their education, and experience. Also with the failure of Congress to honor our seniors with pharmaceutical coverage policy, it's more important than ever to take pro-active steps to safeguard your health. Continued use of GHR will make a radical difference in your health, HGH is particularly helpful to the elderly who, given a choice, would rather stay independent in their own home, strong, healthy and alert enough to manage their own affairs, exercise and stay involved in their communities. Frank, age 85, walks two miles a day, plays golf, belongs to a dance club for seniors, had a girl friend again and doesn't need Viagra, passed his driver's test and is hardly ever home when we call - GHR delivers."

HGH is known to relieve symptoms of Asthma, Angina, Chronic Fatigue, Constipation, Lower back pain and Sciatica, Cataracts and Macular Degeneration, Menopause, Fibromyalgia, Regular and Diabetic Neuropathy, Hepatitis, helps Kidney Dialysis and Heart and Stroke recovery.

**For more information or to order call**
**877-849-4777**
**www.biehealth.us**

These statements have not been evaluated by the FDA. Copyright © 2000. Code OFA.

- Municipalities are changing codes to allow miniature goats as pets.

*In-demand pets . . .*

- small mammals—guinea pigs, hamsters, rabbits
- reptiles—bearded dragons, geckos, snakes
- birds

## TOPS IN PET TOYS

- playthings made of firehose material
- chew toys with crannies for dabs of natural nut butters
- recyclable toys (returned for re-manufacturing)

## PAMPERING FOR PAWS

- Doggy day care centers offer rubber floors to ease older pooches' joints.

- Hotels download a guest's pet photos from social media, display the pics in the guest's room, and offer maps to pet-friendly restaurants.

- Realtors appeal to dog owners with videos of a seller's dog "showing" the home—as well as local parks.

- Dating sites match like-minded pet owners ("Should pets sleep in an owner's bed?") or connect dogs with other canines in the area.

## THE BEST PET TECH

- collars with sensors that open pet doors if the pet is near or alert vets if a pet is licking or scratching excessively
- video games through which players take over a doggy day care center and learn about caring for different breeds

## PET AND PEOPLE PERKS

Pet owners will not only take better care of their pets but also expect the flexibility to live, work, travel, and spend more time with them.

*–Steve Feldman, president, Human Animal Bond Research Institute*

*The trends . . .*

- vests with metal spikes and Kevlar or nylon whiskers to prevent dogs from being carried away by coyotes or eagles
- companies that hire people to walk employees' dogs, reserve space for the dogs at meetings, and set up dog-free zones for allergy sufferers

*(continued)*

FOLLOW US:

■ in electric campers that we maneuver remotely to change campsites or hitch up to a tow vehicle

■ in vehicles that warn of items left behind or request that rubbish be removed

### TECH FOR THE TIMES

■ Autonomous autos drop passengers at a designated spot in a lot, then park elsewhere and return for them when needed.

## CULTURE

Apps will pair vision-impaired people with sighted volunteers for assistance in getting around urban areas.

### IT'S A TREE COUNTRY

■ We're renting potted Christmas trees to be returned to the nursery after the holidays.

■ Cities are mapping their trees' locations online, with weeding and watering times.

■ App tools measure trees' rainwater over a month, and people commit to watering trees regularly.

■ Scientists are mixing the DNA of ancient giant sequoias and redwoods and planting the disease-resistant seeds.

■ Municipalities are planting shade trees in yards at no charge if residents agree to water them.

### WE'RE ON THE MOVE . . .

■ in vintage hot rods and roadsters with electric power trains

■ in older cars retrofitted with smart technology

### BY THE NUMBERS

**$50 billion:** expected growth of air taxi market over the next 5 years

**300 miles:** range per charge of an all-electric pickup truck

**79%** of us want to work from elsewhere (not home or office)

**10:** online accounts the average American can not access, monthly, due to forgotten passwords

Photo: Prostock-Studio/Getty Images

FOLLOW US:

■ Robots are taught via photos to recognize cigarette butts and remove them from beaches.

*On the horizon . . .*

■ loud devices that will make waves to push toxic particles into the atmosphere and leave healthier air below

■ trucks that will store exhaust on board to offload later and/or store underground

■ speakers that will emit sound waves to block street noise from apartments

## GROUP PROJECTS

■ Volunteers are collecting discarded glass bottles to be crushed into sand and used as construction material.

## SMART IDEAS

■ signs on town benches that invite people to sit and chat

■ compilations of daily date-stamped 1-second videos, shot over months or years

■ hotel guest rooms used as workspaces during office hours

## FASHION

Demand for all-natural eco-materials—from mushroom fabrics to pineapple leather—will spark new collaborations between farmers and fashion houses.

*–Skyler Hubler, senior cultural strategist, TBWA\Worldwide*

## TODAY'S TRAPPINGS

■ paint-flecked vintage painters' overalls or clothes and shoes with newly splattered paint

### BUZZWORDS
**Farm-to-closet:** clothing made by apparel companies that invest in regenerative farming

■ workout garb with weights sewn into the fabric

■ hiking boots made from regenerative (recycled) leather or with outsoles that can be removed and recycled

## THE LOOKS FOR WOMEN

■ mismatched clothes: striped shirts with flowered pants or *(continued)*

skirts and blouses with same-color polka dots

- bib overalls
- leather sandals, with cotton ankle socks

## THE LOOKS FOR MEN

- Western: ornate cowboy boots, straight-cut jeans, snap-front shirts
- single-color outfits: pink, beige, crimson, or emerald

- cashmere baseball caps in navy, gray, or black
- black leggings with sport coats

## SEW NICE CLOTHES, WITH . . .

- knitwear with scannable tags that tell the story of the sheep that produced the wool (e.g., when they were last shorn, whether they had lambs, etc.)
- "yo-yo" guarantees: the option to return jeans for a larger or smaller size in the future (the denim is resold or recycled)
- guaranteed repairs for the life of a garment
- compostable or water-soluble packaging
- on-demand manufacturing, with discounts for orders that can wait

## SECOND ACTS

- new and used garments placed together in ads and on store racks
- used clothing sold by the pound
- secondhand clothing for sale on supermarket shelves

## IN DEMAND BY ALL

- mosquito-proof fabrics
- flax and hemp cloth
- human hair "yarn" textiles ■

## BY THE NUMBERS

**31%** of Americans never want to wear a button-down shirt or dress pants again.

**10%** would take a pay cut rather than have to get dressed for work every day.

**60%** think that we should know the materials used in a garment.

**38%** know the materials used in their garments.

**23%** repair their clothing.

**$51 billion:** estimated value of secondhand clothing market in 2023 (up from **$24 billion** in 2019)

FOLLOW US:

'TABASCO' PEPPERS RATE BETWEEN 30,000 AND 50,000 ON THE SCOVILLE SCALE OF HEAT LEVELS.

# TURN UP
# THE HEAT!

## BY DANISE COON

C hile peppers span centuries and cultures. They originated as small, round, berrylike fruit on wild vining plants in the Amazon rain forest between Bolivia and Brazil thousands of years ago. Indigenous peoples gathered and later cultivated the peppers, and birds helped to disperse the seeds. Through natural and human selection, every size, shape, and color of chile that we enjoy today originated from these tiny, very hot fruit.

*(continued)*

'AJI'

'BHUT JOLOKIA'

HABANERO

'NUMEX BIG JIM'

'ROCOTO'

'TRINIDAD MORUGA SCORPION'

## HOT STUFF FIVE WAYS

There are five species of domesticated chiles:

• *Capsicum annuum* houses most of the more commonly used peppers, including bell. Most peppers are sweet or hot, the latter being the type that produce capsaicin. Bell peppers do not produce capsaicin and thus are considered sweet.

Also in this group are the serrano, cherry, jalapeño, and famous New Mexican–type pepper known by many

> **DID YOU KNOW?**
> Store-bought pepperoni and other red meats, makeup, fish and canary foods, and many other products contain the natural coloring agent extracted from red chiles. If you use patches or cream to relieve muscle aches, you'll find that their effective ingredient is likely to be capsaicin extracted from chiles.

as the Hatch chile, not to be confused with its Anaheim counterpart.

These two names— Hatch and Anaheim— are almost misnomers in the world of chiles. "Hatch" pepper is not an actual variety; varieties such as 'NuMex Big Jim', 'NuMex Sandia' ("NuMex" indicates that the fruit is a hybrid), and 'New Mexico 6-4' are grown in New Mexico's Hatch Valley. The Anaheim pepper, grown in Anaheim, California, is another type of New

Mexican pepper. A farmer named Emilio Ortega is credited with having brought seeds from the New Mexican pepper to Anaheim, where it thrived. After years of cultivation in this area, it has become its own variety.

• *C. chinense* includes some of the hottest chiles in the world, including the habanero and the Scotch bonnet, as well as 'Trinidad Moruga Scorpion' and 'Bhut Jolokia'; the last two are known as "superhots," with Scoville Heat Unit counts above 1 million. (The Scoville Heat Unit is a measurement on the eponymous scale invented by a chemist named Wilbur Scoville. The higher the number of Scoville Heat Units assigned, the hotter the pepper is. Today, liquid chromatography is used to detect molecules of

## NATURE'S SEED-SAVERS

Birds are the natural disseminators of chiles. Unlike mammals, birds do not have receptors in their mouths or on their tongue to feel the burn from capsaicin. Birds can eat a lot of very hot chiles and pass the seeds intact through their digestive systems; mammals' digestive systems crush the seed and its embryo. Scientists believe that capsaicin—the alkaloid that gives chiles their distinctive heat—evolved in chiles to keep mammals from eating them.

capsaicin and give each type of chile its own measurement value.)

• *C. baccatum* includes the 'Aji', which is mainly grown and used in South America.

• 'Tabasco' peppers, from which Tabasco sauce is made, are *C. frutescens*.

• *C. pubescens* includes the 'Rocoto' and 'Manzano', both stuffing peppers used mainly in Peru and Chile.

## GROWING HOT OR HOTTER

Chiles are relatively easy to grow and can thrive in most hardiness zones. However, gardeners in Zones 1a through 3b and most of Canada should start seedlings indoors to allow from 120 to 150 days to harvest for most *C. annuum* and 150 to 180 days for most *C. chinense*; the growing times for all

| Anaheim Bell Cherry Hatch | Jalapeño Serrano | 'Aji' 'Manzano' 'Rocoto' 'Tabasco' | Habanero Scotch Bonnet | 'Bhut Jolokia' 'Trinidad Moruga Scorpion' |

other species of chiles fall in between 120 and 180 days.

Most *C. annuum* seeds will germinate in 10 to 14 days in a fine seedling mix that is kept moist (not soggy). *C. chinense* typically needs 16 to 28 days to germinate. Using bottom heat can reduce germination time for all chile seeds.

Most varieties of chile peppers can be grown in full sun in raised beds, directly in ground, or in pots. Use well-draining soil that is high in organic matter and has a neutral pH. (It is difficult to grow chiles in clay soil, which must be amended for success.) Apply a well-balanced fertilizer every 2 weeks during the active growing season. Chiles prefer moist soil that is allowed to dry slightly between waterings; the roots of chile plants can not tolerate wet or soggy conditions.

Harvest chiles at the ripe green stage or the fully ripe stage, which can be red, yellow, orange, brown, white, or any shade in between.

Freshly harvested chiles can be used raw in salads, stews, soups, or sauces, except for the long, green, New Mexican chiles, which must be roasted so that their thick outer skin can be peeled off. (This roasting process is a cultural event in New Mexico that runs from mid-August through September, during the green chile harvest season.) Chiles can be used fresh or dried.

**CHILE PEPPER *RISTRA***

## WELCOME SIGNS

In New Mexico, dried, red, New Mexican-type chiles are used to make the iconic *ristra* that many people hang on their front door as a "Welcome" sign or in the kitchen to be used in cooking or for decoration.

To make a *ristra,* use string to tie together clusters of three to five red, ripe (not dried), New Mexican-type chiles with the stem on. Tie each cluster to a 3- to 4-foot double strand of string. Continue tying peppers together in clusters and then onto the string, being sure to keep a little space between the clusters, until you have reached the desired length. It takes about 130 to 150 chiles to make a 2½-foot *ristra.* ∎

---

**Danise Coon** is a native New Mexican and research associate for the New Mexico State University Extension Plant Sciences Department. She has more than 20 years of experience in chile pepper science and has helped to develop more than a dozen varieties of chiles for home gardeners and high-scale production.

# THE OLD FARMER'S GUIDE TO

## SEEDS, PLANTS, AND BULBS

### Breck's
*Direct to you from Holland since 1818*

Gardeners have trusted Breck's for more than two centuries. We offer affordable, top-quality Dutch bulbs, perennials, and more.

**Brecks.com**

### Park Seed Company
Plant superior seeds, grow more delicious food. *Shop exclusive Whopper seeds plus 1,100 varieties of organic, heirloom, non-GMO seeds for successful growing.* Direct to you since 1865.

**ParkSeed.com**

### Sow True Seed
*Open-pollinated Heirloom & Organic Seeds*

With 500 varieties of vegetable, herb and flower seeds, we have proudly supported food security and seed diversity since 2009.

**SowTrueSeed.com**
**828-254-0708**

### Burgess Seed & Plant Co.
*Your one-stop garden shop*

Celebrating over 100 years of serving American gardeners, we offer a wide range of plants, seeds, bulbs, and other supplies at value prices.

**EBurgess.com**

### Totally Tomatoes
*We Totally Love Tomatoes!*
See our complete catalog of seeds and plants online, including tomatoes, peppers, herbs, and much more. Take 15% Off with code: ALMANAC23

**TotallyTomatoes.com**
**800-345-5977**

### Earth-friendly Lawn & Garden Solutions
The original partner for an eco-friendly lifestyle, Gardens Alive! offers products and advice rooted in nature and tested by gardeners.

**GardensAlive.com**

39

## PICK YOUR PERFECT

BY
DOREEN G.
HOWARD

WITH
ALMANAC
EDITORS

# PERENNIALS

### HOW TO ENJOY CAREFREE, LONG-LASTING COLOR UNDER MOST CLIMATIC CONDITIONS IN THE U.S. AND CANADA

When you plant a flowering perennial, you expect it to perform magnificently year after year, with little or no attention, right? But will it? Maybe. Put that plant in a climate that it doesn't like—and watch out! It is liable to become finicky and attract diseases, refuse to flower, or even rot in the ground. Here's why: Local soil, temperature range, and rainfall can make or break a perennial. As you plan your garden, take note of the climatic conditions in your area and seek native or adapted flowers.

The areas here are based broadly on our weather regions; gardeners in Alaska and Hawaii may find options for micro-climatic conditions. Also, consider your immediate vicinity. To learn about new varieties developed to withstand the rigors of your climate, visit your local garden center.

The plants listed are chosen for long bloom, cutting, beauty, color en masse, or ease of growing; some fit more than one category. *(continued)*

**WHEN PERENNIALS BECOME ESTABLISHED, MAINTENANCE IS MINIMAL: A LITTLE FERTILIZER ONCE OR TWICE A YEAR, AN OCCASIONAL PRUNING, AND THINNING EVERY COUPLE OF YEARS.**

**1** NEW ENGLAND ASTER

**5** OBEDIENT PLANT

2 BUTTERFLY WEED

3 JOE PYE WEED

4 RUSSIAN SAGE

6 DELPHINIUM

7 CUTLEAF CONEFLOWER

8 WOOD LILY

# GARDENING

## 1. THE NORTHEAST

Gardeners in New England, the Upper Great Lakes, and eastern Canada experience a range of weather extremes. Winters are cold and summers are cool to warm, so cold tolerance is a must. Gardeners are advised to pay close attention to zone recommendations; if a plant is borderline, it probably won't make it. More reliable are tough native perennials or plants that originated in cold climates or perennials that have deep or spreading root systems; these can regenerate from root bits that don't die in deep freezes.

- 'Purple Dome' New England aster* *(Symphyotrichum novae-angliae)*
- Fern-leaf bleeding heart* *(Dicentra eximia)*
- Garden phlox*: pink, purple, and white *(Phlox paniculata)*
- Musk mallow *(Malva moschata)*

FERN-LEAF BLEEDING HEART

GARDEN PHLOX

MUSK MALLOW

OX EYE DAISY

BLACK-EYED SUSAN

PURPLE MEXICAN SAGE

## 2. THE MID-ATLANTIC/OHIO VALLEY

Throughout this area, native perennials such as black-eyed Susan stretch endlessly across fields. Savvy gardeners fill their perennial beds with these; some display them proudly on their vehicles: In Virginia, some auto license plates feature native flowers.

- Butterfly weed* *(Asclepias tuberosa)*
- Ox eye daisy *(Leucanthemum vulgare)*
- Black-eyed Susan* *(Rudbeckia hirta)*
- Purple Mexican sage *(Salvia leucantha)*          (continued)

*Indicates a native plant.*

LENTEN ROSE

JAPANESE ANEMONE

SWAMP SUNFLOWER

## 3. THE DEEP SOUTH

Gardeners in this area have to contend with mild winters, which is problematic for many perennials because most of them require a few months of dormancy. Perennials can look different in the South: The plants are small—the heat beats them down—and they tend to be shorter than they might be elsewhere. The bloom period is short, too—with luck, about 1 to 2 weeks.

- Joe Pye weed*
  (*Eutrochium purpureum*)
- Lenten rose
  (*Helleborus orientalis*)
- Swamp sunflower*
  (*Helianthus angustifolius*)
- 'Honorine Jobert' Japanese anemone (*Anemone* x *hybrida*)

## 4. THE MIDWEST/GREAT PLAINS/PRAIRIES

The Midwest and contiguous areas north into Canada are famous for arctic winds in January and withering heat waves in July. Plants have to be both cold- and heat-tolerant or be protected. Many gardeners use their house as a thermal sink (absorbing heat during the day and radiating it back to the plants at night). To survive the severe winters, perennials must be heavily mulched with porous materials such as hay or evergreen boughs. This shields the plants and soil from the sun, prevents ground thaw, and allows air circulation. In the summer, mulch with denser materials, such as shredded leaves or wood chips, to cool the soil and prevent evaporation. Put heat-sensitive perennials in beds that receive afternoon shade.

- Russian sage (*Perovskia atriplicifolia*)
- 'Magnus' purple coneflower*
  (*Echinacea purpurea*)
- 'Autumn Joy' sedum
  (*Hylotelephium* [aka *Sedum*] *spectabile*)
- Perennial sweet pea (*Lathyrus latifolius*)

*(continued)*

PURPLE CONEFLOWER

PERENNIAL SWEET PEA

SEDUM

Photos: 3. from top: OnTheRunPhoto/Getty Images; DutchlightNetherlands/Getty Images; mauribo/Getty Images.
4. clockwise from top: Meindert van der Haven/Getty Images; seven75/Getty Images; Whiteway/Getty Images.

# FIREWOOD ALERT!

### You have the power to protect forests and trees!

# BUY IT WHERE YOU BURN IT.

Pests like the invasive emerald ash borer can hitchhike in your firewood. You can prevent the spread of these damaging insects and diseases by following these firewood tips:

▶ Buy locally harvested firewood at or near your destination.

▶ Buy certified heat-treated firewood ahead of time, if available.

▶ Gather firewood on site when permitted.

## What might be in your firewood?

**SPONGY MOTH\*** is a devastating pest of oaks and other trees. Moths lay tan patches of eggs on firewood, campers, vehicles, patio furniture — anything outside! When these items are moved to new areas, this pest gets a free ride.

**SPOTTED LANTERNFLY** sucks sap from dozens of tree and plant species. This pest loves tree-of-heaven but will feed on black walnut, white oak, sycamore, and grape. Like the spongy moth, this pest lays clusters of eggs on just about any dry surface, from landscaping stone to firewood!

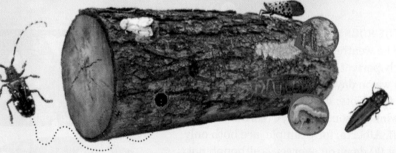

**ASIAN LONGHORNED BEETLE** will tunnel through, and destroy, over 20 species of trees — especially maple trees. The larvae of this beetle bore into tree branches and trunks, making it an easy pest to accidentally transport in firewood.

**EMERALD ASH BORER** — the infamous killer of ash trees — is found in forests and city trees across much of the eastern and central United States. This insect is notoriously good at hitching rides in infested firewood. Don't give this tree-killing bug a ride to a new forest, or a new state!

DONTMOVEFIREWOOD.org

This graphic is for illustrative purposes only. Many of these pests will only infest certain types of trees, making it very unlikely for a single log to contain all species as shown.

Visit dontmovefirewood.org for more information.

\*Spongy moth was formerly named "gypsy moth"

*Indicates a native plant.*

BEARDED IRIS

YARROW

WORMWOOD

### 5. TEXAS/OKLAHOMA

This area's temperate spring sometimes stretches into June, when extreme heat then overtakes the summer months. To cool the soil, many gardeners top all of their beds with plenty of mulch in the belief that any perennial does better with it. Heat-resistant varieties and native plants that thrive in hot, dry areas are recommended.

- Obedient plant* *(Physostegia virginiana)*
- German bearded iris *(Iris germanica)*
- 'Paprika' yarrow *(Achillea millefolium)*
- 'Powis Castle' wormwood *(Artemisia arborescens)*

### 6. THE ROCKY MOUNTAINS

The weather in the mountains is nearly perfect for many perennials, with warm days and cool nights in the summer. Note: *nearly* perfect. The growing seasons in Vail, Colorado, and Banff, Alberta, for example, are both only about 90 days, on average—although not the same days. The first fall freeze comes to Vail around September 5; Banff's first freeze arrives around August 19. Beware of plants that promise early- and late-season color.

- 'Magic Fountains' delphinium *(Delphinium elatum)*
- Iceland poppy *(Papaver nudicaule)*
- Colorado columbine* *(Aquilegia caerulea)*
- 'Lami Dark Purple' dead nettle *(Lamium maculatum)* *(continued)*

ICELAND POPPY

COLORADO COLUMBINE

DEAD NETTLE

 Photos: **5.** clockwise from top left: cjmckendry/Getty Images; Jennifer Yakey-Ault/Getty Images; nickkurzenko/Getty Images. **6.** from top: constantgardener/Getty Images; Linda Jo Heilman/Getty Images; Bluestone Perennials.

# CoQ10's Failure Leaves Millions Wanting

## Use this Pill to Supercharge Your Brain and Think Better than Ever

Millions of Americans take the supplement known as CoQ10. It's the "jet fuel" that supercharges your cells' power generators, known as mitochondria.

As you age, you have fewer mitochondria than you did when you were young. In fact, by age 67, you have just 20% of the mitochondria you had at age 25. But if you're taking CoQ10, there's something important you should know.

As powerful as CoQ10 is, there is a critical thing it fails to do... It can't create new mitochondria to replace the ones you lost.

### Taking CoQ10 is not enough

"There's a little-known NASA nutrient that multiplies the number of new power generators in your cells by up to 55%," says Dr. Al Sears, medical director of the Sears Institute for Anti-Aging Medicine in Royal Palm Beach, Florida. "Science once thought this was impossible. But now you can maintain a youthful brain and body again."

"I tell my patients the most important thing I can do is increase their 'health span.' This is the length of time you can live with all your youthful abilities and faculties intact."

### Multiply the "Power Generators" in Your Cells

Dr. Sears recently released an energy-supporting supplement based on this NASA nutrient that has become so popular, he's having trouble keeping it in stock.

Dr. Sears is the author of over 500 scientific papers on anti-aging and recently spoke at the Palm Beach Health & Wellness Festival featuring Dr. Oz and special guest Suzanne Somers. Thousands of people listened to Dr. Sears speak on his anti-aging breakthroughs and attended his book signing at the event.

Medical professionals as well as the general public were astonished to hear about the newly discovered nutrient that multiplies mitochondria... Shattering the limitations of traditional CoQ10 supplements.

### Why Mitochondria Matter

A single cell in your body can contain between 200 to 2,000 mitochondria on average, with the "energy hungry" organs like the heart and brain having hundreds of thousands. These metabolically active organs are the first to feel threatened when mitochondria decline.

But because of natural aging, stress, and poor diet, these power generators produce less and less energy over time. In fact, the Mitochondria Research Society reports 50 million U.S. adults notice more intense, age-related changes because of aging mitochondria.

Common ailments often associated with aging — like memory loss, declining vision, and fatigue — can all be connected to a decrease in mitochondria.

### Birth of New Mitochondria

Dr. Sears combined the most powerful form of CoQ10 available — called ubiquinol — with a unique, newly discovered natural compound called PQQ that has the remarkable ability to grow new mitochondria. Together, the two powerhouses are now available in a supplement called **Ultra Accel** II.

Discovered by a NASA probe in space dust, PQQ (Pyrroloquinoline quinone) stimulates something called "mitochondrial biogenesis" — a unique process that actually boosts the number of healthy mitochondria in your cells.

In a study published in the Journal of Nutrition, mice fed PQQ grew a staggering number of new mitochondria, showing an increase of more than 55% in just eight weeks.

The mice with the strongest mitochondria showed few signs of aging — even when they were the equivalent of 80 years old.

### Science Stands Behind the Power of PQQ

Biochemical Pharmacology reports that PQQ is up to 5,000 times more efficient in sustaining energy production than common antioxidants.

"With the PQQ in **Ultra Accel** II, I have energy I never thought possible at my age," says Colleen R., one of Dr. Sears' patients. "I am in my 70s but feel

**NASA-discovered nutrient is stunning the medical world by activating more youthful energy, vitality and health than CoQ10.**

40 again. I think clearly, move with real energy and sleep like a baby."

The demand for this supplement is so high, Dr. Sears is having trouble keeping it in stock. "My patients tell me they feel better than they have in years. This is ideal for people who are feeling or looking old and run down... or for those who are tired or growing more forgetful. It surprises many you can support a long and robust health span simply by adding this simple routine of taking **Ultra Accel** II every day."

"The most rewarding aspect of practicing medicine is watching my patients get the joy back in their lives. **Ultra Accel** II sends a wake-up call to every cell in their bodies... And they actually feel young again."

### How to Get Ultra Accel

To secure the hot, new **Ultra Accel** formula, buyers should contact the Sears Health Hotline at **1-800-714-0700 TODAY**. "It's not available in retail stores yet," says Dr. Sears. "The Hotline allows us to ship directly to the customer." Dr. Sears feels so strongly about **Ultra Accel**, all orders are backed by a 100% money-back guarantee. "Just send me back the bottle and any unused product within 90 days from purchase date, and I'll send you all your money back."

Call NOW at **1-800-714-0700** to secure your supply of **Ultra Accel**. Use Promo Code **OFAUA0822** when you call. Lines are frequently busy, but all calls will be answered!

# GARDENING

## 7. THE SOUTHWEST

Here plants have to survive with little or no water and live in the adobe clay of coastal areas or thin sandy soil of interior deserts. Instead of arguing with the land, gardeners are advised to make peace with it by planting only what will grow easily. Any plant that doesn't need rich, amended soil or abundant water will thrive in the hot, dry Southwest. Look for perennials labeled "Xeriscape" or "native."

- Cutleaf coneflower* *(Rudbeckia laciniata)*
- Blanket flower* *(Gaillardia pinnatifida)*
- Bee balm* *(Monarda)*
- Harebell* *(Campanula rotundifolia)*

HELLEBORE

ORANGE SEDGE

TREE MALLOW

## 8. THE NORTHWEST

Plants bloom 2 to 3 weeks longer in the Pacific Northwest than they do elsewhere—but they also tend to suffer from too much rain in winter. Gardeners here lose more plants to root rot than to winter cold. One solution is to create mini-berms on which to plant: Spread a 12- to 18-inch-thick layer of sand on the ground and top it with another 12 inches of garden soil. With the improved drainage, your perennials should be about 20 percent larger than normal. Given that outcome, allow more space between plants than is recommended because they get much bigger.

- Wood lily* *(Lilium philadelphicum)*
- Hellebore *(Helleborus foetidus)*
- 'Barnsley' tree mallow *(Lavatera thuringiaca)*
- Orange sedge *(Carex flagellifera)* ∎

BLANKET FLOWER

BEE BALM

HAREBELL

**Doreen G. Howard,** who gardened in nearly every climate zone in the United States, was a frequent contributor to Almanac publications.

Photos: **7.** from top: IngaL/Getty Images; Hana Richterova/Getty Images; Dougall_Photography/Getty Images. **8.** clockwise from top: emer1940/Getty Images; Dobies; John Caley/Getty Images.

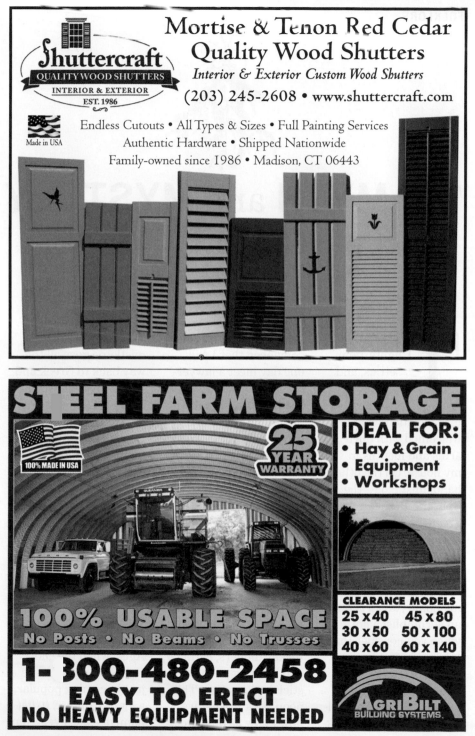
49

# The **MYTH** and **MYSTERY** of **MISTLETOE**

## Or, would you stand under a "dung twig"?

### BY KAREN BERTELSEN • ILLUSTRATIONS BY TIM ROBINSON

Twinkling lights, poinsettias, and shortbread cookies are all Christmas traditions that are welcomed with open arms and mouths in my house. On the other hand, mistletoe—the Spin-the-Bottle of the greenery world—has never once hung from any of my doorways. I will squash several full-size pine trees into my home (which is quite an accomplishment when you consider that I do not in fact live in a national park), and I bake enough gingerbread to build entire villages. I watch Hallmark holiday movies until I'm convinced that I will one day meet a lawyer-turned-rancher who has a side hobby of making artisan Christmas ornaments out of wood that he carved from the tree planted by his now-deceased parents.

But I don't hang mistletoe. The lovely traditions with which so many of us grew up have their evergreen-scented roots in the Victorian era. The 1800s brought us Christmas trees and popularized turkey dinners, caroling, and hanging poop on a stick in doorways. This poop stick is what we now know as mistletoe.

The history of mistletoe goes all the way back to Greek and Norse mythology, with a lengthy stay in paganism before seeping into Christianity. In fact, the bubbling cauldron of exaggerations, myths, and misleading information surrounding mistletoe goes so far back that I'm afraid I'm going to have to stick with the boring facts as I tell the tale of this festive foliage.

**THE NAME**
In the early Middle Ages, when the Old English language was just becoming popular, a lot of stuff had to get named—like, everything

in the world had to be assigned a word. It took me 2 months to name my cat, so I'm having a really hard time imagining the undertaking of naming every single thing in existence.

Whoever got put in charge of naming mistletoe decided to name it based on the way it grows. It was widely believed that mistletoe was planted by birds who ate its berries and then pooped them out onto tree branches, which is where mistletoe grows— on trees. So, the guy naming mistletoe called it "misteltan," which gets its meaning from the Anglo-Saxon words *mistel* (meaning dung) and *tan* (meaning twig). This, of course, translates to "dung twig," and since nothing says "let's make out" more than poop sticks, the tradition of kissing under mistletoe was born.

## THE KISSING

The custom of kissing beneath the mistletoe first became popular among the serving class in England before it was adopted by the upper class. Actually—you

know what?—let me rephrase that: It was popular among the men in both classes. The women, I'm sure, would have preferred to eat their own hair than stand anywhere near the mistletoe. First of all, they'd probably already endured a really long day of avoiding unwanted kissing, and, second of all, according to the "rules," anywhere mistletoe was hung, a man was given the privilege of kissing any woman he wanted to. Lest you think that it

seems like the privilege was a teensy bit off balance in this scenario, you can take comfort in knowing that the woman was given the privilege of saying no. But if she did so, it was said that she would endure a lifetime of bad luck, not marry within that year, and essentially set herself up to be a warty spinster till the end.

## THE PLANT

This plant that we've all come to know as the symbol of love, fertility, and smooches (you know, the

If you end up under the mistletoe in Europe, be sure to keep your lips closed and have handy a medical kit stocked with all of your basic poison antidote essentials.

poop twig) is a real-life horror show. The plant is so terrifying that we should really be associating it with Halloween or the scariest holiday of them all—Black Friday.

There are more than 1,300 species of mistletoe that grow on every continent other than Antarctica, but that's not the scary part. The real problem is that the mistletoe species that we associate with kissing is a parasitic or semi-parasitic plant that germinates on tree branches before attaching itself to the circulatory system of its host and sucking the life out of it. Merry Christmas.

You might be wondering how those seeds really get on the branches to germinate. Many of them do in fact land there after being pooped out by birds that have eaten mistletoe berries, but certain mistletoe species have another way of seed-spreading. When the moment is right and their seeds are ready, these mistletoes will projectile-vomit their seeds at almost 60 miles per hour across the landscape, infecting whatever tree might happen to be in their path.

## THE POISON

Oh. And if you're in Europe, it's poisonous. Therefore, if you do

The holidays are a time for hoping that the next year will be as good or better than the last. A time for happiness and family and, yes, maybe even standing under the mistletoe.

willingly end up under the mistletoe, be sure to keep your lips closed and have handy a medical kit stocked with all of your basic poison antidote essentials. The American variety of mistletoe might give you a little stomach distress, but that's about it.

**BUT WAIT!**
Ready for this seemingly unredeemable plant to parasitically attach itself to that spot in your heart reserved for love? Mistletoe can kill cancer cells. This has been proven only in test tubes, but doctors have been prescribing mistletoe extract for cancer patients in the United Kingdom and elsewhere in Europe for decades. Mistletoe's potential for killing cancer has been the subject of study in a clinical trial at Johns Hopkins University. This remedy hasn't been approved by the U.S. Food and Drug Administration or even 100% proven in patients, but it offers hope.

And the holidays are a time for hope. A time for hoping that the next year will be as good or better than the last. A time for happiness and family and, yes, maybe even standing under the mistletoe. Doing so may not be for just anyone, you understand, but if that lawyer/rancher happens to be walking down the hall with a wooden ornament in his hands, for instance . . . well, this might not be such a bad tradition after all. ∎

**Karen Bertelsen** of Hamilton, Ontario, is the founder of the lifestyle blog The Art of Doing Stuff.

# Facts and Lore

- There are more than 1,300 species of mistletoe in the world. Dwarf species are native to the western United States and Canada.
- Birds that consume (and excrete) mistletoe berries include cedar waxwings, American robins, hermit thrushes, mourning doves, and eastern bluebirds.
- The great purple, thicket, and Johnson's hairstreak butterflies live in and on mistletoe.
- Norse (ancient Scandinavian) mythology holds that the plant symbolizes love and that no harm should come to those who stand underneath it.
- Ancient Druids (Celtic cultures) hung mistletoe over doorways to ward off evil spirits during winter solstice festivities.
- American writer Washington Irving (1783–1859) popularized the European custom of kissing under the mistletoe among early Americans by referring to it in his short story "Christmas Eve" in 1820.
- Most mistletoe species will thrive on almost any deciduous tree, but they flourish on the soft wood of old apple trees.
- The branches of mature parasitic mistletoe growing on a tree can sometimes take the shape of a basket as much as 5 feet wide and up to 50 pounds in weight. Such an infestation, sometimes called a "witch's broom," can kill its host tree. -K. B.

55

# WHY BIRDS FEATHER THEIR NESTS

## ...AND OTHER SECRETS OF AVIAN ABODES

### BY KATHERINE SWARTS

Believe it or not, birds do not live in nests as people live in houses. Most wild birds do not have permanent homes: They move around as suits their situation. Nests are built not as long-term homes but as nurseries where eggs and babies stay until the young birds can survive in the open.

Except for egg-incubating parents and families with nestlings, birds rarely sleep in their nests, either; in fact, few songbirds return to a nest after the young can fly. (One reason: The "nursery" can accumulate excessive wear and tear. Some birds, such as mourning doves, build flimsy nests that barely hold together for the 3-week incubate-and-brood period.) A few larger species do reuse nests, but only during actual nesting seasons, returning year after year to build fresh "egg sections" on top. Some bald eagle

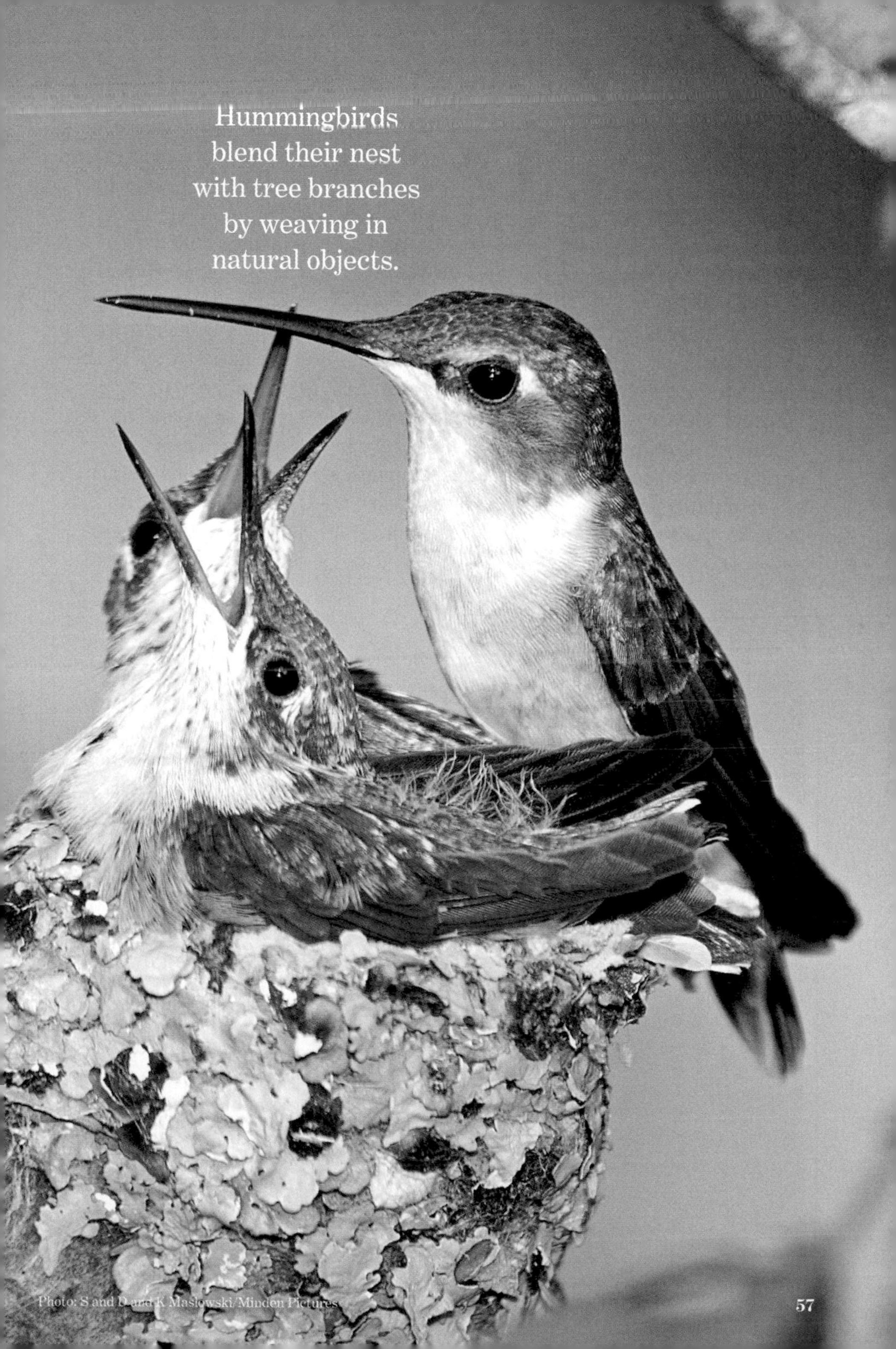

Hummingbirds blend their nest with tree branches by weaving in natural objects.

Photo: S and D and K Maslowski/Minden Pictures

nests "grow" for over 30 years and reach 8 feet in diameter!

At bedtime, birds go to roosts—whatever safe, comfortable places they can find, whether this means a well-sheltered tree branch or a cozy hole under an eave. Whether they're nesting or roosting, birds know how to select and furnish a place for their survival.

## PROTECTION AGAINST PREDATION

Especially with eggs or helpless young in the nest, birds are constant targets for predators, from larger birds to climbing snakes to domestic cats. To outsmart these enemies, birds rely on two tactics: camouflage and making a nest difficult to reach.

• Hummingbirds' nests are woven from natural objects to blend in with tree branches. Common materials include lichens, leaf scraps, and "thread" plucked from spider webs (which also lets the nest stretch as the young grow).

• Cactus wrens are well named: The sharp-spined cholla cactus that they favor for nest locations discourages predators from investigating too closely. These birds build empty "dummy" nests in addition to their real ones, banking on predators being unable to locate them among the decoys.

• Flycatchers weave snakeskin (or discarded snakeskin-like plastic strips) into their nests, a practice that has a scarecrow-like effect against squirrels and other nest raiders.

• Many seabirds lay pear-shape eggs on cliffs where few predators can climb. The eggs' shape keeps them from rolling off the cliff. Thousands of birds will nest within wing's-reach of each

Cactus wrens build nests in the sharp-spined cholla cactus to discourage predators.

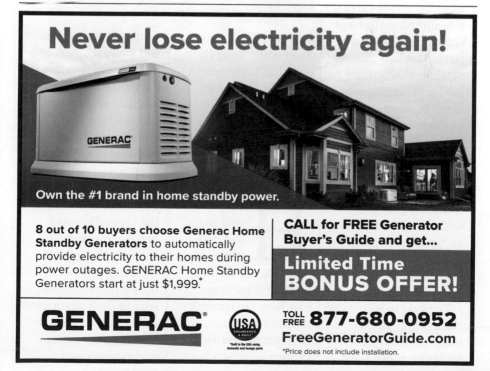

other for a safety-in-numbers effect (many species that nest near beaches or wetlands gather in similar loose-flock arrangements).

A big, tough neighbor also discourages predators from trying a nest raid. House sparrows are known to slip their nests between the twigs in bald eagle nests; black-chinned hummingbirds nest near Cooper's hawks; snow geese in Canada will choose sites in a snowy owl's territory; egrets in southern wetlands build nests above alligator ponds to keep egg-eating raccoons away. The best "guard neighbors" are either too big to be interested in a comparatively tiny nest or (as with nonclimbing alligators) unable to reach the nest themselves.

Black-necked stilts (small, long-legged, wetland birds) will fake an "incubation pose" to decoy predators from their real nest locations.

To avoid being "followed home," many birds vary the routes by which they

Royal terns nest within wing's-reach of each other for protection.

approach their nests and roosts. Before entering a tree hole or nest box, they often perch on the entrance to check inside from a safe fly-away position.

## PROTECTION AGAINST WEATHER

Heat waves, cold snaps, and high water cause problems for birds just as for humans. Feathers are naturally weather-resistant, so much of a bird's protection depends on

simply staying clean and well groomed. For nesting and roosting, they have other tricks.

• Loons, grebes, and coots, which nest in wetlands, build "floating nests" of aquatic vegetation as insurance against flooding. As it decays, the vegetation also generates extra warmth for the nest.

• Canada jays, a boreal forest species, situate their nests for southern exposure to ensure extra sunlight and warmth in the

Photo: Tom Mangelsen/Minden Pictures

chilly Canada–Alaska climate.

Nestling songbirds hatch with their insulating feathers yet to grow, so parents line the nest with warm materials, including their own feathers and feathers from other birds. Some "plucky" species will actually pull insulating fur from dogs and other animals.

Tufted titmice are notorious for doing this.

On frigid nights, birds snuggle into old nest holes or whatever warm spots they can find, often piling into groups for extra insulation.

Like most animals (and humans), birds spend a lot of time resting in the shade (preferably near a cool water dip) on very hot days.

Thanks to a natural "locking tendon" in their legs and feet, perching birds can stay on branches during strong winds (and even in their sleep) without much effort.

When the weather turns extreme, birds head for thick vegetation, sheltered tree cavities, or any available port—as did the Cooper's hawk that a Houston taxi driver found crouched in his cab during Hurricane Harvey in 2017.

Wetland nesters like grebes build "floating nests" of aquatic vegetation as insurance against flooding.

### PROTECTION IN URBAN ENVIRONS

Birds excel in nesting and roosting for survival not just in wild settings. Many species have mastered the art of living near humans.

• Wrens are famous for their nesting ingenuity. They like tree holes and nest boxes but have been found incubating in door wreaths, on car bumpers, and in the pockets of coats left hanging outside.

• Barn swallows frequently nest under

Photo: Michael Quinton/Minden Pictures

63

the eaves of human-occupied buildings. (I once witnessed a pair feeding their young over a ticket booth at SeaWorld San Antonio.) They seem to sense that humans will indulge them while also scaring predators away.

• Purple martins, the largest swallows in North America, have practically abandoned wild nesting, opting for colonies based in nest boxes. Other colony-nesting swallows attach mud nests under traffic overpasses in enormous numbers, oblivious to the cars and trucks roaring overhead.

• Peregrine falcons and red-tailed hawks have been highly successful in using skyscraper ledges as nest sites.

Many birds weave human discards—paper, candy wrappers, twine—into their nests. House finches have even been observed pulling wires from window screens. ■

**Katherine Swarts** is a longtime birder and a resident of Houston, Texas—home to nesting and roosting birds from purple martins to robins, from cardinals to bald eagles.

## PROTECTION THAT YOU CAN PROVIDE

Regardless of whether they typically live near us, birds appreciate our help with their safe quarters. Here's what you can do.

• If there are old trees in your yard, leave them standing unless they are a genuine safety hazard. Birds love them for nesting holes, perches, and edible-insect attractors.

A HOUSE WREN PREPPING A NEST BOX

• Buy or build nest boxes. Read the instructions carefully: Small differences in size and positioning can make big differences in whether birds use a box.

• Plant native flora on your property, including adequate cover for songbirds hiding from predators. Add a running water feature for additional bird-attraction value.

• Resist the temptation to keep souvenirs when cleaning out boxes after nesting season. There are bird-protection laws (notably the Migratory Bird Treaty Act of 1918) against unauthorized possession of feathers, eggshells, or nests from most native North American birds.

• If you want your nest box to double as a winter roost, clean it of any harmful dirt or parasites; plug extra ventilation holes to keep the cold out; and raise the box to 10 feet off the ground (birds feel safer up high).

• You can also install a separate roost box for winter use: Check online or at a wildlife center for instructions.

Have fun watching your feathered neighbors make themselves at home!  *-K. S.*

Photo: Daphne Kinzler/Minden Pictures

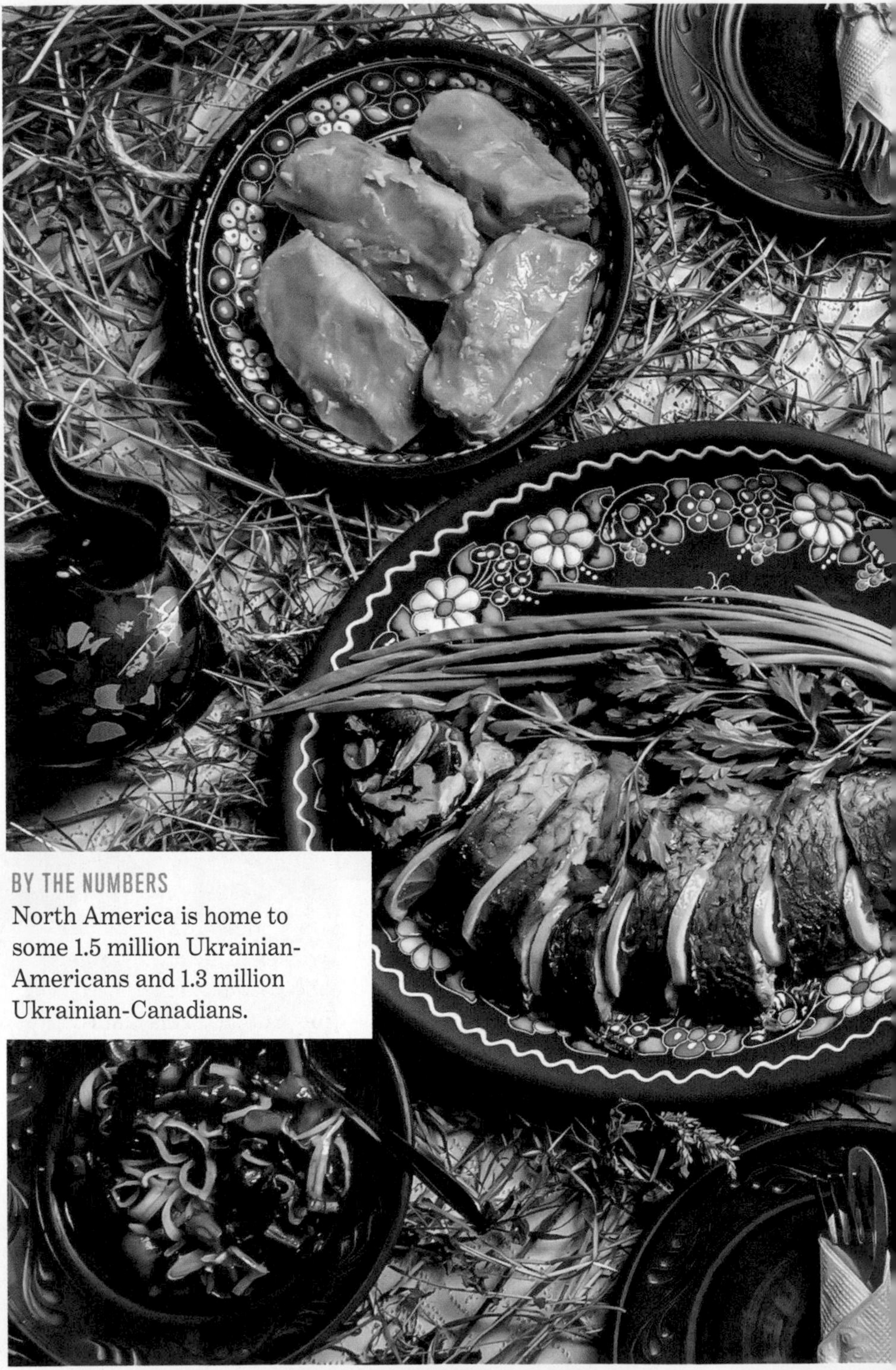

BY THE NUMBERS

North America is home to some 1.5 million Ukrainian-Americans and 1.3 million Ukrainian-Canadians.

# DELICIOUS DISHES FROM A UKRAINIAN CHRISTMAS

One in an occasional series on cultural traditions

BY BETTY SCHILL

For some 79 percent of Ukrainian-Americans and -Canadians, Christmas is the favorite or most important holiday of the year—and for good reason. A time for family, feasting, and celebration, the Ukrainian Christmas tradition begins on December 24 (or January 6 in the Gregorian calendar for certain denominations) and involves a 12-course dinner called *Sviata Vecheria,* or Holy Supper. This tradition differs in detail from family to family, but certain aspects remain the same. The number of dishes is symbolic of the 12 Apostles, and aspects of the meal evoke the Nativity scene.

*(continued)*

Kolachi

Kutia

T his meal begins when the first star of the evening appears, symbolizing the trek of the three Wise Men. In farming communities, the head of the household might bring in a sheaf of wheat, called a *didukh* (grandfather spirit), a symbol of the gathering together of the family. In cities, this tradition has been modified and the sheaf replaced by a few stalks of wheat in a vase. In some Ukrainian homes, hay is put under the table or under the tablecloth as a reminder of Christ's humble birth in a manger.

W hen all of the family is at the table, they sing the Ukrainian carol *"Boh predvichny"* ("God Eternal") and then offer a prayer to bless the food. A lit candle burns in a window to welcome any homeless people. An extra place at the table is set for the souls of those family members who have died. A *kolach* (braided, ring-shape bread) with a candle in the middle serves as the centerpiece of the table.

*(continued)*

Borsch

**T**he totally meatless dinner starts with *kutia,* a preparation of cooked wheat dressed with honey, poppy seeds, and nuts. Many other traditional Ukrainian dishes may then also be served, including *borsch* (beet soup); baked or fried fish; pickled herring; *holubtsi* (stuffed cabbage); *varenyky* (filled dumplings, similar to Polish *pierogies*); *pidpenky* (mushrooms in gravy); and mashed beans. The dinner ends with a dessert of stewed dried fruit (compote) and *pampushky* (poppy-seed buns) or *makivnyk* (poppy-seed roll). Everyone must have at least a small serving of each dish.

**A**fter the meal, according to custom, the family joins in singing Christmas carols and general merrymaking. The evening culminates in attendance at mass, often beginning before midnight and ending after.

This holiday season, try something different with a few traditional Ukrainian dishes.

*(see recipes, page 198)*

# 2022 RECIPE CONTEST WINNERS

We asked you for your best recipes using bananas, excluding breads, and we received many delicious dishes. Sincere thanks to all of you who took the time to submit recipes— we wish that we could acknowledge you all!

FIRST PRIZE (TIE)
**BANANA-STUFFED PEANUT
BUTTER FRENCH TOAST**
*(recipe on page 76)*

**STYLING AND PHOTOGRAPHY:
SAMANTHA JONES/QUINN BREIN COMMUNICATIONS**

FIRST PRIZE (TIE)
**SPICY BANANA
SHRIMP STIR-FRY**
*(recipe on page 76)*

*(continued)*

SECOND PRIZE
**GO BANANAS POPS**
*(recipe on page 77)*

THIRD PRIZE
**EASY STICKY
BANANA SQUARES**
*(recipe on page 77)*

*(continued)*

## BANANA-STUFFED PEANUT BUTTER FRENCH TOAST

2 eggs
$1/4$ cup milk
$1/2$ cup peanut butter, divided
1 tablespoon sugar
$1/4$ teaspoon ground cinnamon
4 slices bread
1 medium banana, cut into $1/4$-inch slices
1 tablespoon butter
confectioners' sugar, for sprinkling
maple syrup, for serving (optional)

In a bowl, whisk together eggs, milk, $1/4$ cup of peanut butter, sugar, and cinnamon.

Spread remaining peanut butter on two bread slices and top with bananas. Cover with remaining bread to make two sandwiches.

In a frying pan over medium heat, melt butter.

Dunk each side of the sandwiches into egg mixture, allowing mixture to slightly soak into both sides. Place in pan and cook for 3 to 4 minutes per side, or until golden.

Serve sprinkled with confectioners' sugar and drizzled with maple syrup (if using).

**Makes 2 servings.**

*–Anna Benefiel, Stayton, Oregon*

## SPICY BANANA SHRIMP STIR-FRY
**DRESSING:**
3 tablespoons extra-virgin olive oil
2 teaspoons fresh lime juice
2 teaspoons minced or grated fresh ginger
2 teaspoons soy sauce
2 teaspoons agave syrup or honey
salt and freshly ground black pepper, to taste

**STIR-FRY:**
$1/2$ pound angel hair pasta
$1\frac{1}{2}$ tablespoons canola oil
2 tablespoons finely minced red onion
1 serrano pepper, seeded and finely minced
2 cloves garlic, minced
2 ripe bananas, cut into $1/2$-inch pieces
$1\frac{1}{2}$ cups diced fresh pineapple
1 pound medium shrimp, peeled and deveined
salt and freshly ground black pepper, to taste
$1/4$ cup chopped fresh cilantro, for garnish

*For dressing:* In a bowl, whisk together all of the ingredients. Set aside.

*For stir-fry:* Cook pasta according to directions. Drain and keep warm.

Meanwhile, in a wok or large skillet over medium-high heat, warm canola oil. Add onions and peppers and stir-fry for 1 to 2 minutes. Add garlic and stir-fry for 30 seconds more. Add bananas, pineapple, and shrimp and continue to stir-fry until shrimp are fully cooked. Season with salt and black pepper. Add pasta to wok and toss to combine.

Re-whisk dressing, then stir into wok mixture. Turn off heat and let sit for 1 to 2 minutes. Taste again for seasonings, adding more salt and black pepper if desired. Garnish with cilantro and serve.

**Makes 4 servings.**

*–Frank Millard, Edgerton, Wisconsin*

SECOND PRIZE: $200
# GO BANANAS POPS

3 medium bananas, ripe but firm
3 tablespoons finely chopped dry
  roasted peanuts
3 tablespoons coarsely crushed
  mini pretzels
2 tablespoons mini semisweet
  chocolate chips
1 package (10 ounces) sea salt
  caramel baking chips
1 teaspoon vegetable oil
special equipment:
  9 pop or craft sticks for handles

Line a baking sheet with wax paper.

Cut ends off bananas and then cut crosswise into thirds. Insert a pop stick halfway into one cut end of each banana piece.

In a bowl, combine peanuts, pretzels, and chocolate chips.

In a heatproof bowl, toss together caramel chips and oil. Set bowl over a saucepan of simmering water (water not touching bowl). Once chips soften, stir until melted and smooth.

Dip banana pieces into melted caramel until coated, using a small spoon to help to evenly coat them. Push bananas into peanut mixture and, using your fingers, sprinkle mixture over bananas, turning each one to evenly coat. Place bananas on prepared baking sheet and freeze for 20 minutes, or until firm.

**Makes 9 servings.**
*–Cole Goerg, Neenah, Wisconsin*

THIRD PRIZE: $100
# EASY STICKY BANANA SQUARES

1½ cups all-purpose flour
⅔ cup butter, softened
3 tablespoons brown sugar
¼ cup (½ stick) butter
1 package (10 ounces) mini
  marshmallows
4 medium bananas, cut into
  ¼-inch slices

Preheat oven to 350°F. Spray an 8-inch baking dish with nonstick cooking spray.

In a bowl, combine flour, softened butter, and brown sugar. Stir until crumbly; press into prepared baking dish. Bake for 15 minutes, then set aside to cool.

In a nonstick saucepan over medium-low heat, melt butter. Add marshmallows and stir until melted. Remove from heat and gently stir in bananas. Quickly spread over crust. Allow to cool completely before slicing into squares. Cover and refrigerate leftovers.

**Makes 12 squares.**
*–Loretta Russell, Edmonton, Alberta* ■

## ENTER THE 2023 RECIPE CONTEST: GINGER

Got a great recipe using ginger that's loved by family and friends? Send it in and it could win! See contest rules on page 251.

FARMERS SHARE
THEIR STORIES,
INSPIRATIONS,
AND DREAMS.

# MAKING A

## TIDAL 9 FISHERIES
### NORTH HAVEN, MAINE

**W**hen Karen Cooper saw a friend eating seaweed salad a few years ago, it seemed pretty unappetizing. Then she tried it and found it to be quite tasty; she had no idea that she'd grow it one day.

Lobster fishing in Maine's Penobscot Bay has been Cooper's livelihood for 30 years (she's a 3rd-generation lobsterman, fishing up to 200 traps). She loves it: "It's the fun of not knowing. You go out every day and find out if you set the traps in the right place. Are they full of lobsters or not?"

Looking to make some off-season money, Cooper became curious about seaweed and got an aquaculture lease to harvest and sell kelp. This required almost no capital investment (only the cost of the chain and line) and logistically was a perfect fit. Lobstering runs from June through October; kelp is seeded in November and harvested in

May. "So, we are working on the water all year 'round," she notes.

The kelp thrived: The microscopic seeds looked like slime for weeks but grew many feet long. "I don't even have a houseplant, other than a few shrubs outside—I can't grow anything, but if it has to do with the ocean, I can probably do it," Cooper reports. Today, she harvests and sells 15,000 pounds of kelp annually.

This successful side venture spurred Cooper to start another one—harvesting sea salt and selling it in jars at local gift shops. This is all a reflection of the diversification that will be required of the next generation of lobstermen—including her nephew, who helps to harvest the kelp: "He loves lobster fishing," Cooper says, "but it's not going to be around forever, so he needs to think about what he can do to make a living on the ocean." *(continued)*

Photo: Hannah McGowan

# GROW OF IT

BY KAREN
DAVIDSON AND
STACEY
KUSTERBECK

"I CAN'T GROW
ANYTHING, BUT IF
IT HAS TO DO WITH
THE OCEAN, I CAN
PROBABLY DO IT."

## LIFE WATER GARDENS
### NORWAY HOUSE, MANITOBA

The town of Norway House is rich in history as the inland depot of the Hudson's Bay Company, but to this day, it's in perennial need of fresh vegetables. While the Cree Nation is surrounded by the bounties of fishing, trapping, and logging, its cultural gardening history strays little beyond root vegetables. Any aboveground crop risks being nipped at –5°C (23°F) in the third week of June, and any remaining hope can be strangled with the same lows as early as September 5.

In 2019, exactly this kind of cold weather was a reminder that the 8,000 citizens of Norway House lacked secure, affordable food. This motivated Virginia Muswagon and Ian Maxwell to start Life Water Gardens. As co-managers, they tend a prefabricated container outfitted for growing lettuces, kale, pak choi, and herbs hydroponically year-round.

"At first, I was curious about planting seeds into rockwool that felt like firm candy floss," recalls Muswagon, "and I was surprised by the microscopic size of mint seeds." Ever resourceful, she bent a drinking straw into a tiny shovel for planting three to five mint seeds into each nesting cube.

Those rookie days have now evolved into the routine harvesting of 450 herbs and greens plants each week. The local hospital and school have been converted into customers by the consistent quality of the produce. Flame-colored lettuces for burgers and salads sell like "Wildfire" (which is the lettuce mix's name).

The community at large is somewhere between agnostic and enthusiastic about the whole enterprise. As Maxwell explains, "There's still disbelief that these pristine vegetables are real and that they're grown right here in the north."

Muswagon, however, is determined to make believers out of her neighbors. Her hook? At promotional events, she serves a kale–Saskatoon berry smoothie. *(continued)*

"THERE'S STILL DISBELIEF THAT THESE PRISTINE VEGETABLES ARE REAL."

Photo: Life Water Gardens

## NORMA'S PRODUCE AT PENN FARM
### COLONIAL BEACH, VIRGINIA

As migrant farmworkers, Dora and Leopoldo Beltran followed the harvest across five U.S. states for decades. When one farm owner retired 20 years ago, he encouraged the Beltrans to take over the operation, which sold tomatoes and squash wholesale. They eventually

"IT MAKES IT WORTHWHILE WHEN WE CAN MEET OUR CUSTOMERS AND SEE THAT SOMEONE IS ENJOYING WHAT WE DO."

bought 46 acres and leased 35 more beside Virginia's Rappahannock River.

Naming their enterprise after their firstborn, Norma, the new owners made two big decisions right away: to grow dozens of varieties of fruit, vegetables, and herbs and to sell directly to consumers. Today, they sell some

40,000 pounds of produce per week at nine area farmers' markets. "Now, we have a fully operational farm where we can decide what we want to do with the land," comments their son, Leopoldo Jr. The changes have paid off: "It makes it worthwhile when we can meet our customers and see that someone is enjoying what we do," he says.

Some regulars preorder seasonal produce online for convenience. Others appreciate some expert help in choosing their selections. "One customer says, 'Do your magic,' knowing that I will pick out the best cantaloupe for him," he reports.

Five years ago, the family made another big change, installing four high tunnels, which enable them to farm in the winter. Being able to sell year-round has proven to be a big advantage. "This is what people want—not just beets and carrots that will survive the cold, but a variety of things—asparagus and fresh salads, for example," continues Leopoldo Jr. "In April, we have tomatoes, squash, and cucumbers months ahead of everybody else."

The elder Beltrans still are in charge, but Leopoldo Jr. is preparing to take over and expand operations even more with value-added products (jams, jellies, and pickled vegetables), community-supported agriculture, fruit orchards, and flowers. "We are always open to finding different ways to sell what we grow and add to what we are already doing," he says. *(continued)*

**"If you're looking for some extra cash for whatever reason, your home's equity just might be the right solution."**

Tom Selleck, Actor and AAG Paid Spokesperson

# WEATHER THE FINANCIAL STORM

Shield Yourself from Economic Uncertainty with a Reverse Mortgage Loan

Supplement your income with the added protection of a reverse mortgage loan. Use the extra cash to:

✓ **Eliminate your mortgage payment**
Borrowers remain responsible for paying homeowners insurance and property taxes, maintaining the home, and complying with the loan terms.

✓ **Fight inflation**

✓ **Cover everyday expenses such as gas, groceries, and more**

✓ **Pay off existing higher-interest debt, medical bills, and in-home care**

## Call (800) 491-0466
**Receive Your FREE Information Guide.**

# GILL FAMILY ORCHARDS
## KELOWNA, BRITISH COLUMBIA

I n 2018, Mani Gill abandoned a safe job—a 10-year banking career—to return to his family's farmer roots near Kelowna.

"This is what I was meant to do," says Gill. "It's not work—it's a passion."

This work ethic comes naturally from his parents, who immigrated from India's Punjab region to the Okanagan Valley in the 1980s to work as laborers. As a young teenager, Gill recalls, he picked cherries, changed water pivots, and drove a tractor under the blazing sun near Osoyoos, which—with its desertlike geography—is often cited as the hottest place in Canada. Before long, his parents had acquired their own acreage, moving 80 miles north to the cooler temperatures of Kelowna.

Today, Gill and his brother Jasmeet manage 100 acres of vineyards and orchards. None of them expected the unusual heat dome of 2021 that settled over the valley in late June, with temperatures that spiked to 45°C (113°F) for several days.

This nature-borne oven meant that the early-maturing cherry varieties of some growers basically became baked on the trees and rendered unmarketable. Fortunately, the Gill family was able to employ microjet sprinklers at ground level to keep their orchards cooled. Their 'Lapins' and 'Staccato' cherry varieties were saved, although at smaller-than-usual sizes. Another beneficial factor was that the orchards are planted in an east–west direction, which meant that the tree canopies protected the maturing fruit.

"Climate change is happening," comments Gill. "We've never seen these temperatures in Kelowna before."

Thanks to access to irrigation water, the Gill family has managed to sustain their orchards and vineyards.

"Every year, there's something new to face, whether it's frost or heat. It's part of the business," observes Gill. "Next year, we'll be prepared."

Rather than counting work hours, he and his wife Kamal are now counting their blessings while raising their two children. *(continued)*

"THIS IS WHAT I WAS MEANT TO DO. IT'S NOT WORK— IT'S A PASSION."

Photo: Gill Family Orchards

# SAUNDERS FAMILY FARM & VINEYARD
## BEAMSVILLE, ONTARIO

*D*o *no harm, embrace life.* Ann-Marie Saunders's motto is as natural as the millennia-old limestone escarpment that overlooks her family's farm. Purchased by her parents in the mid-1960s, their certified-organic, 12-acre vineyard is a work in progress by regenerative standards. As she explains, many conventional agricultural practices are interventionist, using pesticides to kill unwanted weeds or insects, while regenerative practices are preservationist.

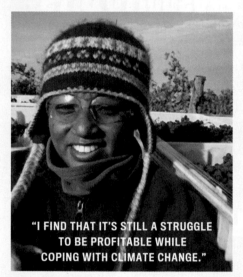

**"I FIND THAT IT'S STILL A STRUGGLE TO BE PROFITABLE WHILE COPING WITH CLIMATE CHANGE."**

"This is a way of harnessing biology rather than using reductive chemistry," notes Saunders. "It feels experimental in some senses, but it's a way to keep everything alive."

For example, grapevines, brush, and leaves are shredded and composted for a year. Once in spring and once in fall,

the compost is bagged and placed in a 300-gallon brewer, where it is then aerated for a day along with vermicompost and water. Brimming with life-giving microbes, the steeped compost tea is then sprayed onto the soil. For further soil enrichment, Muscovy duck manure is sourced from the neighbor's farm.

To aid in soil regeneration, the vineyard walkways are planted with clay-busting daikon radishes, nitrogen-fixing clovers, and pollinator-attracting buckwheat. Along with vegetation such as naturally wild carrots, these plants are allowed to grow to waist height before being mown down about twice annually. What looks to be a messy plant menagerie is—upon closer inspection—buzzing with beneficial insects, some of which eat into the populations of leaf-sucking bugs such as aphids, leafhoppers, and mites.

"Another reason to keep the plant mixture long is to prevent soil erosion," reports Saunders. "After heavy rains, we have no runoff, no puddles."

Come fall, their hand-harvested grapes are sought by local winemakers who value their ecological methods. Incessant rains can diminish yields, but it's the winemakers who ultimately determine how a vintage fares.

"I find that it's still a struggle to be profitable while coping with climate change," adds Saunders. "The biggest challenge, however, lies in being patient with existing systems that are sometimes slow to change." *(continued)*

Photo: Saunders Family Farm & Vineyard

# Prevagen®
## Improves Memory*¹

# #1 PHARMACIST RECOMMENDED
## MEMORY SUPPORT BRAND

Prevagen® is America's best-selling brain support supplement‡ and has been clinically shown to help with mild memory loss associated with aging.*¹

**Prevagen Improves Memory**

**REGULAR STRENGTH**

SUPPORTS:
- ☑ Healthy Brain Function*
- ☑ Sharper Mind*
- ☑ Clearer Thinking*

**ONE CAPSULE DAILY**
Dietary Supplement
30 Capsules

Clinically Tested Ingredient*

PREVAGEN
*Pharmacy Times*
#1 PHARMACIST RECOMMENDED BRAND!
MEMORY SUPPORT
2022-2023

**Prevagen is available at stores nationwide.**

*Walgreens*  **CVS/pharmacy**  **RITE AID**  **Walmart** ⅍

## ASKIN LAND AND LIVESTOCK
### LUSK, WYOMING

When trying to get a foothold in the ranching business as a recent college graduate, Sage Askin had plenty of knowledge (a degree in rangeland ecology and watershed management, plus five minors: forestry, reclamation and restoration ecology, agro-ecology, soil science, and wildlife and fisheries biology) and years of experience in raising steers and working on a ranch. He had very few assets, though—just $1,000 from his last paycheck, a paid-for pickup, a trailer, and a horse.

He tried to obtain a revolving line of credit to buy land. "With no equity, they looked at me as if I were crazy when I asked for $300,000 to follow my dream," says Askin. Soaring land prices stood in the way. "Just 10 or 20 years ago, you could still buy land with the crop produced. No longer is this the case, with ag land in America often two or three times its 'productive value,'" observes Askin.

Instead of giving up on ranching, Askin decided to run an ad saying "Ranch lease wanted—Young aspiring rancher" in a local newspaper. Today, Sage and Faith Askin run a diversified operation on 75,000 acres of leased land: They offer custom grazing and run three bands of sheep on seven different ranches. "The dream didn't change, but the road has not been the way that I'd envisioned," says Askin.

They and 13 employees follow an intensive regenerative adaptive grazing program, with cattle moved every 1 to 3 days in springtime and some pastures rested for the entire year. "We can make the soil better, which makes the plants better, which benefits us all," notes Askin, who offers this advice to young ranchers: "Network every chance that you get—and don't be afraid to take the plunge and do something different." ∎

"DON'T BE AFRAID TO TAKE THE PLUNGE AND DO SOMETHING DIFFERENT."

---

Canadian profiles are by **Karen Davidson,** editor of *The Grower,* a leading Canadian horticultural magazine, and frequent contributor to the Almanac. U.S. profiles are by **Stacey Kusterbeck,** a regular contributor to the Almanac.

Thank you for reading *The Old Farmer's Almanac*.

# BUT WAIT, THERE'S MORE!

### Get instant **FREE** access to *EXTRA!*

*EXTRA!* from *The Old Farmer's Almanac* is our monthly digital magazine for your tablet, mobile phone, and computer. It features all-new and exclusive content with the Almanac's unique perspective—because once a year is not enough!

### EVERY MONTH, *EXTRA!* GIVES READERS:

- *extra* seasonal calendar facts and astronomical highlights
- *extra* gardening tips, secrets, and advice
- *extra* ideas for living better naturally
- *extra* quick-and-easy, great-tasting recipes
- *extra* doses of the Almanac's "pleasant degree of humor"

From cover to cover, month to month, *EXTRA!* delivers wit and wisdom as only the *Almanac* can—with a wink and a smile.

## VISIT ALMANAC.COM/EXTRA/FREETOJOIN

This is not a trial and we won't ask for a credit card. It only takes an email address to begin enjoying your monthly *EXTRA!* digital magazine. A $9.99 retail value.

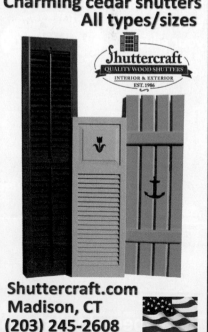

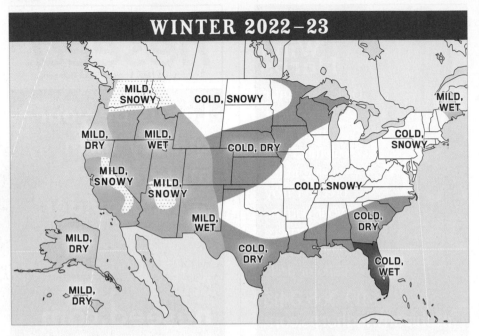

# WINTER 2022-23

- MILD, SNOWY
- COLD, SNOWY
- MILD, WET
- MILD, DRY
- MILD, WET
- COLD, SNOWY
- MILD, SNOWY
- COLD, DRY
- MILD, SNOWY
- COLD, SNOWY
- MILD, WET
- COLD, DRY
- MILD, DRY
- COLD, DRY
- COLD, WET
- MILD, DRY

These weather maps correspond to the winter and summer predictions in the General Weather Forecast (opposite) and on the regional forecast pages, 206–223. To learn more about how we make our forecasts, turn to page 202.

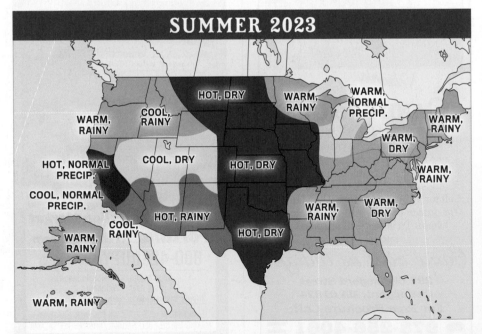

# SUMMER 2023

- HOT, DRY
- WARM, RAINY
- WARM, NORMAL PRECIP.
- WARM, RAINY
- COOL, RAINY
- WARM, RAINY
- WARM, DRY
- HOT, NORMAL PRECIP.
- COOL, DRY
- HOT, DRY
- WARM, RAINY
- COOL, NORMAL PRECIP.
- HOT, RAINY
- WARM, RAINY
- WARM, DRY
- COOL, RAINY
- HOT, DRY
- WARM, RAINY
- WARM, RAINY

Maps: AccuWeather, Inc.

# THE GENERAL WEATHER REPORT AND FORECAST

## FOR REGIONAL FORECASTS, SEE PAGES 206-223.

What's shaping the weather? Recent Solar Cycle 24 had the lowest level of solar activity in more than 100 years. We are now early in Cycle 25, which is expected to peak around July 2025 and also bring diminished activity, which historically has meant cooler temperatures, on average, across Earth. We believe that most of the U.S. will be colder than normal this winter, although summer will be mostly warmer than usual. In addition to a neutral to perhaps weak El Niño, important weather influences will include a continued warm phase of the Atlantic Multidecadal Oscillation (AMO), a neutral to positive North Atlantic Oscillation (NAO), and a negative Pacific Decadal Oscillation (PDO). Oscillations are linked ocean–atmosphere patterns that can have long-term effects on the weather.

**WINTER** will be milder than normal across eastern Maine, from the Rockies to the West Coast, and across Alaska and Hawaii. It will be colder than normal across much of the country between the East Coast and Rockies. Precipitation will be above normal from Maine to southeastern Virginia, in Florida, from the lower Great Lakes into Missouri, and from western Minnesota to the northern Rockies, southward into the southern Rockies, and westward to the California coast and near or below normal elsewhere. Snowfall will be greater than normal from central New England through northern North Carolina, from the Lower Great Lakes and the Ohio and Tennessee Valleys into the southern Plains, from the northern Plains into eastern Washington, and across the higher terrain of the southern Rockies and California and near or less than normal in most other areas that receive snow.

**SPRING** will be warmer than normal in much of New England, from the Ohio Valley through the Deep South and Florida, from the High Plains down through Texas, along the West Coast, and across Alaska and Hawaii and near normal or cooler elsewhere. Rainfall will be above normal from southern New England through northern Florida, in the Upper Midwest, from the Deep South into the southern Plains and northward through the High Plains, and across much of the U.S. West and Hawaii and near or below normal elsewhere.

**SUMMER** will be cooler than normal in the northern and central Rockies and Great Basin and along the central and southern California coast and near normal or warmer elsewhere. Rainfall will be above normal from New England through the mid-Atlantic coast, in the Upper Midwest, from the Ohio Valley southward to the Deep South, from the northern Rockies through the Pacific Northwest, from the Desert Southwest to the southern California coast, and across Alaska and Hawaii and near or below normal elsewhere.

The best chances for **TROPICAL STORMS** will be in Texas in late July and the Deep South and Texas in late August.

**AUTUMN** will be cooler than normal from Maine to Virginia and westward into the Appalachians and from the Intermountain West through the Pacific Northwest and near normal or warmer elsewhere. Precipitation will be above normal in the Lower Lakes, from the High Plains to the Desert Southwest, and across Hawaii and northern Alaska and near or below normal elsewhere.

TO GET A SUMMARY OF THE RESULTS OF OUR FORECAST FOR LAST WINTER, TURN TO PAGE 204.

WEATHER

# THE OLD FARMER'S ALMANAC

*Established in 1792 and published every year thereafter*
ROBERT B. THOMAS, *founder* (1766–1846)

YANKEE PUBLISHING INC.
**EDITORIAL AND PUBLISHING OFFICES**
P.O. Box 520, 1121 Main Street, Dublin, NH 03444
Phone: 603-563-8111 • Fax: 603-563-8252

EDITOR *(13th since 1792):* Janice Stillman
CREATIVE DIRECTOR: Colleen Quinnell
MANAGING EDITOR: Jack Burnett
SENIOR EDITORS: Sarah Perreault, Heidi Stonehill
ASSOCIATE EDITOR: Tim Goodwin
WEATHER GRAPHICS AND CONSULTATION:
AccuWeather, Inc.

V.P., NEW MEDIA AND PRODUCTION:
Paul Belliveau
PRODUCTION DIRECTOR: David Ziarnowski
PRODUCTION MANAGER: Brian Johnson
SENIOR PRODUCTION ARTISTS:
Jennifer Freeman, Rachel Kipka, Janet Selle

**WEB SITE: ALMANAC.COM**
SENIOR DIGITAL EDITOR: Catherine Boeckmann
ASSOCIATE DIGITAL EDITOR: Christopher Burnett
SENIOR WEB DESIGNER: Amy O'Brien
DIGITAL MARKETING SPECIALIST: Holly Sanderson
E-MAIL MARKETING SPECIALIST: Eric Bailey
E-COMMERCE MARKETING DIRECTOR: Alan Henning
PROGRAMMING: Peter Rukavina

**CONTACT US**
We welcome your questions and comments about articles in and topics for this Almanac. Mail all editorial correspondence to Editor, The Old Farmer's Almanac, P.O. Box 520, Dublin, NH 03444-0520; fax us at 603-563-8252; or contact us through Almanac.com/Contact. *The Old Farmer's Almanac* can not accept responsibility for unsolicited manuscripts and will not acknowledge any hard-copy queries or manuscripts that do not include a stamped and addressed return envelope.

All printing inks used in this edition of *The Old Farmer's Almanac* are soy-based. This product is recyclable. Consult local recycling regulations for the right way to do it.

*Thank you for buying this Almanac! We hope that you find it "useful, with a pleasant degree of humor." Thanks, too, to everyone who had a hand in it, including advertisers, distributors, printers, and sales and delivery people.*

No part of this Almanac may be reproduced in whole or in part, or stored in a retrieval system, or transmitted in any form or by any means (electronic, mechanical, photocopying, recording, or other) without written permission of the publisher.

# THE OLD FARMER'S ALMANAC

## OUR CONTRIBUTORS

**BOB BERMAN,** our astronomy editor, leads annual tours to Chilean observatories as well as to view solar eclipses and the northern lights. He is the author of *Zoom* (Little Brown, 2015) and *Earth-Shattering: Violent Supernovas, Galactic Explosions, Biological Mayhem, Nuclear Meltdowns, and Other Hazards to Life in Our Universe* (Little Brown, 2019).

**JACK BURNETT,** the Almanac's managing editor, writes the weather doggerel verse that runs down the center of the Right-Hand Calendar Pages.

**BETHANY E. COBB,** our astronomer, is an Associate Professor of Honors and Physics at George Washington University. In addition to conducting research on gamma-ray bursts and teaching astronomy and physics courses to non–science majors, she enjoys rock climbing, figure skating, and reading science fiction.

**CELESTE LONGACRE,** our astrologer, often refers to astrology as "a study of timing, and timing is everything." A New Hampshire native, she has been a practicing astrologer for more than 40 years. Her book, *Celeste's Garden Delights* (2015), is available at CelesteLongacre.com.

Meteorologists **BOB SMERBECK** and **BRIAN THOMPSON** made the weather predictions, in consultation with Michael Steinberg, our meteorologist since 1996. Bob and Brian bring not just a total of 51 years of forecasting expertise to the task but also some unique early accomplishments: a portable, wood-and-PVC-pipe tornado machine built by Bob and prescient 5-day forecasts made by Brian—in fourth grade.

**TED WILLIAMS,** a Massachusetts-based nature writer, pens the Farmer's Calendar essays. He serves on the Circle of Chiefs of the Outdoor Writers Association of America and is national chair of the Native Fish Coalition as well as the author of *Earth Almanac* (Storey Publishing, 2020).

## THE OLD
# FARMER'S ALMANAC

*Established in 1792 and published every year thereafter*
ROBERT B. THOMAS, *founder* (1766–1846)

YANKEE PUBLISHING INC.
P.O. Box 520, 1121 Main Street, Dublin, NH 03444
Phone: 603-563-8111 • Fax: 603-563-8252

PUBLISHER *(23rd since 1792):* Sherin Pierce
EDITOR IN CHIEF: Judson D. Hale Sr.

### FOR DISPLAY ADVERTISING RATES
Go to Almanac.com/AdvertisingInfo or
call 800-895-9265, ext. 109

Stephanie Bernbach-Crowe • 914-827-0015
Steve Hall • 800-736-1100, ext. 320

### FOR CLASSIFIED ADVERTISING
Cindy Levine, RJ Media • 212-986-0016

SENIOR AD PRODUCTION COORDINATOR:
Janet Selle • 800-895-9265, ext. 168

### PUBLIC RELATIONS
Quinn Brein • 206-842-8922
Ginger Vaughan • ginger@quinnbrein.com

### CONSUMER ORDERS & INFO
Call 800-ALMANAC (800-256-2622)
or go to Almanac.com/Shop

### RETAIL SALES
Stacey Korpi • 800-895-9265, ext. 160
Janice Edson, ext. 126

### DISTRIBUTORS
NATIONAL: Comag Marketing Group
Smyrna, GA
BOOKSTORE: HarperCollins Publishers
New York, NY
NEWSSTAND CONSULTANT: PSCS Consulting
Linda Ruth • 603-924-4407

Old Farmer's Almanac publications are available
for sales promotions or premiums. Contact Beacon
Promotions, info@beaconpromotions.com.

YANKEE PUBLISHING INCORPORATED
AN EMPLOYEE-OWNED COMPANY

Jamie Trowbridge, *President;* Paul Belliveau,
Ernesto Burden, Judson D. Hale Jr.,
Brook Holmberg, Jennie Meister, Sherin Pierce,
*Vice Presidents.*

# IN MEMORIAM

**T**im Clark (1950–2021) began work as an editor and writer at Yankee Publishing in 1980. During his 41 years here, he was a prolific contributor to both *Yankee* magazine and the Almanac, but his desire to provide useful information with our "pleasant degree of humor," plus a lifelong interest in folklore, made him singularly suited to the Almanac. This was Tim. When a story idea or strange angle on a topic came to him, he lit up. His Almanac chronicles covered the origins of napping, the nuances of noise, the fastest man's last death-defying ride, 20/20 vision (for 2020), and the end of the Civil War, among many others. Folklore was his forte; his essays on beekeeping, teeth, "shoe-perstitions," and the Moon, as well as all manner of home remedies, lent credibility and charm to many mysterious traditions and practices.

His inimitable how to's—have a baby, clean your chimney, tell when someone's lying, become a prophet, avoid dying, prevent balding, fall asleep, appear to know more than you really do, and be immortal—are legendary in Almanac annals. Even his silly inquiries, like "How Happy *Is* a Clam?" on page 188, make a certain sense. Still, Tim may have taken greatest joy and pride in writing the weather doggerel on the Right-Hand Calendar Pages. So fond of this form was he that he composed his corporate retirement farewell in verse *(below)* a year and half before he died. He wrote it for us, his colleagues, yes, but also for anyone who might ever be in need of a smile. Rest in peace and boundless curiosity, Tim.

*And so my Yankee sojourn ends,*
*With thanks to you, my loving friends,*
*Expressed in this neglected genre,*
*With due respect and utmost honor.*
*For you, I'd send a fulsome bloggerel,*
*Compose a tuneful Indian raggarel,*
*Consume a New Year's Eve*
*    eggnoggerel,*
*Revive the long-extinguished quaggarel.*
*Here's a toast in Navy groggerel:*
*May all you live high on the hoggerel,*
*Leap slim and spry as any froggerel,*
*Heroes of a Viking saggarel!*
*No more: Before I start to sloggerel,*
*My arteries begin to cloggerel,*
*Become a bump upon a loggerel,*
*I'll halt this halting hound of doggerel.* ∎

# ECLIPSES

There will be four eclipses in 2023, two of the Sun and two of the Moon. Solar eclipses are visible only in certain areas and require eye protection to be viewed safely. Lunar eclipses are technically visible from the entire night side of Earth, but during a penumbral eclipse, the dimming of the Moon's illumination is slight. See the **Astronomical Glossary, page 110,** for explanations of the different types of eclipses.

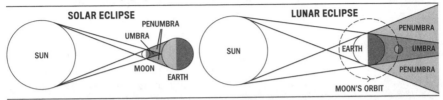

**APRIL 19-20: ANNUAL TOTAL ECLIPSE OF THE SUN.** This hybrid eclipse, which is seen as annular or total depending on viewing location along its path, is not visible from North America. (It is visible only from the southern Indian Ocean, parts of Antarctica, most of Australasia, Indonesia, Philippines, most of Oceania, and the western Pacific Ocean.)

**MAY 5: PENUMBRAL ECLIPSE OF THE MOON.** This eclipse is not visible from North America. (The eclipse is visible only from Antarctica, Oceania, Australasia, Asia, Europe, Africa, and South Georgia and the South Sandwich Islands.)

**OCTOBER 14: ANNULAR ECLIPSE OF THE SUN.** This eclipse is at least partially visible from most of North America. The annular phase is visible in a narrow path that runs through Oregon, Nevada, Utah, Arizona, New Mexico, and Texas. The eclipse begins at 11:04 A.M. EDT (8:04 A.M. PDT) and ends at 4:55 P.M. EDT (1:55 P.M. PDT).

**OCTOBER 28: PARTIAL ECLIPSE OF THE MOON.** This eclipse is visible from northeastern North America. The Moon will rise during the eclipse and observers will only see a penumbral eclipse. The Moon will enter the penumbra at 2:00 P.M. EDT and the umbra at 3:35 P.M. EDT. The Moon will leave the umbra at 4:54 P.M. EDT and the penumbra at 6:28 P.M. EDT.

**TRANSIT OF MERCURY.** Mercury's proximity to the Sun makes it difficult to observe. In 2023, Mercury is best viewed from the Northern Hemisphere just after sunset in the second week of April and shortly before sunrise in late September. Spot Mercury close to Jupiter after sunset on March 26, 27, or 28. Look for a conjunction between Mercury and Venus on the evening of July 26—Mars will also be nearby.

## THE MOON'S PATH

The Moon's path across the sky changes with the seasons. Full Moons are very high in the sky (at midnight) between November and February and very low in the sky between May and July.

### FULL-MOON DATES (ET)

|       | 2023   | 2024 | 2025 | 2026   | 2027 |
|-------|--------|------|------|--------|------|
| JAN.  | 6      | 25   | 13   | 3      | 22   |
| FEB.  | 5      | 24   | 12   | 1      | 20   |
| MAR.  | 7      | 25   | 14   | 3      | 22   |
| APR.  | 6      | 23   | 12   | 1      | 20   |
| MAY   | 5      | 23   | 12   | 1 & 31 | 20   |
| JUNE  | 3      | 21   | 11   | 29     | 18   |
| JULY  | 3      | 21   | 10   | 29     | 18   |
| AUG.  | 1 & 30 | 19   | 9    | 28     | 17   |
| SEPT. | 29     | 17   | 7    | 26     | 15   |
| OCT.  | 28     | 17   | 6    | 26     | 15   |
| NOV.  | 27     | 15   | 5    | 24     | 13   |
| DEC.  | 26     | 15   | 4    | 23     | 13   |

# BRIGHT STARS

## TRANSIT TIMES

This table shows the time (ET) and altitude of a star as it transits the meridian (i.e., reaches its highest elevation while passing over the horizon's south point) at Boston on the dates shown. The transit time on any other date differs from that of the nearest date listed by approximately 4 minutes per day. To find the time of a star's transit for your location, convert its time at Boston using Key Letter C **(see Time Corrections, page 238).**

| STAR | CONSTELLATION | MAGNITUDE | JAN. 1 | MAR. 1 | MAY 1 | JULY 1 | SEPT. 1 | NOV. 1 | ALTITUDE (DEGREES) |
|------|---------------|-----------|--------|--------|-------|--------|---------|--------|---------------------|
| Altair | Aquila | 0.8 | **12:52** | 9:00 | 6:00 | 2:00 | **9:52** | **5:52** | 56.3 |
| Deneb | Cygnus | 1.3 | **1:42** | 9:50 | 6:50 | 2:50 | **10:42** | **6:43** | 92.8 |
| Fomalhaut | Psc. Aus. | 1.2 | **3:58** | **12:06** | 9:06 | 5:06 | 1:03 | **8:59** | 17.8 |
| Algol | Perseus | 2.2 | **8:08** | **4:16** | **1:16** | 9:17 | 5:13 | 1:13 | 88.5 |
| Aldebaran | Taurus | 0.9 | **9:36** | **5:44** | **2:44** | 10:44 | 6:40 | 2:40 | 64.1 |
| Rigel | Orion | 0.1 | **10:14** | **6:22** | **3:22** | 11:22 | 7:18 | 3:19 | 39.4 |
| Capella | Auriga | 0.1 | **10:17** | **6:25** | **3:25** | 11:25 | 7:21 | 3:21 | 93.6 |
| Bellatrix | Orion | 1.6 | **10:25** | **6:33** | **3:33** | 11:33 | 7:29 | 3:29 | 54.0 |
| Betelgeuse | Orion | var. 0.4 | **10:54** | **7:03** | **4:03** | **12:03** | 7:59 | 3:59 | 55.0 |
| Sirius | Can. Maj. | −1.4 | **11:44** | **7:52** | **4:52** | **12:52** | 8:49 | 4:49 | 31.0 |
| Procyon | Can. Min. | 0.4 | 12:42 | **8:46** | **5:46** | **1:47** | 9:43 | 5:43 | 52.9 |
| Pollux | Gemini | 1.2 | 12:48 | **8:53** | **5:53** | **1:53** | 9:49 | 5:49 | 75.7 |
| Regulus | Leo | 1.4 | 3:11 | **11:15** | **8:15** | **4:15** | **12:12** | 8:12 | 59.7 |
| Spica | Virgo | var. 1.0 | 6:27 | 2:35 | **11:31** | **7:32** | **3:28** | 11:28 | 36.6 |
| Arcturus | Boötes | −0.1 | 7:17 | 3:25 | 12:26 | **8:22** | **4:18** | **12:18** | 66.9 |
| Antares | Scorpius | var. 0.9 | 9:31 | 5:39 | 2:39 | **10:36** | **6:32** | **2:32** | 21.3 |
| Vega | Lyra | 0 | 11:38 | 7:46 | 4:46 | **12:46** | **8:38** | **4:38** | 86.4 |

*TIME OF TRANSIT (ET) — BOLD = P.M. LIGHT = A.M.*

## RISE AND SET TIMES

To find the time of a star's rising at Boston on any date, subtract the interval shown at right from the star's transit time on that date; add the interval to find the star's setting time. To find the rising and setting times for your city, convert the Boston transit times above using the Key Letter shown at right before applying the interval **(see Time Corrections, page 238).** Deneb, Algol, Capella, and Vega are circumpolar stars—they never set but appear to circle the celestial north pole.

| STAR | INTERVAL (H.M.) | RISING KEY | RISING DIR.* | SETTING KEY | SETTING DIR.* |
|------|-----------------|------------|--------------|-------------|---------------|
| Altair | 6 36 | B | EbN | E | WbN |
| Fomalhaut | 3 59 | E | SE | D | SW |
| Aldebaran | 7 06 | B | ENE | D | WNW |
| Rigel | 5 33 | D | EbS | B | WbS |
| Bellatrix | 6 27 | B | EbN | D | WbN |
| Betelgeuse | 6 31 | B | EbN | D | WbN |
| Sirius | 5 00 | D | ESE | B | WSW |
| Procyon | 6 23 | B | EbN | D | WbN |
| Pollux | 8 01 | A | NE | E | NW |
| Regulus | 6 49 | B | EbN | D | WbN |
| Spica | 5 23 | D | EbS | B | WbS |
| Arcturus | 7 19 | A | ENE | E | WNW |
| Antares | 4 17 | E | SEbE | A | SWbW |

*b = "by"

# "I haven't been this excited since I got my first bicycle!"

## Introducing *ZOOMER!*

**The portable, folding, battery-powered chair that offers easy one-handed operation**

Remember when you were a child and got your first bicycle? I do. It gave me a sense of independence . . . I felt like I could go anywhere, and it was so much easier and more enjoyable than walking. Well, at my age, that bike wouldn't do me much good. Fortunately, there's a new invention that gives me the freedom and independence to go wherever I want . . . safely and easily. It's called the Zoomer, and it's changed my life.

After just one trip around your home in the Zoomer, you'll marvel at how easy it is to navigate. It is designed to maneuver in tight spaces like doorways, between furniture, and around corners. It can go over thresholds and works great on any kind of floor or carpet. It's not bulky or cumbersome, so it can roll right up to a table or desk– there's no need to transfer to a chair. Its

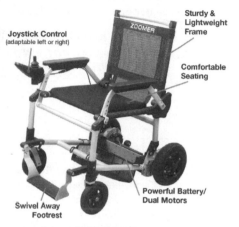

Joystick Control (adaptable left or right)

Sturdy & Lightweight Frame

Comfortable Seating

Powerful Battery/ Dual Motors

Swivel Away Footrest

sturdy yet lightweight aluminum frame makes it durable and comfortable. Its dual motors power it at up to 3.7 miles per hour and its automatic electromagnetic brakes stop on a dime. The rechargeable battery powers it for up to 8 miles on a single charge. Plus, its exclusive foldable design enables you to transport it easily and even store it in a closet or under a bed when it's not in use.

Why spend another day letting mobility issues hamper your lifestyle? Call now and find out how you can have your very own Zoomer.

**Now available with sporty two-arm lever steering** (Zinger Chair)

**Ready to get your own Zoomer? We'd love to talk to you.**

Call now toll free and order one today! **1-888-235-6822**

Please mention code 117050 when ordering.

# THE TWILIGHT ZONE/METEOR SHOWERS

Twilight is the time when the sky is partially illuminated preceding sunrise and again following sunset. The ranges of twilight are defined according to the Sun's position below the horizon. **Civil twilight** occurs when the Sun's center is between the horizon and 6 degrees below the horizon (visually, the horizon is clearly defined). **Nautical twilight** occurs when the center is between 6 and 12 degrees below the horizon (the horizon is distinct). **Astronomical twilight** occurs when the center is between 12 and 18 degrees below the horizon (sky illumination is imperceptible). When the center is at 18 degrees (**dawn** or **dark**) or below, there is no illumination.

## LENGTH OF ASTRONOMICAL TWILIGHT (HOURS AND MINUTES)

| LATITUDE | JAN. 1–APR. 10 | APR. 11–MAY 2 | MAY 3–MAY 14 | MAY 15–MAY 25 | MAY 26–JULY 22 | JULY 23–AUG. 3 | AUG. 4–AUG. 14 | AUG. 15–SEPT. 5 | SEPT. 6–DEC. 31 |
|---|---|---|---|---|---|---|---|---|---|
| 25°N to 30°N | 1 20 | 1 23 | 1 26 | 1 29 | 1 32 | 1 29 | 1 26 | 1 23 | 1 20 |
| 31°N to 36°N | 1 26 | 1 28 | 1 34 | 1 38 | 1 43 | 1 38 | 1 34 | 1 28 | 1 26 |
| 37°N to 42°N | 1 33 | 1 39 | 1 47 | 1 52 | 1 59 | 1 52 | 1 47 | 1 39 | 1 33 |
| 43°N to 47°N | 1 42 | 1 51 | 2 02 | 2 13 | 2 27 | 2 13 | 2 02 | 1 51 | 1 42 |
| 48°N to 49°N | 1 50 | 2 04 | 2 22 | 2 42 | – | 2 42 | 2 22 | 2 04 | 1 50 |

**TO DETERMINE THE LENGTH OF TWILIGHT:** The length of twilight changes with latitude and the time of year. See the **Time Corrections, page 238,** to find the latitude of your city or the city nearest you. Use that figure in the chart above with the appropriate date to calculate the length of twilight in your area.

**TO DETERMINE ARRIVAL OF DAWN OR DARK:** Calculate the sunrise/sunset times for your locality using the instructions in **How to Use This Almanac, page 116.**

Subtract the length of twilight from the time of sunrise to determine when dawn breaks. Add the length of twilight to the time of sunset to determine when dark descends.

### EXAMPLE:
#### BOSTON, MASS. (LATITUDE 42°22')

| | |
|---|---|
| Sunrise, August 1 | 5:36 A.M. ET |
| Length of twilight | - 1 52 |
| Dawn breaks | 3:44 A.M. |
| Sunset, August 1 | 8:04 P.M. ET |
| Length of twilight | +1 52 |
| Dark descends | 9:56 P.M. |

## PRINCIPAL METEOR SHOWERS

| SHOWER | BEST VIEWING | POINT OF ORIGIN | DATE OF MAXIMUM* | NO. PER HOUR** | ASSOCIATED COMET |
|---|---|---|---|---|---|
| **Quadrantid** | **Predawn** | N | Jan. 4 | 25 | – |
| Lyrid | Predawn | S | Apr. 22 | 10 | Thatcher |
| Eta Aquarid | Predawn | SE | May 4 | 10 | Halley |
| Delta Aquarid | Predawn | S | July 30 | 10 | – |
| **Perseid** | **Predawn** | **NE** | **Aug. 11-13** | **50** | **Swift-Tuttle** |
| Draconid | Late evening | NW | Oct. 9 | 6 | Giacobini-Zinner |
| Orionid | Predawn | S | Oct. 21-22 | 15 | Halley |
| Northern Taurid | Late evening | S | Nov. 9 | 3 | Encke |
| Leonid | Predawn | S | Nov. 17-18 | 10 | Tempel-Tuttle |
| Andromedid | Late evening | S | Nov. 25-27 | 5 | Biela |
| **Geminid** | **All night** | **NE** | **Dec. 13-14** | **75** | – |
| Ursid | Predawn | N | Dec. 22 | 5 | Tuttle |

*May vary by 1 or 2 days  **In a moonless, rural sky  **Bold** = most prominent

# NEW PROSTATE PILL HELPS RELIEVE SYMPTOMS WITHOUT DRUGS OR SURGERY

## Combats all-night bathroom urges and embarrassment... Yet most doctors don't even know about it!

By Health Writer Peter Metler

Thanks to a brand new discovery made from a rare prostate relief plant; thousands of men across America are taking their lives back from "prostate hell". This remarkable new natural supplement helps you:

- **MINIMIZE** constant urges to urinate
- **END** embarrassing sexual "let-downs"
- **SUPPORT** a strong, healthy urine flow
- **GET** a restful night of uninterrupted sleep
- **STOP** false alarms, dribbles
- **ENJOY** a truly empty bladder

More men than ever before are dealing with prostate problems that range from annoying to downright EMBARRASSING! But now, research has discovered a new solution so remarkable that helps alleviate symptoms associated with an enlarged prostate (sexual failure, lost sleep, bladder discomfort and urgent runs to the bathroom). Like nothing before!

Yet 9 out of 10 doctors don't know about it! Here's why: Due to strict managed health care constrictions, many MD's are struggling to keep their practices afloat. "Unfortunately, there's no money in prescribing natural products. They aren't nearly as profitable," says a confidential source. Instead, doctors rely on toxic drugs that help, but could leave you sexually "powerless" (or a lot worse)!

On a CNN Special, Medical Correspondent Dr. Steve Salvatore shocked America by quoting a statistic from the prestigious Journal of American Medical Association that stated, "... about 60% of men who go under the knife for a prostatectomy are left UNABLE to perform sexually!"

### PROSTATE PROBLEM SOLVED!

But now you can now beat the odds. And enjoy better sleep, a powerful urine stream and a long and healthy love life. The secret? You need to load your diet with essential Phyto-Nutrients, (traditionally found in certain fruits, vegetables and grains).

The problem is, most Phyto-Nutrients never get into your bloodstream. They're destroyed

### HERE ARE 6 WARNING SIGNS YOU BETTER NOT IGNORE

- ✓ Waking up 2 to 6 times a night to urinate
- ✓ A constant feeling that you have to "go"... but can't
- ✓ A burning sensation when you do go
- ✓ A weak urine stream
- ✓ A feeling that your bladder is never completely empty
- ✓ Embarrassing sputtering, dripping & staining

by today's food preparation methods (cooking, long storage times and food additives).

### YEARS OF RESEARCH

Thankfully, a small company (Wellness Logix™) out of Maine, is on a mission to change that. They've created a product that arms men who suffer with prostate inflammation with new hope. And it's fast becoming the #1 Prostate formula in America.

*Prostate IQ™* gives men the super-concentrated dose of Phyto-Nutrients they need to beat prostate symptoms. "You just can't get them from your regular diet" says Daniel. It's taken a long time to understand how to capture the prostate relieving power of this amazing botanical. But their hard work paid off. *Prostate IQ™* is different than any other prostate supplement on the market...

### DON'T BE FOOLED BY CHEAP FORMULATIONS!

Many hope you won't notice, but a lot of prostate supplements fall embarrassingly short with their dosages. The formulas may be okay, but they won't do a darn thing for you unless you take 10 or more tablets a day. *Prostate IQ™* contains a whopping 300mg of this special "Smart Prostate Plant". So it's loaded with Phyto-Nutrients. Plus, it gets inside your bloodstream faster and stays inside for maximum results!

THESE STATEMENTS HAVE NOT BEEN EVALUATED BY THE FDA. THESE PRODUCTS ARE NOT INTENDED TO DIAGNOSE, TREAT, CURE OR PREVENT ANY DISEASE. OFFER NOT AVAILABLE TO RESIDENTS OF IOWA.

# THE VISIBLE PLANETS

Listed here for Boston are viewing suggestions for and the rise and set times (ET) of Venus, Mars, Jupiter, and Saturn on specific days each month, as well as when it is best to view Mercury. Approximate rise and set times for other days can be found by interpolation. Use the Key Letters at the right of each listing to convert the times for other localities **(see pages 116 and 238).**

**GET ALL PLANET RISE AND SET TIMES BY POSTAL CODE VIA ALMANAC.COM/2023.**

## VENUS

Venus is often called our "sister planet," based on the fact that it's not only our nearest planetary world but also nearly identical to us in mass as well as size. Starting off in January as an evening star, Venus is at its dimmest magnitude of the year before brightening steadily to a shadow-casting magnitude –4.7 through most of July. Then, after an inferior conjunction on August 13, it's a riveting morning star for the final 4 months of the year, attaining another dazzling maximum magnitude –4.8 in mid-September. Always enhancing the on-going spectacle, Venus delivers glorious conjunctions, or meet-ups, with the crescent Moon, various planets, and several bright zodiacal stars throughout the year.

| | | | | | | | | | | | | |
|---|---|---|---|---|---|---|---|---|---|---|---|---|
| Jan. 1 | set | 5:41 | A | Apr. 1 | set | 10:24 | E | July 1 | set | 10:39 | D | Oct. 1 | rise | 3:02 | B |
| Jan. 11 | set | 6:06 | B | Apr. 11 | set | 10:48 | E | July 11 | set | 10:04 | D | Oct. 11 | rise | 3:02 | B |
| Jan. 21 | set | 6:32 | B | Apr. 21 | set | 11:09 | E | July 21 | set | 9:20 | D | Oct. 21 | rise | 3:08 | B |
| Feb. 1 | set | 7:00 | B | May 1 | set | 11:26 | E | Aug. 1 | set | 8:20 | D | Nov. 1 | rise | 3:20 | C |
| Feb. 11 | set | 7:25 | C | May 11 | set | 11:37 | E | Aug. 11 | rise | 6:23 | B | Nov. 11 | rise | 2:34 | C |
| Feb. 21 | set | 7:50 | C | May 21 | set | 11:41 | E | Aug. 21 | rise | 5:16 | B | Nov. 21 | rise | 2:51 | D |
| Mar. 1 | set | 8:09 | D | June 1 | set | 11:37 | E | Sept. 1 | rise | 4:14 | B | Dec. 1 | rise | 3:10 | D |
| Mar. 11 | set | 8:33 | D | June 11 | set | 11:24 | E | Sept. 11 | rise | 3:35 | B | Dec. 11 | rise | 3:31 | D |
| Mar. 21 | set | 9:58 | D | June 21 | set | 11:05 | E | Sept. 21 | rise | 3:12 | B | Dec. 21 | rise | 3:53 | D |
| | | | | | | | | | | | | Dec. 31 | rise | 4:15 | E |

## MARS

This is a bad year for Mars—and a strange one. The Red Planet, which is actually orange with tan or cocoa-color areas, comes nearest Earth every 26 months. So, years when Mars is brilliant and eye-catching alternate with those like 2023, when it has no close encounter, or opposition, with Earth at all. On January 1, Mars starts off in Taurus at a very brilliant magnitude –1.2, having had its close approach (opposition) just 3 weeks earlier, on December 8. Then it steadily fades, never getting back to even 1st magnitude after April, and has its conjunction behind the Sun on November 18. Indeed, there won't be a Mars opposition in 2024 either, meaning that we will experience a rare 2-year absence of a Martian close encounter.

| | | | | | | | | | | | | |
|---|---|---|---|---|---|---|---|---|---|---|---|---|
| Jan. 1 | set | 5:11 | E | Apr. 1 | set | 2:08 | E | July 1 | set | 10:52 | D | Oct. 1 | set | 7:00 | B |
| Jan. 11 | set | 4:27 | E | Apr. 11 | set | 1:50 | E | July 11 | set | 10:27 | D | Oct. 11 | set | 6:36 | B |
| Jan. 21 | set | 3:50 | E | Apr. 21 | set | 1:31 | E | July 21 | set | 10:02 | D | Oct. 21 | set | 6:14 | B |
| Feb. 1 | set | 3:15 | E | May 1 | set | 1:11 | E | Aug. 1 | set | 9:34 | D | Nov. 1 | set | 5:50 | B |
| Feb. 11 | set | 2:48 | E | May 11 | set | 12:51 | E | Aug. 11 | set | 9:08 | D | Nov. 11 | set | 4:30 | B |
| Feb. 21 | set | 2:25 | E | May 21 | set | 12:30 | E | Aug. 21 | set | 8:43 | C | Nov. 21 | rise | 6:39 | E |
| Mar. 1 | set | 2:08 | E | June 1 | set | 12:05 | E | Sept. 1 | set | 8:15 | C | Dec. 1 | rise | 6:36 | E |
| Mar. 11 | set | 1:48 | E | June 11 | set | 11:40 | E | Sept. 11 | set | 7:49 | C | Dec. 11 | rise | 6:33 | E |
| Mar. 21 | set | 2:29 | E | June 21 | set | 11:17 | E | Sept. 21 | set | 7:24 | C | Dec. 21 | rise | 6:29 | E |
| | | | | | | | | | | | | Dec. 31 | rise | 6:24 | E |

**BOLD = P.M.** LIGHT = A.M.

## JUPITER

Unlike fast-moving Mercury and Venus and the chameleon Mars, Jupiter is steadier and more predictable. Earth's much faster speed causes it to pass the Gas Giant every 13 months. At such oppositions, Jupiter grows brighter and bigger but not spectacularly so. This makes the planet's opposition on November 3 an occasion of note, especially since optimum viewing conditions will last for a few weeks. Jupiter's brilliance, an impressive magnitude –2.9, is topped this year only by that of Venus, so its conjunctions with the Moon and other planets are eye-catching affairs.

| | | | | | | | | | | | | | | |
|---|---|---|---|---|---|---|---|---|---|---|---|---|---|
| Jan. 1 | set | 11:06 | C | Apr. 1 | set | 7:44 | D | July 1 | rise | 1:43 | B | Oct. 1 | rise | 7:53 | B |
| Jan. 11 | set | 10:33 | C | Apr. 11 | rise | 6:18 | B | July 11 | rise | 1:08 | B | Oct. 11 | rise | 7:11 | B |
| Jan. 21 | set | 10:02 | C | Apr. 21 | rise | 5:44 | B | July 21 | rise | 12:33 | B | Oct. 21 | rise | 6:28 | B |
| Feb. 1 | set | 9:29 | C | May 1 | rise | 5:10 | B | Aug. 1 | rise | 11:50 | B | Nov. 1 | rise | 5:41 | B |
| Feb. 11 | set | 9:00 | C | May 11 | rise | 4:37 | B | Aug. 11 | rise | 11:13 | B | Nov. 11 | set | 5:46 | D |
| Feb. 21 | set | 8:31 | C | May 21 | rise | 4:03 | B | Aug. 21 | rise | 10:36 | B | Nov. 21 | set | 5:00 | D |
| Mar. 1 | set | 8:09 | C | June 1 | rise | 3:26 | B | Sept. 1 | rise | 9:54 | B | Dec. 1 | set | 4:15 | D |
| Mar. 11 | set | 7:41 | D | June 11 | rise | 2:52 | B | Sept. 11 | rise | 9:14 | B | Dec. 11 | set | 3:32 | D |
| Mar. 21 | set | 8:14 | D | June 21 | rise | 2:18 | B | Sept. 21 | rise | 8:34 | B | Dec. 21 | set | 2:50 | D |
| | | | | | | | | | | | | Dec. 31 | set | 2:10 | D |

## SATURN

The Ringed Planet starts the year low in the west at dusk, in Aquarius. After its conjunction with Venus on January 22, Saturn sinks lower into twilight before becoming lost by month's end. It emerges in the east as a morning star in April, to remain visible for the rest of the year. Saturn's rings are angled at an intermediate position, observable through any telescope with more than 30× magnification. The planet comes up before midnight in July, brightening until its opposition on August 27. In December, Saturn stands on the meridian, due south, at its highest position at nightfall. Look for it to meet the Moon on December 17.

| | | | | | | | | | | | | | | |
|---|---|---|---|---|---|---|---|---|---|---|---|---|---|
| Jan. 1 | set | 7:46 | B | Apr. 1 | rise | 5:08 | D | July 1 | rise | 11:18 | D | Oct. 1 | set | 3:38 | B |
| Jan. 11 | set | 7:12 | B | Apr. 11 | rise | 4:31 | D | July 11 | rise | 10:38 | D | Oct. 11 | set | 2:56 | B |
| Jan. 21 | set | 6:38 | B | Apr. 21 | rise | 3:54 | D | July 21 | rise | 9:58 | D | Oct. 21 | set | 2:15 | B |
| Feb. 1 | set | 6:02 | B | May 1 | rise | 3:16 | D | Aug. 1 | rise | 9:13 | D | Nov. 1 | set | 1:31 | B |
| Feb. 11 | set | 5:29 | B | May 11 | rise | 2:39 | D | Aug. 11 | rise | 8:32 | D | Nov. 11 | set | 11:48 | B |
| Feb. 21 | rise | 6:30 | D | May 21 | rise | 2:01 | D | Aug. 21 | rise | 7:51 | D | Nov. 21 | set | 11:10 | B |
| Mar. 1 | rise | 6:01 | D | June 1 | rise | 1:19 | D | Sept. 1 | set | 5:46 | B | Dec. 1 | set | 10:33 | B |
| Mar. 11 | rise | 5:24 | D | June 11 | rise | 12:40 | D | Sept. 11 | set | 5:03 | B | Dec. 11 | set | 9:56 | B |
| Mar. 21 | rise | 5:48 | D | June 21 | rise | 11:57 | D | Sept. 21 | set | 4:20 | B | Dec. 21 | set | 9:21 | B |
| | | | | | | | | | | | | Dec. 31 | set | 8:46 | B |

## MERCURY

From Earth, Mercury's observed year appears to be only about 4 months long: It spends about 2 months as a morning star visible before dawn and then, after a hiatus, emerges as an evening star low in the west after sunset. Between these windows of visibility, the planet is either behind the Sun or in front of it, lost in glare. To be observable, Mercury must be at least 5 degrees above the horizon 40 minutes before sunrise or after sunset and boast a brilliance of at least 1st magnitude. This year, its most favorable evening star conditions happen in mid-April, while in the predawn eastern sky, Mercury will be best in early September.

**DO NOT CONFUSE:** *Mars with Taurus's brightest star, Aldebaran, on Feb. 3. Both are orange, but Mars is brighter and higher. • Jupiter with Venus on Feb. 28 and March 1, when they meet at nightfall in the west for the year's best conjunction. Venus is brighter. • Mercury with Mars on Aug. 3, low in the west after sunset. Both are orange, but Mercury is brighter. • Uranus with the stars in Taurus on Nov. 13. Uranus is the green "star" halfway between Jupiter and the Pleiades star cluster.*

# ASTRONOMICAL GLOSSARY

**APHELION (APH.):** The point in a planet's orbit that is farthest from the Sun.

**APOGEE (APO.):** The point in the Moon's orbit that is farthest from Earth.

**CELESTIAL EQUATOR (EQ.):** The imaginary circle around the celestial sphere that can be thought of as the plane of Earth's equator projected out onto the sphere.

**CELESTIAL SPHERE:** An imaginary sphere projected into space that represents the entire sky, with an observer on Earth at its center. All celestial bodies other than Earth are imagined as being on its inside surface.

**CIRCUMPOLAR:** Always visible above the horizon, such as a circumpolar star.

**CONJUNCTION:** The time at which two or more celestial bodies appear closest in the sky. **Inferior (Inf.):** Mercury or Venus is between the Sun and Earth. **Superior (Sup.):** The Sun is between a planet and Earth. Actual dates for conjunctions are given on the **Right-Hand Calendar Pages, 121–147;** the best times for viewing the closely aligned bodies are given in **Sky Watch** on the **Left-Hand Calendar Pages, 120–146.**

**DECLINATION:** The celestial latitude of an object in the sky, measured in degrees north or south of the celestial equator; comparable to latitude on Earth. This Almanac gives the Sun's declination at noon.

**ECLIPSE, LUNAR:** The full Moon enters the shadow of Earth, which cuts off all or part of the sunlight reflected off the Moon. **Total:** The Moon passes completely through the umbra (central dark part) of Earth's shadow. **Partial:** Only part of the Moon passes through the umbra. **Penumbral:** The Moon passes through only the penumbra (area of partial darkness surrounding the umbra). See **page 102** for more information about eclipses.

**ECLIPSE, SOLAR:** Earth enters the shadow of the new Moon, which cuts off all or part of the Sun's light. **Total:** Earth passes through the umbra (central dark part) of the Moon's shadow, resulting in totality for observers within a narrow band on Earth. **Annular:** The Moon appears silhouetted against the Sun, with a ring of sunlight showing around it. **Partial:** The Moon blocks only part of the Sun.

**ECLIPTIC:** The apparent annual path of the Sun around the celestial sphere. The plane of the ecliptic is tipped 23½° from the celestial equator.

**ELONGATION:** The difference in degrees between the celestial longitudes of a planet and the Sun. **Greatest Elongation (Gr. Elong.):** The greatest apparent distance of a planet from the Sun, as seen from Earth.

**EPACT:** A number from 1 to 30 that indicates the Moon's age on January 1 at Greenwich, England; used in determining the date of Easter.

**EQUINOX:** When the Sun crosses the celestial equator. This event occurs two times each year: **Vernal** is around March 20 and **Autumnal** is around September 22.

**EVENING STAR:** A planet that is above the western horizon at sunset and less than 180° east of the Sun in right ascension.

**GOLDEN NUMBER:** A number in the 19-year Metonic cycle of the Moon, used in determining the date of Easter. See **page 149** for this year's Golden Number.

**MAGNITUDE:** A measure of a celestial object's brightness. **Apparent magnitude** measures the brightness of an object as seen from Earth. Objects with an apparent magnitude of 6 or less are observable to the naked eye. The lower the magnitude, the greater the brightness; an object with a magnitude of –1, e.g., is brighter than one with a magnitude of +1.

*(continued)*

111

# ASTRONOMICAL GLOSSARY

**MIDNIGHT:** Astronomically, the time when the Sun is opposite its highest point in the sky. Both 12 hours before and after noon (so, technically, both A.M. and P.M.), midnight in civil time is usually treated as the beginning of the day. It is displayed as 12:00 A.M. on 12-hour digital clocks. On a 24-hour cycle, 00:00, not 24:00, usually indicates midnight.

**MOON ON EQUATOR:** The Moon is on the celestial equator.

**MOON RIDES HIGH/RUNS LOW:** The Moon is highest above or farthest below the celestial equator.

**MOONRISE/MOONSET:** When the Moon rises above or sets below the horizon.

**MOON'S PHASES:** The changing appearance of the Moon, caused by the different angles at which it is illuminated by the Sun. **First Quarter:** Right half of the Moon is illuminated. **Full:** The Sun and the Moon are in opposition; the entire disk of the Moon is illuminated. **Last Quarter:** Left half of the Moon is illuminated. **New:** The Sun and the Moon are in conjunction; the Moon is darkened because it lines up between Earth and the Sun.

**MOON'S PLACE, Astronomical:** The position of the Moon within the constellations on the celestial sphere at midnight. **Astrological:** The position of the Moon within the tropical zodiac, whose twelve 30° segments (signs) along the ecliptic were named more than 2,000 years ago after constellations within each area. Because of precession and other factors, the zodiac signs no longer match actual constellation positions.

**MORNING STAR:** A planet that is above the eastern horizon at sunrise and less than 180° west of the Sun in right ascension.

**NODE:** Either of the two points where a celestial body's orbit intersects the ecliptic. **Ascending:** When the body is moving from south to north of the ecliptic. **Descending:** When the body is moving from north to south of the ecliptic.

**OCCULTATION (OCCN.):** When the Moon or a planet eclipses a star or planet.

**OPPOSITION:** The Moon or a planet appears on the opposite side of the sky from the Sun (elongation 180°).

**PERIGEE (PERIG.):** The point in the Moon's orbit that is closest to Earth.

**PERIHELION (PERIH.):** The point in a planet's orbit that is closest to the Sun.

**PRECESSION:** The slowly changing position of the stars and equinoxes in the sky caused by a slight wobble as Earth rotates around its axis.

**RIGHT ASCENSION (R.A.):** The celestial longitude of an object in the sky, measured eastward along the celestial equator in hours of time from the vernal equinox; comparable to longitude on Earth.

**SOLSTICE, Summer:** When the Sun reaches its greatest declination (23½°) north of the celestial equator, around June 21. **Winter:** When the Sun reaches its greatest declination (23½°) south of the celestial equator, around December 21.

**STATIONARY (STAT.):** The brief period of apparent halted movement of a planet against the background of the stars shortly before it appears to move backward/westward (retrograde motion) or forward/eastward (direct motion).

**SUN FAST/SLOW:** When a sundial is ahead of (fast) or behind (slow) clock time.

**SUNRISE/SUNSET:** The visible rising/setting of the upper edge of the Sun's disk across the unobstructed horizon of an observer whose eyes are 15 feet above ground level.

**TWILIGHT:** See **page 106.** ∎

*Note: These definitions apply to the Northern Hemisphere; some do not hold true for locations in the Southern Hemisphere.*

113

# 2022

## JANUARY
```
 S  M  T  W  T  F  S
                   1
 2  3  4  5  6  7  8
 9 10 11 12 13 14 15
16 17 18 19 20 21 22
23 24 25 26 27 28 29
30 31
```

## FEBRUARY
```
 S  M  T  W  T  F  S
       1  2  3  4  5
 6  7  8  9 10 11 12
13 14 15 16 17 18 19
20 21 22 23 24 25 26
27 28
```

## MARCH
```
 S  M  T  W  T  F  S
       1  2  3  4  5
 6  7  8  9 10 11 12
13 14 15 16 17 18 19
20 21 22 23 24 25 26
27 28 29 30 31
```

## APRIL
```
 S  M  T  W  T  F  S
                1  2
 3  4  5  6  7  8  9
10 11 12 13 14 15 16
17 18 19 20 21 22 23
24 25 26 27 28 29 30
```

## MAY
```
 S  M  T  W  T  F  S
 1  2  3  4  5  6  7
 8  9 10 11 12 13 14
15 16 17 18 19 20 21
22 23 24 25 26 27 28
29 30 31
```

## JUNE
```
 S  M  T  W  T  F  S
          1  2  3  4
 5  6  7  8  9 10 11
12 13 14 15 16 17 18
19 20 21 22 23 24 25
26 27 28 29 30
```

## JULY
```
 S  M  T  W  T  F  S
                1  2
 3  4  5  6  7  8  9
10 11 12 13 14 15 16
17 18 19 20 21 22 23
24 25 26 27 28 29 30
31
```

## AUGUST
```
 S  M  T  W  T  F  S
    1  2  3  4  5  6
 7  8  9 10 11 12 13
14 15 16 17 18 19 20
21 22 23 24 25 26 27
28 29 30 31
```

## SEPTEMBER
```
 S  M  T  W  T  F  S
             1  2  3
 4  5  6  7  8  9 10
11 12 13 14 15 16 17
18 19 20 21 22 23 24
25 26 27 28 29 30
```

## OCTOBER
```
 S  M  T  W  T  F  S
                   1
 2  3  4  5  6  7  8
 9 10 11 12 13 14 15
16 17 18 19 20 21 22
23 24 25 26 27 28 29
30 31
```

## NOVEMBER
```
 S  M  T  W  T  F  S
       1  2  3  4  5
 6  7  8  9 10 11 12
13 14 15 16 17 18 19
20 21 22 23 24 25 26
27 28 29 30
```

## DECEMBER
```
 S  M  T  W  T  F  S
             1  2  3
 4  5  6  7  8  9 10
11 12 13 14 15 16 17
18 19 20 21 22 23 24
25 26 27 28 29 30 31
```

# 2023

## JANUARY
```
 S  M  T  W  T  F  S
 1  2  3  4  5  6  7
 8  9 10 11 12 13 14
15 16 17 18 19 20 21
22 23 24 25 26 27 28
29 30 31
```

## FEBRUARY
```
 S  M  T  W  T  F  S
          1  2  3  4
 5  6  7  8  9 10 11
12 13 14 15 16 17 18
19 20 21 22 23 24 25
26 27 28
```

## MARCH
```
 S  M  T  W  T  F  S
          1  2  3  4
 5  6  7  8  9 10 11
12 13 14 15 16 17 18
19 20 21 22 23 24 25
26 27 28 29 30 31
```

## APRIL
```
 S  M  T  W  T  F  S
                   1
 2  3  4  5  6  7  8
 9 10 11 12 13 14 15
16 17 18 19 20 21 22
23 24 25 26 27 28 29
30
```

## MAY
```
 S  M  T  W  T  F  S
    1  2  3  4  5  6
 7  8  9 10 11 12 13
14 15 16 17 18 19 20
21 22 23 24 25 26 27
28 29 30 31
```

## JUNE
```
 S  M  T  W  T  F  S
             1  2  3
 4  5  6  7  8  9 10
11 12 13 14 15 16 17
18 19 20 21 22 23 24
25 26 27 28 29 30
```

## JULY
```
 S  M  T  W  T  F  S
                   1
 2  3  4  5  6  7  8
 9 10 11 12 13 14 15
16 17 18 19 20 21 22
23 24 25 26 27 28 29
30 31
```

## AUGUST
```
 S  M  T  W  T  F  S
       1  2  3  4  5
 6  7  8  9 10 11 12
13 14 15 16 17 18 19
20 21 22 23 24 25 26
27 28 29 30 31
```

## SEPTEMBER
```
 S  M  T  W  T  F  S
             1  2
 3  4  5  6  7  8  9
10 11 12 13 14 15 16
17 18 19 20 21 22 23
24 25 26 27 28 29 30
```

## OCTOBER
```
 S  M  T  W  T  F  S
 1  2  3  4  5  6  7
 8  9 10 11 12 13 14
15 16 17 18 19 20 21
22 23 24 25 26 27 28
29 30 31
```

## NOVEMBER
```
 S  M  T  W  T  F  S
          1  2  3  4
 5  6  7  8  9 10 11
12 13 14 15 16 17 18
19 20 21 22 23 24 25
26 27 28 29 30
```

## DECEMBER
```
 S  M  T  W  T  F  S
                1  2
 3  4  5  6  7  8  9
10 11 12 13 14 15 16
17 18 19 20 21 22 23
24 25 26 27 28 29 30
31
```

# 2024

## JANUARY
```
 S  M  T  W  T  F  S
    1  2  3  4  5  6
 7  8  9 10 11 12 13
14 15 16 17 18 19 20
21 22 23 24 25 26 27
28 29 30 31
```

## FEBRUARY
```
 S  M  T  W  T  F  S
             1  2  3
 4  5  6  7  8  9 10
11 12 13 14 15 16 17
18 19 20 21 22 23 24
25 26 27 28 29
```

## MARCH
```
 S  M  T  W  T  F  S
                1  2
 3  4  5  6  7  8  9
10 11 12 13 14 15 16
17 18 19 20 21 22 23
24 25 26 27 28 29 30
31
```

## APRIL
```
 S  M  T  W  T  F  S
    1  2  3  4  5  6
 7  8  9 10 11 12 13
14 15 16 17 18 19 20
21 22 23 24 25 26 27
28 29 30
```

## MAY
```
 S  M  T  W  T  F  S
          1  2  3  4
 5  6  7  8  9 10 11
12 13 14 15 16 17 18
19 20 21 22 23 24 25
26 27 28 29 30 31
```

## JUNE
```
 S  M  T  W  T  F  S
                   1
 2  3  4  5  6  7  8
 9 10 11 12 13 14 15
16 17 18 19 20 21 22
23 24 25 26 27 28 29
30
```

## JULY
```
 S  M  T  W  T  F  S
    1  2  3  4  5  6
 7  8  9 10 11 12 13
14 15 16 17 18 19 20
21 22 23 24 25 26 27
28 29 30 31
```

## AUGUST
```
 S  M  T  W  T  F  S
             1  2  3
 4  5  6  7  8  9 10
11 12 13 14 15 16 17
18 19 20 21 22 23 24
25 26 27 28 29 30 31
```

## SEPTEMBER
```
 S  M  T  W  T  F  S
 1  2  3  4  5  6  7
 8  9 10 11 12 13 14
15 16 17 18 19 20 21
22 23 24 25 26 27 28
29 30
```

## OCTOBER
```
 S  M  T  W  T  F  S
          1  2  3  4  5
 6  7  8  9 10 11 12
13 14 15 16 17 18 19
20 21 22 23 24 25 26
27 28 29 30 31
```

## NOVEMBER
```
 S  M  T  W  T  F  S
                1  2
 3  4  5  6  7  8  9
10 11 12 13 14 15 16
17 18 19 20 21 22 23
24 25 26 27 28 29 30
```

## DECEMBER
```
 S  M  T  W  T  F  S
 1  2  3  4  5  6  7
 8  9 10 11 12 13 14
15 16 17 18 19 20 21
22 23 24 25 26 27 28
29 30 31
```

# A CALENDAR OF THE HEAVENS FOR 2023

−Beth Krommes

CALENDAR

The **Calendar Pages (120–147)** are the heart of *The Old Farmer's Almanac.* They present sky sightings and astronomical data for the entire year and are what make this book a true almanac, a "calendar of the heavens." In essence, these pages are unchanged since 1792, when Robert B. Thomas published his first edition. The long columns of numbers and symbols reveal all of nature's precision, rhythm, and glory, providing an astronomical look at the year 2023.

## HOW TO USE THE CALENDAR PAGES

The astronomical data on the **Calendar Pages (120–147)** are calculated for Boston (where Robert B. Thomas learned to calculate the data for his first Almanac). Guidance for calculating the times of these events for your locale appears on **pages 116–117.** Note that the results will be *approximate.* Find the *exact* time of any astronomical event at your locale via **Almanac.com/2023.** You can also go to **Almanac.com/SkyMap** to print each month's "Sky Map," which may be useful for viewing with "Sky Watch" in the Calendar Pages.

For a list of 2023 holidays and observances, see **pages 148–149.** Also check out the **Glossary of Almanac Oddities** on **pages 150–151,** which describes some of the more obscure entries traditionally found on the **Right-Hand Calendar Pages (121–147).**

**ABOUT THE TIMES:** All times are given in ET (Eastern Time), except where otherwise noted as AT (Atlantic Time, +1 hour), CT (Central Time, –1), MT (Mountain Time, –2), PT (Pacific Time, –3), AKT (Alaska Time, –4), or HAT (Hawaii-Aleutian Time, –5). Between 2:00 A.M., March 12, and 2:00 A.M., November 5, Daylight Saving Time is assumed in those locales where it is observed.

**ABOUT THE TIDES:** Tide times for Boston appear on **pages 120–146;** for Boston tide heights, see **pages 121–147.** Tide Corrections for East Coast locations appear on **pages 236–237.** Tide heights and times for locations across the United States and Canada are available via **Almanac.com/2023.**

# The Left-Hand Calendar Pages, 120 to 146

On these pages are the year's astronomical predictions for Boston (42°22' N, 71°3' W). Learn how to calculate the times of these events for your locale here or via **Almanac.com/2023**.

## A SAMPLE MONTH

**SKY WATCH:** The paragraph at the top of each Left-Hand Calendar Page describes the best times to view conjunctions, meteor showers, planets, and more. (Also see **How to Use the Right-Hand Calendar Pages, page 118.**)

| | | | | | | | | | | | | | | |
|---|---|---|---|---|---|---|---|---|---|---|---|---|---|---|
| | | | **1** | | **2** | | **3** | **4** | **5** | | **6** | | **7** | **8** |
| DAY OF YEAR | DAY OF MONTH | DAY OF WEEK | ☀ RISES H. M. | RISE KEY | ☀ SETS H. M. | SET KEY | LENGTH OF DAY H. M. | SUN FAST M. | SUN DECLINATION ° ' | HIGH TIDE TIMES BOSTON | ☾ RISES H. M. | RISE KEY | ☾ SETS H. M. | SET KEY | ☾ ASTRON. PLACE | ☾ AGE |
| 60 | 1 | Fr. | 6:20 | D | 5:34 | C | 11 14 | 4 | 7 s. 30 | 7¼ 8 | 3:30 | E | 12:58 | B | SAG | 25 |
| 61 | 2 | Sa. | 6:18 | D | 5:35 | C | 11 17 | 4 | 7 s. 07 | 8¼ 9 | 4:16 | E | 1:51 | B | SAG | 26 |
| 62 | 3 | **F** | 6:17 | D | 5:36 | C | 11 19 | 4 | 6 s. 44 | 9¼ 9¾ | 4:56 | E | 2:47 | B | CAP | 27 |
| 63 | 4 | M. | 6:15 | D | 5:37 | C | 11 22 | 4 | 6 s. 21 | 10 10½ | 5:31 | E | 3:45 | C | CAP | 28 |

**1.** To calculate the sunrise time in your locale: Choose a day. Note its Sun Rise Key Letter. Find your (nearest) city on **page 238**. Add or subtract the minutes that correspond to the Sun Rise Key Letter to/from the sunrise time for Boston.[†]

### EXAMPLE:

To calculate the sunrise time in Denver, Colorado, on day 1:

| | |
|---|---|
| Sunrise, Boston, with Key Letter D (above) | 6:20 A.M. ET |
| Value of Key Letter D for Denver (p. 238) | + 11 minutes |
| Sunrise, Denver | 6:31 A.M. MT |

To calculate your sunset time, repeat, using Boston's sunset time and its Sun Set Key Letter value.

**2.** To calculate the length of day: Choose a day. Note the Sun Rise and Sun Set Key Letters. Find your (nearest) city on **page 238**. Add or subtract the minutes that correspond to the Sun Set Key Letter to/from Boston's length of day. *Reverse* the sign (e.g., minus to plus) of the Sun Rise Key Letter minutes. Add or subtract it to/from the first result.

### EXAMPLE:

To calculate the length of day in Richmond, Virginia, on day 1:

| | |
|---|---|
| Length of day, Boston (above) | 11h.14m. |
| Sunset Key Letter C for Richmond (p. 242) | + 25m. |
| | 11h.39m. |
| Reverse sunrise Key Letter D for Richmond (p. 242, +17 to -17) | - 17m. |
| Length of day, Richmond | 11h.22m. |

**3.** Use Sun Fast to change sundial time to clock time. A sundial reads natural (Sun) time, which is neither Standard nor Daylight time. To calculate clock time on a sundial in Boston, subtract the minutes given in this column; add the minutes when preceded by an asterisk [*].

–Beth Krommes

[†] For locations where Daylight Saving Time is never observed, subtract 1 hour from results between the second Sunday of March and first Sunday of November.

To convert the time to your (nearest) city, use Key Letter C on **page 238.**

**EXAMPLE:**

To change sundial to clock time in Boston or Salem, Oregon, on day 1:

| | |
|---|---|
| Sundial reading (Boston or Salem) | 12:00 noon |
| Subtract Sun Fast (p. 116) | - 4 minutes |
| Clock time, Boston | 11:56 A.M. ET** |
| Use Key Letter C for Salem (p. 241) | + 27 minutes |
| Clock time, Salem | 12:23 P.M. PT** |

**Note: Add 1 hour to the results in locations where Daylight Saving Time is currently observed.

**4.** This column gives the degrees and minutes of the Sun from the celestial equator at noon ET.

**5.** This column gives the approximate times of high tide in Boston. For example, the first high tide occurs at 7:15 A.M. and the second occurs at 8:00 P.M. the same day. (A dash indicates that high tide occurs on or after midnight and is recorded on the next day.) Figures for calculating approximate high tide times for localities other than Boston are given in the **Tide Corrections** table on **page 236.**

**6.** To calculate the moonrise time in your locale: Choose a day. Note the Moon Rise Key Letter. Find your (nearest) city on **page 238.** Add or subtract the minutes that correspond to the Moon Rise Key Letter to/from the moonrise time given for Boston.

| LONGITUDE OF CITY | CORRECTION MINUTES | LONGITUDE OF CITY | CORRECTION MINUTES |
|---|---|---|---|
| 58°–76° | 0 | 116°–127° | +4 |
| 77°–89° | +1 | 128°–141° | +5 |
| 90°–102° | +2 | 142°–155° | +6 |
| 103°–115° | +3 | | |

(A dash indicates that the moonrise occurs on/after midnight and is recorded on the next day.) Find the longitude of your (nearest) city on **page 238.** Add a correction in minutes for your city's longitude (see table, bottom left). Use the same procedure with Boston's moonset time and the Moon Set Key Letter value to calculate the time of moonset in your locale.[†]

**EXAMPLE:**

To calculate the time of moonset in Lansing, Michigan, on day 1:

| | |
|---|---|
| Moonset, Boston, with Key Letter B (p. 116) | 12:58 P.M. ET |
| Value of Key Letter B for Lansing (p. 240) | + 53 minutes |
| Correction for Lansing longitude, 84°33' | + 1 minute |
| Moonset, Lansing | 1:52 P.M. ET |

**7.** This column gives the Moon's *astronomical* position among the constellations (not zodiac) at midnight. For *astrological* data, see **pages 224–227.**

Constellations have irregular borders; on successive nights, the midnight Moon may enter one, cross into another, and then move to a new area of the previous. It visits the 12 zodiacal constellations, as well as Auriga **(AUR),** a northern constellation between Perseus and Gemini; Cetus **(CET),** which lies south of the zodiac, just south of Pisces and Aries; Ophiuchus **(OPH),** primarily north of the zodiac but with a small corner between Scorpius and Sagittarius; Orion **(ORI),** whose northern limit first reaches the zodiac between Taurus and Gemini; and Sextans **(SEX),** which lies south of the zodiac except for a corner that just touches it near Leo.

**8.** This column gives the Moon's age: the number of days since the previous new Moon. (The average length of the lunar month is 29.53 days.) *(cont.)*

# The Right-Hand Calendar Pages, 121 to 147

The Right-Hand Calendar Pages contain celestial events; religious observances; proverbs and poems; civil holidays; historical events; folklore; tide heights; weather prediction rhymes; Farmer's Calendar essays; and more.

## A SAMPLE MONTH

| | 1 | 2 | 3 | 4 | 5 | 6 | 7 | 8 | 9 | 10 |
|---|---|---|---|---|---|---|---|---|---|---|

| 1 | Fr. | ALL FOOLS' • *If you want to make a fool of yourself, you'll find a lot of people ready to help you.* | *Flakes* | an inch long, who v |
| 2 | Sa. | Tap dancer Charles "Honi" Coles born, 1911 • Tides {9.5 {9.0 | *alive!* | in fresh water, pro pond across the |
| 3 | **B** | 2nd S. of Easter • Writer F. Scott Fitzgerald married Zelda Sayre, 1920 | *Spring's* | emerged a month |
| 4 | M. | Annunciation[T] • ♂♆☽ • *Ben Hur* won 11 Academy Awards, 1960 | *arrived!* | to spend the next 3 |
| 5 | Tu. | ☽ AT ☋ • Blizzard left 27.2" snow, St. John's, Nfld., 1999 • Tides {10.8 {10.8 | *Or is this* | on land before ret their wet world. |
| 6 | W. | ☽ ON EQ. • ♂♀☽ • Twin mongoose lemurs born, Busch Gardens, Tampa, Fla., 2012 | *warmth* | You can't mis |

**1.** The bold letter is the Dominical Letter (from A to G), a traditional ecclesiastical designation for Sunday determined by the date on which the year's first Sunday falls. For 2023, the Dominical Letter is **A**.

**2.** Civil holidays and astronomical events.

**3.** Religious feasts: A[T] indicates a major feast that the church has this year temporarily transferred to a date other than its usual one.

**4.** Sundays and special holy days.

**5.** Symbols for notable celestial events. For example, ♂♆☽ on the 4th day means that a conjunction (♂) of Neptune (♆) and the Moon (☽) occurs.

**6.** Proverbs, poems, and adages.

**7.** Noteworthy historical events, folklore, and legends.

**8.** High tide heights, in feet, at Boston, Massachusetts.

**9.** Weather prediction rhyme.

**10.** Farmer's Calendar essay.

## Celestial Symbols

| | | | | |
|---|---|---|---|---|
| ☉ Sun | ⊕ Earth | ♅ Uranus | ♂ Conjunction | ☋ Descending node |
| ○●☽ Moon | ♂ Mars | ♆ Neptune | (on the same | ☍ Opposition |
| ☿ Mercury | ♃ Jupiter | ♇ Pluto | celestial longitude) | (180 degrees |
| ♀ Venus | ♄ Saturn | | ☊ Ascending node | from Sun) |

## PREDICTING EARTHQUAKES

Note the dates in the Right-Hand Calendar Pages when the Moon rides high or runs low. The date of the high begins the most likely 5-day period of earthquakes in the Northern Hemisphere; the date of the low indicates a similar 5-day period in the Southern Hemisphere. Also noted are the 2 days each month when the Moon is on the celestial equator, indicating the most likely time for earthquakes in either hemisphere.

### EARTH AT PERIHELION AND APHELION

**Perihelion:** January 4, 2023 (EST). Earth will be 91,403,034 miles from the Sun. **Aphelion:** July 6, 2023 (EDT). Earth will be 94,506,364 miles from the Sun.

# Why We Have Seasons

–Beth Krommes

The seasons occur because as Earth revolves around the Sun, its axis remains tilted at 23.5 degrees from the perpendicular. This tilt causes different latitudes on Earth to receive varying amounts of sunlight throughout the year.

In the Northern Hemisphere, the summer solstice marks the beginning of summer and occurs when the North Pole is tilted toward the Sun. The winter solstice marks the beginning of winter and occurs when the North Pole is tilted away from the Sun.

The equinoxes occur when the hemispheres equally face the Sun. At this time, the Sun rises due east and sets due west. The vernal equinox marks the beginning of spring; the autumnal equinox marks the beginning of autumn.

In the Southern Hemisphere, the seasons are the reverse of those in the Northern Hemisphere.

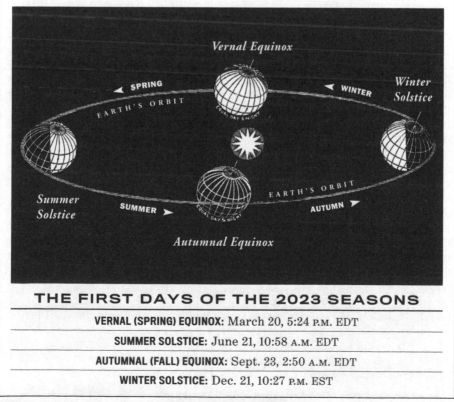

## THE FIRST DAYS OF THE 2023 SEASONS

**VERNAL (SPRING) EQUINOX:** March 20, 5:24 P.M. EDT

**SUMMER SOLSTICE:** June 21, 10:58 A.M. EDT

**AUTUMNAL (FALL) EQUINOX:** Sept. 23, 2:50 A.M. EDT

**WINTER SOLSTICE:** Dec. 21, 10:27 P.M. EST

# NOVEMBER 2022

**SKY WATCH:** Now and for the remainder of the year, the action happens solely in the evening sky, except for on the night of the 7th–8th, when a very nice total eclipse of the Moon is at least partially visible from the entire U.S. and Canada during the second half of the night. West of the Mississippi, the eclipse may be seen in its entirety. The Moon features prominently throughout this month, as it dangles below Saturn on the 1st, closely below Jupiter on the 4th, above Mars on the 10th, below Mars on the 11th, to the left of Virgo's blue star Spica on the 21st, below Saturn again on the 28th, and halfway between Jupiter and Saturn on the 30th.

| | | | | |
|---|---|---|---|---|
| ☽ FIRST QUARTER | 1st day | 2:37 A.M. | ● NEW MOON | 23rd day 5:57 P.M. |
| ○ FULL MOON | 8th day | 6:02 A.M. | ☽ FIRST QUARTER | 30th day 9:37 A.M. |
| ☾ LAST QUARTER | 16th day | 8:27 A.M. | | |

*After 2:00 A.M. on November 6, Eastern Standard Time is given.*

**GET THESE PAGES WITH TIMES SET TO YOUR ZIP CODE VIA ALMANAC.COM/2023.**

| DAY OF YEAR | DAY OF MONTH | DAY OF WEEK | ☀ RISES H. M. | RISE KEY | ☀ SETS H. M. | SET KEY | LENGTH OF DAY H. M. | SUN FAST M. | SUN DECLINATION ° ' | HIGH TIDE TIMES BOSTON | | ☾ RISES H. M. | RISE KEY | ☾ SETS H. M. | SET KEY | ☾ ASTRON. PLACE | ☾ AGE |
|---|---|---|---|---|---|---|---|---|---|---|---|---|---|---|---|---|---|
| 305 | 1 | Tu. | 7:18 | D | 5:37 | B | 10 19 | 32 | 14 s. 34 | 5½ | 5¾ | 2:44 | E | — | - | CAP | 7 |
| 306 | 2 | W. | 7:19 | D | 5:36 | B | 10 17 | 32 | 14 s. 53 | 6½ | 6¾ | 3:15 | E | 12:27 | B | CAP | 8 |
| 307 | 3 | Th. | 7:20 | D | 5:35 | B | 10 15 | 32 | 15 s. 12 | 7½ | 8 | 3:41 | D | 1:42 | C | AQU | 9 |
| 308 | 4 | Fr. | 7:21 | E | 5:34 | B | 10 13 | 32 | 15 s. 30 | 8½ | 9 | 4:03 | D | 2:55 | D | AQU | 10 |
| 309 | 5 | Sa. | 7:22 | E | 5:33 | B | 10 11 | 32 | 15 s. 49 | 9½ | 10 | 4:25 | C | 4:05 | D | PSC | 11 |
| 310 | 6 | **B** | 6:24 | E | 4:31 | B | 10 07 | 32 | 16 s. 07 | 9¼ | 9¾ | 3:47 | C | 4:15 | E | PSC | 12 |
| 311 | 7 | M. | 6:25 | E | 4:30 | B | 10 05 | 32 | 16 s. 24 | 10 | 10½ | 4:10 | B | 5:24 | E | PSC | 13 |
| 312 | 8 | Tu. | 6:26 | E | 4:29 | B | 10 03 | 32 | 16 s. 42 | 10¾ | 11¼ | 4:36 | B | 6:33 | E | ARI | 14 |
| 313 | 9 | W. | 6:27 | E | 4:28 | B | 10 01 | 32 | 16 s. 59 | 11½ | — | 5:06 | B | 7:41 | E | TAU | 15 |
| 314 | 10 | Th. | 6:29 | E | 4:27 | B | 9 58 | 32 | 17 s. 16 | 12 | 12 | 5:43 | A | 8:47 | E | TAU | 16 |
| 315 | 11 | Fr. | 6:30 | E | 4:26 | B | 9 56 | 32 | 17 s. 32 | 12¾ | 12¾ | 6:26 | A | 9:49 | E | TAU | 17 |
| 316 | 12 | Sa. | 6:31 | E | 4:25 | B | 9 54 | 32 | 17 s. 48 | 1½ | 1½ | 7:17 | A | 10:45 | E | GEM | 18 |
| 317 | 13 | **B** | 6:32 | E | 4:24 | B | 9 52 | 31 | 18 s. 04 | 2¼ | 2¼ | 8:14 | B | 11:32 | E | GEM | 19 |
| 318 | 14 | M. | 6:34 | E | 4:23 | B | 9 49 | 31 | 18 s. 20 | 3 | 3 | 9:16 | B | 12:11 | E | GEM | 20 |
| 319 | 15 | Tu. | 6:35 | E | 4:22 | B | 9 47 | 31 | 18 s. 35 | 3¾ | 3¾ | 10:19 | B | 12:43 | E | CAN | 21 |
| 320 | 16 | W. | 6:36 | E | 4:21 | B | 9 45 | 31 | 18 s. 50 | 4¾ | 4¾ | 11:23 | C | 1:10 | E | LEO | 22 |
| 321 | 17 | Th. | 6:37 | E | 4:20 | B | 9 43 | 31 | 19 s. 05 | 5½ | 5¾ | — | - | 1:33 | E | LEO | 23 |
| 322 | 18 | Fr. | 6:39 | E | 4:20 | B | 9 41 | 31 | 19 s. 19 | 6½ | 6½ | 12:28 | C | 1:54 | D | LEO | 24 |
| 323 | 19 | Sa. | 6:40 | E | 4:19 | B | 9 39 | 30 | 19 s. 33 | 7¼ | 7½ | 1:33 | D | 2:15 | C | VIR | 25 |
| 324 | 20 | **B** | 6:41 | E | 4:18 | B | 9 37 | 30 | 19 s. 47 | 8 | 8¼ | 2:40 | D | 2:36 | C | VIR | 26 |
| 325 | 21 | M. | 6:42 | E | 4:17 | B | 9 35 | 30 | 20 s. 00 | 8¾ | 9¼ | 3:50 | E | 2:59 | B | VIR | 27 |
| 326 | 22 | Tu. | 6:43 | E | 4:17 | A | 9 34 | 30 | 20 s. 13 | 9½ | 10 | 5:03 | E | 3:25 | B | VIR | 28 |
| 327 | 23 | W. | 6:45 | E | 4:16 | A | 9 31 | 29 | 20 s. 26 | 10¼ | 10¾ | 6:21 | E | 3:58 | B | LIB | 0 |
| 328 | 24 | Th. | 6:46 | E | 4:16 | A | 9 30 | 29 | 20 s. 38 | 11 | 11½ | 7:40 | E | 4:41 | A | SCO | 1 |
| 329 | 25 | Fr. | 6:47 | E | 4:15 | A | 9 28 | 29 | 20 s. 50 | 11¾ | — | 8:57 | E | 5:35 | A | OPH | 2 |
| 330 | 26 | Sa. | 6:48 | E | 4:15 | A | 9 27 | 28 | 21 s. 01 | 12¼ | 12½ | 10:05 | E | 6:42 | B | SAG | 3 |
| 331 | 27 | **B** | 6:49 | E | 4:14 | A | 9 25 | 28 | 21 s. 12 | 1¼ | 1½ | 11:01 | E | 7:57 | B | SAG | 4 |
| 332 | 28 | M. | 6:50 | E | 4:14 | A | 9 24 | 28 | 21 s. 22 | 2¼ | 2¼ | 11:44 | E | 9:15 | B | CAP | 5 |
| 333 | 29 | Tu. | 6:52 | E | 4:13 | A | 9 21 | 27 | 21 s. 33 | 3¼ | 3¼ | 12:18 | E | 10:32 | C | CAP | 6 |
| 334 | 30 | W. | 6:53 | E | 4:13 | A | 9 20 | 27 | 21 s. 42 | 4¼ | 4½ | 12:46 | D | 11:46 | C | AQU | 7 |

# NOVEMBER

*Fill your hearts with old-time cheer:*
*Heaven be thanked for one more year.*
**–G. P. Lathrop**

| DAY OF MONTH | DAY OF WEEK | DATES, FEASTS, FASTS, ASPECTS, TIDE HEIGHTS, AND WEATHER | |
|---|---|---|---|
| 1 | Tu. | All Saints' • ☌♄☾ • Space Coast's 321 area code went into effect, Brevard Co., Fla., 1999 • {9.1 / 10.2 | *Mild* |
| 2 | W. | All Souls' • Howard Hughes's *Hercules* (aka *Spruce Goose*) wooden aircraft flew 1 mile, 1947 • {9.1 / 10.1 | *and* |
| 3 | Th. | *Common sense is not always true.* • Tides {9.4 / 10.0 | *drizzly.* |
| 4 | Fr. | ☌♃☾ • ☌♆☾ • Composer Felix Mendelssohn died, 1847 • {9.8 / 10.1 | *Suddenly* |
| 5 | Sa. | Sadie Hawkins Day • ☾ ON EQ. • Susan B. Anthony cast ballot, earning $100 fine, 1872 | *grisly:* |
| 6 | **B** | **22nd S. af. P.** • **DAYLIGHT SAVING TIME ENDS, 2:00 A.M.** • {10.6 / 10.1 | *raining* |
| 7 | M. | Magnitude 6.3 earthquake struck off coast of Vancouver Island, B.C., 2012 • {10.8 / 10.0 | *and sleeting* |
| 8 | Tu. | **ELECTION DAY** • **FULL BEAVER** ○ • **ECLIPSE** ☾ • ☾ AT ☊ • ☌♅☾ • ☿ IN SUP. ☌ | |
| 9 | W. | ♅ AT ☍ • Great Boston fire began, 1872 • 1st launch of NASA's Saturn V rocket, 1967 • {10.7 / — | *and* |
| 10 | Th. | Montreal Canadiens' Armand Mondou awarded 1st penalty shot in NHL, 1934 • Tides {9.6 / 10.5 | *freezing,* |
| 11 | Fr. | St. Martin of Tours • **VETERANS DAY** • ☌♂☾ • Tides {9.3 / 10.3 | *before* |
| 12 | Sa. | Indian Summer • ☾ **RIDES HIGH** • *Rain at seven, fine at eleven.* • {8.9 / 9.9 | *easing.* |
| 13 | **B** | **23rd S. af. P.** • Wall of Vietnam Veterans Memorial dedicated, D.C., 1982 • {8.6 / 9.6 | *Don't* |
| 14 | M. | ☾ AT APO. • Insulin co-discoverer Sir Frederick Banting born, 1891 • Tides {8.3 / 9.2 | *drop* |
| 15 | Tu. | Artist Georgia O'Keeffe born, 1887 • 49 tornadoes tore through Midwest, 2005 • {8.2 / 9.0 | *your* |
| 16 | W. | Last Hawaiian king, Kalakaua, born, 1836 • Tides {8.1 / 8.8 | *guard—* |
| 17 | Th. | St. Hugh of Lincoln • 1st U.S. patent for clock granted to Eli Terry, 1797 • Tides {8.3 / 8.8 | *snowing* |
| 18 | Fr. | St. Hilda of Whitby • 1st dated book printed in England, *Dictes or Sayengis of the Philosophres,* 1477 | *hard!* |
| 19 | Sa. | ☾ ON EQ. • Cat, missing for 3 yrs., reunited w/ owner after walking into hospital, Berlin, N.H., 2020 | *You'll* |
| 20 | **B** | **24th. S. af. P.** • Princess Elizabeth (later, Queen Elizabeth II) wed Lt. Philip Mountbatten, 1947 | *suffer* |
| 21 | M. | "Tweety Bird" cartoon character debuted, 1942 • {10.2 / 9.6 | *without* |
| 22 | Tu. | ☾ AT ☋ • ☌☿♀ • Filmmaker Gil Cardinal died, 2015 • {10.7 / 9.9 | *a* |
| 23 | W. | St. Clement • **NEW** ● • *Pleasant hours fly fast.* • Tides {11.2 / 10.0 | *muffler!* |
| 24 | Th. | **THANKSGIVING DAY** • ☌☿☾ • ☌♀☾ • ♃ STAT. • {11.6 / 10.1 | *May* |
| 25 | Fr. | ☾ AT PERIG. • Record 4-min., 17.9-sec. mile run by P. Robinson in Antarctica (–13°F windchill), 2017 | *your* |
| 26 | Sa. | ☾ RUNS LOW • *Peanuts* cartoonist Charles Schulz born, 1922 • Tides {10.0 / 11.7 | *feast* |
| 27 | **B** | **1st S. of Advent** • ☌♇☾ • Announced: UK's Prince Harry engaged to Meghan Markle, 2017 | |
| 28 | M. | ☌♄☾ • 1st ad via skywriting, N.Y.C., 1922 • {9.7 / 11.1 | *be feastly:* |
| 29 | Tu. | *Pong* coin-operated video game debuted, 1972 • Tides {9.5 / 10.7 | *Outside's* |
| 30 | W. | St. Andrew • ♂ AT CLOSEST APPROACH • 405-lb. yellowfin tuna caught, Magdalena Bay, Mexico, 2010 | *beastly!* |

## Farmer's Calendar

You can measure a kestrel's life span on one hand. But if you're handy, you can increase the chances that this smallest falcon may have a place to lay its eggs, as my neighbor did some 30 years ago.

In 1989, Dave nailed together boards from rough-cut pine, with a hole big enough for his fist to fit. He stationed the box 16 feet up his telephone pole. The first spring, the place stayed vacant. But the second year and ever since, kestrels have been in residence—arriving as early as March 25 or delayed until April 16—depending on the amount of bare ground nearby. Kestrels need snowless patches to hunt mice and other small rodents, and, as the season warms, insects. In late June, Dave spies the nestlings' faces squeezed into the opening; by mid-July, the box is again hollow. In autumn, Dave fetches a ladder to clean his chimney, then he leans it against the pole and climbs up to rake out old bedding. From his pocket he delivers a fistful of clean shavings. On this dim, chill afternoon, he's preparing for the next handful of kestrels that will perch at this opening, taking their first peek at the world.

CALENDAR

# DECEMBER 2022

**SKY WATCH:** The Moon is again the star of the celestial show throughout this month, as it dangles below Jupiter on the 1st; floats closely and beautifully above Mars on the 7th, when it is full; dangles below Saturn on the 26th; hangs below Jupiter on the 28th; and stands to the left of Jupiter on the 29th. (It is again beautifully close to Mars on January 3, 2023.) Unfortunately, the Moon plays the role of villain for the Geminid meteors on December 13, when its fat gibbous phase casts unwelcome light. During the final week of the year, Venus may be glimpsed as it returns as an evening star, very low in the southwest. Winter in the Northern Hemisphere begins with the solstice on December 21 at 4:48 P.M. EST.

| ○ **FULL MOON** | 7th day 11:08 P.M. | ● **NEW MOON** | 23rd day 5:17 A.M. |
| ◑ **LAST QUARTER** | 16th day 3:56 A.M. | ◐ **FIRST QUARTER** | 29th day 8:21 P.M. |

*All times are given in Eastern Standard Time.*

**GET THESE PAGES WITH TIMES SET TO YOUR ZIP CODE VIA ALMANAC.COM/2023.**

| DAY OF YEAR | DAY OF MONTH | DAY OF WEEK | ☼ RISES H. M. | RISE KEY | ☼ SETS H. M. | SET KEY | LENGTH OF DAY H. M. | SUN FAST M. | SUN DECLINATION ° ' | HIGH TIDE TIMES BOSTON | | ☾ RISES H. M. | RISE KEY | ☾ SETS H. M. | SET KEY | ☾ ASTRON. PLACE | ☾ AGE |
|---|---|---|---|---|---|---|---|---|---|---|---|---|---|---|---|---|---|
| 335 | 1 | Th. | 6:54 | E | 4:13 | A | 9 19 | 27 | 21 s. 52 | 5¼ | 5½ | 1:09 | D | — | - | AQU | 8 |
| 336 | 2 | Fr. | 6:55 | E | 4:12 | A | 9 17 | 26 | 22 s. 01 | 6¼ | 6¾ | 1:31 | C | 12:57 | D | PSC | 9 |
| 337 | 3 | Sa. | 6:56 | E | 4:12 | A | 9 16 | 26 | 22 s. 09 | 7¼ | 7¾ | 1:52 | C | 2:05 | E | PSC | 10 |
| 338 | 4 | **B** | 6:57 | E | 4:12 | A | 9 15 | 25 | 22 s. 17 | 8 | 8¾ | 2:14 | B | 3:13 | E | PSC | 11 |
| 339 | 5 | M. | 6:58 | E | 4:12 | A | 9 14 | 25 | 22 s. 25 | 9 | 9½ | 2:38 | B | 4:21 | E | ARI | 12 |
| 340 | 6 | Tu. | 6:59 | E | 4:12 | A | 9 13 | 25 | 22 s. 32 | 9¾ | 10¼ | 3:07 | B | 5:28 | E | ARI | 13 |
| 341 | 7 | W. | 7:00 | E | 4:11 | A | 9 11 | 24 | 22 s. 39 | 10¼ | 11 | 3:40 | A | 6:35 | E | TAU | 14 |
| 342 | 8 | Th. | 7:01 | E | 4:11 | A | 9 10 | 24 | 22 s. 45 | 11 | 11¾ | 4:21 | A | 7:38 | E | TAU | 15 |
| 343 | 9 | Fr. | 7:02 | E | 4:11 | A | 9 09 | 23 | 22 s. 51 | 11¾ | — | 5:09 | A | 8:36 | E | TAU | 16 |
| 344 | 10 | Sa. | 7:02 | E | 4:11 | A | 9 09 | 23 | 22 s. 56 | 12¼ | 12¼ | 6:05 | A | 9:27 | E | GEM | 17 |
| 345 | 11 | **B** | 7:03 | E | 4:12 | A | 9 09 | 22 | 23 s. 01 | 1 | 1 | 7:05 | B | 10:09 | E | GEM | 18 |
| 346 | 12 | M. | 7:04 | E | 4:12 | A | 9 08 | 22 | 23 s. 06 | 1¾ | 1¾ | 8:07 | B | 10:43 | E | CAN | 19 |
| 347 | 13 | Tu. | 7:05 | E | 4:12 | A | 9 07 | 22 | 23 s. 10 | 2½ | 2½ | 9:11 | B | 11:11 | E | LEO | 20 |
| 348 | 14 | W. | 7:06 | E | 4:12 | A | 9 06 | 21 | 23 s. 14 | 3¼ | 3¼ | 10:14 | C | 11:36 | E | LEO | 21 |
| 349 | 15 | Th. | 7:06 | E | 4:12 | A | 9 06 | 21 | 23 s. 17 | 4 | 4 | 11:17 | D | 11:57 | E | LEO | 22 |
| 350 | 16 | Fr. | 7:07 | E | 4:13 | A | 9 06 | 20 | 23 s. 19 | 4¾ | 5 | — | - | 12:17 | D | VIR | 23 |
| 351 | 17 | Sa. | 7:08 | E | 4:13 | A | 9 05 | 20 | 23 s. 22 | 5½ | 5¾ | 12:21 | D | 12:37 | C | VIR | 24 |
| 352 | 18 | **B** | 7:08 | E | 4:13 | A | 9 05 | 19 | 23 s. 23 | 6¼ | 6¾ | 1:28 | E | 12:58 | C | VIR | 25 |
| 353 | 19 | M. | 7:09 | E | 4:14 | A | 9 05 | 19 | 23 s. 25 | 7¼ | 7¾ | 2:38 | E | 1:22 | B | VIR | 26 |
| 354 | 20 | Tu. | 7:09 | E | 4:14 | A | 9 05 | 18 | 23 s. 25 | 8 | 8½ | 3:52 | E | 1:51 | B | LIB | 27 |
| 355 | 21 | W. | 7:10 | E | 4:15 | A | 9 05 | 18 | 23 s. 26 | 8¾ | 9½ | 5:10 | E | 2:28 | B | LIB | 28 |
| 356 | 22 | Th. | 7:10 | E | 4:15 | A | 9 05 | 17 | 23 s. 26 | 9¾ | 10¼ | 6:29 | E | 3:17 | A | SCO | 29 |
| 357 | 23 | Fr. | 7:11 | E | 4:16 | A | 9 05 | 17 | 23 s. 25 | 10½ | 11¼ | 7:44 | E | 4:19 | A | SAG | 0 |
| 358 | 24 | Sa. | 7:11 | E | 4:16 | A | 9 05 | 16 | 23 s. 24 | 11½ | — | 8:48 | E | 5:33 | B | SAG | 1 |
| 359 | 25 | **B** | 7:12 | E | 4:17 | A | 9 05 | 16 | 23 s. 22 | 12 | 12¼ | 9:38 | E | 6:54 | B | CAP | 2 |
| 360 | 26 | M. | 7:12 | E | 4:18 | A | 9 06 | 15 | 23 s. 20 | 1 | 1¼ | 10:17 | E | 8:15 | C | CAP | 3 |
| 361 | 27 | Tu. | 7:12 | E | 4:18 | A | 9 06 | 15 | 23 s. 18 | 2 | 2 | 10:48 | E | 9:33 | C | AQU | 4 |
| 362 | 28 | W. | 7:13 | E | 4:19 | A | 9 06 | 14 | 23 s. 15 | 2¾ | 3 | 11:13 | D | 10:47 | D | AQU | 5 |
| 363 | 29 | Th. | 7:13 | E | 4:20 | A | 9 07 | 14 | 23 s. 11 | 3¾ | 4 | 11:36 | D | 11:57 | D | PSC | 6 |
| 364 | 30 | Fr. | 7:13 | E | 4:21 | A | 9 08 | 13 | 23 s. 08 | 4¾ | 5¼ | 11:57 | C | — | - | CET | 7 |
| 365 | 31 | Sa. | 7:13 | E | 4:21 | A | 9 08 | 13 | 23 s. 03 | 5¾ | 6¼ | 12:19 | C | 1:05 | E | PSC | 8 |

# THE TWELFTH MONTH • 2022 DECEMBER DECEMBER HATH 31 DAYS

*Holly, fir, and spruce boughs / Green upon the wall,*
*Spotless snow upon the road— / More going to fall.*
**–Unknown**

| DAY OF MONTH | DAY OF WEEK | DATES, FEASTS, FASTS, ASPECTS, TIDE HEIGHTS, AND WEATHER | |
|---|---|---|---|
| 1 | Th. | ☌♃☾ • ☌♆☾ • Writer/USN Capt. Edward L. Beach died, 2002 • 9.5 / 9.8 | *Numb* |
| 2 | Fr. | St. Viviana • ☾ ON EQ. • 1st pizza party in space, ISS, 2017 • Tides 9.7 / 9.6 | *and* |
| 3 | Sa. | *If things were to be done twice, all would be wise.* • 9.9 / 9.4 | *number,* |
| 4 | **B** | **2nd S. of Advent** • ♆ STAT. • Tides 10.2 / 9.4 | *with flakes* |
| 5 | M. | ☾ AT ☊ • ☌⛢☾ • Ship *Mary Celeste* found abandoned, 1872 • 10.4 / 9.3 | *aswirl;* |
| 6 | Tu. | St. Nicholas • Everglades Nat'l Park dedicated, Fla., 1947 • Tides 10.4 / 9.2 | *bluster* |
| 7 | W. | St. Ambrose • **National Pearl Harbor Remembrance Day** • **FULL COLD** ○ • OCCN. ♂☾ | |
| 8 | Th. | ♂ AT ☍ • 896 couples in N.H./Mo./Colo. kissed under mistletoe, setting world record, 2019 | *ceases,* |
| 9 | Fr. | ☾ RIDES HIGH • Canada's 1st coin club, Numismatic Society of Montreal, formed, 1862 • 10.3 / — | *sun* |
| 10 | Sa. | St. Eulalia • Poet Emily Dickinson born, 1830 • Tides 8.0 / 10.1 | *increases.* |
| 11 | **B** | **3rd S. of Advent** • ☾ AT APO. • *Good words cost naught.* • 8.7 / 9.9 | *Hang* |
| 12 | M. | **Our Lady of Guadalupe** • *Apollo 17* astronauts discovered orange soil on Moon, 1972 • 8.6 / 9.7 | *your* |
| 13 | Tu. | St. Lucia • National Day of the Horse • Tides 8.5 / 9.4 | *holly:* |
| 14 | W. | Ember Day • Halcyon Days begin. • *Mariner 2* passed Venus (1st successful planetary flyby), 1962 | *Don't* |
| 15 | Th. | Baseball player Dick Stuart died, 2002 • Tides 8.4 / 8.9 | *go* |
| 16 | Fr. | Ember Day • Lillian Disney (wife of Walt Disney) died, 1997 • Tides 8.6 / 8.7 | *out* |
| 17 | Sa. | Ember Day • ☾ ON EQ. • France formally recognized American independence, 1777 | *without* |
| 18 | **B** | **4th S. of Advent** • Chanukah begins at sundown • Tides 9.3 / 8.8 | *your* |
| 19 | M. | ☾ AT ☋ • 1st season of National Hockey League (NHL), 1917 • Tides 9.7 / 9.0 | *brolly!* |
| 20 | Tu. | Beware the Pogonip. • J. Russell Coffey, oldest known U.S. WWI veteran at time, died at age 109, 2007 | *Leave* |
| 21 | W. | St. Thomas • **Winter Solstice** • ☿ GR. ELONG. (20° EAST) • Tides 10.9 / 9.5 | *Santa* |
| 22 | Th. | U.S. first lady Claudia "Lady Bird" Johnson born, 1912 • Tides 11.4 / 9.8 | *a* |
| 23 | Fr. | NEW ● • ☾ RUNS LOW • Saturn's moon Rhea discovered, 1672 • Tides 11.7 / 10.0 | *snack* |
| 24 | Sa. | ☾ AT PERIG. • ☌☿☾ • ☌♀☾ • ☌♇☾ • Tides 12.0 / — | *to* |
| 25 | **B** | **Christmas** • *If windy on Christmas Day, trees will bring much fruit.* • Tides 10.1 / 11.9 | *be* |
| 26 | M. | St. Stephen • **Boxing Day (Canada)** • **First Day of Kwanzaa** • ☌♄☾ • 10.1 / 11.7 | *sure* |
| 27 | Tu. | St. John • Chemist Louis Pasteur born, 1822 • 141-lb. 8-oz. Pacific sailfish caught on 4# test line, Piñas Bay, Panama, 1992 | |
| 28 | W. | Holy Innocents • ☌♆☾ • ☿ STAT. • Comic book writer Stan Lee born, 1922 | *he comes* |
| 29 | Th. | ☾ ON EQ. • ☌☿♀ • ☌♃☾ • *Dec. 28–29:* 25.5" snow in 24 hrs., Victoria, B.C., 1996 | *back.* |
| 30 | Fr. | Samoa skipped this day to move from eastern to western side of International Date Line, 2011 • 9.8 / 9.5 | *Adieu,* |
| 31 | Sa. | St. Sylvester • Gymnast Gabby Douglas born, 1995 • Tides 9.8 / 9.0 | *'22!* |

## Farmer's Calendar

Plowing the roads of Cabot, Vermont, is the second-best job Walter "Rusty" Churchill's ever had. First best? Dairy farming, which he did for 30 years. He didn't know what he'd do after he sold his cows. He thought about taking a shift at the Cabot Creamery; then someone mentioned a job opening at the town garage and encouraged Rusty to throw his name in for it. They hired another guy, but he didn't last. So that's how, for over a decade now, Rusty's knack for spreading lime and manure and tilling soil makes him an ace at scattering salt and sand and plowing for his hometown. The hours are similar—Thanksgiving, Christmas, New Year's, Easter—he works them all. But, he admits, it's satisfying to clear a path after a huge storm: "Then it seems like you're doing something." Rusty's route includes some of the town's 65 miles of blacktop, hilltop, and back roads. "There aren't too many out this early," he says of clearing snow long before sunrise. "You've got Creamery help—they have a shift that starts at 4:00 A.M.—and milk trucks. Otherwise, it's just me. Kinda peaceful. As long as the radio works, I'm all set."

# JANUARY

**SKY WATCH:** The year begins with our two nearest planetary neighbors displaying opposite properties. January 1 finds Mars at its brightest of the entire year, while Venus is at its dimmest of 2023. However, Venus is on an upward trajectory, appearing higher and brighter each evening. Saturn is the closest bright "star" far above Venus. Observers will enjoy watching Venus and Saturn draw closer every night before a meeting on the 22nd. Meanwhile, the year's closest Moon occurs on the 21st at a surface-to-surface distance from Earth of just 216,500 miles. Unfortunately, the Moon is in its new phase and therefore not visible. During late January, spectacle abounds at nightfall in the southern sky featuring the Moon, three planets, and eight of the brightest stars, all surrounding Orion.

○ **FULL MOON** 6th day 6:08 P.M.　● **NEW MOON** 21st day 3:53 P.M.
◐ **LAST QUARTER** 14th day 9:10 P.M.　◑ **FIRST QUARTER** 28th day 10:19 A.M.

*All times are given in Eastern Standard Time.*

**GET THESE PAGES WITH TIMES SET TO YOUR ZIP CODE VIA ALMANAC.COM/2023.**

| DAY OF YEAR | DAY OF MONTH | DAY OF WEEK | ☀ RISES H. M. | RISE KEY | ☀ SETS H. M. | SET KEY | LENGTH OF DAY H. M. | SUN FAST M. | SUN DECLINATION ° ' | HIGH TIDE TIMES BOSTON | | ☽ RISES H. M. | RISE KEY | ☽ SETS H. M. | SET KEY | ☽ ASTRON. PLACE | ☽ AGE |
|---|---|---|---|---|---|---|---|---|---|---|---|---|---|---|---|---|---|
| 1 | 1 | **A** | 7:13 | E | 4:22 | A | 9 09 | 12 | 22 s. 58 | 6¾ | 7¼ | 12:42 | B | 2:13 | E | ARI | 9 |
| 2 | 2 | M. | 7:13 | E | 4:23 | A | 9 10 | 12 | 22 s. 53 | 7½ | 8¼ | 1:09 | B | 3:20 | E | ARI | 10 |
| 3 | 3 | Tu. | 7:13 | E | 4:24 | A | 9 11 | 11 | 22 s. 47 | 8½ | 9¼ | 1:41 | A | 4:26 | E | TAU | 11 |
| 4 | 4 | W. | 7:13 | E | 4:25 | A | 9 12 | 11 | 22 s. 41 | 9¼ | 10 | 2:19 | A | 5:30 | E | TAU | 12 |
| 5 | 5 | Th. | 7:13 | E | 4:26 | A | 9 13 | 10 | 22 s. 35 | 10 | 10¾ | 3:05 | A | 6:30 | E | TAU | 13 |
| 6 | 6 | Fr. | 7:13 | E | 4:27 | A | 9 14 | 10 | 22 s. 28 | 10¾ | 11¼ | 3:58 | A | 7:22 | E | GEM | 14 |
| 7 | 7 | Sa. | 7:13 | E | 4:28 | A | 9 15 | 10 | 22 s. 20 | 11¼ | — | 4:56 | B | 8:07 | E | GEM | 15 |
| 8 | 8 | **A** | 7:13 | E | 4:29 | A | 9 16 | 9 | 22 s. 12 | 12 | 12 | 5:58 | B | 8:44 | E | CAN | 16 |
| 9 | 9 | M. | 7:13 | E | 4:30 | A | 9 17 | 9 | 22 s. 04 | 12½ | 12¾ | 7:02 | B | 9:14 | E | CAN | 17 |
| 10 | 10 | Tu. | 7:13 | E | 4:31 | A | 9 18 | 8 | 21 s. 55 | 1¼ | 1¼ | 8:05 | C | 9:39 | E | LEO | 18 |
| 11 | 11 | W. | 7:12 | E | 4:32 | A | 9 20 | 8 | 21 s. 46 | 1¾ | 2 | 9:07 | C | 10:01 | D | LEO | 19 |
| 12 | 12 | Th. | 7:12 | E | 4:33 | A | 9 21 | 8 | 21 s. 36 | 2½ | 2¾ | 10:10 | D | 10:21 | D | LEO | 20 |
| 13 | 13 | Fr. | 7:12 | E | 4:34 | A | 9 22 | 7 | 21 s. 26 | 3¼ | 3½ | 11:14 | D | 10:41 | C | VIR | 21 |
| 14 | 14 | Sa. | 7:11 | E | 4:35 | A | 9 24 | 7 | 21 s. 15 | 4 | 4¼ | — | - | 11:00 | C | VIR | 22 |
| 15 | 15 | **A** | 7:11 | E | 4:37 | A | 9 26 | 6 | 21 s. 04 | 4¾ | 5¼ | 12:20 | E | 11:22 | B | VIR | 23 |
| 16 | 16 | M. | 7:10 | E | 4:38 | A | 9 28 | 6 | 20 s. 53 | 5½ | 6 | 1:30 | E | 11:48 | B | LIB | 24 |
| 17 | 17 | Tu. | 7:10 | E | 4:39 | A | 9 29 | 6 | 20 s. 41 | 6½ | 7¼ | 2:43 | E | 12:19 | B | LIB | 25 |
| 18 | 18 | W. | 7:09 | E | 4:40 | B | 9 31 | 5 | 20 s. 29 | 7½ | 8¼ | 4:00 | E | 1:01 | A | SCO | 26 |
| 19 | 19 | Th. | 7:09 | E | 4:41 | B | 9 32 | 5 | 20 s. 17 | 8¼ | 9¼ | 5:16 | E | 1:54 | A | OPH | 27 |
| 20 | 20 | Fr. | 7:08 | E | 4:43 | B | 9 35 | 5 | 20 s. 04 | 9¼ | 10 | 6:26 | E | 3:03 | A | SAG | 28 |
| 21 | 21 | Sa. | 7:07 | E | 4:44 | B | 9 37 | 5 | 19 s. 51 | 10¼ | 11 | 7:23 | E | 4:22 | B | SAG | 0 |
| 22 | 22 | **A** | 7:07 | E | 4:45 | B | 9 38 | 4 | 19 s. 37 | 11¼ | 11¾ | 8:09 | E | 5:46 | B | CAP | 1 |
| 23 | 23 | M. | 7:06 | E | 4:46 | B | 9 40 | 4 | 19 s. 23 | 12 | — | 8:44 | E | 7:08 | C | CAP | 2 |
| 24 | 24 | Tu. | 7:05 | E | 4:48 | B | 9 43 | 4 | 19 s. 09 | 12¾ | 1 | 9:13 | D | 8:27 | D | AQU | 3 |
| 25 | 25 | W. | 7:04 | E | 4:49 | B | 9 45 | 4 | 18 s. 54 | 1½ | 1¾ | 9:37 | D | 9:42 | D | AQU | 4 |
| 26 | 26 | Th. | 7:04 | E | 4:50 | B | 9 46 | 3 | 18 s. 39 | 2½ | 2¾ | 10:00 | C | 10:53 | E | CET | 5 |
| 27 | 27 | Fr. | 7:03 | E | 4:52 | B | 9 49 | 3 | 18 s. 23 | 3¼ | 3¾ | 10:22 | C | — | - | PSC | 6 |
| 28 | 28 | Sa. | 7:02 | E | 4:53 | B | 9 51 | 3 | 18 s. 08 | 4¼ | 4¾ | 10:45 | B | 12:03 | E | ARI | 7 |
| 29 | 29 | **A** | 7:01 | E | 4:54 | B | 9 53 | 3 | 17 s. 52 | 5 | 5¾ | 11:11 | B | 1:11 | E | ARI | 8 |
| 30 | 30 | M. | 7:00 | E | 4:55 | B | 9 55 | 3 | 17 s. 35 | 6 | 6¾ | 11:41 | A | 2:19 | E | TAU | 9 |
| 31 | 31 | Tu. | 6:59 | E | 4:57 | B | 9 58 | 2 | 17 s. 19 | 7 | 7¾ | 12:18 | A | 3:24 | E | TAU | 10 |

# JANUARY

*Happy, happy New Year!...*
*We with a welcome greet, / His knocking at our door.*
**–Rev. A. William Fiske**

| DAY OF MONTH | DAY OF WEEK | DATES, FEASTS, FASTS, ASPECTS, TIDE HEIGHTS, AND WEATHER | |
|---|---|---|---|
| 1 | **A** | 1st S. af. Ch. • Holy Name • **New Year's Day** • ☾ at ☊ • ☌♀♇ • occn. ⛢☾ | *New* |
| 2 | M. | Ga. became 4th U.S. state, 1788 • 28-lb. 13-oz. tautog caught, Ocean City, Md., 2015 | *Year's babe in* |
| 3 | Tu. | ☌♂☾ • Environmental activist Greta Thunberg born, 2003 • Tides {9.9 / 8.6 | *swaddling* |
| 4 | W. | St. Elizabeth Ann Seton • ⊕ at perihelion • {10.0 / 8.6 | *clothes* |
| 5 | Th. | Twelfth Night • ☾ rides high • Reggie Jackson elected to National Baseball Hall of Fame, 1993 | *needs a* |
| 6 | Fr. | **Epiphany** • **Full Wolf** ○ • *Jan. 6–8:* Nor'easter w/ record snow hit U.S. East Coast, 1996 | *parka* |
| 7 | Sa. | Orthodox Christmas (Julian) • Distaff Day • ☿ in inf. ☌ • Tides {10.0 / 8.7 | *for the* |
| 8 | **A** | **1st S. af. Ep.** • ☾ at apo. • Entertainer Elvis Presley born, 1935 • {10.0 / — | *snows!* |
| 9 | M. | Plough Monday • Conn. became 5th U.S. state, 1788 • {8.7 / 9.9 | *Great* |
| 10 | Tu. | Thomas Paine's *Common Sense* published, 1776 • {8.7 / 9.8 | *for* |
| 11 | W. | *Man's best candle is his understanding.* • Tides {8.7 / 9.5 | *skating,* |
| 12 | Th. | ♂ stat. • Charleston Museum, 1st museum in America, founded, Charleston, S.C., 1773 | *but cold is* |
| 13 | Fr. | St. Hilary • ☾ on eq. • Meeting to organize National Geographic Society, D.C., 1888 | *grating.* |
| 14 | Sa. | 40,000 pounds liquid chocolate flooded I-40 due to overturned tanker near Flagstaff, Ariz., 2019 • {9.0 / 8.7 | *Shovelers* |
| 15 | **A** | **2nd S. af. Ep.** • *The wind keeps not always in one quarter.* • {9.1 / 8.5 | *muttering,* |
| 16 | M. | **Martin Luther King Jr.'s Birthday, observed** • ☾ at ☋ • Tides {9.4 / 8.4 | *flurries* |
| 17 | Tu. | U.S. statesman Benjamin Franklin born, 1706 • Singer Eartha Kitt born, 1927 • {9.7 / 8.5 | *fluttering.* |
| 18 | W. | ☌♇☉ • ☿ stat. • Meteorite (0.66 lb.) crashed through doctors' office, Lorton, Va., 2010 | *Brief* |
| 19 | Th. | Mother Joseph of the Sacred Heart died, 1902 • Actress Jean Stapleton born, 1923 | *spell of* |
| 20 | Fr. | ☾ runs low • ☌☿☾ • Naomi Fraley, "We Can Do It!" 1943 poster inspiration, died, 2018 | *dripping,* |
| 21 | Sa. | **New** ● • ☾ at perig. • ☌♇☾ • Tides {11.7 / 9.9 | *then icy hand* |
| 22 | **A** | **3rd S. af. Ep.** • **Lunar New Year (China)** • ☌♀♄ • ⛢ stat. | *gripping,* |
| 23 | M. | ☌♀☾ • ☌♄☾ • Eldfell volcano began to form, Heimaey Island, Iceland, 1973 | *refusing* |
| 24 | Tu. | Gold discovered at Sutter's Mill, starting California Gold Rush, Coloma, Calif., 1848 • {10.5 / 11.8 | *to ever* |
| 25 | W. | Conversion of Paul • ☌♃☾ • ☌♆☾ • January thaw typically begins about now. | *let go.* |
| 26 | Th. | Sts. Timothy & Titus • ☾ on eq. • Tides {10.5 / 10.6 | *Clear and* |
| 27 | Fr. | *Jan. 26–29:* Atmospheric river caused major West Coast storm, 2021 • Tides {10.3 / 9.9 | *frigid,* |
| 28 | Sa. | St. Thomas Aquinas • ☾ at ☊ • ☌⛢☾ • Astronomer Helen Hogg died, 1993 | *everything* |
| 29 | **A** | **4th S. af. Ep.** • *Hearts may agree though heads differ.* • {9.8 / 8.6 | *rigid.* |
| 30 | M. | occn. ♂☾ • ☿ gr. elong. (25° west) • Aviator Orville Wright died, 1948 | *More snow,* |
| 31 | Tu. | Raccoons mate now. • *Explorer 1,* 1st successful U.S. satellite, launched, 1958 • {9.4 / 8.0 | *you know?!* |

## Farmer's Calendar

Legend has it that on Twelfth Night (January 5), wild animals can speak. This is certainly true for chickadees, not that they shut up during the rest of the year. If you learn their language, they'll even tell you what they're doing.

Winter is the best time to study these garrulous little birds because they have the silent woods mostly to themselves. Now they flit about in small flocks, hanging from boughs and plucking insect eggs. They have at least 15 distinct vocalizations, and each bird has a dominance rank within the flock.

The familiar "chickadee" call may mean "Hi, how are you all doing?" "Dee-dee-dee dee-dee" signals alarm. (Eavesdropping nuthatches will "retweet" these alarm calls to their neighbors.) A "Chi-besh" means "Get away—I outrank you."

Members out of visual range keep in contact with a high-pitched "tseet-tseet." The sweet, clear "fee-bee" song of the male (often confused with the raspier song of the male eastern phoebe and heard more as winter progresses) indicates early breeding behavior.

A bird that spots a predator freezes the flock with this warning, spoken in perfect English: "See! See! See! See!"

# FEBRUARY

**SKY WATCH:** As evening twilight fades on the 1st, Saturn may finally be too low, its long evening star apparition ending. On the 3rd, the Moon meets Pollux, the brighter of the legendary Gemini twins. Mars, dimming but still very bright at magnitude –0.2, remains above Taurus's famous orange star, Aldebaran, and outshines it. From the 7th to the 28th, brightening Venus draws closer to Jupiter. On the 27th, the crescent Moon closely meets Mars, while Venus and Jupiter come together nearby. On the 28th, the night's brightest stars begin to merge to create an amazing configuration. This Venus/Jupiter conjunction shouldn't be missed, although they are so low in the fading evening twilight that they require a totally unblocked western horizon for viewing.

○ **FULL MOON** 5th day 1:29 P.M.  ● **NEW MOON** 20th day 2:06 A.M.
☽ **LAST QUARTER** 13th day 11:01 A.M.  ☾ **FIRST QUARTER** 27th day 3:06 A.M.

*All times are given in Eastern Standard Time.*

GET THESE PAGES WITH TIMES SET TO YOUR ZIP CODE VIA ALMANAC.COM/2023.

| DAY OF YEAR | DAY OF MONTH | DAY OF WEEK | ☀ RISES H. M. | RISE KEY | ☀ SETS H. M. | SET KEY | LENGTH OF DAY H. M. | SUN FAST M. | SUN DECLINATION ° ' | HIGH TIDE TIMES BOSTON | | ☾ RISES H. M. | RISE KEY | ☾ SETS H. M. | SET KEY | ☾ ASTRON. PLACE | ☾ AGE |
|---|---|---|---|---|---|---|---|---|---|---|---|---|---|---|---|---|---|
| 32 | 1 | W. | 6:58 | E | 4:58 | B | 10 00 | 2 | 17 s. 02 | 8 | 8¾ | 1:01 | A | 4:25 | E | TAU | 11 |
| 33 | 2 | Th. | 6:57 | E | 4:59 | B | 10 02 | 2 | 16 s. 44 | 8¾ | 9½ | 1:52 | A | 5:19 | E | GEM | 12 |
| 34 | 3 | Fr. | 6:56 | E | 5:01 | B | 10 05 | 2 | 16 s. 27 | 9¾ | 10¼ | 2:49 | B | 6:06 | E | GEM | 13 |
| 35 | 4 | Sa. | 6:55 | D | 5:02 | B | 10 07 | 2 | 16 s. 09 | 10¼ | 11 | 3:50 | B | 6:45 | E | CAN | 14 |
| 36 | 5 | **A** | 6:54 | D | 5:03 | B | 10 09 | 2 | 15 s. 51 | 11 | 11½ | 4:54 | B | 7:17 | E | CAN | 15 |
| 37 | 6 | M. | 6:52 | D | 5:05 | B | 10 13 | 2 | 15 s. 32 | 11¾ | — | 5:57 | C | 7:43 | E | LEO | 16 |
| 38 | 7 | Tu. | 6:51 | D | 5:06 | B | 10 15 | 2 | 15 s. 14 | 12¼ | 12¼ | 7:00 | C | 8:06 | E | LEO | 17 |
| 39 | 8 | W. | 6:50 | D | 5:07 | B | 10 17 | 2 | 14 s. 55 | 12¾ | 1 | 8:03 | D | 8:27 | D | LEO | 18 |
| 40 | 9 | Th. | 6:49 | D | 5:08 | B | 10 19 | 2 | 14 s. 36 | 1¼ | 1½ | 9:06 | D | 8:46 | C | VIR | 19 |
| 41 | 10 | Fr. | 6:47 | D | 5:10 | B | 10 23 | 2 | 14 s. 16 | 2 | 2¼ | 10:11 | E | 9:05 | C | VIR | 20 |
| 42 | 11 | Sa. | 6:46 | D | 5:11 | B | 10 25 | 2 | 13 s. 57 | 2½ | 3 | 11:18 | E | 9:26 | B | VIR | 21 |
| 43 | 12 | **A** | 6:45 | D | 5:12 | B | 10 27 | 2 | 13 s. 37 | 3¼ | 3¾ | — | - | 9:49 | B | VIR | 22 |
| 44 | 13 | M. | 6:44 | D | 5:14 | B | 10 30 | 2 | 13 s. 17 | 4 | 4½ | 12:28 | E | 10:17 | B | LIB | 23 |
| 45 | 14 | Tu. | 6:42 | D | 5:15 | B | 10 33 | 2 | 12 s. 56 | 5 | 5¾ | 1:41 | E | 10:52 | B | SCO | 24 |
| 46 | 15 | W. | 6:41 | D | 5:16 | B | 10 35 | 2 | 12 s. 36 | 6 | 6¾ | 2:55 | E | 11:38 | A | OPH | 25 |
| 47 | 16 | Th. | 6:39 | D | 5:18 | B | 10 39 | 2 | 12 s. 15 | 7 | 7¾ | 4:06 | E | 12:38 | A | SAG | 26 |
| 48 | 17 | Fr. | 6:38 | D | 5:19 | B | 10 41 | 2 | 11 s. 54 | 8 | 8¾ | 5:08 | E | 1:50 | B | SAG | 27 |
| 49 | 18 | Sa. | 6:37 | D | 5:20 | B | 10 43 | 2 | 11 s. 33 | 9 | 9¾ | 5:58 | E | 3:11 | B | CAP | 28 |
| 50 | 19 | **A** | 6:35 | D | 5:21 | B | 10 46 | 2 | 11 s. 11 | 10 | 10¾ | 6:37 | E | 4:35 | C | CAP | 29 |
| 51 | 20 | M. | 6:34 | D | 5:23 | B | 10 49 | 2 | 10 s. 50 | 11 | 11½ | 7:09 | E | 5:57 | C | AQU | 0 |
| 52 | 21 | Tu. | 6:32 | D | 5:24 | B | 10 52 | 2 | 10 s. 28 | 11¾ | — | 7:36 | D | 7:16 | D | AQU | 1 |
| 53 | 22 | W. | 6:31 | D | 5:25 | B | 10 54 | 2 | 10 s. 06 | 12¼ | 12¾ | 8:00 | C | 8:31 | E | PSC | 2 |
| 54 | 23 | Th. | 6:29 | D | 5:26 | B | 10 57 | 3 | 9 s. 44 | 1 | 1½ | 8:22 | C | 9:44 | E | PSC | 3 |
| 55 | 24 | Fr. | 6:28 | D | 5:28 | B | 11 00 | 3 | 9 s. 22 | 2 | 2¼ | 8:46 | B | 10:56 | E | PSC | 4 |
| 56 | 25 | Sa. | 6:26 | D | 5:29 | B | 11 03 | 3 | 9 s. 00 | 2¾ | 3¼ | 9:11 | B | — | - | ARI | 5 |
| 57 | 26 | **A** | 6:25 | D | 5:30 | C | 11 05 | 3 | 8 s. 38 | 3½ | 4¼ | 9:40 | B | 12:06 | E | ARI | 6 |
| 58 | 27 | M. | 6:23 | D | 5:31 | C | 11 08 | 3 | 8 s. 15 | 4½ | 5¼ | 10:15 | A | 1:14 | E | TAU | 7 |
| 59 | 28 | Tu. | 6:21 | D | 5:33 | C | 11 12 | 3 | 7 s. 52 | 5½ | 6¼ | 10:56 | A | 2:18 | E | TAU | 8 |

# FEBRUARY

*Love is a plant of holier birth*
*Than aught that takes its root on earth.*
–**Henry Neele**

| DAY OF MONTH | DAY OF WEEK | DATES, FEASTS, FASTS, ASPECTS, TIDE HEIGHTS, AND WEATHER | |
|---|---|---|---|
| 1 | W. | St. Brigid • Space Shuttle *Columbia* disaster, 2003 • Tides {9.4 8.1 | *Beyond* |
| 2 | Th. | Candlemas • Groundhog Day • ☾ RIDES HIGH • {9.5 8.2 | *a shadow* |
| 3 | Fr. | *A February spring is not worth a pin.* • Tides {9.6 8.4 | *of doubt,* |
| 4 | Sa. | ☾ AT APO. • 5,622 ice lanterns displayed, setting world record, State College, Pa., 2017 | *winter is* |
| 5 | **A** | **Septuagesima** • FULL SNOW ○ • Journalist Ralph McGill born, 1898 | *now about.* |
| 6 | M. | Barbara Ann Scott won Canada's 1st Olympic gold medal for figure skating, 1948 | *Cold spell's* |
| 7 | Tu. | 1st ballet performance *(The Deserter)* in U.S., Bowery Theater, N.Y.C., 1827 • {9.0 10.0 | *got sock-o,* |
| 8 | W. | College of William & Mary chartered, 1693 • Tides {9.1 9.9 | *chill takes* |
| 9 | Th. | ☾ ON EQ. • U.S. president William Harrison born, 1773 • {9.2 9.7 | *its toll!* |
| 10 | Fr. | ☌☿♇ • Treaty of Paris signed, formally ending French and Indian War, 1763 | *Time for* |
| 11 | Sa. | 1st La-Z-Boy reclining chair designed, 1928 • *Landsat 8* satellite launched, 2013 • {9.4 9.1 | *hot choco and* |
| 12 | **A** | **Sexagesima** • ☾ AT ☋ • U.S. president Abe Lincoln born, 1809 | *a souper bowl!* |
| 13 | M. | Test pilot Chuck Yeager born, 1923 • *Love knows no measure.* • {9.5 8.4 | *Extra covers* |
| 14 | Tu. | Sts. Cyril & Methodius • **Valentine's Day** • {9.6 8.3 | *for lovers.* |
| 15 | W. | **National Flag of Canada Day** • ☌♀♆ • Social reformer Susan B. Anthony born, 1820 | *Sometimes* |
| 16 | Th. | ☾ RUNS LOW • ☌♄☉ • Nylon ("Linear Condensation Polymers") patented, 1937 | *cold,* |
| 17 | Fr. | ☌♇☾ • Winter's back breaks. • –60°F, Esker, Lab., 1973 • Tides {10.6 9.1 | *sometimes* |
| 18 | Sa. | ☌☿☾ • Artist Louis Comfort Tiffany born, 1848 • F4 tornado struck Van Wert Co., Ohio, 1992 | *mild,* |
| 19 | **A** | **Quinquagesima** • ☾ AT PERIG. • ☌♄☾ • Copernicus born, 1473 | *sometimes* |
| 20 | M. | **Presidents' Day** • NEW ● • Abolitionist Frederick Douglass died, 1895 | *sunny,* |
| 21 | Tu. | Shrove Tuesday • ☌♆☾ • Half-cent denomination discontinued in U.S., 1857 • {11.8 — | *seldom* |
| 22 | W. | Ash Wednesday • ☾ ON EQ. • ☌♀☾ • ☌♃☾ • G. Washington born, 1732 | *wild.* |
| 23 | Th. | USS *Osmond Ingram,* 1st U.S. naval vessel named for enlisted man, launched, 1919 • {11.1 11.1 | *Now a* |
| 24 | Fr. | St. Matthias • ☾ AT ☊ • Programmer/game designer Sid Meier born, 1954 | *freeze* |
| 25 | Sa. | ☌♅☾ • Architect Christopher Wren died, 1723 • Tides {10.5 9.6 | *will* |
| 26 | **A** | **1st S. in Lent** • *Never is a long day.* • {10.1 8.9 | *shiver* |
| 27 | M. | Orthodox Lent begins • ☌♂☾ • Tides {9.6 8.3 | *your* |
| 28 | Tu. | St. Romanus • Skunks mate now. • Last episode of *M*A*S*H* aired on TV, 1983 | *knees.* |

*Q: What did one lightbulb say to the other on Valentine's Day?*
*A: I love you a whole watt.*

## Farmer's Calendar

Among the treasures to be collected from the winter woods are pinecones—the reproductive structures of an ancient genus that preceded flowering plants by more than 150 million years and whose Carboniferous Period contemporaries are now coal. The cones that you'll want to pick up are the larger females that have dried and dropped their seeds.

Hard pines such as the red, lodgepole, shortleaf, longleaf, slash, ponderosa, pitch, loblolly, and Coulter generally produce woody, thick-scale cones armored with prickers. Soft pines such as the eastern white, western white, sugar, whitebark, limber, foxtail, bristlecone, and pinyon usually produce softer, smoother, more elongated cones. A sugar pine cone can be 2 feet long. A Coulter pine cone can weigh 11 pounds.

Dry, seedless cones of hard pines make superb bird feeders. Fill all nooks with natural peanut butter, then roll them in birdseed. Soft-pine cones are best for fire starters. Hook wires to the tops of dry, seedless ones and soak them in melted paraffin or candle wax. Add crayons for the desired cone color. For white flames, coat waxed cones with Epsom salts; for yellow flames, table salt; for violet flames, salt substitute.

# MARCH

**SKY WATCH:** On the 1st, Venus and Jupiter are breathtakingly close to each other, low in the west 40 minutes after sunset, creating the year's finest conjunction. On the 2nd, they're visibly separating. During March, Jupiter sinks lower while Venus climbs a bit higher each evening. The crescent Moon dangles below Venus on the 23rd and above it on the 24th. Also on the 24th, binocular users can look for green planet Uranus to the left of the Moon. Since there are no green stars, the color should make it easily identifiable. On the 28th, look for the Moon to hover just above fading Mars. They're part of the impressive gathering of stars and planets that surround Orion in the southwest at nightfall. Spring begins with the vernal equinox on the evening of the 20th at 5:24 P.M. EDT.

| ○ FULL MOON | 7th day | 7:40 A.M. | ● NEW MOON | 21st day | 1:23 P.M. |
|---|---|---|---|---|---|
| ☽ LAST QUARTER | 14th day | 10:08 P.M. | ☾ FIRST QUARTER | 28th day | 10:32 P.M. |

*After 2:00 A.M. on March 12, Eastern Daylight Time is given.*

**GET THESE PAGES WITH TIMES SET TO YOUR ZIP CODE VIA ALMANAC.COM/2023.**

| DAY OF YEAR | DAY OF MONTH | DAY OF WEEK | ☀ RISES H. M. | RISE KEY | ☀ SETS H. M. | SET KEY | LENGTH OF DAY H. M. | SUN FAST M. | SUN DECLINATION ° ' | HIGH TIDE TIMES BOSTON | | ☽ RISES H. M. | RISE KEY | ☽ SETS H. M. | SET KEY | ☽ ASTRON. PLACE | ☽ AGE |
|---|---|---|---|---|---|---|---|---|---|---|---|---|---|---|---|---|---|
| 60 | 1 | W. | 6:20 | D | 5:34 | C | 11 14 | 4 | 7 s. 30 | 6½ | 7¼ | 11:45 | A | 3:15 | E | GEM | 9 |
| 61 | 2 | Th. | 6:18 | D | 5:35 | C | 11 17 | 4 | 7 s. 07 | 7½ | 8¼ | 12:40 | A | 4:04 | E | GEM | 10 |
| 62 | 3 | Fr. | 6:17 | D | 5:36 | C | 11 19 | 4 | 6 s. 44 | 8½ | 9 | 1:41 | B | 4:46 | E | GEM | 11 |
| 63 | 4 | Sa. | 6:15 | D | 5:37 | C | 11 22 | 4 | 6 s. 21 | 9¼ | 9¾ | 2:44 | B | 5:19 | E | CAN | 12 |
| 64 | 5 | **A** | 6:13 | D | 5:39 | C | 11 26 | 4 | 5 s. 58 | 10 | 10½ | 3:48 | C | 5:47 | E | LEO | 13 |
| 65 | 6 | M. | 6:12 | D | 5:40 | C | 11 28 | 5 | 5 s. 34 | 10½ | 11 | 4:52 | C | 6:11 | E | LEO | 14 |
| 66 | 7 | Tu. | 6:10 | D | 5:41 | C | 11 31 | 5 | 5 s. 11 | 11¼ | 11¾ | 5:55 | D | 6:32 | D | LEO | 15 |
| 67 | 8 | W. | 6:08 | D | 5:42 | C | 11 34 | 5 | 4 s. 48 | 11¾ | — | 6:59 | D | 6:52 | D | VIR | 16 |
| 68 | 9 | Th. | 6:07 | C | 5:43 | C | 11 36 | 5 | 4 s. 24 | 12¼ | 12½ | 8:04 | E | 7:11 | C | VIR | 17 |
| 69 | 10 | Fr. | 6:05 | C | 5:45 | C | 11 40 | 6 | 4 s. 01 | 12¾ | 1 | 9:10 | E | 7:31 | C | VIR | 18 |
| 70 | 11 | Sa. | 6:03 | C | 5:46 | C | 11 43 | 6 | 3 s. 37 | 1¼ | 1¾ | 10:19 | E | 7:53 | B | VIR | 19 |
| 71 | 12 | **A** | 7:02 | C | 6:47 | C | 11 45 | 6 | 3 s. 14 | 3 | 3½ | — | - | 9:19 | B | LIB | 20 |
| 72 | 13 | M. | 7:00 | C | 6:48 | C | 11 48 | 6 | 2 s. 50 | 3¾ | 4¼ | 12:31 | E | 9:51 | B | LIB | 21 |
| 73 | 14 | Tu. | 6:58 | C | 6:49 | C | 11 51 | 7 | 2 s. 26 | 4½ | 5¼ | 1:44 | E | 10:32 | A | SCO | 22 |
| 74 | 15 | W. | 6:56 | C | 6:50 | C | 11 54 | 7 | 2 s. 03 | 5½ | 6¼ | 2:54 | E | 11:25 | A | OPH | 23 |
| 75 | 16 | Th. | 6:55 | C | 6:52 | C | 11 57 | 7 | 1 s. 39 | 6½ | 7½ | 3:58 | E | 12:31 | A | SAG | 24 |
| 76 | 17 | Fr. | 6:53 | C | 6:53 | C | 12 00 | 8 | 1 s. 15 | 7¾ | 8½ | 4:50 | E | 1:46 | B | SAG | 25 |
| 77 | 18 | Sa. | 6:51 | C | 6:54 | C | 12 03 | 8 | 0 s. 51 | 8¾ | 9½ | 5:33 | E | 3:06 | B | CAP | 26 |
| 78 | 19 | **A** | 6:50 | C | 6:55 | C | 12 05 | 8 | 0 s. 28 | 9¾ | 10½ | 6:06 | E | 4:28 | C | CAP | 27 |
| 79 | 20 | M. | 6:48 | C | 6:56 | C | 12 08 | 8 | 0 s. 04 | 10¾ | 11¼ | 6:34 | D | 5:47 | D | AQU | 28 |
| 80 | 21 | Tu. | 6:46 | C | 6:57 | C | 12 11 | 9 | 0 N. 19 | 11¾ | — | 6:59 | D | 7:04 | D | AQU | 0 |
| 81 | 22 | W. | 6:44 | C | 6:59 | C | 12 15 | 9 | 0 N. 43 | 12¼ | 12½ | 7:22 | C | 8:19 | E | CET | 1 |
| 82 | 23 | Th. | 6:43 | C | 7:00 | C | 12 17 | 9 | 1 N. 06 | 1 | 1¼ | 7:45 | C | 9:33 | E | PSC | 2 |
| 83 | 24 | Fr. | 6:41 | C | 7:01 | C | 12 20 | 10 | 1 N. 30 | 1¾ | 2¼ | 8:10 | B | 10:46 | E | ARI | 3 |
| 84 | 25 | Sa. | 6:39 | C | 7:02 | C | 12 23 | 10 | 1 N. 54 | 2½ | 3 | 8:38 | B | 11:57 | E | ARI | 4 |
| 85 | 26 | **A** | 6:37 | C | 7:03 | C | 12 26 | 10 | 2 N. 17 | 3¼ | 3¾ | 9:10 | B | — | - | TAU | 5 |
| 86 | 27 | M. | 6:36 | C | 7:04 | C | 12 28 | 10 | 2 N. 41 | 4 | 4¾ | 9:50 | A | 1:05 | E | TAU | 6 |
| 87 | 28 | Tu. | 6:34 | C | 7:05 | D | 12 31 | 11 | 3 N. 04 | 4¾ | 5½ | 10:36 | A | 2:06 | E | TAU | 7 |
| 88 | 29 | W. | 6:32 | C | 7:06 | D | 12 34 | 11 | 3 N. 27 | 5¾ | 6½ | 11:30 | A | 3:00 | E | GEM | 8 |
| 89 | 30 | Th. | 6:30 | C | 7:08 | D | 12 38 | 11 | 3 N. 51 | 6¾ | 7½ | 12:29 | B | 3:44 | E | GEM | 9 |
| 90 | 31 | Fr. | 6:29 | C | 7:09 | D | 12 40 | 12 | 4 N. 14 | 7¾ | 8½ | 1:32 | B | 4:21 | E | CAN | 10 |

**CALENDAR**

*O March that blusters and March that blows,*
*What color under your footsteps glows!*
–Celia Thaxter, of spring flowers

| DAY OF MONTH | DAY OF WEEK | DATES, FEASTS, FASTS, ASPECTS, TIDE HEIGHTS, AND WEATHER | |
|---|---|---|---|
| 1 | W. | Ember Day • St. David • ☾ rides high • Tides {8.9 / 7.8} | *Sunny* |
| 2 | Th. | St. Chad • ☌☿♄ • ☌♀♃ • Tides {8.9 / 7.9} | *chill* |
| 3 | Fr. | Ember Day • ☾ at apo. • Madeleine de Verchères (defended family fort at age 14) born, 1678 | *lingers* |
| 4 | Sa. | Ember Day • Granite Railway chartered, Quincy, Mass., 1826 • {9.4 / 8.5} | *before* |
| 5 | **A** | **2nd S. in Lent** • Misao Okawa (who lived to be 117 yrs. old), born, 1898 | *rain-soaked* |
| 6 | M. | U.S. Football League (USFL) began its 1st season, 1983 • Tides {9.9 / 9.1} | *fingers* |
| 7 | Tu. | St. Perpetua • FULL WORM ○ • Comet Kohoutek discovered, 1973 | *again* |
| 8 | W. | ☾ on Eq. • *Much would have more and lost all.* • {10.0 / —} | *seek* |
| 9 | Th. | Hummingbirds migrate north now. • Tides {9.7 / 9.9} | *a comfortable* |
| 10 | Fr. | Ojibwe writer Richard Wagamese died, 2017 • Tides {9.8 / 9.7} | *mitten.* |
| 11 | Sa. | ☾ at ☋ • Inventor Philo T. Farnsworth died, 1971 • {10.0 / 9.5} | *Snowing* |
| 12 | **A** | **3rd S. in Lent** • Daylight Saving Time begins, 2:00 A.M. • {10.0 / 9.2} | *again—* |
| 13 | M. | U.S. first lady Abigail Fillmore born, 1798 • Tides {10.0 / 8.8} | *Remember* |
| 14 | Tu. | Pelican Island National Wildlife Refuge (Fla.), 1st in U.S., established, 1903 • {9.9 / 8.5} | *back then* |
| 15 | W. | ☾ runs low • ☌♆☉ • Beware the ides of March. • {9.8 / 8.3} | *when* |
| 16 | Th. | ☌☿♆ • Mathematician/navigator Nathaniel Bowditch died, 1838 • {9.9 / 8.4} | *everyone* |
| 17 | Fr. | St. Patrick's Day • ☌♇☾ • ☿ in sup. ☌ • {10.1 / 8.8} | *wasn't* |
| 18 | Sa. | Agricultural engineer Wesley Buchele born, 1920 • {10.5 / 9.4} | *frostbitten?* |
| 19 | **A** | **4th S. in Lent** • ☾ at perig. • ☌♄☾ • Tides {10.9 / 10.0} | *Equinox* |
| 20 | M. | St. Joseph[T] • Vernal Equinox • 32.5" snow, Juneau, Alaska, 1948 | *vernal* |
| 21 | Tu. | NEW ● • ☾ on Eq. • ☌☿☾ • ☌♆☾ • Tides {11.4 / —} | *springs* |
| 22 | W. | Ramadan begins at sundown • ☌♃☾ • Mime Marcel Marceau born, 1923 | *hope eternal* |
| 23 | Th. | ☾ at ☊ • *When you do not know what to do—wait.* • Tides {11.3 / 11.1} | *for just* |
| 24 | Fr. | ☌♀☾ • ☌♅☾ • 18.7-inch-long goldfish set world record, 2003 • {11.3 / 10.6} | *one warm* |
| 25 | Sa. | **Annunciation** • Chess grandmaster Daniel Yanofsky born, 1925 • {11.0 / 10.0} | *breeze* |
| 26 | **A** | **5th S. in Lent** • *Thunder in spring, Cold will bring.* • Tides {10.6 / 9.3} | *or two.* |
| 27 | M. | 5.75" rain, Nashville, Tenn., 2021 • Tides {10.0 / 8.7} | *Ha, ha, ha—* |
| 28 | Tu. | ☾ rides high • ☌☿♃ • ☌♂☾ • Tides {9.5 / 8.2} | *Guess what?* |
| 29 | W. | Due to ice jam, Niagara Falls stopped flowing for 1st time in recorded history, 1848 | *It's more rain* |
| 30 | Th. | Artist Vincent van Gogh born, 1853 • Tides {8.8 / 7.8} | *and snow* |
| 31 | Fr. | ☾ at apo. • ☌♀♅ • Chipmunks emerge from hibernation now. • {8.8 / 8.0} | *for you!* |

## Farmer's Calendar

Sapsicles—those shards of frozen sap that hang from broken branches of sugar maples, red maples, sweet birches, black walnuts, box elders, and butternuts—seem made for consumption by kids and kids-at-heart. If you concentrate, you can taste the coming spring.

Sapsicles are sweeter than liquid sap because the sugar has been concentrated by evaporation. Look for them on late-winter days after cold nights. When sapsicles melt a bit, you may be sharing them with mourning cloaks, one of the few butterfly species abroad in the warm winter woods. They've pupated during the previous spring or summer and have been hibernating in tree cavities, bark, moss, or leaf litter.

According to some connoisseurs, sweet-birch sapsicles have a faint wintergreen flavor; box-elder sapsicles are said to be vaguely reminiscent of vanilla. Red-maple and black walnut sapsicles are considered superb.

The best 'sicles are produced by sugar maples, which grow from Nova Scotia to Tennessee and west to Ontario and Minnesota. Some of these are 5 feet in diameter and still bear the V-shape scars made by Native Americans who collected their sap to make sugar.

**SKY WATCH:** Mercury's brilliant magnitude –1.0 may offer a glimpse soon after sunset despite its extremely low elevation in the west. It gains height each evening but loses brilliance. Mercury's best evening of 2023 is probably on the 11th, when it's at its highest position and still shining at magnitude 0—but it will be dazzling Venus above that draws everyone's attention. Then come a series of close meetings with the crescent Moon: below Mercury on the 20th, halfway between Mercury and Venus on the 21st, below Venus on the 22nd, above Venus on the 23rd, between Mars and Venus on the 24th, and with Mars on the 25th. An annular total eclipse, not visible from the U.S. or Canada, appears as total over westernmost Australia and a string of nearby islands on the 20th (local time).

○ **FULL MOON** 6th day 12:35 A.M.  ● **NEW MOON** 20th day 12:13 A.M.
◑ **LAST QUARTER** 13th day 5:11 A.M.  ◐ **FIRST QUARTER** 27th day 5:20 P.M.

*All times are given in Eastern Daylight Time.*

**GET THESE PAGES WITH TIMES SET TO YOUR ZIP CODE VIA ALMANAC.COM/2023.**

| DAY OF YEAR | DAY OF MONTH | DAY OF WEEK | ☼ RISES H.M. | RISE KEY | ☼ SETS H.M. | SET KEY | LENGTH OF DAY H.M. | SUN FAST M. | SUN DECLINATION ° ′ | HIGH TIDE TIMES BOSTON | | ☾ RISES H.M. | RISE KEY | ☾ SETS H.M. | SET KEY | ASTRON. PLACE | ☾ AGE |
|---|---|---|---|---|---|---|---|---|---|---|---|---|---|---|---|---|---|
| 91 | 1 | Sa. | 6:27 | C | **7:10** | D | 12 43 | 12 | 4 N. 37 | 8¾ | 9½ | **2:36** | B | 4:50 | E | CAN | 11 |
| 92 | 2 | **A** | 6:25 | C | **7:11** | D | 12 46 | 12 | 5 N. 00 | 9¾ | 10¼ | **3:40** | C | 5:15 | E | LEO | 12 |
| 93 | 3 | M. | 6:24 | C | **7:12** | D | 12 48 | 13 | 5 N. 23 | 10½ | 10¾ | **4:44** | C | 5:37 | D | LEO | 13 |
| 94 | 4 | Tu. | 6:22 | C | **7:13** | D | 12 51 | 13 | 5 N. 46 | 11 | 11½ | **5:48** | D | 5:57 | D | LEO | 14 |
| 95 | 5 | W. | 6:20 | C | **7:14** | D | 12 54 | 13 | 6 N. 09 | 11¾ | — | **6:53** | D | 6:16 | C | VIR | 15 |
| 96 | 6 | Th. | 6:18 | B | **7:15** | D | 12 57 | 13 | 6 N. 32 | 12 | 12½ | **7:59** | E | 6:36 | C | VIR | 16 |
| 97 | 7 | Fr. | 6:17 | B | **7:17** | D | 13 00 | 14 | 6 N. 54 | 12½ | 1 | **9:09** | E | 6:57 | B | VIR | 17 |
| 98 | 8 | Sa. | 6:15 | B | **7:18** | D | 13 03 | 14 | 7 N. 17 | 1¼ | 1¾ | **10:22** | E | 7:22 | B | LIB | 18 |
| 99 | 9 | **A** | 6:13 | B | **7:19** | D | 13 06 | 14 | 7 N. 39 | 1¾ | 2½ | **11:35** | E | 7:53 | B | LIB | 19 |
| 100 | 10 | M. | 6:12 | B | **7:20** | D | 13 08 | 14 | 8 N. 01 | 2½ | 3¼ | — | – | 8:31 | A | OPH | 20 |
| 101 | 11 | Tu. | 6:10 | B | **7:21** | D | 13 11 | 15 | 8 N. 23 | 3¼ | 4 | 12:47 | E | 9:20 | A | OPH | 21 |
| 102 | 12 | W. | 6:08 | B | **7:22** | D | 13 14 | 15 | 8 N. 45 | 4¼ | 5 | 1:52 | E | 10:21 | A | SAG | 22 |
| 103 | 13 | Th. | 6:07 | B | **7:23** | D | 13 16 | 15 | 9 N. 07 | 5¼ | 6 | 2:48 | E | 11:32 | B | SAG | 23 |
| 104 | 14 | Fr. | 6:05 | B | **7:25** | D | 13 20 | 15 | 9 N. 29 | 6¼ | 7¼ | 3:32 | E | **12:49** | B | CAP | 24 |
| 105 | 15 | Sa. | 6:04 | B | **7:26** | D | 13 22 | 16 | 9 N. 50 | 7½ | 8¼ | 4:07 | E | **2:08** | C | CAP | 25 |
| 106 | 16 | **A** | 6:02 | B | **7:27** | D | 13 25 | 16 | 10 N. 12 | 8½ | 9¼ | 4:36 | E | **3:26** | C | AQU | 26 |
| 107 | 17 | M. | 6:00 | B | **7:28** | D | 13 28 | 16 | 10 N. 33 | 9½ | 10¼ | 5:01 | D | **4:41** | D | AQU | 27 |
| 108 | 18 | Tu. | 5:59 | B | **7:29** | D | 13 30 | 16 | 10 N. 54 | 10½ | 11 | 5:24 | C | **5:56** | E | PSC | 28 |
| 109 | 19 | W. | 5:57 | B | **7:30** | D | 13 33 | 17 | 11 N. 15 | 11½ | 11¾ | 5:46 | C | **7:09** | E | PSC | 29 |
| 110 | 20 | Th. | 5:56 | B | **7:31** | D | 13 35 | 17 | 11 N. 35 | 12¼ | — | 6:09 | B | **8:23** | E | ARI | 0 |
| 111 | 21 | Fr. | 5:54 | B | **7:32** | D | 13 38 | 17 | 11 N. 56 | 12½ | 1 | 6:35 | B | **9:36** | E | ARI | 1 |
| 112 | 22 | Sa. | 5:53 | B | **7:34** | D | 13 41 | 17 | 12 N. 16 | 1¼ | 1¾ | 7:06 | B | **10:46** | E | TAU | 2 |
| 113 | 23 | **A** | 5:51 | B | **7:35** | D | 13 44 | 17 | 12 N. 36 | 2 | 2½ | 7:43 | A | **11:52** | E | TAU | 3 |
| 114 | 24 | M. | 5:50 | B | **7:36** | D | 13 46 | 18 | 12 N. 56 | 2¾ | 3¼ | 8:27 | A | — | – | TAU | 4 |
| 115 | 25 | Tu. | 5:48 | B | **7:37** | D | 13 49 | 18 | 13 N. 16 | 3½ | 4¼ | 9:18 | A | 12:50 | E | AUR | 5 |
| 116 | 26 | W. | 5:47 | B | **7:38** | D | 13 51 | 18 | 13 N. 35 | 4¼ | 5 | 10:16 | B | 1:39 | E | GEM | 6 |
| 117 | 27 | Th. | 5:45 | B | **7:39** | D | 13 54 | 18 | 13 N. 54 | 5¼ | 6 | 11:18 | B | 2:19 | E | CAN | 7 |
| 118 | 28 | Fr. | 5:44 | B | **7:40** | E | 13 56 | 18 | 14 N. 13 | 6 | 7 | **12:22** | B | 2:52 | E | CAN | 8 |
| 119 | 29 | Sa. | 5:42 | B | **7:41** | E | 13 59 | 18 | 14 N. 32 | 7 | 7¾ | **1:26** | C | 3:18 | E | LEO | 9 |
| 120 | 30 | **A** | 5:41 | B | **7:43** | E | 14 02 | 18 | 14 N. 50 | 8 | 8¾ | **2:29** | C | 3:41 | E | LEO | 10 |

CALENDAR

# THE FOURTH MONTH · 2023 APRIL APRIL HATH 30 DAYS

*Hark! the cock crows, and yon bright star*
*Tells us the day himself's not far.*
–Charles Cotton

| DAY OF MONTH | DAY OF WEEK | DATES, FEASTS, FASTS, ASPECTS, TIDE HEIGHTS, AND WEATHER | |
|---|---|---|---|
| 1 | Sa. | **All Fools'** • Composer Sergei Rachmaninoff born, 1873 • {8.9 / 8.3 | *Foolin' with* |
| 2 | A | **Palm Sunday** • 199.5+ mph wind gust, Cannon Mtn., N.H., 1973 • {9.2 / 8.7 | *flurries,* |
| 3 | M. | *The fool's p[illegible]sure costs him dear.* • Tides {9.5 / 9.2 | *but warming,* |
| 4 | Tu. | Canadian st[illegible] Jules Léger bor[illegible] • U.S. civil rights leader Martin Luther King Jr. assassinated, 1968 | *no* |
| 5 | W. | Passover begins at sundown • ☾ EQ. [illegible] Camel deputized, L.A. Cty. [illegible]riff's Dept., Calif., 2003 | *worries.* |
| 6 | Th. | Maundy Thursday • FULL PINK ○ • Mu[illegible] Tammy Wyne[illegible] 1998 • {9.9 / 9.9 | *Showers,* |
| 7 | Fr. | **Good Friday** • ☾ AT ☋ • Tides [illegible] | *then* |
| 8 | Sa. | Painter Pablo Picasso died, 1973 • Tides {9.[illegible] | *sunny for* |
| 9 | A | **Easter** • *A rainy Easter betokens a good harvest.* [illegible] | *[illegible]ke Easter* |
| 10 | M. | Easter Monday • Naturalist Jack Miner born, 1865 • {10.5 / 9.3 | *[illegible]ny.* |
| 11 | Tu. | ☾ RUNS LOW • ☌♃☉ • ☿ GR. ELONG. (20° EAST) • Thundersnow, Minn., S.Dak., Wis., 2019 | *Bu[illegible]* |
| 12 | W. | Charles Gayler received patent for fireproof iron chest, 1833 • Tides {10.3 / 8.7 | *and* |
| 13 | Th. | ☌♇☾ • U.S. president Thomas Jefferson born, 1743 • Tides {10.1 / 8.7 | *forth,* |
| 14 | Fr. | Dr. Harry Plotz's discovery of cause of typhus formally announced, 1915 • {10.0 / 8.9 | *south* |
| 15 | Sa. | ☾ AT PERIG. • ☌♄☾ • Actress Elizabeth Montgomery born, 1933 • {10.1 / 9.3 | *and* |
| 16 | A | **2nd S. of Easter** • **Orthodox Easter** • Tides {10.3 / 9.9 | *north,* |
| 17 | M. | ☌♆☾ • Eastern U.S. heat wave: 80°F, Portland, Maine; 97°F, Newark, N.J., 2002 | *spring* |
| 18 | Tu. | ☾ ON EQ. • "Old" Yankee Stadium opened, N.Y.C., 1923 • Tides {10.7 / 11.0 | *comes* |
| 19 | W. | ☌♃☾ • Death of oldest known spider (43-yr.-old trapdoor species) announced, 2018 | *forth.* |
| 20 | Th. | NEW ● • ECLIPSE ☉ • ☾ AT ☊ • Tides {10.7 / — | *Sun* |
| 21 | Fr. | ☌☿☾ • ☌♅☾ • ☿ STAT. • Tides {11.3 / 10.4 | *and* |
| 22 | Sa. | **Earth Day** • TV producer Aaron Spelling born, 1923 • Tides {11.2 / 10.0 | *sprinkles,* |
| 23 | A | 3rd S. of Easter • ☌♀☾ • 1st YouTube video, "Me at the zoo," uploaded, 2005 | *willy-nilly;* |
| 24 | M. | St. George[T] • Almanac founder Robert B. Thomas born, 1766 • Spain declared war on U.S., 1898 | *first it's* |
| 25 | Tu. | St. Mark • ☾ RIDES HIGH • ☌♂☾ • Tides {9.9 / 8.6 | *warm,* |
| 26 | W. | Poplars leaf out about now. • *Deep rivers move in silence; shallow brooks are noisy.* • {9.5 / 8.3 | *then* |
| 27 | Th. | Astronomer John Russell Hind discovered new variable star in Ophiuchus, 1848 • {9.1 / 8.1 | *it's* |
| 28 | Fr. | ☾ AT APO. • Hailstorms hit parts of Tex. and Okla., with 6.4" hailstone falling in Hondo, Tex., 2021 | *chilly.* |
| 29 | Sa. | UK's Prince William married Catherine "Kate" Middleton, 2011 • Tides {8.7 / 8.3 | *April's been* |
| 30 | A | **4th S. of Easter** • U.S. Dept. of the Navy established, 1798 | *a daffo-dilly!* |

## Farmer's Calendar

While a bumblebee may not be the first insect that you see in the spring, it's likely to be the first that you hear. The buzz starts on some hushed morning over snow-bent grass or sun-washed earth split by swelling bulbs.

These big bumblebees are fertilized queens, sole survivors from last autumn. The flight of each is slow and purposeful, not wild and erratic as in the operatic score "Flight of the Bumblebee."

The queen is searching for a nest site—perhaps an abandoned chipmunk burrow—which she'll stuff with grass [illegible] moss. Next, she'll make a t[illegible]e-size wax pot and fill it w[illegible]nectar. Finally, she'll knead [illegible]en and nectar into "bee b[illegible]d." The nectar will sustain h[illegible]hile she's brooding. Larvae [illegible] eat the bread.

The bumblebee's fur allows it to live in colder climates than most other insects. One species, *Bombus polaris,* has been reported 62 miles from the North Pole.

North Americans are fond of bumblebees. They're harbingers of fine weather, resemble winged teddy bears, and are so good-natured that getting one to sting you is a major undertaking. But most important, they're ours. Unlike honeybees, they are natives.

# MAY

**SKY WATCH:** Venus, shining at a dazzling magnitude –4.1, stands visibly high in the west at nightfall on the 1st. In the predawn eastern sky, Mercury also reaches its greatest Sun-separation; however, at magnitude 5, it's much too faint to be seen. The 5th brings a penumbral lunar eclipse, the kind that doesn't change the full Moon's appearance. Unfortunately, it's not visible from the U.S. or Canada. Look for Venus above the Moon on the 22nd and below it on the 23rd. On this same night, the crescent Moon floats between Mars and Venus. At nightfall on the 31st, Mars hovers to the upper left of brilliant Venus, with both of Earth's nearest neighbors having now crossed into Leo.

○ **FULL MOON** 5th day 1:34 P.M.     ● **NEW MOON** 19th day 11:53 A.M.

◑ **LAST QUARTER** 12th day 10:28 A.M.     ◐ **FIRST QUARTER** 27th day 11:22 A.M.

*All times are given in Eastern Daylight Time.*

**GET THESE PAGES WITH TIMES SET TO YOUR ZIP CODE VIA ALMANAC.COM/2023.**

| DAY OF YEAR | DAY OF MONTH | DAY OF WEEK | ☼ RISES H.M. | RISE KEY | ☼ SETS H.M. | SET KEY | LENGTH OF DAY H.M. | SUN FAST M. | SUN DECLINATION ° ′ | HIGH TIDE TIMES BOSTON | | ☽ RISES H.M. | RISE KEY | ☽ SETS H.M. | SET KEY | ☽ ASTRON. PLACE | ☽ AGE |
|---|---|---|---|---|---|---|---|---|---|---|---|---|---|---|---|---|---|
| 121 | 1 | M. | 5:40 | B | 7:44 | E | 14 04 | 19 | 15 N. 08 | 9 | 9½ | 3:33 | D | 4:01 | D | LEO | 11 |
| 122 | 2 | Tu. | 5:38 | B | 7:45 | E | 14 07 | 19 | 15 N. 26 | 9¾ | 10 | 4:37 | D | 4:20 | D | VIR | 12 |
| 123 | 3 | W. | 5:37 | B | 7:46 | E | 14 09 | 19 | 15 N. 44 | 10½ | 10¾ | 5:44 | E | 4:40 | C | VIR | 13 |
| 124 | 4 | Th. | 5:36 | B | 7:47 | E | 14 11 | 19 | 16 N. 02 | 11¼ | 11½ | 6:53 | E | 5:00 | C | VIR | 14 |
| 125 | 5 | Fr. | 5:34 | B | 7:48 | E | 14 14 | 19 | 16 N. 19 | 12 | — | 8:05 | E | 5:24 | B | LIB | 15 |
| 126 | 6 | Sa. | 5:33 | B | 7:49 | E | 14 16 | 19 | 16 N. 36 | 12 | 12½ | 9:21 | E | 5:53 | B | LIB | 16 |
| 127 | 7 | **A** | 5:32 | B | 7:50 | E | 14 18 | 19 | 16 N. 52 | 12¾ | 1¼ | 10:36 | E | 6:29 | A | SCO | 17 |
| 128 | 8 | M. | 5:31 | B | 7:51 | E | 14 20 | 19 | 17 N. 09 | 1½ | 2¼ | 11:45 | E | 7:15 | A | OPH | 18 |
| 129 | 9 | Tu. | 5:30 | B | 7:52 | E | 14 22 | 19 | 17 N. 25 | 2¼ | 3 | — | - | 8:13 | A | SAG | 19 |
| 130 | 10 | W. | 5:28 | B | 7:54 | E | 14 26 | 19 | 17 N. 40 | 3 | 4 | 12:45 | E | 9:23 | B | SAG | 20 |
| 131 | 11 | Th. | 5:27 | B | 7:55 | E | 14 28 | 19 | 17 N. 56 | 4 | 4¾ | 1:32 | E | 10:39 | B | CAP | 21 |
| 132 | 12 | Fr. | 5:26 | B | 7:56 | E | 14 30 | 19 | 18 N. 11 | 5 | 6 | 2:10 | E | 11:57 | C | CAP | 22 |
| 133 | 13 | Sa. | 5:25 | B | 7:57 | E | 14 32 | 19 | 18 N. 26 | 6¼ | 7 | 2:40 | E | **1:14** | C | AQU | 23 |
| 134 | 14 | **A** | 5:24 | B | 7:58 | E | 14 34 | 19 | 18 N. 41 | 7¼ | 8 | 3:05 | D | **2:28** | D | AQU | 24 |
| 135 | 15 | M. | 5:23 | B | 7:59 | E | 14 36 | 19 | 18 N. 55 | 8¼ | 8¾ | 3:28 | D | **3:41** | D | PSC | 25 |
| 136 | 16 | Tu. | 5:22 | B | 8:00 | E | 14 38 | 19 | 19 N. 09 | 9¼ | 9¾ | 3:50 | C | **4:53** | E | PSC | 26 |
| 137 | 17 | W. | 5:21 | A | 8:01 | E | 14 40 | 19 | 19 N. 22 | 10¼ | 10½ | 4:12 | C | **6:05** | E | PSC | 27 |
| 138 | 18 | Th. | 5:20 | A | 8:02 | E | 14 42 | 19 | 19 N. 36 | 11 | 11¼ | 4:36 | B | **7:17** | E | ARI | 28 |
| 139 | 19 | Fr. | 5:19 | A | 8:03 | E | 14 44 | 19 | 19 N. 49 | 12 | — | 5:04 | B | **8:28** | E | ARI | 0 |
| 140 | 20 | Sa. | 5:18 | A | 8:04 | E | 14 46 | 19 | 20 N. 01 | 12 | 12¾ | 5:38 | A | **9:36** | E | TAU | 1 |
| 141 | 21 | **A** | 5:17 | A | 8:05 | E | 14 48 | 19 | 20 N. 13 | 12¾ | 1½ | 6:19 | A | **10:38** | E | TAU | 2 |
| 142 | 22 | M. | 5:17 | A | 8:06 | E | 14 49 | 19 | 20 N. 25 | 1½ | 2¼ | 7:08 | A | **11:32** | E | GEM | 3 |
| 143 | 23 | Tu. | 5:16 | A | 8:07 | E | 14 51 | 19 | 20 N. 37 | 2¼ | 3 | 8:04 | A | — | - | GEM | 4 |
| 144 | 24 | W. | 5:15 | A | 8:08 | E | 14 53 | 19 | 20 N. 48 | 3 | 3¾ | 9:05 | B | **12:16** | E | GEM | 5 |
| 145 | 25 | Th. | 5:14 | A | 8:09 | E | 14 55 | 19 | 20 N. 59 | 3¾ | 4½ | 10:08 | B | **12:51** | E | CAN | 6 |
| 146 | 26 | Fr. | 5:14 | A | 8:09 | E | 14 55 | 19 | 21 N. 10 | 4½ | 5¼ | 11:12 | B | **1:20** | E | LEO | 7 |
| 147 | 27 | Sa. | 5:13 | A | 8:10 | E | 14 57 | 18 | 21 N. 20 | 5½ | 6¼ | **12:15** | C | **1:44** | E | LEO | 8 |
| 148 | 28 | **A** | 5:12 | A | 8:11 | E | 14 59 | 18 | 21 N. 29 | 6¼ | 7 | **1:18** | C | **2:05** | D | LEO | 9 |
| 149 | 29 | M. | 5:12 | A | 8:12 | E | 15 00 | 18 | 21 N. 39 | 7¼ | 7¾ | **2:21** | D | **2:24** | D | VIR | 10 |
| 150 | 30 | Tu. | 5:11 | A | 8:13 | E | 15 02 | 18 | 21 N. 48 | 8¼ | 8½ | **3:26** | D | **2:43** | C | VIR | 11 |
| 151 | 31 | W. | 5:11 | A | 8:14 | E | 15 03 | 18 | 21 N. 56 | 9 | 9¼ | **4:33** | E | 3:03 | C | VIR | 12 |

THE FIFTH MONTH • 2023 **MAY** MAY HATH 31 DAYS

*A deep mysterious sympathy doth bind*
*The human heart to Nature's beauties all.*
–**Robert Nicoll**

| DAY OF MONTH | DAY OF WEEK | DATES, FEASTS, FASTS, ASPECTS, TIDE HEIGHTS, AND WEATHER | |
|---|---|---|---|
| 1 | M. | Sts. Philip & James • MAY DAY • ☿ IN INF. ☌ • {9.0 / 9.1 | *Mayp'les* |
| 2 | Tu. | St. Athanasius • ☾ ON EQ. • ♇ STAT. • Tides {9.2 / 9.5 | *done* |
| 3 | W. | *A wet May will fill a byre full of hay.* • Tides {9.4 / 10.0 | *budding,* |
| 4 | Th. | ☾ AT ☋ • Pringles can designer Fredric Baur died, 2008 • Tides {9.6 / 10.4 | *watch* |
| 5 | Fr. | Vesak • FULL FLOWER ○ • ECLIPSE ☾ • Tides {9.7 / — | *out* |
| 6 | Sa. | *Hindenburg* disaster, 1937 • Swimmer Ethelda Bleibtrey died, 1978 • 8.74" rain, Groton, S.Dak., 2007 | *for* |
| 7 | A | **5th S. of Easter** • U.S. chief justice Salmon P. Chase died, 1873 | *flooding!* |
| 8 | M. | St. Julian of Norwich • Treaty of Washington signed, 1871 • Tides {11.0 / 9.6 | *Rainy* |
| 9 | Tu. | St. Gregory of Nazianzus • ☾ RUNS LOW • ☌⛢☉ • Tides {11.0 / 9.4 | *but* |
| 10 | W. | ☌♇☾ • 1st submerged voyage around world completed by submarine USS *Triton,* 1960 | *balmy,* |
| 11 | Th. | Three • ☾ AT PERIG. • Minn. became 32nd U.S. state, 1858 • Composer Irving Berlin born, 1888 | *warm* |
| 12 | Fr. | Chilly • U.S. and Canada signed NORAD agreement, 1958 • Tides {10.4 / 9.3 | *just* |
| 13 | Sa. | Saints • ☌♄☾ • Cranberries in bud now. • {10.2 / 9.5 | *like* |
| 14 | A | **Rogation Sunday** • MOTHER'S DAY • ☌♆☾ • ☿ STAT. | *Mommy.* |
| 15 | M. | ☾ ON EQ. • Mercury-Atlas 9 *(Faith 7)* launched, 1963 • Tides {10.0 / 10.3 | *Still* |
| 16 | Tu. | Artist Alfred Pellan born, 1906 • Canadian Victoria Cross unveiled, 2008 • {10.0 / 10.7 | *getting* |
| 17 | W. | ☾ AT ☊ • ☌☿☾ • OCCN. ♃☾ • Tides {10.1 / 11.0 | *mild—* |
| 18 | Th. | **Ascension** • ☌⛢☾ • Research suggested Stonehenge built around 1848 B.C., 1952 | *We'll* |
| 19 | Fr. | St. Dunstan • NEW ● • *Advice should precede the act.* • {9.9 / — | *have no* |
| 20 | Sa. | Engineer William Hewlett born, 1913 • Tides {11.1 / 9.7 | *grumbling* |
| 21 | A | 1st S. af. Asc. • Stranded driver played drums on side of I-695 until help arrived, Baltimore, Md., 2013 | *about* |
| 22 | M. | VICTORIA DAY (CANADA) • ☾ RIDES HIGH • Deadly EF5 tornado struck Joplin, Mo., 2011 | *lightning* |
| 23 | Tu. | ☌♀☾ • S.C. became 8th U.S. state, 1788 • {10.3 / 8.9 | *wild and* |
| 24 | W. | ☌♂☾ • Brooklyn Bridge opened, N.Y.C., 1883 • Tides {9.9 / 8.6 | *thunder* |
| 25 | Th. | St. Bede • **Orthodox Ascension** • Shavuot begins at sundown • ☾ AT APO. | *rumbling!* |
| 26 | Fr. | *Challenger* Expedition completed, 1876 • Astronaut Sally Ride born, 1951 • {9.2 / 8.4 | *Warm* |
| 27 | Sa. | 1st automatic soda fountain dispenser introduced, Chicago World's Fair, Ill., 1933 • {9.0 / 8.5 | *memories* |
| 28 | A | **Whit S. • Pentecost** • Athlete Jim Thorpe born, 1888 | *dear* |
| 29 | M. | MEMORIAL DAY, OBSERVED • ☾ ON EQ. • ☿ GR. ELONG. (25° WEST) • Wis. became 30th U.S. state, 1848 | |
| 30 | Tu. | *Flowers are the pledges of fruit.* • 3-lb. 1-oz. blackedge moray caught, Gulf of Mexico, Tex., 1999 | *but storms* |
| 31 | W. | Visit. of Mary • Ember Day • World Otter Day • {8.9 / 9.8 | *interfere.* |

## Farmer's Calendar

When buds unfurl east of the Rockies, gray catbirds arrive in congregations aptly called "mewings." Calls of the male teem with melodious, often nocturnal, songs that mimic at least 100 sounds, including mechanical clatter and bird and frog vocalizations. One catbird that resided near a cemetery where "Taps" was frequently played learned part of the score.

The catbird usually sings a mimicked phrase once, while its cousin, the mockingbird, repeats it three or four times. "Catbirds," observed early 20th-century ornithologist Chester Reed, "seem determined to find out what you are doing, and why you are doing it, and also what you are going to do next. . . . It is in turn a merry jester, a fine musician, a mocking sprite, and a screaming termagant."

Few birds provide a better excuse for cooling it with the clippers, for thickets thereby preserved provide nesting sites. Watch the wild courtship chases. Puffed up and tail lowered, the male bows until his bill touches the ground, lifts his tail, sashays, struts, and flashes his chestnut rump patch. Both sexes construct "practice nests," but the final one is usually built by the female.

CALENDAR

# JUNE

**SKY WATCH:** In dusk's fading twilight on the 4th, Venus stands 45 degrees from the Sun, in Cancer, at magnitude –4.4. A much dimmer Mars can be seen to its upper left. On the 14th, early risers can see a Jupiter/crescent Moon conjunction in the predawn twilight. On the 21st, 40 minutes after the Sun sets at its rightmost possible position, a gorgeous three-way conjunction of Venus, Mars, and the crescent Moon occurs. On the next evening, the 22nd, a dim Mars hovers halfway between the crescent Moon and Venus. Venus's absolute maximum brilliance arrives on the 30th and is maintained through July 20. Summer in the Northern Hemisphere begins with the solstice on the 21st at 10:58 A.M. EDT.

| | | | | | |
|---|---|---|---|---|---|
| ○ FULL MOON | 3rd day | 11:42 P.M. | ● NEW MOON | 18th day | 12:37 A.M. |
| ◑ LAST QUARTER | 10th day | 3:31 P.M. | ◐ FIRST QUARTER | 26th day | 3:50 A.M. |

*All times are given in Eastern Daylight Time.*

**GET THESE PAGES WITH TIMES SET TO YOUR ZIP CODE VIA ALMANAC.COM/2023.**

| DAY OF YEAR | DAY OF MONTH | DAY OF WEEK | ☼ RISES H. M. | RISE KEY | ☼ SETS H. M. | SET KEY | LENGTH OF DAY H. M. | SUN FAST M. | SUN DECLINATION ° | ' | HIGH TIDE TIMES BOSTON | | ☾ RISES H. M. | RISE KEY | ☾ SETS H. M. | SET KEY | ☾ ASTRON. PLACE | ☾ AGE |
|---|---|---|---|---|---|---|---|---|---|---|---|---|---|---|---|---|---|---|
| 152 | 1 | Th. | 5:10 | A | **8:14** | E | 15 04 | 18 | 22 N. | 05 | 9¾ | **10** | **5:44** | E | 3:25 | B | VIR | 13 |
| 153 | 2 | Fr. | 5:10 | A | **8:15** | E | 15 05 | 18 | 22 N. | 13 | 10½ | **10¾** | **6:59** | E | 3:51 | B | LIB | 14 |
| 154 | 3 | Sa. | 5:09 | A | **8:16** | E | 15 07 | 17 | 22 N. | 20 | 11½ | **11½** | **8:15** | E | 4:23 | B | SCO | 15 |
| 155 | 4 | **A** | 5:09 | A | **8:17** | E | 15 08 | 17 | 22 N. | 27 | **12¼** | — | **9:29** | E | 5:06 | A | SCO | 16 |
| 156 | 5 | M. | 5:08 | A | **8:17** | E | 15 09 | 17 | 22 N. | 34 | 12¼ | **1** | **10:35** | E | 6:01 | A | SAG | 17 |
| 157 | 6 | Tu. | 5:08 | A | **8:18** | E | 15 10 | 17 | 22 N. | 40 | 1 | **1¾** | **11:29** | E | 7:08 | B | SAG | 18 |
| 158 | 7 | W. | 5:08 | A | **8:19** | E | 15 11 | 17 | 22 N. | 46 | 2 | **2¾** | — | - | 8:25 | B | SAG | 19 |
| 159 | 8 | Th. | 5:07 | A | **8:19** | E | 15 12 | 17 | 22 N. | 51 | 3 | **3¾** | 12:10 | E | 9:45 | B | CAP | 20 |
| 160 | 9 | Fr. | 5:07 | A | **8:20** | E | 15 13 | 16 | 22 N. | 57 | 3¾ | **4¾** | 12:43 | E | 11:03 | C | AQU | 21 |
| 161 | 10 | Sa. | 5:07 | A | **8:20** | E | 15 13 | 16 | 23 N. | 01 | 4¾ | **5½** | 1:10 | D | **12:19** | D | AQU | 22 |
| 162 | 11 | **A** | 5:07 | A | **8:21** | E | 15 14 | 16 | 23 N. | 05 | 6 | **6½** | 1:33 | D | **1:32** | D | AQU | 23 |
| 163 | 12 | M. | 5:07 | A | **8:21** | E | 15 14 | 16 | 23 N. | 09 | 7 | **7½** | 1:55 | C | **2:43** | E | CET | 24 |
| 164 | 13 | Tu. | 5:07 | A | **8:22** | E | 15 15 | 16 | 23 N. | 13 | 8 | **8½** | 2:17 | C | **3:54** | E | PSC | 25 |
| 165 | 14 | W. | 5:07 | A | **8:22** | E | 15 15 | 15 | 23 N. | 16 | 9 | **9¼** | 2:40 | B | **5:05** | E | ARI | 26 |
| 166 | 15 | Th. | 5:07 | A | **8:23** | E | 15 16 | 15 | 23 N. | 19 | 10 | **10¼** | 3:06 | B | **6:15** | E | ARI | 27 |
| 167 | 16 | Fr. | 5:07 | A | **8:23** | E | 15 16 | 15 | 23 N. | 21 | 10¾ | **11** | 3:37 | B | **7:24** | E | TAU | 28 |
| 168 | 17 | Sa. | 5:07 | A | **8:24** | E | 15 17 | 15 | 23 N. | 23 | 11¾ | **11¾** | 4:15 | A | **8:28** | E | TAU | 29 |
| 169 | 18 | **A** | 5:07 | A | **8:24** | E | 15 17 | 15 | 23 N. | 24 | **12½** | — | 5:01 | A | **9:24** | E | TAU | 0 |
| 170 | 19 | M. | 5:07 | A | **8:24** | E | 15 17 | 14 | 23 N. | 25 | 12½ | **1** | 5:54 | A | **10:11** | E | GEM | 1 |
| 171 | 20 | Tu. | 5:07 | A | **8:24** | E | 15 17 | 14 | 23 N. | 26 | 1 | **1¾** | 6:54 | B | **10:50** | E | GEM | 2 |
| 172 | 21 | W. | 5:07 | A | **8:25** | E | 15 18 | 14 | 23 N. | 26 | 1¾ | **2½** | 7:57 | B | **11:21** | E | CAN | 3 |
| 173 | 22 | Th. | 5:08 | A | **8:25** | E | 15 17 | 14 | 23 N. | 26 | 2½ | **3¼** | 9:00 | B | **11:46** | E | CAN | 4 |
| 174 | 23 | Fr. | 5:08 | A | **8:25** | E | 15 17 | 13 | 23 N. | 25 | 3¼ | **4** | 10:04 | C | — | - | LEO | 5 |
| 175 | 24 | Sa. | 5:08 | A | **8:25** | E | 15 17 | 13 | 23 N. | 24 | 4 | **4¾** | 11:06 | C | 12:08 | D | LEO | 6 |
| 176 | 25 | **A** | 5:08 | A | **8:25** | E | 15 17 | 13 | 23 N. | 22 | 4¾ | **5½** | **12:08** | D | 12:28 | D | LEO | 7 |
| 177 | 26 | M. | 5:09 | A | **8:25** | E | 15 16 | 13 | 23 N. | 20 | 5¾ | **6¼** | **1:10** | D | 12:46 | D | VIR | 8 |
| 178 | 27 | Tu. | 5:09 | A | **8:25** | E | 15 16 | 13 | 23 N. | 18 | 6½ | **7** | **2:15** | E | 1:05 | C | VIR | 9 |
| 179 | 28 | W. | 5:10 | A | **8:25** | E | 15 15 | 12 | 23 N. | 15 | 7½ | **7¾** | **3:23** | E | 1:25 | C | VIR | 10 |
| 180 | 29 | Th. | 5:10 | A | **8:25** | E | 15 15 | 12 | 23 N. | 12 | 8¼ | **8½** | **4:34** | E | 1:49 | B | LIB | 11 |
| 181 | 30 | Fr. | 5:11 | A | **8:25** | E | 15 14 | 12 | 23 N. | 09 | 9¼ | **9½** | **5:50** | E | 2:18 | B | LIB | 12 |

 To use this page, see p. 116; for Key Letters, see p. 238. LIGHT = A.M. **BOLD** = P.M. 

# JUNE

*Flocks of happy-hearted birds*
*Talking in melodious words.*
–**Frank Dempster Sherman**

| DAY OF MONTH | DAY OF WEEK | DATES, FEASTS, FASTS, ASPECTS, TIDE HEIGHTS, AND WEATHER | |
|---|---|---|---|
| 1 | Th. | ☾ AT ☋ • U.S. Navy Capt. James Lawrence ordered, "Don't give up the ship!" (War of 1812), 1813 | *In the* |
| 2 | Fr. | Ember Day • *An ounce of patience is worth a pound of brains.* • Tides { 9.3 / 10.7 | *garden's* |
| 3 | Sa. | Ember Day • **FULL STRAWBERRY** ○ • Hale Telescope dedicated, Palomar Obs., Calif., 1948 | *thrall,* |
| 4 | **A** | Trinity • Orthodox Pentecost • ☌☿⛢ • ♀ GR. ELONG. (45° EAST) • { 9.6 / — | *atop the* |
| 5 | M. | St. Boniface • ☾ RUNS LOW • Singer Conway Twitty died, 1993 | *rows,* |
| 6 | Tu. | D-Day, 1944 • ☾ AT PERIG. • Tides { 11.5 / 9.7 | *cool drops* |
| 7 | W. | ☌♇☾ • Painter Paul Gauguin born, 1848 • { 11.4 / 9.7 | *fall,* |
| 8 | Th. | U.S. Bald Eagle Protection Act approved, 1940 • { 11.3 / 9.7 | *and* |
| 9 | Fr. | ☌♄☾ • Racehorse Secretariat won Triple Crown, 1973 • Tides { 10.9 / 9.8 | *everything* |
| 10 | Sa. | Possible day of Benjamin Franklin's kite and key experiment, 1752 • Tides { 10.6 / 9.9 | *grows.* |
| 11 | **A** | Corpus Christi • Orthodox All Saints' • ☾ ON EQ. • ☌♆☾ • { 10.2 / 10.1 | *Brisk and* |
| 12 | M. | St. Barnabas[T] • Jiroemon Kimura, world's oldest man at time, died at age 116 yrs. 54 days, 2013 | *sunny* |
| 13 | Tu. | ☾ AT ☊ • Yukon Territory created, 1898 • { 9.6 / 10.5 | *for that* |
| 14 | W. | St. Basil • **FLAG DAY** • ☌♃☾ • Tides { 9.4 / 10.6 | *home run–y!* |
| 15 | Th. | ☌⛢☾ • *A swarm of bees in June, Is worth a silver spoon.* • Tides { 9.3 / 10.7 | *Temps now* |
| 16 | Fr. | ☌☿☾ • Andrew Jackson Jr. issued patent for eye protectors for chickens, 1903 • { 9.3 / 10.7 | *good* |
| 17 | Sa. | Artist Maurits Cornelis Escher born, 1898 • { 9.2 / 10.6 | *Ol' Glory-ous* |
| 18 | **A** | 3rd S. af. P. • **FATHER'S DAY** • **NEW** ● • ☾ RIDES HIGH • ♄ STAT. | *before* |
| 19 | M. | **JUNETEENTH NATIONAL INDEPENDENCE DAY** • Mathematician/philosopher Blaise Pascal born, 1623 | *clouds* |
| 20 | Tu. | W.Va. became 35th U.S. state, 1863 • Tides { 10.3 / 8.9 | *then* |
| 21 | W. | **SUMMER SOLSTICE** • ☌♀☾ • N.H. became 9th U.S. state, 1788 • Ferris wheel debuted, 1893 | *rain* |
| 22 | Th. | St. Alban • ☾ AT APO. • ☌♂☾ • Tides { 9.9 / 8.8 | *victorious.* |
| 23 | Fr. | Storms brought flooding to midwestern Ontario, 2017 • Tides { 9.6 / 8.7 | *Hay's in* |
| 24 | Sa. | Nativ. John the Baptist • **MIDSUMMER DAY** • { 9.4 / 8.8 | *the field,* |
| 25 | **A** | **4th S. af. P.** • Va. became 10th U.S. state, 1788 • Tides { 9.1 / 8.9 | *sunny and* |
| 26 | M. | ☾ ON EQ. • *Love is blind but sees afar.* • Tides { 8.9 / 9.0 | *warm—* |
| 27 | Tu. | Paddington Bear children's writer Michael Bond died, 2017 • Tides { 8.7 / 9.3 | *Do get it* |
| 28 | W. | St. Irenaeus • ☾ AT ☋ • Independence National Historical Park created, Philadelphia, Pa., 1948 | *in* |
| 29 | Th. | Sts. Peter & Paul • 44" snow, Livingston Ranger Station, Alta., 1963 • { 8.7 / 10.0 | *before the* |
| 30 | Fr. | International Asteroid Day • Tides { 8.8 / 10.4 | *next storm!* |

## Farmer's Calendar

Never take children on "nature walks." The term smacks of schoolwork. Take them on "expeditions" and do so with a stated purpose, even if it's a diversion. Catch pollywogs, for example. Collect chrysalids. Feed slapped mosquitos to water striders.

The most indelible natural history lessons are taught by actions, not words. It took me years to unlearn the lesson taught to me by my grandmother, who, upon encountering a large snapping turtle crossing our woodlot one long-ago June day, fetched an ax-toting woodsman to separate the reptile from its head.

Decades later, a male cousin asked me to kill a milk snake because "snakes alarm my lady friends." I declined, explaining that the problem was not snakes but instead wrong lessons.

At Trout Lake Camp in Quebec's Eastern Townships, my young pal Forrest Stearns once dashed up to me, grinning proudly and clutching a writhing garter snake—the first that we'd encountered that year. She had never considered the possibility that someone might recoil in alarm at the sight of a snake because she'd never seen anyone do such a thing. By stopping to admire snakes, her parents had taught her that they're beautiful and special.

# JULY

**SKY WATCH:** Fading evening twilight on the 1st reveals Venus and Mars next to blue Regulus, Leo's brilliant brightest star. Venus maintains its super-bright magnitude of –4.7, while Mars has a close conjunction with Regulus from the 9th to the 11th. At the same time, Mercury begins an evening star apparition, starting very low in the west while sporting a magnitude –1.0. It further brightens and rises each successive evening. The 18th finds Mercury to the left of the thin crescent Moon, with Venus farther left. On the 20th, Mars hovers to the left of the Moon, with Venus directly below them. Pluto reaches opposition just before midnight on the 21st but is much too faint for backyard telescopes.

| ○ **FULL MOON** | 3rd day 7:39 A.M. | ● **NEW MOON** | 17th day 2:32 P.M. |
|---|---|---|---|
| ◑ **LAST QUARTER** | 9th day 9:48 P.M. | ◐ **FIRST QUARTER** | 25th day 6:07 P.M. |

*All times are given in Eastern Daylight Time.*

**GET THESE PAGES WITH TIMES SET TO YOUR ZIP CODE VIA ALMANAC.COM/2023.**

| DAY OF YEAR | DAY OF MONTH | DAY OF WEEK | ☀ RISES H. M. | RISE KEY | ☀ SETS H. M. | SET KEY | LENGTH OF DAY H. M. | SUN FAST M. | SUN DECLINATION ° ' | HIGH TIDE TIMES BOSTON | | ☽ RISES H. M. | RISE KEY | ☽ SETS H. M. | SET KEY | ☽ ASTRON. PLACE | ☽ AGE |
|---|---|---|---|---|---|---|---|---|---|---|---|---|---|---|---|---|---|
| 182 | 1 | Sa. | 5:11 | A | 8:25 | E | 15 14 | 12 | 23 N. 05 | 10 | 10¼ | 7:06 | E | 2:55 | A | OPH | 13 |
| 183 | 2 | **A** | 5:12 | A | 8:25 | E | 15 13 | 12 | 23 N. 01 | 11 | 11 | 8:17 | E | 3:44 | A | OPH | 14 |
| 184 | 3 | M. | 5:12 | A | 8:25 | E | 15 13 | 11 | 22 N. 56 | 11¾ | — | 9:17 | E | 4:47 | A | SAG | 15 |
| 185 | 4 | Tu. | 5:13 | A | 8:24 | E | 15 11 | 11 | 22 N. 51 | 12 | 12¾ | 10:05 | E | 6:02 | B | SAG | 16 |
| 186 | 5 | W. | 5:13 | A | 8:24 | E | 15 11 | 11 | 22 N. 45 | 12¾ | 1½ | 10:42 | E | 7:24 | B | CAP | 17 |
| 187 | 6 | Th. | 5:14 | A | 8:24 | E | 15 10 | 11 | 22 N. 39 | 1¾ | 2½ | 11:12 | E | 8:46 | C | CAP | 18 |
| 188 | 7 | Fr. | 5:15 | A | 8:23 | E | 15 08 | 11 | 22 N. 33 | 2¾ | 3¼ | 11:37 | D | 10:06 | D | AQU | 19 |
| 189 | 8 | Sa. | 5:15 | A | 8:23 | E | 15 08 | 11 | 22 N. 26 | 3½ | 4¼ | 12:00 | C | 11:21 | D | AQU | 20 |
| 190 | 9 | **A** | 5:16 | A | 8:23 | E | 15 07 | 10 | 22 N. 19 | 4½ | 5¼ | — | - | 12:34 | E | CET | 21 |
| 191 | 10 | M. | 5:17 | A | 8:22 | E | 15 05 | 10 | 22 N. 12 | 5½ | 6¼ | 12:22 | C | 1:46 | E | PSC | 22 |
| 192 | 11 | Tu. | 5:17 | A | 8:22 | E | 15 05 | 10 | 22 N. 04 | 6¾ | 7 | 12:44 | B | 2:56 | E | ARI | 23 |
| 193 | 12 | W. | 5:18 | A | 8:21 | E | 15 03 | 10 | 21 N. 55 | 7¾ | 8 | 1:09 | B | 4:07 | E | ARI | 24 |
| 194 | 13 | Th. | 5:19 | A | 8:21 | E | 15 02 | 10 | 21 N. 47 | 8¾ | 9 | 1:39 | B | 5:15 | E | TAU | 25 |
| 195 | 14 | Fr. | 5:20 | A | 8:20 | E | 15 00 | 10 | 21 N. 38 | 9¾ | 9¾ | 2:14 | A | 6:20 | E | TAU | 26 |
| 196 | 15 | Sa. | 5:21 | A | 8:19 | E | 14 58 | 10 | 21 N. 29 | 10½ | 10¾ | 2:57 | A | 7:19 | E | TAU | 27 |
| 197 | 16 | **A** | 5:21 | A | 8:19 | E | 14 58 | 10 | 21 N. 19 | 11¼ | 11½ | 3:48 | A | 8:08 | E | GEM | 28 |
| 198 | 17 | M. | 5:22 | A | 8:18 | E | 14 56 | 10 | 21 N. 09 | 12 | — | 4:45 | A | 8:49 | E | GEM | 0 |
| 199 | 18 | Tu. | 5:23 | A | 8:17 | E | 14 54 | 10 | 20 N. 58 | 12 | 12¾ | 5:47 | B | 9:22 | E | CAN | 1 |
| 200 | 19 | W. | 5:24 | A | 8:17 | E | 14 53 | 9 | 20 N. 47 | 12¾ | 1½ | 6:51 | B | 9:49 | E | CAN | 2 |
| 201 | 20 | Th. | 5:25 | A | 8:16 | E | 14 51 | 9 | 20 N. 36 | 1½ | 2 | 7:54 | C | 10:12 | E | LEO | 3 |
| 202 | 21 | Fr. | 5:26 | A | 8:15 | E | 14 49 | 9 | 20 N. 25 | 2 | 2¾ | 8:57 | C | 10:32 | D | LEO | 4 |
| 203 | 22 | Sa. | 5:27 | A | 8:14 | E | 14 47 | 9 | 20 N. 13 | 2¾ | 3¼ | 9:58 | D | 10:51 | D | LEO | 5 |
| 204 | 23 | **A** | 5:28 | A | 8:13 | E | 14 45 | 9 | 20 N. 01 | 3½ | 4 | 11:00 | D | 11:09 | C | VIR | 6 |
| 205 | 24 | M. | 5:29 | A | 8:12 | E | 14 43 | 9 | 19 N. 48 | 4¼ | 4¾ | 12:02 | E | 11:28 | C | VIR | 7 |
| 206 | 25 | Tu. | 5:30 | A | 8:11 | E | 14 41 | 9 | 19 N. 35 | 5 | 5½ | 1:07 | E | 11:50 | B | VIR | 8 |
| 207 | 26 | W. | 5:31 | A | 8:10 | E | 14 39 | 9 | 19 N. 22 | 5¾ | 6¼ | 2:15 | E | — | - | VIR | 9 |
| 208 | 27 | Th. | 5:31 | A | 8:09 | E | 14 38 | 9 | 19 N. 09 | 6¾ | 7 | 3:27 | E | 12:15 | B | LIB | 10 |
| 209 | 28 | Fr. | 5:32 | A | 8:08 | E | 14 36 | 9 | 18 N. 55 | 7¾ | 8 | 4:42 | E | 12:47 | B | SCO | 11 |
| 210 | 29 | Sa. | 5:33 | A | 8:07 | E | 14 34 | 9 | 18 N. 41 | 8¾ | 9 | 5:54 | E | 1:29 | A | OPH | 12 |
| 211 | 30 | **A** | 5:34 | B | 8:06 | E | 14 32 | 9 | 18 N. 26 | 9¾ | 9¾ | 7:00 | E | 2:24 | A | SAG | 13 |
| 212 | 31 | M. | 5:35 | B | 8:05 | E | 14 30 | 9 | 18 N. 12 | 10½ | 10¾ | 7:54 | E | 3:34 | A | SAG | 14 |

*O month of burning suns and mellow moons,*
*Which warm the heart as would some rare old wine!*
**–Eliot Ryder, of July**

| DAY OF MONTH | DAY OF WEEK | DATES, FEASTS, FASTS, ASPECTS, TIDE HEIGHTS, AND WEATHER | |
|---|---|---|---|
| 1 | Sa. | CANADA DAY • ☿ IN SUP. ☌ • ♆ STAT. • P.E.I. joined Canadian Confederation, 1873 | *Month* |
| 2 | **A** | 5th S. af. P. • ☾ RUNS LOW • Thurgood Marshall, Supreme Court justice, born, 1908 | *number* |
| 3 | M. | Dog Days begin. • FULL BUCK ○ • *Every dog hath its day.* • {9.6 / 11.6 | *seven,* |
| 4 | Tu. | INDEPENDENCE DAY • ☾ AT PERIG. • ☌♇☾ • Tides {9.8 / — | *weather* |
| 5 | W. | Mass. Bay Colony gov. John Winthrop recorded damaging "sudden gust," poss. 1st tornado report in future U.S., 1643 | *from* |
| 6 | Th. | ⊕ AT APHELION • ☌♄☾ • Roy Rogers, "King of the Cowboys," died, 1998 | *Heaven.* |
| 7 | Fr. | ♀ GR. ILLUM. EXT. • Armadillos mate now. • Tides {11.5 / 10.4 | *Warming* |
| 8 | Sa. | ☾ ON EQ. • ☌♆☾ • SSgt. Esther Blake became 1st woman enlisted in USAF, 1948 | *showers* |
| 9 | **A** | 6th S. af. P. • Jim Purol sat in 39,250 seats w/in 48 hrs., setting world record, 2008 | *bring* |
| 10 | M. | ☾ AT ☊ • 134°F, Greenland Ranch, Death Valley, Calif., 1913 • Tides {10.0 / 10.4 | *bowers* |
| 11 | Tu. | ☌♃☾ • U.S. Marine Band established, 1798 • {9.5 / 10.4 | *of* |
| 12 | W. | ☌♅☾ • Cornscateous air is everywhere. • {9.1 / 10.3 | *flowers.* |
| 13 | Th. | 1st season of Stratford Festival began, Ont., 1953 • Tides {8.9 / 10.2 | *Hot!* |
| 14 | Fr. | Bastille Day • CSXT *GoFast* 1st U.S. amateur rocket to reach 385,800' and 3,580 mph, 2014 • {8.8 / 10.2 | *Hotter!* |
| 15 | Sa. | St. Swithin • ☾ RIDES HIGH • *Wheel of Fortune* wheel designer Ed Flesh died, 2011 | *Hottest!* |
| 16 | **A** | 7th. S. af. P. • D. Bailey won 100m dash (9.91 secs.), Canadian TAF Championships, Montreal, Que., 1995 | *And* |
| 17 | M. | NEW ● • *When sheep turn their backs to the wind, it is a sign of rain.* • Tides {8.8 / — | *now* |
| 18 | Tu. | First of Muharram begins at sundown • Activist Nelson Mandela born, 1918 • {10.2 / 8.8 | *hot* |
| 19 | W. | ☌☿☾ • 1st women's rights convention in U.S. began, Seneca Falls, N.Y., 1848 • {10.1 / 8.9 | *it* |
| 20 | Th. | ☾ AT APO. • ☌♀☾ • ♀ STAT. • Tides {10.1 / 9.0 | *not* |
| 21 | Fr. | ☌♂☾ • ♇ AT ☍ • –128.6°F, Vostok Station, Antarctica, 1983 • {9.9 / 9.0 | *is.* |
| 22 | Sa. | St. Mary Magdalene • Humpback whale accidentally caught sea lion in mouth (sea lion OK), Calif., 2019 | *Clouds* |
| 23 | **A** | 8th S. af. P. • ☾ ON EQ. • Baseball player Nomar Garciaparra born, 1973 | *seep* |
| 24 | M. | Marvin the Martian debuted in Bugs Bunny's *Haredevil Hare*, 1948 • EF2 tornado struck Epsom, N.H., 2008 | *as frogs* |
| 25 | Tu. | St. James • ☾ AT ☋ • Black-eyed Susans in bloom now. • {8.9 / 9.4 | *leap.* |
| 26 | W. | St. Anne • ☌☿♀ • N.Y. became 11th U.S. state, 1788 • Tides {8.6 / 9.5 | *Some* |
| 27 | Th. | Ice skater Peggy Fleming born, 1948 • Tides {8.5 / 9.8 | *lightning* |
| 28 | Fr. | 8.2 earthquake SE of Perryville, Alaska, 2021 • {8.5 / 10.1 | *about—* |
| 29 | Sa. | St. Martha • *Spend not where you may save; spare not where you must spend.* • {8.6 / 10.5 | *Swimmers,* |
| 30 | **A** | 9th S. af. P. • ☾ RUNS LOW • Industrialist Henry Ford born, 1863 • {8.9 / 11.0 | *get* |
| 31 | M. | St. Ignatius of Loyola • ☌♇☾ • Roar of MGM's lion Jackie heard for 1st time on screen, 1928 | *out!* |

## Farmer's Calendar

In early summer, America's leopards stalk prey through mid-latitude grass. Farther north, you can still hear them roaring (or perhaps more descriptively, "snoring") from on and even below the surface of ponds and dawdling streams.

These are northern leopard frogs, which inhabit much of southern Canada and the northern United States, as well as the Desert Southwest. Watch for these semiterrestrial amphibians as they hunt crickets, beetles, grasshoppers, worms, spiders, and the like.

You can feed them by hitching a thread to a long stick, loosely tying on a piece of fish or meat, and making the food hop along the ground. They'll snap it up, then stuff it into their mouths with their "hands."

Because of their rapid, zigzag leaps, leopard frogs are a challenge to approach for a closer look. You may get a "chuckle" from them, which they issue only when annoyed.

Once our most abundant frog, the northern leopard frog has declined. According to biologists, causes of this may include deforestation, pollution, and possibly the fact that they were widely collected for food (frog legs) and classroom dissection.

# AUGUST

**SKY WATCH:** Venus and Jupiter have both dropped into the solar glare, ending their lengthy reigns as evening stars. Mercury remains just above the horizon in the western evening twilight at magnitude 0. Mars, six times fainter, hovers above it. The 3rd finds Saturn just above the Moon, which moves on to form a predawn conjunction with Jupiter on the 8th. The Perseid meteor shower arrives on the 11th and 12th; it's best seen after midnight, when rural observers can expect a meteor a minute. The Moon won't interfere, making for excellent viewing conditions. Beginning around the 20th, Venus rises before dawn to become a morning star in the coming months. Saturn reaches opposition on the 27th, at its biggest and brightest of the year.

| | | | |
|---|---|---|---|
| ○ **FULL MOON** | 1st day 2:32 P.M. | ☽ **FIRST QUARTER** 24th day 5:57 A.M. |
| ☽ **LAST QUARTER** | 8th day 6:28 A.M. | ○ **FULL MOON** 30th day 9:36 P.M. |
| ● **NEW MOON** | 16th day 5:38 A.M. | |

*All times are given in Eastern Daylight Time.*

GET THESE PAGES WITH TIMES SET TO YOUR ZIP CODE VIA ALMANAC.COM/2023.

| DAY OF YEAR | DAY OF MONTH | DAY OF WEEK | ☼ RISES H.M. | RISE KEY | ☼ SETS H.M. | SET KEY | LENGTH OF DAY H.M. | SUN FAST M. | SUN DECLINATION ° ′ | HIGH TIDE TIMES BOSTON | ☾ RISES H.M. | RISE KEY | ☾ SETS H.M. | SET KEY | ☾ ASTRON. PLACE | ☾ AGE |
|---|---|---|---|---|---|---|---|---|---|---|---|---|---|---|---|---|
| 213 | 1 | Tu. | 5:36 | B | 8:04 | E | 14 28 | 9 | 17 N. 57 | 11½ 11¾ | 8:36 | E | 4:54 | B | CAP | 15 |
| 214 | 2 | W. | 5:37 | B | 8:03 | E | 14 26 | 10 | 17 N. 41 | 12½ — | 9:10 | E | 6:18 | C | CAP | 16 |
| 215 | 3 | Th. | 5:39 | B | 8:02 | E | 14 23 | 10 | 17 N. 26 | 12½ 1¼ | 9:38 | D | 7:42 | C | AQU | 17 |
| 216 | 4 | Fr. | 5:40 | B | 8:00 | E | 14 20 | 10 | 17 N. 10 | 1½ 2 | 10:02 | D | 9:02 | D | AQU | 18 |
| 217 | 5 | Sa. | 5:41 | B | 7:59 | E | 14 18 | 10 | 16 N. 54 | 2½ 3 | 10:24 | C | 10:19 | D | PSC | 19 |
| 218 | 6 | **A** | 5:42 | B | 7:58 | E | 14 16 | 10 | 16 N. 37 | 3¼ 3¾ | 10:47 | C | 11:33 | E | PSC | 20 |
| 219 | 7 | M. | 5:43 | B | 7:57 | E | 14 14 | 10 | 16 N. 21 | 4¼ 4¾ | 11:12 | B | **12:46** | E | ARI | 21 |
| 220 | 8 | Tu. | 5:44 | B | 7:55 | E | 14 11 | 10 | 16 N. 04 | 5¼ 5¾ | 11:40 | B | **1:58** | E | ARI | 22 |
| 221 | 9 | W. | 5:45 | B | 7:54 | E | 14 09 | 10 | 15 N. 46 | 6¼ 6½ | — | - | **3:08** | E | TAU | 23 |
| 222 | 10 | Th. | 5:46 | B | 7:53 | E | 14 07 | 10 | 15 N. 29 | 7¼ 7½ | 12:14 | A | **4:15** | E | TAU | 24 |
| 223 | 11 | Fr. | 5:47 | B | 7:51 | E | 14 04 | 11 | 15 N. 11 | 8¼ 8½ | 12:54 | A | **5:15** | E | TAU | 25 |
| 224 | 12 | Sa. | 5:48 | B | 7:50 | D | 14 02 | 11 | 14 N. 53 | 9¼ 9½ | 1:43 | A | **6:07** | E | AUR | 26 |
| 225 | 13 | **A** | 5:49 | B | 7:48 | D | 13 59 | 11 | 14 N. 35 | 10¼ 10¼ | 2:38 | A | **6:50** | E | GEM | 27 |
| 226 | 14 | M. | 5:50 | B | 7:47 | D | 13 57 | 11 | 14 N. 17 | 11 11 | 3:39 | B | **7:25** | E | CAN | 28 |
| 227 | 15 | Tu. | 5:51 | B | 7:46 | D | 13 55 | 11 | 13 N. 58 | 11¾ 11¾ | 4:43 | B | **7:53** | E | CAN | 29 |
| 228 | 16 | W. | 5:52 | B | 7:44 | D | 13 52 | 12 | 13 N. 39 | 12¼ — | 5:47 | B | **8:17** | E | LEO | 0 |
| 229 | 17 | Th. | 5:53 | B | 7:43 | D | 13 50 | 12 | 13 N. 20 | 12½ 1 | 6:49 | C | **8:38** | D | LEO | 1 |
| 230 | 18 | Fr. | 5:54 | B | 7:41 | D | 13 47 | 12 | 13 N. 01 | 1 1½ | 7:51 | D | **8:57** | D | LEO | 2 |
| 231 | 19 | Sa. | 5:55 | B | 7:40 | D | 13 45 | 12 | 12 N. 41 | 1¾ 2 | 8:53 | D | **9:15** | C | VIR | 3 |
| 232 | 20 | **A** | 5:56 | B | 7:38 | D | 13 42 | 12 | 12 N. 21 | 2¼ 2¾ | 9:55 | D | **9:33** | C | VIR | 4 |
| 233 | 21 | M. | 5:57 | B | 7:37 | D | 13 40 | 12 | 12 N. 01 | 3 3¼ | 10:58 | E | **9:53** | B | VIR | 5 |
| 234 | 22 | Tu. | 5:59 | B | 7:35 | D | 13 36 | 13 | 11 N. 41 | 3¾ 4 | **12:04** | E | **10:16** | B | VIR | 6 |
| 235 | 23 | W. | 6:00 | B | 7:33 | D | 13 33 | 13 | 11 N. 21 | 4½ 4¾ | **1:13** | E | **10:45** | B | LIB | 7 |
| 236 | 24 | Th. | 6:01 | B | 7:32 | D | 13 31 | 13 | 11 N. 01 | 5¼ 5½ | **2:24** | E | **11:21** | A | LIB | 8 |
| 237 | 25 | Fr. | 6:02 | B | 7:30 | D | 13 28 | 14 | 10 N. 40 | 6¼ 6½ | **3:36** | E | — | - | SCO | 9 |
| 238 | 26 | Sa. | 6:03 | B | 7:29 | D | 13 26 | 14 | 10 N. 19 | 7¼ 7½ | **4:43** | E | 12:09 | A | OPH | 10 |
| 239 | 27 | **A** | 6:04 | B | 7:27 | D | 13 23 | 14 | 9 N. 58 | 8¼ 8½ | **5:41** | E | 1:10 | A | SAG | 11 |
| 240 | 28 | M. | 6:05 | B | 7:25 | D | 13 20 | 15 | 9 N. 37 | 9¼ 9½ | **6:28** | E | 2:23 | B | SAG | 12 |
| 241 | 29 | Tu. | 6:06 | B | 7:24 | D | 13 18 | 15 | 9 N. 16 | 10¼ 10½ | **7:05** | E | 3:45 | B | CAP | 13 |
| 242 | 30 | W. | 6:07 | B | 7:22 | D | 13 15 | 15 | 8 N. 54 | 11¼ 11½ | **7:35** | E | 5:10 | C | CAP | 14 |
| 243 | 31 | Th. | 6:08 | B | 7:20 | D | 13 12 | 16 | 8 N. 33 | 12 — | **8:01** | D | 6:33 | C | AQU | 15 |

# AUGUST

*Jams, and jellies, and juices,*
*Ready for all sweet uses.*
–M. E. B.

| DAY OF MONTH | DAY OF WEEK | DATES, FEASTS, FASTS, ASPECTS, TIDE HEIGHTS, AND WEATHER | |
|---|---|---|---|
| 1 | Tu. | Lammas Day • **FULL STURGEON** ○ • Meter length 1st defined, 1793 • {9.8 / 11.8 | *Sultry* |
| 2 | W. | ☾ AT PERIG. • *Talk much and err much.* • Tides {10.2 / — | *days* |
| 3 | Th. | ☌♄☾ • Calvin Coolidge sworn in as U.S. president by father at Vermont homestead, 1923 | *for* |
| 4 | Fr. | ☌♆☾ • French and Haudenosaunee signed Great Peace of Montreal, 1701 • {11.9 / 10.8 | *country* |
| 5 | Sa. | ☾ ON EQ. • Writer Toni Morrison died, 2019 • Tides {11.6 / 10.9 | *ways—* |
| 6 | **A** | Transfiguration • ☾ AT ☊ • Anne Hathaway, wife of Shakespeare, died, 1623 | *Round* |
| 7 | M. | **Civic Holiday (Canada)** • Bear entered grocery store, Porter Ranch, Calif., 2021 • {10.4 / 10.7 | *up* |
| 8 | Tu. | St. Dominic • ☌♃☾ • ☌⛢☾ • Tides {9.7 / 10.4 | *strays* |
| 9 | W. | ☿ GR. ELONG (27° EAST) • Ragweed in bloom. • Tides {9.1 / 10.1 | *in the* |
| 10 | Th. | St. Lawrence • *A handful of common sense is worth a bushel of learning.* • {8.7 / 9.9 | *haze.* |
| 11 | Fr. | St. Clare • Dog Days end. • Tennis player Bianca Andreescu 1st Canadian to win Rogers Cup in 50 years, 2019 | |
| 12 | Sa. | ☾ RIDES HIGH • Gray squirrels have second litters now. • Tides {8.4 / 9.8 | *Better* |
| 13 | **A** | 11th S. af. P. • ♀ IN INF. ☌ • Tides {8.5 / 9.8 | *mow the* |
| 14 | M. | Oregon Territory organized, 1848 • 1st recorded rain at 10,551', Greenland ice sheet, 2021 • {8.6 / 9.9 | *lawn* |
| 15 | Tu. | Assumption • ☌♀☾ • Nacho inventor Ignacio Anaya García born, 1895 | *at* |
| 16 | W. | NEW ● • ☾ AT APO. • Baseball player Babe Ruth died, 1948 • {9.0 / — | *dawn—* |
| 17 | Th. | Cat Nights commence. • 1st transatlantic balloon flight completed, 1978 • Tides {10.1 / 9.1 | *Storms* |
| 18 | Fr. | ☌☿☾ • ☌♂☾ • Begole, Johnson, and Lucas 1st to summit Mt. Whitney, Sierra Nevada, Calif., 1873 | *and* |
| 19 | Sa. | ☾ ON EQ. • *If kites fly high, fine weather is at hand.* • Tides {9.9 / 9.4 | *showers* |
| 20 | **A** | 12th S. af. P. • Est. F4 tornado hit Austin, Minn., 1928 • Tides {9.7 / 9.5 | *coming* |
| 21 | M. | ☾ AT ☋ • Concert promoter Sid Bernstein died, 2013 | *on!* |
| 22 | Tu. | NASA rec'd 1st photo proving that Neptune had rings, 1989 • Tides {9.1 / 9.6 | *Sun* |
| 23 | W. | ☿ STAT. • Antonia Novello, 1st woman and Hispanic to serve as U.S. Surgeon General, born, 1944 | *spot.* |
| 24 | Th. | St. Bartholomew • Humorist Jerry Clower died, 1998 • {8.6 / 9.7 | *Now comes* |
| 25 | Fr. | Hummingbirds migrate south. • Chef Rachael Ray born, 1968 • Tides {8.4 / 9.8 | *weather* |
| 26 | Sa. | ☾ RUNS LOW • 24-lb. 5-oz. longnose gar caught, Sardis Reservoir, Miss., 1984 • {8.4 / 10.1 | *most* |
| 27 | **A** | 13th S. af. P. • ♄ AT ☍ • Tides {8.6 / 10.5 | *unsettled,* |
| 28 | M. | St. Augustine of Hippo • ☌♇☾ • ⛢ STAT. • Deadly tornado, W. Stockbridge, Mass., 1973 | |
| 29 | Tu. | St. John the Baptist • Goodyear Tire & Rubber Co. incorporated, 1898 | *sometimes dry,* |
| 30 | W. | BLUE ○ • ☾ AT PERIG. • ☌♄☾ • Artist Jacques-Louis David born, 1748 | *sometimes* |
| 31 | Th. | Hurricane Carol made landfall, Long Island, N.Y., and SE Conn., 1954 • Tides {10.8 / — | *wettled.* |

## Farmer's Calendar

When cicadas sing and grass goes gold, daddy longlegs leave their haunts amid dead and living vegetation. In another month, these gangly, nonvenomous arachnids will mate. Sometimes gathering in large clusters, they appear around harvesttime, which is why farmers of yore called them "harvestmen."

Worldwide, there are at least 6,000 species of daddy longlegs, all of which lack the fangs and silk glands of true spiders. Whereas a spider has two distinct body parts, a daddy longlegs has but one. And, unlike a spider, which usually has eight eyes, the daddy longlegs has two, both mounted on a small turret near the front of its body.

A male spider must transfer his sperm to the female on the tip of an armlike appendage called a pedipalp. Daddy longlegs, on the other hand, can copulate.

Unlike spiders, which suck body fluids from prey, a daddy longlegs chews and swallows. In addition to insects and arachnids, it consumes fruit, plants, fungi, and bird droppings.

Its two longest legs are used more for sensory perception than locomotion. According to some countryfolk, you can find a lost cow by noting in which direction the long legs wave.

# SEPTEMBER

**SKY WATCH:** Venus shoots rapidly higher each morning before dawn, reaching its greatest brilliancy of 2023 at midmonth with a shadow-casting magnitude of –4.8. Above the same eastern horizon, look for Mercury to reach its highest position on the 6th. On the 11th, the crescent Moon joins Venus in Cancer. Neptune comes to opposition on the 19th, but a telescope is needed to see its tiny, blue, 8th-magnitude disk. On the 21st, Mercury, in Leo, dangles below Venus. Mercury is now at its best as a morning star, ranging from a brilliant magnitude –0.3 to an even brighter –1.0 at month's end. Fall begins with the autumnal equinox on the morning of the 23rd at 2:50 A.M. EDT.

| ☽ LAST QUARTER | 6th day | 6:21 P.M. | ☾ FIRST QUARTER | 22nd day | 3:32 P.M. |
|---|---|---|---|---|---|
| ● NEW MOON | 14th day | 9:40 P.M. | ○ FULL MOON | 29th day | 5:58 A.M. |

*All times are given in Eastern Daylight Time.*

GET THESE PAGES WITH TIMES SET TO YOUR ZIP CODE VIA ALMANAC.COM/2023.

| DAY OF YEAR | DAY OF MONTH | DAY OF WEEK | ☀ RISES H. M. | RISE KEY | ☀ SETS H. M. | SET KEY | LENGTH OF DAY H. M. | SUN FAST M. | SUN DECLINATION ° ' | HIGH TIDE TIMES BOSTON | | ☾ RISES H. M. | RISE KEY | ☾ SETS H. M. | SET KEY | ☾ ASTRON. PLACE | ☾ AGE |
|---|---|---|---|---|---|---|---|---|---|---|---|---|---|---|---|---|---|
| 244 | 1 | Fr. | 6:09 | B | 7:19 | D | 13 10 | 16 | 8 N. 11 | 12¼ | 12¾ | 8:25 | C | 7:53 | D | AQU | 16 |
| 245 | 2 | Sa. | 6:10 | B | 7:17 | D | 13 07 | 16 | 7 N. 49 | 1¼ | 1¾ | 8:48 | C | 9:11 | E | CET | 17 |
| 246 | 3 | **A** | 6:11 | C | 7:15 | D | 13 04 | 16 | 7 N. 27 | 2 | 2½ | 9:13 | B | 10:27 | E | PSC | 18 |
| 247 | 4 | M. | 6:12 | C | 7:13 | D | 13 01 | 17 | 7 N. 05 | 3 | 3¼ | 9:40 | B | 11:42 | E | ARI | 19 |
| 248 | 5 | Tu. | 6:13 | C | 7:12 | D | 12 59 | 17 | 6 N. 43 | 3¾ | 4¼ | 10:12 | B | 12:55 | E | ARI | 20 |
| 249 | 6 | W. | 6:14 | C | 7:10 | D | 12 56 | 17 | 6 N. 21 | 4¾ | 5 | 10:51 | A | 2:05 | E | TAU | 21 |
| 250 | 7 | Th. | 6:15 | C | 7:08 | D | 12 53 | 18 | 5 N. 58 | 5¾ | 6 | 11:37 | A | 3:09 | E | TAU | 22 |
| 251 | 8 | Fr. | 6:16 | C | 7:07 | D | 12 51 | 18 | 5 N. 36 | 7 | 7 | — | - | 4:05 | E | AUR | 23 |
| 252 | 9 | Sa. | 6:18 | C | 7:05 | D | 12 47 | 18 | 5 N. 13 | 8 | 8 | 12:31 | A | 4:51 | E | GEM | 24 |
| 253 | 10 | **A** | 6:19 | C | 7:03 | D | 12 44 | 19 | 4 N. 50 | 9 | 9 | 1:31 | B | 5:28 | E | GEM | 25 |
| 254 | 11 | M. | 6:20 | C | 7:01 | D | 12 41 | 19 | 4 N. 28 | 9¾ | 10 | 2:34 | B | 5:58 | E | CAN | 26 |
| 255 | 12 | Tu. | 6:21 | C | 7:00 | C | 12 39 | 20 | 4 N. 05 | 10½ | 10¾ | 3:38 | B | 6:23 | E | LEO | 27 |
| 256 | 13 | W. | 6:22 | C | 6:58 | C | 12 36 | 20 | 3 N. 42 | 11¼ | 11¼ | 4:42 | C | 6:44 | D | LEO | 28 |
| 257 | 14 | Th. | 6:23 | C | 6:56 | C | 12 33 | 20 | 3 N. 19 | 11¾ | — | 5:44 | C | 7:03 | D | LEO | 0 |
| 258 | 15 | Fr. | 6:24 | C | 6:54 | C | 12 30 | 21 | 2 N. 56 | 12 | 12¼ | 6:46 | D | 7:21 | C | VIR | 1 |
| 259 | 16 | Sa. | 6:25 | C | 6:52 | C | 12 27 | 21 | 2 N. 33 | 12½ | 1 | 7:48 | D | 7:39 | C | VIR | 2 |
| 260 | 17 | **A** | 6:26 | C | 6:51 | C | 12 25 | 21 | 2 N. 09 | 1¼ | 1½ | 8:51 | E | 7:59 | B | VIR | 3 |
| 261 | 18 | M. | 6:27 | C | 6:49 | C | 12 22 | 22 | 1 N. 46 | 1¾ | 2 | 9:56 | E | 8:21 | B | VIR | 4 |
| 262 | 19 | Tu. | 6:28 | C | 6:47 | C | 12 19 | 22 | 1 N. 23 | 2½ | 2¾ | 11:04 | E | 8:47 | B | LIB | 5 |
| 263 | 20 | W. | 6:29 | C | 6:45 | C | 12 16 | 22 | 1 N. 00 | 3¼ | 3½ | 12:14 | E | 9:20 | A | LIB | 6 |
| 264 | 21 | Th. | 6:30 | C | 6:44 | C | 12 14 | 23 | 0 N. 36 | 4 | 4¼ | 1:25 | E | 10:02 | A | SCO | 7 |
| 265 | 22 | Fr. | 6:31 | C | 6:42 | C | 12 11 | 23 | 0 N. 13 | 4¾ | 5 | 2:32 | E | 10:56 | A | OPH | 8 |
| 266 | 23 | Sa. | 6:32 | C | 6:40 | C | 12 08 | 23 | 0 s. 09 | 5¾ | 6 | 3:31 | E | — | - | SAG | 9 |
| 267 | 24 | **A** | 6:33 | C | 6:38 | C | 12 05 | 24 | 0 s. 33 | 7 | 7¼ | 4:21 | E | 12:03 | A | SAG | 10 |
| 268 | 25 | M. | 6:34 | C | 6:37 | C | 12 03 | 24 | 0 s. 56 | 8 | 8¼ | 5:01 | E | 1:19 | B | CAP | 11 |
| 269 | 26 | Tu. | 6:36 | C | 6:35 | C | 11 59 | 24 | 1 s. 19 | 9 | 9¼ | 5:33 | E | 2:40 | C | CAP | 12 |
| 270 | 27 | W. | 6:37 | C | 6:33 | C | 11 56 | 25 | 1 s. 43 | 10 | 10¼ | 6:00 | D | 4:02 | C | AQU | 13 |
| 271 | 28 | Th. | 6:38 | C | 6:31 | C | 11 53 | 25 | 2 s. 06 | 10¾ | 11¼ | 6:24 | D | 5:23 | D | AQU | 14 |
| 272 | 29 | Fr. | 6:39 | C | 6:30 | C | 11 51 | 25 | 2 s. 29 | 11½ | — | 6:47 | C | 6:42 | D | PSC | 15 |
| 273 | 30 | Sa. | 6:40 | C | 6:28 | C | 11 48 | 26 | 2 s. 53 | 12 | 12½ | 7:11 | C | 8:00 | E | PSC | 16 |

THE NINTH MONTH · 2023 **SEPTEMBER** SEPTEMBER HATH 30 DAYS

*A little stir among the clouds, / Before they rent asunder,—*
*A little rocking of the trees, / And then came on the thunder.*
**–Oliver Wendell Holmes**

| DAY OF MONTH | DAY OF WEEK | DATES, FEASTS, FASTS, ASPECTS, TIDE HEIGHTS, AND WEATHER | |
|---|---|---|---|
| 1 | Fr. | ☾ ON EQ. • ☌♆☾ • *Industry is the parent of success.* • Tides {11.9 / 11.2 | *School* |
| 2 | Sa. | ♀ STAT. • Teacher Christa McAuliffe born, 1948 • Writer J.R.R. Tolkien died, 1973 | *is cool.* |
| 3 | **A** | 14th S. af. P. • ☾ AT ☊ • Cartoonist Mort Walker born, 1923 • {11.3 / 11.3 | *Offer* |
| 4 | M. | LABOR DAY • ☌♃☾ • ♃ STAT. • Google incorporated, 1998 | *labor* |
| 5 | Tu. | ☌⛢☾ • L'Anse aux Meadows National Historic Site declared World Heritage Site, N.L., 1978 | *to your* |
| 6 | W. | ☿ IN INF. ☌ • Louisa Swain of Laramie, Wyo., 1st woman since 1807 (N.J. only) to legally cast vote, 1870 | *neighbor.* |
| 7 | Th. | In midst of craze, Georgia Gibbs sang "The Hula-Hoop Song" on *The Ed Sullivan Show,* 1958 | *All* |
| 8 | Fr. | ☾ RIDES HIGH • Cranberry bog harvest begins, Cape Cod, Mass. • Tides {8.4 / 9.5 | *showers* |
| 9 | Sa. | NFL football game lasted 7 hrs. 8 mins. due to lightning delays, Miami Gardens, Fla., 2018 • {8.2 / 9.4 | *fall* |
| 10 | **A** | 15th S. af. P. • *It is never too late to mend.* • {8.3 / 9.4 | *on apple* |
| 11 | M. | PATRIOT DAY • ☌♀☾ • 21-lb. 15-oz. hogfish caught, Georgetown Hole, Charleston, S.C., 2011 | |
| 12 | Tu. | ☾ AT APO. • Jacqueline Bouvier wed JFK, 1953 • Tides {8.7 / 9.8 | *ladders* |
| 13 | W. | ☌☿☾ • Ice from Boston, Mass., 1st arrived in Calcutta, India, 1833 • {9.0 / 9.9 | *tall.* |
| 14 | Th. | Holy Cross • NEW ● • ☿ STAT. • Tides {9.3 / 10.0 | *A chill* |
| 15 | Fr. | Rosh Hashanah begins at sundown • ☾ ON EQ. • Tides {9.6 / — | *everywhere,* |
| 16 | Sa. | OCCN. ♂☾ • Saturn moon Hyperion discovered, 1848 • {9.9 / 9.7 | *a kite* |
| 17 | **A** | 16th S. af. P. • ☾ AT ☋ • National Pet Bird Day (U.S.) • {9.8 / 9.9 | *in the air,* |
| 18 | M. | Jazz pianist Oscar Peterson performed at Carnegie Hall, N.Y.C., 1949 • {9.6 / 9.9 | *skies* |
| 19 | Tu. | ♆ AT ☍ • ♀ GR. ILLUM. EXT. • Formation of Canadian Air Force approved, 1918 | *turning* |
| 20 | W. | Ember Day • Billie Jean King won "Battle of the Sexes" tennis match vs. Bobby Riggs, Houston, Tex., 1973 | *fair.* |
| 21 | Th. | St. Matthew • *St. Matthew Brings on the cold dew.* • Tides {8.8 / 9.9 | *Now* |
| 22 | Fr. | Ember Day • ☾ RUNS LOW • ☿ GR. ELONG. (18° WEST) • {8.5 / 9.8 | *for* |
| 23 | Sa. | Ember Day • Harvest Home • AUTUMNAL EQUINOX • {8.4 / 9.9 | *the* |
| 24 | **A** | 17th S. af. P. • Yom Kippur begins at sundown • ☌♇☾ • {8.5 / 10.1 | *frost* |
| 25 | M. | Woodchucks hibernate now. • Journalist George Plimpton died, 2003 | *as* |
| 26 | Tu. | ☌♄☾ • Composer George Gershwin born, 1898 • {9.4 / 10.9 | *summer* |
| 27 | W. | St. Vincent de Paul • ☾ AT PERIG. • 2,528-lb. pumpkin set N.Am. record, Deerfield Fair, N.H., 2018 | *gets* |
| 28 | Th. | ☌♆☾ • 6.0-magnitude earthquake, Parkfield, Calif., 2004 • {10.8 / 11.5 | *lost.* |
| 29 | Fr. | St. Michael • Sukkoth begins at sundown • FULL HARVEST ○ • ☾ ON EQ. | *Showers* |
| 30 | Sa. | St. Gregory the Illuminator • ☾ AT ☊ • 1st Nat'l Farm Workers Assoc. convention, 1962 | *stall.* |

## Farmer's Calendar

Some creatures don't have the luxury of waiting until fall to migrate. Broad-winged hawks spiral up on thermals in "kettles" of a hundred or more and then glide for miles. Nighthawks—flying insect eaters related to whippoorwills—may depart before the end of August. Monarch butterflies, stately fliers that conserve energy with strong wingbeats and long glides, are on their way to Mexico and California. With the first hard rains, brook trout, belonging to the salmon family, move upstream to spawn, hurdling over waterfalls and swimming through pools shaded by jewelweed.

Over sunny fields throughout North America, green darners mass for migration. Like all dragonflies, they have four independently powered wings that enable them to hover, fly backward, and attain speeds of more than 30 mph. The first two generations migrate and die. The third doesn't migrate but winters in Florida and the Caribbean. The green darner has a wingspan of from 3 to 4½ inches, but a few dragonflies are larger. One ancestral dragonfly-like insect had a nearly 2½-foot wingspan; it's engraved in a 280-million-year-old fossil.

# OCTOBER

**SKY WATCH:** Venus, now a dazzling morning star, closely meets Leo's blue star, Regulus, on the 8th and 9th and is best seen in the east around 5:00 A.M. On the 14th, an annular solar eclipse sweeps across the western U.S.—always use eye protection for this ring-of-fire eclipse. Venus, in Leo all month, reaches its greatest angular distance from the Sun on the 23rd, with its 46 degrees of separation making the morning star truly eye-catching. The 28th finds the full Moon barely sliding into Earth's shadow, creating a 1 percent eclipse visible mainly from Asia. From the northeastern U.S., its penumbral portion may be visible, but a penumbra rarely alters the Moon's appearance. As a consolation, on this same evening of the 28th, the full Moon closely meets Jupiter in a conjunction.

◑ **LAST QUARTER** 6th day 9:48 A.M. ◐ **FIRST QUARTER** 21st day 11:29 P.M.

● **NEW MOON** 14th day 1:55 P.M. ○ **FULL MOON** 28th day 4:24 P.M.

*All times are given in Eastern Daylight Time.*

**GET THESE PAGES WITH TIMES SET TO YOUR ZIP CODE VIA ALMANAC.COM/2023.**

| DAY OF YEAR | DAY OF MONTH | DAY OF WEEK | ☼ RISES H. M. | RISE KEY | ☼ SETS H. M. | SET KEY | LENGTH OF DAY H. M. | SUN FAST M. | SUN DECLINATION ° | ' | HIGH TIDE TIMES BOSTON | | ☾ RISES H. M. | RISE KEY | ☾ SETS H. M. | SET KEY | ☾ ASTRON. PLACE | ☾ AGE |
|---|---|---|---|---|---|---|---|---|---|---|---|---|---|---|---|---|---|---|
| 274 | 1 | A | 6:41 | C | **6:26** | C | 11 45 | 26 | 3 | s. 16 | 1 | **1¼** | **7:38** | B | 9:17 | E | ARI | 17 |
| 275 | 2 | M. | 6:42 | C | **6:24** | C | 11 42 | 26 | 3 | s. 39 | 1¾ | **2** | **8:08** | B | 10:34 | E | ARI | 18 |
| 276 | 3 | Tu. | 6:43 | C | **6:23** | C | 11 40 | 27 | 4 | s. 02 | 2½ | **2¾** | **8:45** | A | 11:48 | E | TAU | 19 |
| 277 | 4 | W. | 6:44 | D | **6:21** | C | 11 37 | 27 | 4 | s. 26 | 3½ | **3¾** | **9:30** | A | **12:57** | E | TAU | 20 |
| 278 | 5 | Th. | 6:45 | D | **6:19** | C | 11 34 | 27 | 4 | s. 49 | 4¼ | **4½** | **10:22** | A | **1:57** | E | TAU | 21 |
| 279 | 6 | Fr. | 6:46 | D | **6:17** | C | 11 31 | 28 | 5 | s. 12 | 5¼ | **5½** | **11:21** | A | **2:48** | E | GEM | 22 |
| 280 | 7 | Sa. | 6:48 | D | **6:16** | C | 11 28 | 28 | 5 | s. 35 | 6¼ | **6½** | — | - | **3:28** | E | GEM | 23 |
| 281 | 8 | A | 6:49 | D | **6:14** | C | 11 25 | 28 | 5 | s. 58 | 7½ | **7½** | 12:24 | B | **4:01** | E | CAN | 24 |
| 282 | 9 | M. | 6:50 | D | **6:12** | C | 11 22 | 29 | 6 | s. 20 | 8¼ | **8½** | 1:28 | B | **4:27** | E | CAN | 25 |
| 283 | 10 | Tu. | 6:51 | D | **6:11** | C | 11 20 | 29 | 6 | s. 43 | 9¼ | **9¼** | 2:31 | C | **4:49** | E | LEO | 26 |
| 284 | 11 | W. | 6:52 | D | **6:09** | C | 11 17 | 29 | 7 | s. 06 | 10 | **10** | 3:34 | C | **5:09** | D | LEO | 27 |
| 285 | 12 | Th. | 6:53 | D | **6:07** | C | 11 14 | 29 | 7 | s. 28 | 10½ | **10¾** | 4:36 | D | **5:27** | D | LEO | 28 |
| 286 | 13 | Fr. | 6:54 | D | **6:06** | B | 11 12 | 30 | 7 | s. 51 | 11¼ | **11½** | 5:39 | D | **5:45** | C | VIR | 29 |
| 287 | 14 | Sa. | 6:56 | D | **6:04** | B | 11 08 | 30 | 8 | s. 13 | 11¾ | — | 6:42 | E | **6:04** | C | VIR | 0 |
| 288 | 15 | A | 6:57 | D | **6:03** | B | 11 06 | 30 | 8 | s. 35 | 12 | **12¼** | 7:47 | E | **6:26** | B | VIR | 1 |
| 289 | 16 | M. | 6:58 | D | **6:01** | B | 11 03 | 30 | 8 | s. 58 | 12¾ | **1** | 8:55 | E | **6:50** | B | LIB | 2 |
| 290 | 17 | Tu. | 6:59 | D | **5:59** | B | 11 00 | 30 | 9 | s. 20 | 1½ | **1½** | 10:05 | E | **7:21** | A | LIB | 3 |
| 291 | 18 | W. | 7:00 | D | **5:58** | B | 10 58 | 31 | 9 | s. 41 | 2 | **2¼** | 11:16 | E | **8:00** | A | SCO | 4 |
| 292 | 19 | Th. | 7:01 | D | **5:56** | B | 10 55 | 31 | 10 | s. 03 | 2¾ | **3** | **12:25** | E | **8:50** | A | OPH | 5 |
| 293 | 20 | Fr. | 7:03 | D | **5:55** | B | 10 52 | 31 | 10 | s. 25 | 3¾ | **3¾** | **1:27** | E | **9:52** | A | SAG | 6 |
| 294 | 21 | Sa. | 7:04 | D | **5:53** | B | 10 49 | 31 | 10 | s. 46 | 4½ | **4¾** | **2:18** | E | **11:04** | B | SAG | 7 |
| 295 | 22 | A | 7:05 | D | **5:52** | B | 10 47 | 31 | 11 | s. 07 | 5½ | **5¾** | **3:00** | E | — | - | CAP | 8 |
| 296 | 23 | M. | 7:06 | D | **5:50** | B | 10 44 | 31 | 11 | s. 28 | 6¾ | **7** | **3:33** | E | 12:21 | B | CAP | 9 |
| 297 | 24 | Tu. | 7:07 | D | **5:49** | B | 10 42 | 32 | 11 | s. 49 | 7¾ | **8** | **4:01** | E | 1:40 | C | AQU | 10 |
| 298 | 25 | W. | 7:09 | D | **5:47** | B | 10 38 | 32 | 12 | s. 10 | 8¾ | **9** | **4:25** | D | 2:59 | C | AQU | 11 |
| 299 | 26 | Th. | 7:10 | D | **5:46** | B | 10 36 | 32 | 12 | s. 31 | 9½ | **10** | **4:48** | C | 4:16 | D | AQU | 12 |
| 300 | 27 | Fr. | 7:11 | D | **5:44** | B | 10 33 | 32 | 12 | s. 51 | 10½ | **11** | **5:11** | C | 5:33 | E | PSC | 13 |
| 301 | 28 | Sa. | 7:12 | D | **5:43** | B | 10 31 | 32 | 13 | s. 11 | 11¼ | **11¾** | **5:36** | B | 6:50 | E | PSC | 14 |
| 302 | 29 | A | 7:13 | D | **5:42** | B | 10 29 | 32 | 13 | s. 31 | **12** | — | **6:04** | B | 8:07 | E | ARI | 15 |
| 303 | 30 | M. | 7:15 | D | **5:40** | B | 10 25 | 32 | 13 | s. 51 | 12½ | **12¾** | **6:38** | B | 9:24 | E | ARI | 16 |
| 304 | 31 | Tu. | 7:16 | D | **5:39** | B | 10 23 | 32 | 14 | s. 10 | 1½ | **1½** | **7:20** | A | 10:37 | E | TAU | 17 |

 To use this page, see p. 116; for Key Letters, see p. 238. LIGHT = A.M. **BOLD** = P.M. 

> *How just's the motions of these whirling spheres,*
> *Which ne'er can err while time is met by years!*
> –Allan Ramsay, of eclipses

**CALENDAR**

| DAY OF MONTH | DAY OF WEEK | DATES, FEASTS, FASTS, ASPECTS, TIDE HEIGHTS, AND WEATHER | |
|---|---|---|---|
| 1 | A | 18th ☉. af. ℙ. • ♂♃☾ • Pilot pursued UFO over Fargo, N.Dak., 1948 | *Brilliant* |
| 2 | M. | ♂♅☾ • 27-lb. rainbow trout caught, Lake Natoma, Calif., 2005 • Tides {10.9 {11.4 | *and cold* |
| 3 | Tu. | Two zebra escapees returned to pumpkin patch zoo after 2-hour chase, Pingree Grove, Ill., 2021 • {10.3 {11.0 | *never* |
| 4 | W. | St. Francis of Assisi • "Make Way for Ducklings" sculpture, in honor of Robert McCloskey, installed, Boston, Mass., 1987 | |
| 5 | Th. | ☾ RIDES HIGH • Watch for banded woolly bear caterpillars now. • Tides {9.0 {9.4 | *gets old.* |
| 6 | Fr. | Basketball player Rebecca Lobo born, 1973 • {8.5 {9.4 | *Rain,* |
| 7 | Sa. | *Everyone knows best where the shoe pinches him.* • {8.2 {9.1 | *it's plain,* |
| 8 | A | 19th ☉. af. ℙ. • Philanthropist and "Canada's hockey dad" Walter Gretzky born, 1938 | *then* |
| 9 | M. | **COLUMBUS DAY,** OBSERVED • **INDIGENOUS PEOPLES' DAY** • **THANKSGIVING DAY (CANADA)** • ☾ AT APO. | |
| 10 | Tu. | ♂☽☾ • ☿ STAT • Mysterious boom heard in New England, 2021 • {8.6 {9.3 | *sun again.* |
| 11 | W. | Little brown bats hibernate now. • Tides {9.0 {9.5 | *Fine skies* |
| 12 | Th. | **NATIONAL FARMER'S DAY** • "Big Blow" struck Calif./ Oreg./Wash./B.C., 1962 • {9.3 {9.6 | *for* |
| 13 | Fr. | ☾ ON EQ. • Boston Americans (now Red Sox) won the 1st World Series, 1903 • {9.7 {9.4 | *foliage* |
| 14 | Sa. | **NEW ●** • **ECLIPSE ☉** • ☾ AT ☍ • ♂♀☾ • {10.0 {— | *stroll-iage.* |
| 15 | A | 20th ☉. af. ℙ. • ♂♂☾ • Henry Perky rec'd patent for shredded wheat, 1895 | *Pumpkins* |
| 16 | M. | *That which will not be butter must be made into cheese.* • Walt Disney Company founded, 1923 | *plump* |
| 17 | Tu. | St. Ignatius of Antioch • 1st live broadcast of parliamentary proceedings in House of Commons, Canada, 1977 | *feel* |
| 18 | W. | St. Luke • St. Luke's little summer. • Tides {9.3 {10.4 | *showers* |
| 19 | Th. | *If spiders undo their webs, tempests follow.* • {9.1 {10.3 | *dump.* |
| 20 | Fr. | ☾ RUNS LOW • ☿ IN SUP. • ♂ • Sydney Opera House opened, Australia, 1973 • {8.8 {10.1 | *Cider and* |
| 21 | Sa. | ♂℞☾ • Astronomer Jesse Greenstein died, 2002 • {8.6 {10.0 | *doughnuts* |
| 22 | A | 21st ☉. af. ℙ. • Indian lunar space probe Chandrayaan-1 launched, 2008 | *in the sun* |
| 23 | M. | St. James of Jerusalem • ♀ GR. ELONG. (46° WEST) • {8.8 {10.0 | *as squirrels* |
| 24 | Tu. | ♂♄☾ • SS Princess Sophia struck reef off Alaska and sank next day, 1918 • {9.3 {10.2 | *go nuts on* |
| 25 | W. | ☾ AT PERIG. • ♂♆☾ • Carlsbad Cave Nat'l Monument established, N.Mex., 1923 | *the run.* |
| 26 | Th. | ☾ ON EQ. • Jacques Villeneuve won Formula One World Drivers Championship, 1997 | *Limbs* |
| 27 | Fr. | ☾ AT ☊ • Timber rattlesnakes move to winter dens. • Tides {11.1 {10.8 | *baring—* |
| 28 | Sa. | Sts. Simon & Jude • **FULL HUNTER'S ○** • **ECLIPSE ☾** • {11.5 {10.8 | *Beware* |
| 29 | A | 22nd ☉. af. ℙ. • ♂♀☾ • ♂♃☾ • ♂♅☾ • {11.7 {— | *a* |
| 30 | M. | Martha Jefferson, wife of Thomas Jefferson, born, 1748 • Tides {10.6 {11.6 | *big* |
| 31 | Tu. | All Hallows' Eve • **Reformation Day** • Ethnologist James O. Dorsey born, 1848 | *scaring!* |

## Farmer's Calendar

There's a pause after the fall equinox when the nights are warm and limbs along meadow edges bend low with fruit. Among the first to ripen are Concord grapes, one of the most widely planted and oldest variety grapes in North America.

These grapes feed a host of wildlife, including bears, foxes, ruffed grouse, quail, wild turkeys, and many species of songbirds. The unmistakable fragrance of Concord grapes carries so far that the best way to find them is with your nose. There are plenty, so don't hesitate to pick some.

Their tartness makes them perfect for jelly: Place 5 pounds of crushed grapes in a large saucepan. Add 2 cups of water, bring to a boil, then simmer for 10 minutes, stirring occasionally. Strain through cheesecloth, measuring out 5½ cups of juice. Place 3¼ cups of sugar in a large saucepan and stir in one box (1.75 oz.) of low-sugar pectin and the measured juice. Bring to a full boil, stirring constantly. Immediately stir in ¼ cup more sugar. Bring to a full boil for 1 minute, stirring constantly. Remove from heat. Skim foam. Ladle into 8-ounce sterilized jars and cover. Process in a boiling-water bath for 5 minutes.

# NOVEMBER

**SKY WATCH:** Jupiter, in Aries, comes to opposition on the 3rd, rising at sunset; at its biggest and brightest of the year, the Giant World is visible all night. Saturn, in Aquarius, is also seen the entire night; any telescope using at least 30× magnification will capture its glorious rings. Uranus, in Aries, reaches opposition on the 13th, to the left of Jupiter, which is also in Aries. Binocular owners can easily find Uranus by looking for a green "star" halfway between Jupiter and the famous Pleiades star cluster. Since no star is green, identification should be easy. Not many meteors are expected when the Leonid shower peaks at night on the 18th and 19th. Look for the Moon to the right of Jupiter on the 24th.

◐ **LAST QUARTER**   5th day   3:37 A.M.      ● **FIRST QUARTER** 20th day  5:50 A.M.
● **NEW MOON**      13th day  4:27 A.M.      ○ **FULL MOON**    27th day  4:16 A.M.

*After 2:00 A.M. on November 5, Eastern Standard Time is given.*

GET THESE PAGES WITH TIMES SET TO YOUR ZIP CODE VIA ALMANAC.COM/2023.

| DAY OF YEAR | DAY OF MONTH | DAY OF WEEK | ☼ RISES H.M. | RISE KEY | ☼ SETS H.M. | SET KEY | LENGTH OF DAY H. M. | SUN FAST M. | SUN DECLINATION ° ' | HIGH TIDE TIMES BOSTON | | ☽ RISES H.M. | RISE KEY | ☽ SETS H.M. | SET KEY | ☽ ASTRON. PLACE | ☽ AGE |
|---|---|---|---|---|---|---|---|---|---|---|---|---|---|---|---|---|---|
| 305 | 1 | W. | 7:17 | D | 5:38 | B | 10 21 | 32 | 14 s. 29 | 2¼ | 2¼ | 8:10 | A | 11:43 | E | TAU | 18 |
| 306 | 2 | Th. | 7:18 | D | 5:36 | B | 10 18 | 32 | 14 s. 48 | 3 | 3 | 9:07 | A | 12:39 | E | AUR | 19 |
| 307 | 3 | Fr. | 7:20 | D | 5:35 | B | 10 15 | 32 | 15 s. 07 | 4 | 4 | 10:10 | B | 1:25 | E | GEM | 20 |
| 308 | 4 | Sa. | 7:21 | D | 5:34 | B | 10 13 | 32 | 15 s. 26 | 4¾ | 5 | 11:15 | B | 2:01 | E | CAN | 21 |
| 309 | 5 | **A** | 6:22 | E | 4:33 | B | 10 11 | 32 | 15 s. 44 | 4¾ | 4¾ | 11:19 | B | 1:29 | E | CAN | 22 |
| 310 | 6 | M. | 6:23 | E | 4:32 | B | 10 09 | 32 | 16 s. 02 | 5¾ | 5¾ | — | - | 1:53 | E | LEO | 23 |
| 311 | 7 | Tu. | 6:25 | E | 4:31 | B | 10 06 | 32 | 16 s. 20 | 6½ | 6¾ | 12:22 | C | 2:14 | D | LEO | 24 |
| 312 | 8 | W. | 6:26 | E | 4:29 | B | 10 03 | 32 | 16 s. 37 | 7½ | 7¾ | 1:24 | C | 2:32 | D | LEO | 25 |
| 313 | 9 | Th. | 6:27 | E | 4:28 | B | 10 01 | 32 | 16 s. 55 | 8¼ | 8½ | 2:26 | D | 2:50 | C | VIR | 26 |
| 314 | 10 | Fr. | 6:28 | E | 4:27 | B | 9 59 | 32 | 17 s. 12 | 8¾ | 9¼ | 3:29 | D | 3:09 | C | VIR | 27 |
| 315 | 11 | Sa. | 6:30 | E | 4:26 | B | 9 56 | 32 | 17 s. 28 | 9½ | 10 | 4:33 | E | 3:29 | B | VIR | 28 |
| 316 | 12 | **A** | 6:31 | E | 4:25 | B | 9 54 | 32 | 17 s. 45 | 10 | 10½ | 5:41 | E | 3:53 | B | VIR | 29 |
| 317 | 13 | M. | 6:32 | E | 4:24 | B | 9 52 | 32 | 18 s. 01 | 10¾ | 11¼ | 6:52 | E | 4:22 | B | LIB | 0 |
| 318 | 14 | Tu. | 6:33 | E | 4:23 | B | 9 50 | 31 | 18 s. 16 | 11½ | — | 8:04 | E | 4:59 | A | SCO | 1 |
| 319 | 15 | W. | 6:35 | E | 4:22 | B | 9 47 | 31 | 18 s. 32 | 12 | 12 | 9:15 | E | 5:46 | A | OPH | 2 |
| 320 | 16 | Th. | 6:36 | E | 4:22 | B | 9 46 | 31 | 18 s. 47 | 12¾ | 12¾ | 10:21 | E | 6:45 | A | SAG | 3 |
| 321 | 17 | Fr. | 6:37 | E | 4:21 | B | 9 44 | 31 | 19 s. 02 | 1½ | 1½ | 11:16 | E | 7:55 | B | SAG | 4 |
| 322 | 18 | Sa. | 6:38 | E | 4:20 | B | 9 42 | 31 | 19 s. 16 | 2½ | 2½ | 12:00 | E | 9:11 | B | SAG | 5 |
| 323 | 19 | **A** | 6:40 | E | 4:19 | B | 9 39 | 30 | 19 s. 30 | 3¼ | 3½ | 12:36 | E | 10:29 | C | CAP | 6 |
| 324 | 20 | M. | 6:41 | E | 4:18 | B | 9 37 | 30 | 19 s. 44 | 4¼ | 4½ | 1:04 | E | 11:45 | C | CAP | 7 |
| 325 | 21 | Tu. | 6:42 | E | 4:18 | B | 9 36 | 30 | 19 s. 57 | 5¼ | 5¾ | 1:29 | D | — | - | AQU | 8 |
| 326 | 22 | W. | 6:43 | E | 4:17 | B | 9 34 | 30 | 20 s. 10 | 6¼ | 6¾ | 1:51 | D | 1:01 | D | AQU | 9 |
| 327 | 23 | Th. | 6:44 | E | 4:16 | B | 9 32 | 29 | 20 s. 23 | 7¼ | 7¾ | 2:13 | C | 2:15 | D | CET | 10 |
| 328 | 24 | Fr. | 6:46 | E | 4:16 | A | 9 30 | 29 | 20 s. 35 | 8¼ | 8¾ | 2:36 | C | 3:29 | E | PSC | 11 |
| 329 | 25 | Sa. | 6:47 | E | 4:15 | A | 9 28 | 29 | 20 s. 47 | 9 | 9¾ | 3:02 | B | 4:44 | E | ARI | 12 |
| 330 | 26 | **A** | 6:48 | E | 4:15 | A | 9 27 | 28 | 20 s. 58 | 9¾ | 10½ | 3:33 | B | 6:00 | E | ARI | 13 |
| 331 | 27 | M. | 6:49 | E | 4:14 | A | 9 25 | 28 | 21 s. 09 | 10¾ | 11¼ | 4:11 | A | 7:15 | E | TAU | 14 |
| 332 | 28 | Tu. | 6:50 | E | 4:14 | A | 9 24 | 28 | 21 s. 20 | 11½ | — | 4:58 | A | 8:25 | E | TAU | 15 |
| 333 | 29 | W. | 6:51 | E | 4:13 | A | 9 22 | 27 | 21 s. 30 | 12 | 12¼ | 5:53 | A | 9:26 | E | TAU | 16 |
| 334 | 30 | Th. | 6:52 | E | 4:13 | A | 9 21 | 27 | 21 s. 40 | 12¾ | 1 | 6:54 | A | 10:17 | E | GEM | 17 |

# NOVEMBER

*The Frost Spirit comes! and the quiet lake shall feel*
*The torpid touch of his glazing breath.*
–**John Greenleaf Whittier**

| DAY OF MONTH | DAY OF WEEK | DATES, FEASTS, FASTS, ASPECTS, TIDE HEIGHTS, AND WEATHER | |
|---|---|---|---|
| 1 | W. | All Saints' • Boston Female Medical Col., 1st U.S. medical school for women, opened, Boston, Mass., 1848 | *Flurries* |
| 2 | Th. | All Souls' • ☾ RIDES HIGH • 1st titanium mill opened, Toronto, Ohio, 1957 • {9.3 10.3 | *again;* |
| 3 | Fr. | ♃ AT ☍ • Bob Kane, co-creator of *Batman* comic, died, 1998 • Tides {8.8 9.7 | *the bear* |
| 4 | Sa. | Sadie Hawkins Day • ♄ STAT. • Royal Montreal Golf Club founded, 1873 | *makes* |
| 5 | **A** | **23rd S. af. P.** • **DAYLIGHT SAVING TIME ENDS, 2:00 A.M.** • {8.2 9.0 | *its den.* |
| 6 | M. | ☾ AT APO. • 1st recorded sighting of supernova in Cassiopeia, 1572 • {8.2 8.8 | *St. Martin's* |
| 7 | Tu. | **ELECTION DAY** • Singer-songwriter Leonard Cohen died, 2016 • {8.4 8.8 | *summer,* |
| 8 | W. | Rodrigo Koxa surfed 80' wave, setting world record, Nazaré, Portugal, 2017 • Tides {8.7 8.9 | *but* |
| 9 | Th. | ☾ ON EQ. • ☌♀☾ • Alice Coachman, 1st Black woman to win Olympic gold medal, born, 1923 | *showers* |
| 10 | Fr. | *If red the Sun begin his race, Be sure the rain will fall apace.* • Tides {9.5 9.2 | *a bummer.* |
| 11 | Sa. | St. Martin of Tours • **VETERANS DAY** • ☾ AT ☋ • {9.9 9.3 | *Veterans* |
| 12 | **A** | **24th S. af. P.** • Indian Summer • Tides {10.2 9.4 | *we thank* |
| 13 | M. | NEW ● • ☌♂☾ • ♅ AT ☍ • Tides {10.5 9.4 | *as pull cords* |
| 14 | Tu. | ☌☿☾ • UK's Prince Charles born, 1948 • {10.7 — | *we yank* |
| 15 | W. | America Recycles Day • Astronomer Sir William Herschel born, 1738 • {9.4 10.8 | *to start up* |
| 16 | Th. | ☾ RUNS LOW • *Skylab 4* launched, 1973 • {9.3 10.8 | *ye olde* |
| 17 | Fr. | St. Hugh of Lincoln • Deadly tornado outbreak spawned 55 in Ill. and Ind., 2013 | *snowblower* |
| 18 | Sa. | St. Hilda of Whitby • ☌♂⊙ • ☌♇☾ • Astronaut Alan Shepard born, 1923 | *in temps* |
| 19 | **A** | **25th S. af. P.** • U.S. pres. Abraham Lincoln delivered Gettysburg Address, 1863 | *getting* |
| 20 | M. | ☌♄☾ • *Gratitude is the heart's memory.* • {9.1 10.0 | *lower and* |
| 21 | Tu. | ☾ AT PERIG. • *Nov. 19–21:* The "Long Storm" dropped 18" snow on N.Y.C., 1798 • {9.3 9.9 | *lower.* |
| 22 | W. | ☾ ON EQ. • ☌♆☾ • Wiley Post, 1st pilot to fly solo around world, born, 1898 | *Time for* |
| 23 | Th. | St. Clement • **THANKSGIVING DAY** • Tides {10.2 9.9 | *some turkey,* |
| 24 | Fr. | ☾ AT ☊ • Baseball player Steve Yeager born, 1948 • Pilot reported UFO, north Baffin Island, Nunavut, 2018 | *but* |
| 25 | Sa. | ☌♃☾ • Naturalist Kenneth Brugger, finder of Mex. winter home of monarch butterflies, died, 1998 | *rain* |
| 26 | **A** | **26th S. af. P.** • ☌♅☾ • Thelma Chalifoux 1st Métis woman to become Canadian senator, Alta., 1997 | |
| 27 | M. | FULL BEAVER ○ • *A soft answer turneth away wrath.* • Tides {11.3 9.8 | *and snow* |
| 28 | Tu. | 1st U.S. automobile race held, Chicago, Ill., 1895 • {11.2 — | *lurky.* |
| 29 | W. | ☾ RIDES HIGH • Writer C. S. Lewis born, 1898 • {9.6 10.9 | *Mild,* |
| 30 | Th. | St. Andrew • 1st solar eclipse known to be recorded (Ireland), 3340 B.C. • {9.3 10.5 | *child!* |

## Farmer's Calendar

When nor'easters send Atlantic predator fish streaming south, winter flounder—aka mud dabs, blackbacks, lemon sole—begin their own migration, easing in from deep water to bays and estuaries from the Gulf of St. Lawrence to North Carolina. Protected from frigid water by "antifreeze" proteins in their blood, they'll spawn in winter, their eggs sinking unlike the buoyant offspring of most marine fish.

Winter flounder rest on the bottom, venturing higher in the water column less frequently than most members of the order. Early in their lives, their left eye migrates to the right side of their heads. Lying on their white blind sides, they're camouflaged against (or in) mud or sand. The first, and only, thing you're likely to see is their bulging eyes.

These fish lack the sharp teeth of their cousins, halibut and fluke, and their thick lips are permanently puckered, as if waiting for a kiss.

Few fish make better table fare, and now is the time to pursue them. Use small, long-shank hooks. Sea worms work best, but garden worms are nearly as effective and easier to come by. Flounders like bright colors, so paint your sinkers red.

CALENDAR

# DECEMBER

**SKY WATCH:** All this month, Jupiter is visible at night. Saturn, now solely an evening star, stands on the meridian due south at nightfall, in Aquarius. A bright star far to Saturn's lower left is the 1st magnitude star, Fomalhaut. During December's first few mornings, Venus—a morning star—guides observers to Virgo's blue main star, Spica, to its right. The 13th brings the year's best meteor shower, the Geminids, under perfect, moonless, dark conditions. Rural observers can see a meteor a minute at any time of night. On the 17th, the Moon dangles below Saturn before moving on to meet Jupiter on the 21st and 22nd. Winter in the Northern Hemisphere begins with the solstice on the night of the 21st at 10:27 P.M. EST.

| | | |
|---|---|---|
| ◗ **LAST QUARTER** | 5th day | 12:49 A.M. |
| ◑ **FIRST QUARTER** | 19th day | 1:39 P.M. |
| ● **NEW MOON** | 12th day | 6:32 P.M. |
| ○ **FULL MOON** | 26th day | 7:33 P.M. |

*All times are given in Eastern Standard Time.*

**GET THESE PAGES WITH TIMES SET TO YOUR ZIP CODE VIA ALMANAC.COM/2023.**

| DAY OF YEAR | DAY OF MONTH | DAY OF WEEK | ☀ RISES H.M. | RISE KEY | ☀ SETS H.M. | SET KEY | LENGTH OF DAY H.M. | SUN FAST M. | SUN DECLINATION ° ' | HIGH TIDE TIMES BOSTON | | ☽ RISES H.M. | RISE KEY | ☽ SETS H.M. | SET KEY | ☽ ASTRON. PLACE | ☽ AGE |
|---|---|---|---|---|---|---|---|---|---|---|---|---|---|---|---|---|---|
| 335 | 1 | Fr. | 6:53 | E | 4:13 | A | 9 20 | 27 | 21 s. 49 | 1½ | 1¾ | 7:59 | B | 10:57 | E | GEM | 18 |
| 336 | 2 | Sa. | 6:54 | E | 4:12 | A | 9 18 | 26 | 21 s. 59 | 2½ | 2½ | 9:05 | B | 11:29 | E | CAN | 19 |
| 337 | 3 | **A** | 6:56 | E | 4:12 | A | 9 16 | 26 | 22 s. 07 | 3¼ | 3¼ | 10:08 | C | 11:55 | E | LEO | 20 |
| 338 | 4 | M. | 6:57 | E | 4:12 | A | 9 15 | 26 | 22 s. 15 | 4 | 4¼ | 11:11 | C | 12:17 | D | LEO | 21 |
| 339 | 5 | Tu. | 6:58 | E | 4:12 | A | 9 14 | 25 | 22 s. 23 | 5 | 5 | — | - | 12:36 | D | LEO | 22 |
| 340 | 6 | W. | 6:59 | E | 4:12 | A | 9 13 | 25 | 22 s. 30 | 5¾ | 6 | 12:12 | D | 12:54 | D | VIR | 23 |
| 341 | 7 | Th. | 6:59 | E | 4:12 | A | 9 13 | 24 | 22 s. 37 | 6½ | 7 | 1:14 | D | 1:12 | C | VIR | 24 |
| 342 | 8 | Fr. | 7:00 | E | 4:11 | A | 9 11 | 24 | 22 s. 44 | 7¼ | 7¾ | 2:17 | E | 1:31 | C | VIR | 25 |
| 343 | 9 | Sa. | 7:01 | E | 4:11 | A | 9 10 | 23 | 22 s. 50 | 8 | 8½ | 3:23 | E | 1:53 | B | VIR | 26 |
| 344 | 10 | **A** | 7:02 | E | 4:11 | A | 9 09 | 23 | 22 s. 55 | 8¾ | 9½ | 4:32 | E | 2:20 | B | LIB | 27 |
| 345 | 11 | M. | 7:03 | E | 4:12 | A | 9 09 | 23 | 23 s. 00 | 9½ | 10¼ | 5:44 | E | 2:54 | B | LIB | 28 |
| 346 | 12 | Tu. | 7:04 | E | 4:12 | A | 9 08 | 22 | 23 s. 05 | 10¼ | 11 | 6:57 | E | 3:37 | A | SCO | 0 |
| 347 | 13 | W. | 7:05 | E | 4:12 | A | 9 07 | 22 | 23 s. 09 | 11 | 11¾ | 8:07 | E | 4:33 | A | OPH | 1 |
| 348 | 14 | Th. | 7:05 | E | 4:12 | A | 9 07 | 21 | 23 s. 13 | 11¾ | — | 9:08 | E | 5:41 | B | SAG | 2 |
| 349 | 15 | Fr. | 7:06 | E | 4:12 | A | 9 06 | 21 | 23 s. 16 | 12½ | 12½ | 9:58 | E | 6:58 | B | SAG | 3 |
| 350 | 16 | Sa. | 7:07 | E | 4:13 | A | 9 06 | 20 | 23 s. 19 | 1¼ | 1½ | 10:37 | E | 8:17 | C | CAP | 4 |
| 351 | 17 | **A** | 7:08 | E | 4:13 | A | 9 05 | 20 | 23 s. 21 | 2¼ | 2¼ | 11:08 | E | 9:36 | C | CAP | 5 |
| 352 | 18 | M. | 7:08 | E | 4:13 | A | 9 05 | 19 | 23 s. 23 | 3 | 3¼ | 11:34 | D | 10:51 | D | AQU | 6 |
| 353 | 19 | Tu. | 7:09 | E | 4:14 | A | 9 05 | 19 | 23 s. 24 | 4 | 4¼ | 11:56 | D | — | - | AQU | 7 |
| 354 | 20 | W. | 7:09 | E | 4:14 | A | 9 05 | 18 | 23 s. 25 | 5 | 5¼ | 12:18 | C | 12:05 | D | PSC | 8 |
| 355 | 21 | Th. | 7:10 | E | 4:15 | A | 9 05 | 18 | 23 s. 26 | 6 | 6½ | 12:40 | C | 1:18 | E | PSC | 9 |
| 356 | 22 | Fr. | 7:10 | E | 4:15 | A | 9 05 | 17 | 23 s. 26 | 7 | 7½ | 1:04 | B | 2:31 | E | ARI | 10 |
| 357 | 23 | Sa. | 7:11 | E | 4:16 | A | 9 05 | 17 | 23 s. 25 | 7¾ | 8½ | 1:33 | B | 3:45 | E | ARI | 11 |
| 358 | 24 | **A** | 7:11 | E | 4:16 | A | 9 05 | 16 | 23 s. 24 | 8¾ | 9½ | 2:07 | A | 4:58 | E | TAU | 12 |
| 359 | 25 | M. | 7:12 | E | 4:17 | A | 9 05 | 16 | 23 s. 23 | 9½ | 10¼ | 2:50 | A | 6:09 | E | TAU | 13 |
| 360 | 26 | Tu. | 7:12 | E | 4:17 | A | 9 05 | 15 | 23 s. 21 | 10½ | 11 | 3:41 | A | 7:13 | E | TAU | 14 |
| 361 | 27 | W. | 7:12 | E | 4:18 | A | 9 06 | 15 | 23 s. 19 | 11¼ | 11¾ | 4:40 | A | 8:08 | E | AUR | 15 |
| 362 | 28 | Th. | 7:13 | E | 4:19 | A | 9 06 | 14 | 23 s. 16 | 11¾ | — | 5:44 | B | 8:53 | E | GEM | 16 |
| 363 | 29 | Fr. | 7:13 | E | 4:20 | A | 9 07 | 14 | 23 s. 12 | 12½ | 12½ | 6:50 | B | 9:28 | E | CAN | 17 |
| 364 | 30 | Sa. | 7:13 | E | 4:20 | A | 9 07 | 13 | 23 s. 09 | 1¼ | 1¼ | 7:55 | C | 9:56 | E | CAN | 18 |
| 365 | 31 | **A** | 7:13 | E | 4:21 | A | 9 08 | 13 | 23 s. 04 | 2 | 2 | 8:58 | C | 10:19 | E | LEO | 19 |

To use this page, see p. 116; for Key Letters, see p. 238. LIGHT = A.M. **BOLD = P.M.** 2023

CALENDAR

THE TWELFTH MONTH • 2023 **DECEMBER** DECEMBER HATH 31 DAYS

*Hark! on the frozen ear of night, / The sleighs with silver bells—*
*On yonder hill top's snowy height, / The merry music swells.*
**–Richard George Holland**

| DAY OF MONTH | DAY OF WEEK | DATES, FEASTS, FASTS, ASPECTS, TIDE HEIGHTS, AND WEATHER | |
|---|---|---|---|
| 1 | Fr. | *Always put the saddle on the right horse.* • Tides {9.0 10.1 | *C-c-c-cold* |
| 2 | Sa. | St. Viviana • Skier Bode Miller won his 33rd World Cup race, 2011 • {8.7 9.7 | *and spitting,* |
| 3 | **A** | **1st S. of Advent** • *Pioneer 10* spacecraft's closest approach to Jupiter (EST), 1973 | *snow* |
| 4 | M. | ☾ AT APO. • ☿ GR. ELONG. (21° EAST) • National Cookie Day (U.S.) • Tides {8.4 8.9 | *showers* |
| 5 | Tu. | Six U.S. Navy planes (Flight 19 and Training 49) disappeared over Bermuda Triangle, 1945 • {8.4 8.7 | *hitting,* |
| 6 | W. | St. Nicholas • ☾ ON EQ. • ♆ STAT. • 1st U.S. presidential address via radio, 1923 | *then* |
| 7 | Th. | St. Ambrose • Chanukah begins at sundown • **NATIONAL PEARL HARBOR REMEMBRANCE DAY** | *the* |
| 8 | Fr. | ☾ AT ☋ • Bank of Canada announced human rights activist Viola Desmond to appear on $10 note, 2016 | *real* |
| 9 | Sa. | ☌♀☾ • "Weary Willie" clown Emmett Kelly born, 1898 • {9.5 8.7 | *heavy stuff.* |
| 10 | **A** | **2nd S. of Advent** • Treaty of Paris officially ended Spanish-American war, 1898 | *Chill* |
| 11 | M. | Astronomer Annie Jump Cannon born, 1863 • Tides {10.3 9.0 | *abating, more* |
| 12 | Tu. | **OUR LADY OF GUADALUPE** • **NEW** ● • ☌♂☾ • ☿ STAT. | *snow waiting.* |
| 13 | W. | St. Lucia • ☾ RUNS LOW • *Apollo 17*'s lunar rover reached 11.18 mph, setting record, 1972 | *Enough!* |
| 14 | Th. | Halcyon Days begin. • ☌☿☾ • Canadian Capt. Paul Triquet's WWII valor earned him later Victoria Cross, 1943 | |
| 15 | Fr. | ☌♇☾ • Leaning Tower of Pisa reopened after 11 years of repair, Italy, 2001 • {9.4 11.2 | *Flakes with* |
| 16 | Sa. | ☾ AT PERIG. • Boston Tea Party, 1773 • Tides {9.5 11.1 | *mildness;* |
| 17 | **A** | **3rd S. of Advent** • ☌♄☾ • Tides {9.5 10.8 | *snowstorm* |
| 18 | M. | *A fire hard to kindle indicates bad weather.* • Tides {9.6 10.4 | *with wildness—* |
| 19 | Tu. | ☌♆☾ • Beware the Pogonip. • Writer Emily Brontë died, 1848 • {9.7 10.0 | *Oh, well!* |
| 20 | W. | Ember Day • ☾ ON EQ. • At 81+, Queen Elizabeth II became oldest monarch in UK history, 2007 | *Clear* |
| 21 | Th. | St. Thomas • **WINTER SOLSTICE** • ☾ AT ☊ • Tides {10.0 9.4 | *sky* |
| 22 | Fr. | Ember Day • ☌♃☾ • ☿ IN INF. ☌ • Tides {10.3 9.2 | *for* |
| 23 | Sa. | Ember Day • ☌♅☾ • *A Visit From St. Nicholas* 1st published, 1823 • {10.5 9.2 | *Rudolph's* |
| 24 | **A** | **4th S. of Advent** • Entrepreneur Johns Hopkins died, 1873 • {10.7 9.2 | *flight for* |
| 25 | M. | **Christmas** • 2.6" snow, Tucson, Ariz., 1987 • Tides {10.8 9.2 | *Noël!* |
| 26 | Tu. | St. Stephen • **BOXING DAY (CANADA)** • **FIRST DAY OF KWANZAA** • **FULL COLD** ○ • ☾ RIDES HIGH | |
| 27 | W. | St. John • ☌☿♂ • Aeronautics pioneer Sir George Cayley born, 1773 | *Freezing and* |
| 28 | Th. | Holy Innocents • Endangered Species Act (U.S.) became law, 1973 | *snow showers* |
| 29 | Fr. | Isaac Roberts's photo of Great Nebula in Andromeda (M31) 1st to show its spiral structure, 1888 | *galore—* |
| 30 | Sa. | *One touch of nature makes the whole world kin.* –Shakespeare • {8.9 10.0 | *Now we leap* |
| 31 | **A** | **1st S. af. Ch.** • ♃ STAT. • Singer Donna Summer born, 1948 | *to 2024!* |

## Farmer's Calendar

House mice, ship stowaways from Eurasia, infest human dwellings. Our cleaner, woodland-dwelling natives—white-footed mice—merely visit. If you live anywhere from Nova Scotia to Virginia and west to the Rockies, they are likely to enter your camp or house like poltergeists when the first frosts stiffen the grass.

Trying to block them is futile. By starlight, they always find openings unseen and unknown. You may see one of these creatures in the light of the dying fire, flowing over floor and hearth, pausing to preen its fur and tail, twitching its impossibly long whiskers, and fixing you with huge, obsidian eyes.

Your "polterguest" may even play music for you, especially if leaves have blown in through a door or window. For reasons not understood, they'll drum on them with their paws, creating a melodious buzz.

White-footed mice provide a service to forests by excreting spores of fungi that they eat. These fungi enhance the ability of trees to take up necessary nutrients.

Because these animals don't hibernate, they need a warm place. Beware: They'll poop, may chew soap, and can carry illnesses such as Lyme disease.

# HOLIDAYS AND OBSERVANCES

## 2023 HOLIDAYS
### FEDERAL HOLIDAYS ARE LISTED IN BOLD.

CALENDAR

**JAN. 1: New Year's Day**

**JAN. 7:** Orthodox Christmas (Julian)

**JAN. 16: Martin Luther King Jr.'s Birthday, observed**

**FEB. 2:** Groundhog Day

**FEB. 12:** Abraham Lincoln's Birthday

**FEB. 14:** Valentine's Day

**FEB. 15:** Susan B. Anthony's Birthday *(Fla.)*

**FEB. 20: Presidents' Day**

**FEB. 21:** Mardi Gras *(Baldwin & Mobile counties, Ala.; La.)*

**FEB. 22:** George Washington's Birthday

**MAR. 2:** Texas Independence Day

**MAR. 7:** Town Meeting Day *(Vt.)*

**MAR. 8:** International Women's Day

**MAR. 12:** Daylight Saving Time begins at 2:00 A.M.

**MAR. 17:** St. Patrick's Day
Evacuation Day *(Suffolk Co., Mass.)*

**MAR. 27:** Seward's Day *(Alaska)*

**MAR. 31:** César Chávez Day

**APR. 3:** Pascua Florida Day, observed

**APR. 17:** Patriots Day *(Maine, Mass.)*

**APR. 21:** San Jacinto Day *(Tex.)*

**APR. 22:** Earth Day

**APR. 28:** National Arbor Day

**MAY 5:** Cinco de Mayo

**MAY 8:** Truman Day *(Mo.)*

**MAY 14:** Mother's Day

**MAY 20:** Armed Forces Day

**MAY 22:** National Maritime Day
Victoria Day *(Canada)*

**MAY 29: Memorial Day, observed**

**JUNE 1:** First day of Pride Month

**JUNE 5:** World Environment Day

**JUNE 12:** King Kamehameha I Day, observed *(Hawaii)*

**JUNE 14:** Flag Day

**JUNE 17:** Bunker Hill Day *(Suffolk Co., Mass.)*

**JUNE 18:** Father's Day

**JUNE 19: Juneteenth National Independence Day**

**JUNE 20:** West Virginia Day

**JULY 1:** Canada Day

**JULY 4: Independence Day**

**JULY 22:** National Day of the Cowboy

**JULY 24:** Pioneer Day *(Utah)*

**AUG. 1:** Colorado Day

**AUG. 7:** Civic Holiday *(parts of Canada)*

**AUG. 16:** Bennington Battle Day *(Vt.)*

**AUG. 19:** National Aviation Day

**AUG. 26:** Women's Equality Day

**SEPT. 4: Labor Day**

**SEPT. 9:** Admission Day *(Calif.)*

**SEPT. 10:** Grandparents Day

**SEPT. 11:** Patriot Day

**SEPT. 17:** Constitution Day

**SEPT. 21:** International Day of Peace

**SEPT. 30:** National Day for Truth and Reconciliation *(Canada)*

**OCT. 2:** Child Health Day

**OCT. 9: Columbus Day, observed**
Indigenous Peoples' Day *(parts of U.S.)*
Leif Eriksson Day
Thanksgiving Day *(Canada)*

**OCT. 12:** National Farmer's Day

**OCT. 18:** Alaska Day

**OCT. 24:** United Nations Day

**OCT. 27:** Nevada Day

**OCT. 31:** Halloween

**NOV. 4:** Will Rogers Day *(Okla.)*

**NOV. 5:** Daylight Saving Time ends at 2:00 A.M.

**NOV. 7:** Election Day

**NOV. 11: Veterans Day**
Remembrance Day *(Canada)*

**NOV. 19:** Discovery of Puerto Rico Day
**NOV. 23:** Thanksgiving Day
**NOV. 24:** Acadian Day *(La.)*
**DEC. 7:** National Pearl Harbor Remembrance Day

**DEC. 15:** Bill of Rights Day
**DEC. 17:** Wright Brothers Day
**DEC. 25:** Christmas Day
**DEC. 26:** Boxing Day *(Canada)*
First day of Kwanzaa

## Movable Religious Observances

**FEB. 5:** Septuagesima Sunday
**FEB. 21:** Shrove Tuesday
**FEB. 22:** Ash Wednesday
**MAR. 22:** Ramadan begins at sundown
**APR. 2:** Palm Sunday
**APR. 5:** Passover begins at sundown
**APR. 7:** Good Friday
**APR. 9:** Easter
**APR. 16:** Orthodox Easter
**MAY 14:** Rogation Sunday

**MAY 18:** Ascension Day
**MAY 28:** Whitsunday–Pentecost
**JUNE 4:** Trinity Sunday
**JUNE 11:** Corpus Christi
**SEPT. 15:** Rosh Hashanah begins at sundown
**SEPT. 24:** Yom Kippur begins at sundown
**DEC. 3:** First Sunday of Advent
**DEC. 7:** Chanukah begins at sundown

# CHRONOLOGICAL CYCLES

Dominical Letter **A**
Epact **8**
Golden Number (Lunar Cycle) **10**
Roman Indiction **1**
Solar Cycle (Julian Calendar) **16**
Year of Julian Period **6736**

–Beth Krommes

# ERAS

| ERA | YEAR | BEGINS |
|---|---|---|
| Byzantine | 7532 | September 14 |
| Jewish (A.M.)* | 5784 | September 15 |
| Chinese (Lunar) [Year of the Rabbit] | 4721 | January 22 |
| Roman (A.U.C.) | 2776 | January 14 |
| Nabonassar | 2772 | April 18 |
| Japanese | 2683 | January 1 |
| Grecian (Seleucidae) | 2335 | September 14 (or October 14) |
| Indian (Saka) | 1945 | March 22 |
| Diocletian | 1740 | September 12 |
| Islamic (Hegira)* | 1445 | July 18 |
| Bahá'í* | 180 | March 20 |

*Year begins at sundown.

# GLOSSARY OF ALMANAC ODDITIES

Many readers have expressed puzzlement over the rather obscure entries that appear on our **Right-Hand Calendar Pages, 121–147.** These "oddities" have long been fixtures in the Almanac, and we are pleased to provide some definitions. Once explained, they may not seem so odd after all!

**EMBER DAYS:** These are the Wednesdays, Fridays, and Saturdays that occur in succession following (1) the First Sunday in Lent; (2) Whitsunday–Pentecost; (3) the Feast of the Holy Cross, September 14; and (4) the Feast of St. Lucia, December 13. The word *ember* is perhaps a corruption of the Latin *quatuor tempora,* "four times." The four periods are observed by some Christian denominations for prayer, fasting, and the ordination of clergy.

Folklore has it that the weather on each of the 3 days foretells the weather for the next 3 months; that is, in September, the first Ember Day, Wednesday, forecasts the weather for October; Friday predicts November; and Saturday foretells December.

**DISTAFF DAY (JANUARY 7):** This was the day after Epiphany, when women were expected to return to their spinning following the Christmas holiday. A distaff is the staff that women used for holding the flax or wool in spinning. Hence, the term "distaff" refers to women's work or the maternal side of the family.

**PLOUGH MONDAY (JANUARY):** Traditionally, the first Monday after Epiphany was called Plough Monday because it was the day when men returned to their plough, or daily work, following the Christmas holiday. (Every few years, Plough Monday and Distaff Day fall on the same day.) It was customary at this time for farm laborers to draw a plough through the village, soliciting money for a "plough light,"

–Beth Krommes

which was kept burning in the parish church all year. This traditional verse captures the spirit of it:

> *Yule is come and Yule is gone,*
> *and we have feasted well;*
> *so Jack must to his flail again*
> *and Jenny to her wheel.*

**THREE CHILLY SAINTS (MAY):** Mamertus, Pancras, and Gervais were three early Christian saints whose feast days, on May 11, 12, and 13, respectively, are traditionally cold; thus they have come to be known as the Three Chilly Saints. An old French saying translates to "St. Mamertus, St. Pancras, and St. Gervais do not pass without a frost."

**MIDSUMMER DAY (JUNE 24):** To the farmer, this day is the midpoint of the growing season, halfway between planting and harvest. The Anglican Church considered it a "Quarter Day," one of the four major divisions of the liturgical year. It also marks the feast day of St. John the Baptist. (Midsummer Eve is an occasion for festivity and celebrates fertility.)

**CORNSCATEOUS AIR (JULY):** First used by early almanac makers, this term signifies warm, damp air. Although it signals ideal climatic conditions for growing corn, warm, damp air poses a danger to those affected by asthma and other respiratory problems.

**DOG DAYS (JULY 3–AUGUST 11):** These 40 days are traditionally the year's hottest and unhealthiest. They once coincided with the year's heliacal (at sunrise) rising of the Dog Star, Sirius. Ancient folks thought that the "combined heat" of Sirius and the Sun caused summer's swelter.

**LAMMAS DAY (AUGUST 1):** Derived from the Old English *hlaf maesse,* meaning "loaf mass," Lammas Day marked the beginning of the harvest. Traditionally, loaves of bread were baked from the first-ripened grain and brought to the churches to be consecrated. In Scotland, Lammastide fairs became famous as the time when trial marriages could be made. These marriages could end after a year with no strings attached.

**CAT NIGHTS COMMENCE (AUGUST 17):** This term harks back to the days when people believed in witches. An Irish legend says that a witch could turn into a cat and regain herself eight times, but on the ninth time (August 17), she couldn't change back and thus began her final life permanently as a cat. Hence the saying "A cat has nine lives."

**HARVEST HOME (SEPTEMBER):** In Britain and other parts of Europe, this marked the conclusion of the harvest and a period of festivals for feasting and thanksgiving. It was also a time to hold elections, pay workers, and collect rents. These festivals usually took place around the autumnal equinox. Certain groups in the United States, e.g., the Pennsylvania Dutch, have kept the tradition alive.

**ST. LUKE'S LITTLE SUMMER (OCTOBER):** This is a period of warm weather that occurs on or near St. Luke's feast day (usually October 18) and is sometimes called Indian summer.

**INDIAN SUMMER (NOVEMBER):** A period of warm weather following a cold spell or a hard frost, Indian summer can occur between St. Martin's Day (November 11) and November 20. Although there are differing dates for its occurrence, for more than 225 years the Almanac has adhered to the saying "If All Saints' [November 1] brings out winter, St. Martin's brings out Indian summer." The term may have come from early Native Americans, some of whom believed that the condition was caused by a warm wind sent from the court of their southwestern god, Cautantowwit.

**HALCYON DAYS (DECEMBER):** This period of about 2 weeks of calm weather often follows the blustery winds at autumn's end. Ancient Greeks and Romans experienced this weather at about the time of the winter solstice (around December 21), when the halcyon, or kingfisher—having charmed the wind and waves so that waters were especially calm at this time—was thought to brood in a nest floating on the sea.

**BEWARE THE POGONIP (DECEMBER):** The word *pogonip* refers to frozen fog and was coined by Native Americans to describe the frozen fogs of fine ice needles that occur in the mountain valleys of the western United States and Canada. According to tradition, breathing the fog is injurious to the lungs. ∎

–Beth Krommes

# Nature's Germ Killer
## Stop a virus before it starts

Scientists have discovered a natural way to kill germs fast.

Now thousands of people are using it against viruses and bacteria that cause illness.

Colds and many other illnesses start when viruses get in your nose and multiply. If you don't stop them early, they spread and cause misery.

Hundreds of studies confirm copper kills viruses and bacteria almost instantly just by touch.

That's why ancient Greeks and Egyptians used copper to purify water and heal wounds. They didn't know about viruses and bacteria, but now we do.

"The antimicrobial activity of copper is well established." National Institutes of Health.

Scientists say copper's high conductance disrupts the electrical balance in a microbe cell and destroys it in seconds.

The EPA recommended hospitals use copper for touch surfaces like faucets and doorknobs. This cut the spread of MRSA and other illnesses by over half, and saved lives.

The strong scientific evidence gave inventor Doug Cornell an idea. He made a smooth copper probe with a tip to fit in the bottom of the nostril, where viruses collect.

When he felt a tickle in his nose like a cold about to start, he rubbed the copper gently in his nose for 60 seconds.

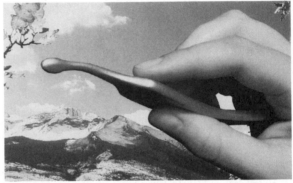

**New research: Copper kills viruses and bacteria.**

"It worked!" he exclaimed. "The cold never happened. I used to get 2-3 bad colds every year. Now I use my device whenever I feel a sign I am about to get sick."

He hasn't had a cold in 10 years.

After his first success with it, he asked relatives and friends to try it. They all said it worked, so he patented CopperZap® and put it on the market.

Soon hundreds of people had tried it. 99% said copper worked if they used it right away at the first sign of bad germs, like a tickle in the nose or a scratchy throat.

As thousands more tried it, some found other things they could use it against.

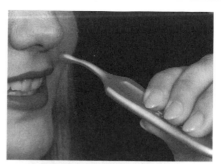

# IT'S

A LEGENDARY EARLY-
20TH-CENTURY TIMEKEEPER
WOULD HAVE LOVED
THE CLOCK OF THE LONG NOW.
OR WOULD SHE?

## ABOUT TIME!

*John Arnold
No. 485*

We all have our time machines. Some take
us back—they're called memories.
Some take us forward—they're called dreams.
*–Jeremy Irons, English actor (b. 1948)*

# JUST LIKE **CLOCKWORK**

As recently as 100 years ago, the world struggled to know what time it was. In London, those who could afford it bought the time of day every week.

Once a week for years, Ruth Belville (1854–1943) would stand at the entryway of a London watchmaker. When the door opened, the storekeeper would greet her with, "Good morning, Miss Belville. How is Arnold today?" Ruth would reply: "Good morning! Arnold is 4 seconds fast." She then would reach into her handbag, grab a pocket watch named Arnold, and pass it to him.

The horologist would use the watch to check the store's main clock before returning the timepiece. Her transaction complete, Ruth would then proceed to other clients: posh shops and fine jewelers, factories and commercial buildings, railroad stations, banks, newspapers, taverns— even two millionaires.

Ruth was in the business of selling time. Knowing the exact hour and minute of the day required astronomical observations and calculations of the type made only by observatories such as the Royal Observatory in Greenwich, England. Without Ruth, people would have needed to travel to Greenwich to find out the proper time.

Every Monday, she would make the 3-hour journey from her cottage in Maidenhead to the Observatory. Reaching its gate by 9 o'clock, she would ring and be greeted by the gate porter. Having handed over her watch to an attendant, she would then have a spot of tea with the gate porter while her timepiece was being compared to the Observatory's master clock. The attendant would then return Arnold to her, along with a certificate stating the difference between its time and that of the Observatory's main clock. With these in hand, Ruth would proceed to her customers in London.

Her father, John Henry Belville (1795–1856), a meteorologist and senior astronomer at the Observatory, had started this peculiar business. The leadership

**155**

there had grown increasingly frustrated by the numerous interruptions caused by local astronomers desperate to know the precise time for their observational work. John had proposed a solution: Bring time to those who desired it.

**A**rnold, a highly accurate chronometer in a gold case, was formally known as John Arnold No. 485, after its maker, who had built it in 1786. Behind Arnold's white enamel face and gold hands sat a range of materials working in sync—brass gears, ruby pivots, and a steel spring.

Legend has it that Arnold had originally been designed as a gift for the Duke of Sussex, a son of George III. The duke thought that the watch was too big; he likened it to a "warming pan" and refused it. However, he was connected to the Observatory, which put Arnold on a path toward John's hands when the time distribution service was created.

John had the watch rebuilt and set into a silver case so that it would be less attractive to thieves. Eventually, providing accuracy to a tenth of a second, he purveyed time to nearly 200 customers who paid annually for his weekly service.

On July 13, 1856, John died, leaving only the watch (no pension) to his third wife, Maria Elizabeth. To support herself and her 2-year-old daughter, Ruth, Maria Elizabeth continued the business for the 100 or so subscribers at the time. (Although the telegraph and other means were by then able to provide the time, many Belville clients found their human connection to be more accurate and reliable.)

**M**aria Elizabeth retired in 1892, at which time Arnold was passed down to 38-year-old Ruth. Described as hale and hearty, Ruth was emotionally tough and resolute and projected a common touch as she moved through a world dominated by

men. Together, Arnold and Ruth—just as had the watch and her parents before her—became trusted fixtures in London life.

As the result of ever increasing competition from other time services using technologies such as the telegraph, wireless communication, and broadcast radio, Ruth was serving only about 50 customers when she retired in 1940. The events of World War II had made it unsafe for her to continue walking the streets—not to mention the fact that she was 86 years old. In total, the Belville family had been in the business of purveying time for nearly 104 years.

By the time of her death 3 years later, Ruth had arranged for Arnold to be donated to the Clockmakers' Company, the horologists' guild. Today, it resides in the Clockmakers' Museum at the Science Museum in London.

*–adapted from* The Alchemy of Us *by Ainissa Ramirez (© 2020 Ainissa Ramirez; published by The MIT Press)*

*(continued)*

Photo: Royal Observatory, Greenwich

TOGETHER, ARNOLD
AND RUTH BECAME
TRUSTED FIXTURES IN
LONDON LIFE.

# MARKING TIME

**H**undreds of feet inside a limestone mountain near Van Horn, Texas, a group of forward thinkers is marking time. They are building a roughly 200-foot-high clock designed to tick for 10,000 years inside a 500-foot vertical shaft carved out of the rock. Construction of The Clock of the Long Now (aka The 10,000-Year Clock) has been ongoing since 2018.

The project was conceived in the 1980s by computer engineer and inventor/designer Danny Hillis as a means to foster long-term thinking. It began to take shape in the '90s with the creation of the Long Now Foundation ("I want to build a clock that ticks once a year," Hillis wrote in 1995) and the eventual construction of an 8-foot-high prototype that began ticking on January 1, 2000.

Why 10,000 years? In an essay written on the Foundation's Web site, board member Kevin Kelly explains: "Ten thousand years is about the age of civilization, so a 10,000-year clock would measure out a future of civilization equal to its past."

With this in mind, the materials—corrosion-resistant, marine-grade, 316 stainless steel; stone; and high-tech ceramics—were chosen to ensure the timepiece's longevity in the dry, dark, stable-temperature environment. "Building something to last 10,000 years requires both a large dose of optimism and a lot of knowledge," observes Kelly.

The Clock of the Long Now will be powered by the Sun and, occasionally, the people who visit it. Its parts—many of which are being machined and assembled in California and Washington state—include a 10,000-pound drive weight (a bronze egg about the size of a small car, filled with concrete); a 6-foot-long titanium pendulum assembly; giant gears, some of which are more than 8 feet in diameter and weigh 1,000 pounds; and, finally, the Geneva wheels that will calculate the more than 3.5 million different chime sequences—one for each day that it is visited over the 10 millennia.

Its 8-foot-diameter face will display actual/current time, and six dials will display the year, century, horizons (revealing the Sun and Moon's rise and set), Sun's position, lunar phase, and stars of the night sky, respectively. At the face's center, a black dome will reveal the day or night sky.

**C**urrent time will always be kept on the clock, but it will be displayed only when the clock is manually "wound." Getting there to do this, however, will not be easy. The entrance is about 1,500 feet above the valley floor, a full day's hike by the Foundation's estimate. Once inside, hikers will travel through a series of tunnels and up steps carved into the mountain (by a special rock-slicing robot), eventually coming to the winding station, where two or three people will be needed to push the capstan that lifts the 5-ton weight.

As of June 2022, the time of the clock's anticipated completion had not yet been announced, although plans for a second one in eastern Nevada had been discussed. Observers may be justified in wondering whether this second endeavor will be a concrete proposal or is simply the result of a group of forward thinkers passing the time. Indeed, only time will tell. ∎

*–Tim Goodwin*

**Tim Goodwin,** associate editor of *The Old Farmer's Almanac,* is usually on time—or so he claims.

"TEN THOUSAND YEARS IS ABOUT THE AGE OF CIVILIZATION, SO A 10,000-YEAR CLOCK WOULD MEASURE OUT A FUTURE OF CIVILIZATION EQUAL TO ITS PAST."

# PROPITIOUS PLANTING DAYS

by Heidi Stonehill

To every thing there is a season, yes, but often there is also a best time or day or tried-and-true planting method passed down through generations of gardeners. (Local weather conditions may be a secondary consideration.) Many of today's gardeners swear by these traditions.

## PLANTING BY THE CALENDAR

**FEBRUARY 14:**
**VALENTINE'S DAY**
Planting peas on this day is believed to bring good luck. Lettuce is traditionally planted on this day.

**MARCH 1-3:**
**BLIND DAYS**
Considered unlucky days to plant seeds.

**GOOD FRIDAY (FRIDAY BEFORE EASTER)**
Folklore tells us that Good Friday is the best day to plant any crop that you want to flourish, including peas, beans, flax, and potatoes. Also, parsley is

said to germinate faster if planted on this day, as the devil holds no power over it at this time.

**MARCH 17:**
**ST. PATRICK'S DAY**
Plant peas on this day, and St. Patrick will bless your garden. Sweet peas planted on this day are said to be especially healthy and

fragrant. This is also a traditional day to plant potatoes, and it is said that if you plant cabbage today, especially before dawn while wearing nightclothes, it will prosper.

**MARCH 21:**
**ST. BENEDICT'S FEAST DAY**
Plant onion sets now for an excellent yield. (St. Benedict is also honored on July 11, but because onions are light sensitive, March 21 is more favorable.)

**MAY 1:**
Cucumbers and watermelons planted before sunrise on this day yield prolifically. Folklore says that if you wear your nightclothes while sowing, the plants will be insect-free.

**MAY 11, 12, 13:**
**THREE CHILLY SAINTS**
The Three Chilly (or Ice or Frost) Saints are traditionally the days on which falls the last cold, or frost, spell before planting season begins and the three coldest days of May. Tradition recommends planting after these days to be sure that plants will be safe from cold and frost damage. In Germany, these days are called *Eismänner* (Iceman Days). Farmers did not plant vulnerable seedlings before the Icemen had come and gone.

**JUNE 29:**
**ST. PAUL'S FEAST DAY**
This is a good day to plant lavender:
*For lavender, bushy,*
*sweet and tall,*

*Tend upon the*
*feast of Paul.*

**JULY 25:**
Plant turnips on this day for success, no matter the weather.
*Sow your turnips the*
*25th of July,*
*You'll make a crop,*
*wet or dry.*

**AUGUST 10:**
**ST. LAWRENCE'S FEAST DAY**
For sweet turnips, plant them on this day.

## PLANTING BY THE QUIRKY LORE

• Swear at basil when planting it. Ancient Greeks and Romans believed that shouting curses at basil while sowing the seeds helped it to thrive. The French phrase *semer le basilic* (literally, "sowing basil") means to rant and rave.

• When broadcasting turnip or corn seed, recite a ditty, a reminder that not all of the seeds will develop into plants that survive to harvest.

**FOR TURNIP:** *One for the fly, one for the devil, and one for I.*

**FOR CORN:** *One for the mouse, one for the crow, one to rot, and one to grow.* Or a variant: *One for the blackbird, one for the crow, one for the cutworm, and two [or three] to grow.*

• Avoid laughing while sowing corn, or the kernels will be irregularly spaced on the cob.

• When planting a peach tree, bury old leather shoes or boots near the roots to give the plant a nutrient boost.

• You must be angry when planting peppers, or they won't grow.

• Plant sweet peas in rows running north to south for best blooms.

• Do not plant onions with potatoes; as a Southern tradition says, "The potatoes will cry their eyes out." ■

**Heidi Stonehill,** a senior editor at *The Old Farmer's Almanac,* laughs at her corncobs with unevenly spaced kernels: "It's part of the joy of gardening!"

# SNEEZE, WHEEZE, ITCH, DRIP:
## IT MUST BE HAY FEVER.

### BY CASTLE FREEMAN JR.

WHEN FLOWERS BLOOM,
**I HOPE YOU'LL NOT SNEEZE,**
AND MAY YOU ALWAYS HAVE
**SOMEONE TO SQUEEZE!**
*–IRISH BLESSING*

Among the multitude of tiresome but nonlethal ailments that famously trouble mankind, hay fever is something of a paradox. It's not a fever, and it has nothing much to do with hay.

It was originally believed by many to be caused by an effluvium—a smell or release of unhealthy air—in and around agricultural mowings. In reality, it's caused not by any infection but by the body's defensive allergic response, usually to various kinds of plant pollen and mold spores. Mistaking these for conventional pathogens like viruses and germs, the body reacts by producing histamines, irritating chemical compounds associated with the immune system, which in turn bring on the sneezing, wheezing, dripping, itching, and other woefully familiar symptoms of the complaint.

The role of pollen in causing hay fever explains why the condition is a summer affliction. Summer—when many trees, flowers, grasses, and other plants are producing pollen—is when *"aestival catarrh"* flourishes. (That's an old-fashioned Latinate name for hay fever; modern medical science calls it "allergic rhinitis.")

But specifically which plants' pollens are the allergens that give rise to hay fever's reaction has been a matter for debate among sufferers and scientists alike and brings up a curious fact about the condition: Hay fever is deceitful. Not only does it afflict us; it decoys us into throwing the blame for our affliction on an innocent party.

In the case of hay fever, the harmless but conspicuous decoy that takes the rap for the allergic reaction behind the malady is goldenrod *(Solidago),* whose familiar large, bright yellow flower clusters on their heavy, nodding heads deck the roadsides and pastures from about midsummer to autumn. People see goldenrod's abundance, note its flowers' appearance at around the beginning of hay fever season, and easily connect the two. *(continued)*

**THE ROLE OF POLLEN IN CAUSING HAY FEVER EXPLAINS WHY THE CONDITION IS A SUMMER AFFLICTION.**

163

Unfortunately, they connect wrong. In fact, goldenrod has little role in causing hay fever. Its pollen is sticky, heavy, and relatively sparse. It is spread by hitching rides on passing animals, birds, and insects and isn't easily inhaled.

The principal hay fever allergen is the pollen of a different plant altogether, one that is little noticed: ragweed *(Ambrosia),* a plain Jane of a species, gray and bushy, whose pollen appears at around the same time as goldenrod's. Unlike that of goldenrod, however, ragweed's pollen, which it produces in enormous quantities, is a light dust and spreads for miles on the wind.

Ragweed and other air- and windborne pollen producers, including birch and ash trees, and molds are the main sources of hay fever's symptoms. This is the reason that the complaint is most common in dry, warm, windy locations. Many sufferers have noticed how, in a dry, sneezable summer, a day or two of steady rain—which effectively hoses down the air and temporarily washes the pollen away—can bring them welcome, although temporary, relief.

Epidemiologically, hay fever is more than a passing nuisance. The American Academy of Allergy, Asthma, & Immunology now estimates that about 7.4 percent of the U.S. population is more or less affected. That's 24 million runny noses; 48 million itchy, weeping eyes; and some astronomical number of sniffles, snorts, and sneezes. Nor are U.S. residents uniquely subject to the condition. One in five Canadians gets it, as well (although ragweed is not as dominant a cause of hay fever in the provinces as it is to the south).

### THE AFFLICTION'S ARISTOCRATIC ORIGINS

In the Old World, the British would seem to suffer even more from hay fever than we do, with one in four in the United Kingdom experiencing

**IN THE U.S., 24 MILLION RUNNY NOSES AND 48 MILLION ITCHY EYES CAN BE ATTRIBUTED TO HAY FEVER EVERY YEAR.**

symptoms, according to a recent report by the BBC. Perhaps it's by a kind of medico-historical karma that hay fever should be prevalent in Great Britain, for it was there that the malady was first investigated and understood scientifically. In 1819, John Bostock (1773–1846), a London physician and researcher— and lifelong hay fever sufferer— published the first authoritative, systematic account of the complaint.

Bostock described the symptoms of hay fever for the first time, which in Britain came to sometimes be called "Bostock catarrh." His scientific paper, titled "Case of a Periodical Affection of the Eyes and Chest," presented a case history that, unbeknownst to its readers, was in fact Bostock's own. The paper established hay fever as a disease entity. Bostock did not, however, suspect the relationship between hay fever and plant pollen, a discovery made 30 years later by another medical Briton, Charles H. Blackley, a physician in Manchester.

In Britain, by the middle of the 19th century, hay fever was well known and had even achieved a measure of celebrity, having taken on the character and reputation of a fashionable disease, like gout. An 1830s monarch, King William IV, was known to have been a sufferer. Blackley wrote in 1873 that most of his patients tended to be either doctors or members of the clergy. Hay fever was "an aristocratic disease," he said, that was "almost wholly confined to the upper classes of society." (Did Blackley reflect that disease in general has a curious affinity for patients who can afford to pay the physician? We can't be sure.)

On our side of the water, the idea of hay fever as a marker of class superiority was soon put in service of a characteristically American purpose: making a buck. Catering to hay fever victims' hypothetical gentility and comparative wealth became a thriving corner of the real estate business. John Bostock had noticed that his own hay fever symptoms were greatly relieved by sea air. In the 19th and early 20th centuries, specialized resorts, hotels, inns, sanitariums, campgrounds, and the like were built all over the United States, especially in mountain and seaside settings, and advertised as havens of summer refuge in low-pollen surroundings. The U.S. Hay Fever Association was organized in 1874 to support victims, often known as "hayfeverites," and promote such facilities to them. Indeed, hay fever became almost a way of life. *(continued)*

**"HAPPY HAYFEVERITES"**
*WASHINGTON EVENING STAR*, SEPTEMBER, 1908

Today, the hayfeverites and their specialized amenities are part of history. Hay fever itself continues, of course, and may even be expanding its reach due to climate change. The medical economics of hay fever have also altered. A bottle of nonprescription antihistamine tablets does a pretty good job of alleviating the worst effects of pollen allergens—and at a rather lower cost than summering in the White Mountains of New Hampshire or on the coast of Maine.

Gone, too, sadly, is the prestige of hay fever, its putative social cachet. Nowadays, evidently, anybody can have it. ∎

Vermont novelist, writer, and keen observer **Castle Freeman Jr.** was for decades the author of our annual "Farmer's Calendar" columns.

**HAY FEVER HAD BECOME ALMOST A WAY OF LIFE.
TODAY, THE HAYFEVERITES ARE PART OF HISTORY.**

# A-CHOO FACTS FOR YOU

## NATURAL REMEDIES

- Naturalist Pliny the Elder (A.D. 23–79) believed that kissing the nostrils of a mule cured hay fever.

- Sip stinging nettle tea to relieve symptoms.

- Eat pineapple, whose enzyme bromelain has anti-inflammatory effects.

- Consume yogurt containing live cultures or foods rich in omega-3 fatty acids (salmon, halibut, tuna, cod, sardines, shrimp, and clams).

- Take one granule of local bee pollen before hay fever season. If no reaction occurs, increase the amount of bee pollen slowly, working your way up to 1 teaspoon per day. (Combine pollen with juice, if desired.)

## PRECAUTIONS

- Stay indoors when the pollen count is high (19th-century physician George M. Beard recommended a "cool, closed, dark room").

- When driving, keep car windows closed.

- When outdoors, wear a hat and wraparound sunglasses.

- When you come in from outdoors, wash your hands and face and run a damp cloth over your hair; take a shower; and/or change clothing.

- Change your pillowcase often.

## CURIOSITIES

- Interglacial deposits in Quebec have been found to contain ragweed pollen (*Ambrosia* spp.) dating from more than 60,000 years ago.

- In North America, the pollen season starts, on average, 3 days sooner than it did in the 1990s. The season is lengthening more at higher latitudes (roughly north of 44°N).

- Symptoms can be felt after exposure to as few as 5 to 20 ragweed pollen grains per million; pollen levels are highest near dawn.

Illustrations: emma/Getty Images

# EGG HATCHING 101

### WHEN TO HATCH EGGS

*If there are thunderstorms while eggs are "setting," the eggs will not hatch.*

–FOLKLORE

Some chicken keepers follow the seasons, purchasing and setting eggs during March and April. However, for centuries, traditional farmers have set eggs year-round and specifically on days when the Moon is growing from new to full in one of three zodiac signs. This practice, which derives partially from folklore and partially from hard-earned experience, follows the belief that the Moon influences the outcome of certain tasks. In this case, the thinking is that chicks hatched from eggs that are set when the waxing (increasing) Moon is in the astrological (not astronomical) signs of Cancer, Scorpio, or Pisces will be healthier and mature more quickly.

The propitious, or favorable, signs and dates for setting eggs this year can be found on page 225. The following steps blend folk adages and practical advice. *(continued)*

One of the most enjoyable parts
of keeping backyard chickens
is hatching chicks and watching them
grow. Hatching chicks requires time,
equipment, energy, and—some
believe—a brightening Moon.

BY CHRIS LESLEY

## NOT JUST ANY EGGS

*Eggs carried in a woman's bonnet
invariably make pullets.*
–Ozark folklore

To hatch chicks, you need eggs that have been fertilized by a rooster. Eggs from a grocery store are not fertilized. If you have a rooster in your flock, the eggs laid by your hens will be fertilized and ready for incubation. If you don't have a rooster but want to hatch fertilized eggs, you can:

• Contact chicken keepers in your area and ask them if you can buy a few fertilized eggs. Purchasing eggs locally will help to ensure that they travel safely.

• Buy fertilized eggs from a breeder and have them shipped through the mail or a courier service. This is ideal if you want to raise a rare breed. However, eggs don't travel well. They may be poorly handled and get jostled in the shipping process, resulting in eggs that don't hatch.

## CHOOSING AN INCUBATOR

*To break a hen from setting, put an
alarm clock in the nest and let it go off.*
–FOLKLORE

Incubators help to maintain the proper temperature and level of humidity needed for eggs to hatch properly. They can range in price from under $100 to several times that; a less expensive model requires more work by the chicken keeper (e.g., manually turning the eggs, monitoring temperature and humidity). A basic, still-air incubator creates warm air but does not circulate it. This can result in cold spots within the incubator, and these may result in the failure of eggs to hatch.

A more expensive forced-air incubator circulates warm air inside the incubator. The result of this is more consistent temperature and humidity levels, which may result in better hatches. *(continued)*

INCUBATORS HELP
TO MAINTAIN THE PROPER
ENVIRONMENT NEEDED
FOR EGGS TO HATCH.

### ESSENTIAL TOOLS

*Cover newly hatched chicks with a sieve and place them in the sunshine a little while, and they will live.*
—FOLKLORE

You will also need a thermometer, a hygrometer (to measure humidity), and a candling device. Some incubators are equipped with a thermometer and hygrometer. However, it's a good idea to double-check the temperature and humidity with separate meters.

A candling device is used to shine light through an egg to ensure that the embryos are growing properly. A flashlight can work perfectly, but some chicken keepers prefer using a specialized piece of equipment to do this.

### PREPARATION

*Setting a hen on a cloudy day will cause all of the chicks to be black.*
—PERSIAN FOLKLORE

Set up the incubator several days in advance of setting the eggs to ensure that it is working properly. The temperature inside the incubator should be between 99° and 102°F. In the first 17 days, the relative humidity in the incubator should be between 50 and 55 percent; on day 18, it should be raised to 70 percent.

### DAY 1: SETTING EGGS

*It's bad luck to set an even number of eggs.*
—FOLKLORE

At a minimum, six eggs should be placed in an incubator at one time. Before placing the eggs in the incubator, use a pencil to draw a mark on one side of each egg. The marks will be helpful when it comes time to turn the eggs. Place each egg in the incubator with its large end up and smaller end down.

### DAYS 1 TO 18: TURNING EGGS

*Never set a hen or an incubator when the wind is blowing from the south, or mighty few of the eggs will hatch.*
—OZARK FOLKLORE

During the first 18 days, each egg should be turned three to five times a day, marking each turn (the marks help to keep track). Turning an egg ensures

DRAWING A MARK ON ONE SIDE OF EACH EGG HELPS WHEN TURNING THEM.

HATCHING YOUR OWN CHICKS IS A DEMANDING BUT ULTIMATELY REWARDING PROCESS.

that the developing chick will not stick to the side of the shell and is resting on top of the yolk.

### DAYS 7 TO 10: CANDLING EGGS

*Candle an egg; if the space
is on the side, it will hatch a hen;
on the top, a rooster.*
−FOLKLORE

In the middle of the incubation period, embryos should be monitored by using a candling device. Several eggs should be checked at once, but none should be out of the incubator for more than 10 minutes.

Blood vessels inside the egg indicate the presence of a healthy embryo. Eggs that are clear on the inside or display a red ring in the egg should be removed from the incubator, as the embryos inside these have died.

### DAYS 18 TO 21: HATCHING EGGS

*Do not set eggs so that they will hatch
during Dog Days [July 3–August 11].*
−FOLKLORE

Between days 18 and 21, the chicks in the incubator are preparing to hatch. The turning process should be stopped on day 18, and the eggs should be left resting on their pointed/narrow end. On day 21, the chicks will probably begin to hatch, but don't be alarmed if they take a bit longer.

Remember: Do not touch chicks when they are hatching or to help them hatch. Pulling off bits of shell that may be attached to a chick can cause fatal bleeding. Leave chicks alone to hatch.

Hatching usually lasts 5 to 7 hours but can take an entire day.

Hatching your own chicks is a demanding but ultimately rewarding process. With the proper materials and by taking into consideration the Moon's phase and position in the zodiacal sky, backyard chicken keepers will likely find themselves with a flock of happy and healthy chicks. ∎

**Chris Lesley,** a fourth-generation chicken keeper, teaches people worldwide how to raise happy, healthy chickens. Her Web site is Chickensandmore.com.

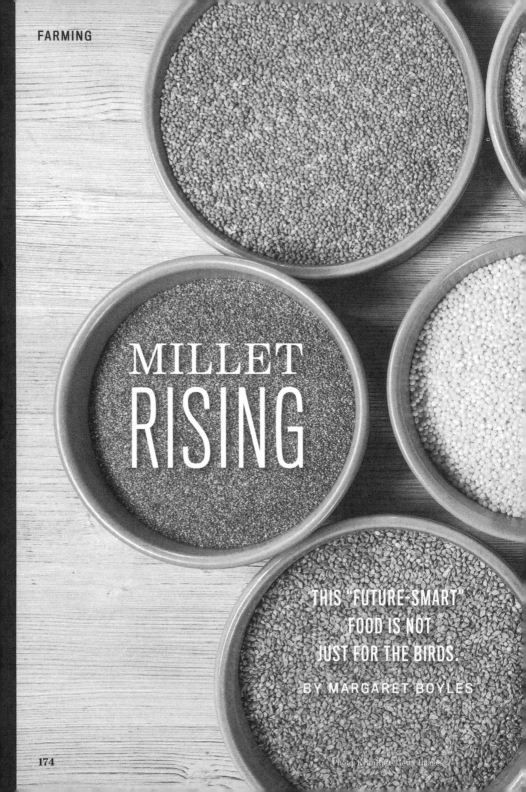

# MILLET
# RISING

THIS "FUTURE-SMART"
FOOD IS NOT
JUST FOR THE BIRDS.

BY MARGARET BOYLES

Stop fretting over quinoa and switch to millets.
–Sangeetha Devi Dundoo, on the health and cost benefits of millets, in Thehindu.com

Millet farm in China

E ndorsing a proposal from India, the United Nations Food and Agriculture Organization (FAO) has designated 2023 as the International Year of Millets.

That's right, millets. "Millet" is an umbrella term embracing as many as 20 species and thousands of local varieties of the small, round, cereal grains that originated independently in China, South Asia, and Africa.

Agricultural, public health, and food security experts use words such as "undervalued," "underresearched," and "underutilized" to describe millets, yet these terms fail to adequately describe how versatile and primed for the future this staple crop really is.

Although only seven species of millet are grown commercially, farmers and subsistence growers around the world grow locally adapted varieties of these ancient cereal grains not only as staple foods but also for grazing, hay, livestock feeds, rotation crops, and cover crops.

All millets are true grains, members of the Poaceae plant family that also includes rice, wheat, corn, oats, rye, and barley. Although millets are considered minor crops globally, people in many regions of Africa, South and Southeast Asia, and the Far East rely on them today as primary staple foods, just as they have for millennia.

Millets thrive in hot, arid environments and lower-fertility soils increasingly unable to support wheat, rice, or corn. They resist insect pests and diseases, and because they mature much more quickly than the dominant grains, millets allow growers in many areas to harvest two or three grain crops in a single growing season or use millet to make up for a failed crop.

This is why, although in many parts of the world millets are considered food for the poor, today they qualify as what the FAO calls a "future-smart" food, well suited to becoming a staple human food crop in an era of climate change.

## MILLET IN THE USA

"Proso millet came to the western U.S. in the late 1800s with immigrant farmers from Europe," says Ron Meyer, a crop advisor with the Colorado State University Cooperative Extension, adding that more than half of the U.S. millet crop is grown in Colorado.

"Early farmers grew it for grazing and hay," he reports. In the late 1960s, a growing demand for birdseed led to an increase in millet acreage. Then, in the 1990s, new research into celiac disease (an autoimmune condition triggered by ingesting gluten, a protein in wheat and some other cereal grains) brought attention to

gluten-free cereals like millet. Because food-grade millet was more profitable than birdseed, acreage increased again.

"But millet is still a

### Is Millet the Oldest Grain Crop?

- From a site in northeastern China, archaeologists have identified proso millet, the primary species grown in the United States, as the first cereal crop that humans domesticated more than 10,000 years ago.
- In northwestern China, a different team unearthed what they believe to be the world's oldest noodles, made from two species of millet.
- Archaeologists have also found evidence of millet beer-brewing in China more than 5,000 years ago.

minor crop," Meyer observes, adding: "We're always looking for improved varieties and new markets."

Among the world's most knowledgeable and enthusiastic proponents of food-grade millet, Dr. Dipak Santra, alternative crops breeder at the University of Nebraska–Lincoln, is eager to develop these new varieties with improved agronomic and nutritional traits. "I'm the only proso millet breeder in an American public university and maybe anywhere in the world," he notes.

This is not a boast. Instead, Santra is commenting on the lack of even small amounts

Dipak Santra at Lane and Chris Stum's millet farm in Towner, CO

of the research funding needed to allow him and others working in the public sphere to acquire the modern genomic tools that would enable rapid development of new millet varieties. In the United States, millet hasn't yet qualified for the public funding that has enabled decades of breeding improvements and marketing initiatives for wheat, corn, and rice.

Santra goes on to note the devilish chicken-and-egg dilemma plaguing millet farmers around the world: "Even if I had the funding, what's the use of developing new millet varieties unless we have a corresponding growth of the long-term, reliable markets that would encourage farmers to grow them?

There are no public marketing initiatives for millet, either."

There are, however, enthusiastic growers and an expanding network of handlers, processors, and markets.

## AN INGREDIENT GUY

Clay Smith, who owns Eastern Colorado Seeds in Burlington, Colorado, has developed markets for proso millet across the Middle East, Europe, Indonesia, and Japan, as well as at home. "U.S. markets are still dominated by livestock feeds and birdseed," he comments, "but domestic sales of food-grade millet picked up during the pandemic—primarily, I think, because people were staying home and

cooking more."

"I'm an ingredient guy," Smith continues, adding that his customers include bird- and animal-feed manufacturers as well as energy bar, granola, and pasta makers and even a whiskey producer. To compete with larger seed companies, Smith has developed an unusual marketing strategy. "I travel around and knock on doors a lot," he reports, noting that he often links his seed grain customers to innovative end markets and gets a farm sale by guaranteeing the farmer a stable, long-term market. "All the farmer has to do is grow the crop," he says.

## COOPERATIVE SALES

Three generations of the Hediger family operate Golden Prairie Millet, which is based in Nunn, Colorado. The operation includes their own farms in Colorado and Montana, plus a loose collaboration of other organic farmers who market food-grade millet in all 50 states. *(continued)*

Golden Prairie Millet crop

Millet mango avocado cucumber salad

Millet pudding with caramelized bananas

## "The Workhorse of the Kitchen"

According to registered dietician Dr. Melissa Wdowik, who teaches nutrition at East Carolina State University and maintains a private consulting practice, "Millet is very nutritious: high in fiber, protein, many minerals, B vitamins, and many antioxidants.

"It's also gluten-free, easily digested, and good for your gut—acting as a prebiotic that feeds friendly bacteria there.

"I love the consistency of cooked millet—neither firm nor mushy—and the fact that it doesn't have much flavor of its own but takes on the flavors of other foods that you cook with it."

Furthermore, Wdowik adds, "It's inexpensive, readily available, and easy to prepare. Use it in place of rice or other grains in stir-fries, soups, and crockpot recipes; serve it for breakfast instead of oatmeal; substitute it for bread crumbs as a topping; work it into desserts; serve it cold in salads. It's so versatile that some cooks have begun calling it 'the workhorse of the kitchen.'"

Millet-based beers from Holidaily Brewing Co.

The Hedigers have been organic wheat farmers since 1989. Three years later, Jean Hediger says, "we got into growing millet because organic production requires crop rotation. Since we plant wheat in the fall, we needed a spring crop."

Already marketing her wheat crop through United Natural Foods, Inc. (UNFI), she started moving the millet through the nationwide distributor as well. "UNFI started asking for more and more millet. We couldn't meet the demand, so we reached out to growers in Nebraska, Kansas, Wyoming, Montana, and the Dakotas and banded together with other organic family farms. As we grew, each farmer allocated more acres to millet. Today, we clean, dehull, package, and market millet from as many as 20 farms, collectively totaling up to 40,000 acres," Hediger notes.

## FOCUS ON FERMENTING

It seems that everywhere farmers and small landholders grow millet, people ferment it into gluten-free beers and wines. Among the best known and most successful of these in the United States is Holidaily Brewing Company in Golden, Colorado. Holidaily was founded in 2016 by Karen Hertz, a craft beer enthusiast who, after surviving both melanoma and thyroid cancer in her early 30s, followed her doctors' recommendations to adopt a gluten-free diet. After taste-testing many gluten-free beers and finding them lacking, she began learning the processes of brewing them herself, eventually partnering with Twila Soles, founder of Grouse Malt House, who'd begun making gluten-free malts using only millet and buckwheat.

"Millet-based beers are much harder to brew than traditional ones," observes

Holidaily's brewmeister, Alan Windhausen, who abandoned plans for medical school in favor of earning a master brewer's certificate at the University of California–Davis. He has worked with Colorado State to develop brewery equipment suitable for millet. "One of the cool things about using millet as a malt is that we can create flavors not available to classic malts," he reports.

## GRAIN ON THE GROW

Global food-supply experts hope that the adjectives "resilient," "sustainable," and "nutritious" will soon come to define millet. Folks whom we interviewed in early to mid-2021 described networks of players beginning to form, creating a still-nascent global infrastructure to elevate these ancient grains. They predicted that food consumers would eventually see an uptick in millet flours and flour blends; millet puffs, flakes, chips, crisps, and crackers; millet energy bars, veggie burgers, and high-end restaurant entrées; mil-

let wines and whiskeys; and millet extracts in hair and skin-care products and perhaps medicines. Some cited ongoing research suggesting that some species of millet may even provide feedstocks for second-generation biofuels made from crop residues that don't com-

### Going With the Grain

- In China, the elderly are advised to eat a bowl of millet before going to bed in order to get a good night's sleep.
- In Summer 2021, India's first "grain ATM" was set up in Gurugram; it can dispense up to 154 pounds of wheat, rice, and millet.

Pearl millet growing in India

Photo: DEEP CHAND/Getty Images

pete with food for land.

"The opportunities for food-grade millet expansion are great," says Clay Smith. "Millet requires as little as a quarter of the input costs of raising a bushel of corn."

Third-generation Towner, Colorado, millet farmer Chris Stum, although disappointed by the failed passage of a 2018 statewide millet marketing order (a legal agreement that would tax all millet farmers in the region, enabling them to use the assessments for research and marketing initiatives), nonetheless echoes Smith's enthusiasm. "I think that we'll see global marketing opportunities expanding for millet as a staple crop for feeding families and livestock," he says. "I'd also like to include it as part of the global environmental conversation, for the important role that it can play in restoring the land and increasing its value." ■

**Margaret Boyles,** a resident of New Hampshire for more than five decades, is an avid gardener who has recently developed a fondness for millet recipes.

# HANGING BY A SILKEN THREAD

## FACTS AND FOLKLORE ABOUT NATURE'S WEB GURUS

BY PAULA E. CUSHING, PH.D.

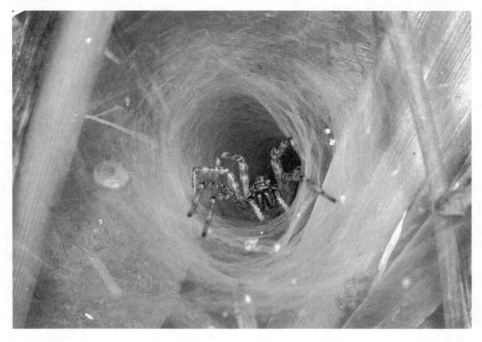

SPIDERS IN THE
FUNNEL WEB FAMILY
(AGELENIDAE) LIVE
IN A SILKEN FUNNEL
WITH A "PLATFORM"
OF SILK AT THE
ENTRANCE.

**S**piders manufacture and use silk in weird and wonderful ways. If Hollywood aimed for accuracy in the *Spiderman* movies, Peter Parker would not release silk from his wrists. Silk would come from an entirely different region of Peter's body. A real spider's silk glands are in the abdomen, and the silk is released from structures at the very rear end of a spider called "spinnerets." Let us all be thankful that, in this case, Hollywood took some liberties with the truth.

## NOZZLED SPINNERETS

Spiders have been on Earth for over 350 million years, and they have been producing silk for all of this time. Inside the abdomen, male and female spiders have up to six different kinds of silk glands, each secreting and storing a slightly different composition of proteinaceous silk. The spider squeezes the liquid protein out of each silk gland into tubes leading to the spinnerets. On the surface of the spinnerets are tiny spigots, each shaped somewhat like the nozzle of a garden hose. The silk protein is still in liquid form as it emerges from the spider

Photo: Satoshi Kuribayashi/Minden Pictures

but changes to a solid when a droplet is put under tension. A spider attaching the droplet to a surface and moving away or pulling the silk from its body using its rear legs provides enough tension to change the liquid droplet to a solid strand of silk.

## ARACHNONAUTS

Although much of their behavior is instinctive, spiders (of the class Arachnida) are amazingly adaptable and can even build fully functional webs in the zero gravity of space. In 1973, two orb-weaving spiders were sent up to the Skylab space station, where they both built functional orb (round) webs despite the lack of gravity cues or wind currents. Then, in both 2008 and 2011, a company called BioServe Space Technologies sent four more orb-weaving spiders to the International Space Station, where they were able to quickly adapt to conditions there.

## MATERIAL WITNESSES

Spider silk is considered the "Holy Grail" of material sciences. It is stronger by unit weight than steel and extremely elastic. For decades, scientists from labs all over the world have been studying spider silk to unlock the keys to its extraordinary properties with the thought that if a material with the same strength and elasticity as spider silk can be mass-manufactured, it could be used for lightweight bulletproof vests; strong, resilient parachutes; or strong natural fibers for medical surgery procedures. The uses of such a material are limited only by the imagination. However, spiders can not be raised en masse to harvest their silk. They are predators that readily cannibalize each other, so trying to rear them together to spool their silk results in one very fat and happy spider.

With the development of molecular research, scientists have determined what genes code for spider silk protein and have even inserted them into various organisms in hope of finding a way to mass-manufacture a material with the same properties as spider silk. A biotechnology company called Nexia has managed to insert the genetic coding for spider silk protein into cells of goats and reared a lineage of

### LITTLE MISS MUFFET'S DISTRESS

Legend has it that the subject of the eponymous nursery rhyme was actually a child named Patience, the stepdaughter of Thomas Muffet, a 16th-century physician who, some believe, used spiders and spiderwebs in his remedies. At that time, a traditional cure for ague, or fever, was to swallow clean cobwebs; patients with a more serious condition might be advised to consume a live spider (wrapped discreetly in a crust of bread for those with weak constitutions). Is it any wonder, then, that the petite miss was frightened by the spider sitting beside her? Every time she got the sniffles, her stepdad probably made her swallow a spider.

## WOUNDED? THERE'S A WEB FOR THAT.

Spiders and their webs have been used for a variety of purposes throughout human history, including to bind wounds. This treatment is likely efficacious because the acidic nature of spider silk means that it is not prone to attack by bacteria or fungi. The next time that you get a cut, clean the wound and then bind it with a layer of spider silk. As long as the silk is fresh and not cluttered with insect carcasses, it can serve as an effective bandage.

## WEB WEATHER

Spiders spinning unusually large webs is a sign of a cold winter to come.

*Spiderwebs floating at autumn sunset / Bring a night frost, on this you may bet.*

Spiders move down from their webs before rain.

goats whose milk included spider silk proteins in liquid form. No lab or company has yet managed to do what spiders do naturally: transform the liquid protein into strands of silk.

## NOT-SO-TANGLED WEBS

To date, over 49,000 species of spiders have been described, and more are discovered every year. Not all weave webs, but they all produce silk. Those that do weave webs do not all make the same type of structure. Web-building spider families are often distinguished by the type of web that they weave, but all web forms have the same goal—to capture insect prey. Here are some examples:

• Spiders in the funnel web family (Agelenidae) live in a silken funnel with a "platform" of silk at the entrance. When an insect blunders onto the platform, the funnel web spider rushes over to bite and inject venom into the insect before then dragging it inside the funnel to be devoured.

• The ogre-faced spider, of the genus *Deinopis* (family Deinopidae), has huge front eyes and good eyesight. This spider hangs upside down in vegetation and uses the first two pairs of its eight legs to grip its square, postage stamp–size web. When it spots an insect walking on the forest floor, it pushes the square web onto the insect and twists the hapless prey into the silk.

• Most orb-weaving spiders in the family Araneidae build a vertically oriented, round web with the hub more or less in the middle, radii projecting outward, and rings of sticky spirals surrounding the hub. However, one kind of orb weaver in New Guinea builds an enormously long web with the hub far above most of the sticky spirals. Because of this web's unusual shape, it is called a "ladder web" and is very effective in capturing moths. Typically, moths can escape a sticky spiderweb because their scale-covered wings don't adhere well to the spirals. But when a moth flies into a ladder web, it topples down the surface of the elongated web, losing scales along the way, until its wings, devoid of their protective covering, get firmly stuck. The web owner can then take its time in coming close to bite its prey and wrap it in silk.

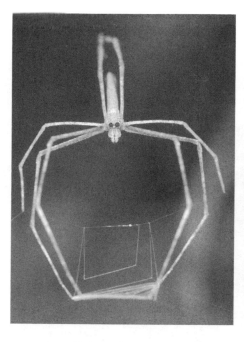 

• Other species of orb-weaving spiders in New Guinea and other parts of Australasia produce webs that are as big as 3 feet in diameter. Native people turn these to their advantage. They bend a flexible branch or bamboo stick into a loop and collect one or more of the giant orb webs, using this silken net to capture fish.

Spiders are real-life action heroes in the animal kingdom. Without them, we would be overwhelmed by insects. Arachnologists Martin Nyffeler of the University of Basel (Switzerland) and Klaus Birkhofer of the Brandenburg (Germany) University of Technology estimate that spiders worldwide catch 400 million to 800 million tons of insects every year! So, the next time that you see a spider in your home or outside, don't swat it or stomp on it. Thank it—it's doing you a service. ■

**THE OGRE-FACED SPIDER (LEFT) PUSHES ITS POSTAGE STAMP-SIZE SQUARE WEB ONTO AN INSECT AND TWISTS THE HAPLESS PREY INTO THE SILK.**

**MOST ORB-WEAVING SPIDERS (RIGHT) IN THE FAMILY ARANEIDAE BUILD A VERTICALLY ORIENTED, ROUND WEB WITH THE HUB MORE OR LESS IN THE MIDDLE.**

**Paula Cushing** is a museum curator and arachnologist living in Colorado. A past president of both the International Society of Arachnology and the American Arachnological Society, she has been researching spiders and other arachnids for decades.

# How Happy *Is* a Clam? (and So Forth)

## BY TIM CLARK

Reprinted from *The 1980 Old Farmer's Almanac.*

### HOW HAPPY IS A CLAM?

We will probably never know exactly what makes a clam happy, but people usually list a long life and true love among their hopes. Thus, by human standards, a clam has good reason to be happy because, according to Dr. Ida Thompson of Princeton University, the clam is the foxy grandpa of the invertebrate kingdom. Dr. Thompson has determined that a clam's bands correspond to the rings found in a tree trunk and can be used to determine its age. By this method, she has discovered that clams live as long as 150 years (assuming that they are not made into chowder), show no signs of aging (other than adding bands), and remain sexually active throughout their lives. In fact, Dr. Thompson is uncertain whether these clams ever die of old age.

### HOW MAD IS A WET HEN?

We called up the folks at Hubbard Farms in Walpole, New Hampshire, one of the nation's leading egg producers, and were asked to explain our business. We said we wanted to know how mad a wet hen becomes. After some confusion, we were referred to the Advertising Director. We repeated the question. There was a long pause.

"Can I get back to

Illustration: Tim Robinson

you?" he asked.

We assured him that he could.

Thirty minutes later, he called triumphantly with the information that indeed, hens do not like to get wet. "They sort of flick their feathers," he explained.

## HOW SCARCE ARE HEN'S TEETH?

Very scarce. In fact, hens do not have teeth. Some say that they were ground down during a severe rainstorm.

## HOW MUCH IS A HILL OF BEANS WORTH?

It depends on the size of the hill. If the hill were 50 feet high, with a diameter at its base of 200 feet, its volume would be 523,599 cubic feet, or 420,627 bushels. At $6.70 per bushel (the closing price of soybeans on the New York commodity exchange as of November 14, 1978), the hill would be worth $2,818,201. That most certainly ain't hay.

A bale of hay the same size would be worth only $390,953. Which just goes to prove that hay ain't worth beans.

## HOW OLD IS AN OLD SAW?

Ancient. Copper saws were first introduced by the Egyptians around 4000 B.C. They were used in the construction of the pyramids.

## HOW FAST IS GREASED LIGHTNING?

According to the *Encyclopedia Britannica*, lightning travels from its point of origin in the sky to Earth's surface at an average speed of 1.5 x $10^5$ meters per second, or about 335,000 miles per hour. Greased lightning is, of course, considerably swifter.

## CAN A SILK PURSE BE MADE OUT OF A SOW'S EAR?

No. But in 1921, Dr. Arthur D. Little of Cambridge, Massachusetts, boiled 1,000 sow's ears into a gelatinous substance, spun it into a fine thread, and produced two purses that had the look and feel of the finest silk. The project, undertaken by Dr. Little to prove that nothing is impossible, led to the development of such popular synthetic fabrics as nylon and rayon.

Dr. Little went on to found the internationally famous industrial consulting firm of Arthur D. Little Co. In 1977, a few engineers at that company decided to go the founder one better and had a contest to produce a flightworthy lead balloon. Three were eventually produced, using lead foil so delicate that "it would break if you breathed on it," according to one witness. One of the balloons was torn during inflation. The other two were successfully flown at the end of tethers. But in the process of reeling them in, one balloon broke away and disappeared over the Atlantic Ocean.

So far, nobody at A. D. Little has attempted to lead a horse to water and then make him drink. "This is not an industrial problem," sniffed a company spokesperson. ■

After publication of this, his first article, **Tim Clark** would go on to become a contributor to and an editor for *Yankee* magazine and *The Old Farmer's Almanac* for another 40 years.

# THE LITTLE-KNOWN JOURNEY OF WILLIE O'REE

## TO BREAK THE NHL'S COLOR BARRIER

BY THOMAS J. WHALEN

**A**lmost everybody knows about Jackie Robinson and the historic role that he played in integrating Major League Baseball. But mention Willie O'Ree, and you'll likely receive a blank look.

This may start to change. On January 19, 2022, the U.S. House of Representatives passed a bill awarding O'Ree the Congressional Gold Medal. A day earlier, the Boston Bruins had retired O'Ree's #22 sweater on the 64th anniversary of the night when the forward from New Brunswick, Canada, had become the first Black person to play in a National Hockey League game.

O'Ree had always felt that he possessed the talent to play in the NHL. A speedy skater with an intuitive feel for the game, O'Ree had played organized hockey since age 5 and scored 22 goals with 12 assists in his first professional season with the Quebec Aces.

His big break came when the Boston Bruins invited him to attend training camp before the start of the 1957–58 season. Although he failed to make the final cut, team officials were impressed enough by his overall performance that they told him that he needed only "a little more seasoning" to reach the big time. *(continued)*

**IN 2022, O'REE WAS AWARDED THE CONGRESSIONAL GOLD MEDAL.**

## "I'M JUST HAPPY TO GET A CHANCE UP HERE–THAT'S ABOUT ALL I CAN SAY."

"They knew what I could do," O'Ree later recalled in his memoir, *The Autobiography of Willie O'Ree: Hockey's Black Pioneer* (Somerville House Books, 2000).

Sure enough, that January, when the Boston Bruins became short a roster player, they called him up from their minor league club for a road contest against the Montreal Canadiens. O'Ree could barely control his excitement. "I could see fans pointing, 'There's that Black kid. He's up with the Bruins,'" O'Ree wrote.

Despite his nervousness, he did nothing to embarrass himself during a rare 3–0 Boston shutout over their hated archrivals. "O'Ree is not only fast, but he's a strong skater," Montreal general manager Frank Selke said after the game. "He looks as if he could go all night."

O'Ree suited up for only one more game as a Bruin that season before being returned to the minors. He was hardly crestfallen. "I'm just happy to get a chance up here—that's about all I can say," he told *The Boston Globe*.

Wearing #22 for the Bruins in 1960–61, O'Ree tallied four goals and 10 assists in 43 games. His first NHL score, a game-winner against Montreal at the Boston Garden on New Year's Day, 1961, proved memorable. On a breakaway, a teammate fed him a perfect pass, which he then deposited under the glove hand of Montreal goaltender Charlie Hodge. For his standout effort, O'Ree received a rousing standing ovation from the home crowd that lasted several minutes.

O'Ree wasn't so well received at other NHL venues. At New York City's venerable Madison Square Garden, for instance, fans showered him with

## BREAKAWAYS FOR #22

■ In 2008, Willie O'Ree, the descendant of people who were enslaved, was awarded the Order of Canada, the highest honor given to a Canadian civilian.

■ In 2018, the NHL introduced the Willie O'Ree Community Hero Award, presented annually to "an individual, who–through the game of hockey–has positively impacted his or her community, culture, or society."

■ O'Ree was inducted into the Hockey Hall of Fame class of

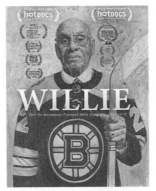

2018 as part of the "Builder" category, which honors those who have made significant contributions to the sport.

■ In 2020, a 90-minute feature film on O'Ree's life, titled *Willie*, was released. It is available on Amazon.

■ On January 18, 2022, the Boston Bruins retired O'Ree's #22 jersey, making him only the 12th player in team history to have his sweater hung in Boston/TD Garden.

racial insults before he even stepped onto the ice. In Chicago, he was targeted for abuse by bruising Blackhawks forward Eric "Elbows" Nesterenko. After calling O'Ree a common epithet, Nesterenko took the butt end of his stick and rammed it into O'Ree's unsuspecting face. A broken nose and two missing front teeth later, O'Ree had had enough. He took his stick and smashed Nesterenko over the head with it. O'Ree's teammates came rushing to his aid as both teams' benches emptied. What followed was a classic hockey donnybrook that ended with O'Ree being sent to the Bruins locker room for medical treatment.

**E**very time I went on the ice, I was faced with racial slurs because of my color," O'Ree admitted to an Anti-Defamation League Youth Congress gathering held in Boston in 2016. "I had black cats thrown on the ice, and people told me to go back to the cotton fields and pick cotton."

O'Ree claimed that he didn't mind. "I didn't let it hurt me," he recalled. "I let it go in one ear and out the other."

O'Ree's dream of hockey glory had almost been cut tragically short. While playing in a junior league game in Guelph, Ontario, as a 20-year-old, he lost most of the sight in his right eye after a deflected puck struck his face. Ignoring the doctor's advice to hang up his skates, O'Ree continued to play despite being at an obvious competitive disadvantage.

"I was a left-hand shot, and I was playing left wing, but I had no right eye," O'Ree explained. He didn't want others to know of his handicap, lest it scare teams away from employing him. "It was my secret," he confided.

**W**hen the Bruins traded O'Ree to the Canadiens before the start of the 1961–62 season, he was personally devastated. Having won five of the preceding six Stanley Cup championships, Montreal was an elite team that had no room for O'Ree on its roster. As a result, O'Ree spent the remainder of his career playing on a series of minor league clubs, including the Los Angeles Blades of the Western Hockey League. He was a major standout for Los Angeles, scoring a career-high 38 goals in 1964–65, but the NHL never gave him a second look.

O'Ree did, however, serve as an inspiration for future NHL players of color like Jarome Iginla and Mike Grier.

"I'm in awe knowing what he went through," Iginla told *USA Today* in 2008. "There is a lot of trash-talking going on [in the game], and I can't imagine what he must have gone through."

O'Ree himself has voiced few regrets. He did, after all, defy the odds, and he'll forever be known as "the Jackie Robinson of hockey." ■

**Thomas J. Whalen** is an associate professor of social sciences at Boston University. This article was originally published on THE CONVERSATION (theconversation.com).

**O'REE SERVED AS AN INSPIRATION FOR FUTURE NHL PLAYERS OF COLOR.**

# FAMILY TREASURES

## HOW TO DOWNSIZE, ORGANIZE, AND SAFEGUARD YOUR KEEPSAKES AND COLLECTIONS

### BY DENISE MAY LEVENICK

Facing a mountain of memorabilia is always a daunting experience. Still, reducing and protecting your family treasures to create a meaningful archive can be done—and here's how to do it.

## KEEP ONLY WHAT'S IMPORTANT

Divide your materials into three categories . . .

- **VITAL** (e.g., photos, letters): These items give key genealogical information about a person, place, or event or confirm or refute family lore.
- **ADDS "COLOR"** (e.g., a brochure about a favorite vacation spot): These artifacts add context and weight to your family history.
- **NOT ARCHIVAL** (e.g., receipts, bill stubs): If something doesn't add personal information, it's probably not worth saving. If it interests only you or perhaps your insurance company, keep it outside the archive.

**TIP**: *Put items into a box and see if other family members want anything. If they don't, you may feel easier about tossing things.*

## PRESERVE AND PROTECT
### PAPER

**PRESERVE:** Sort these items by associated family member, surname, size, or type (e.g., vital records, military papers, school memorabilia).

- Carefully remove staples, paper clips, or other metal; twine; rubber bands; and other types of fasteners.
- Unfold letters for flat storage. Leave brittle ones folded. Keep notes and mail with their envelopes; keep correspondence collections together.
- Scan or photocopy onto acid-free paper any newspaper clippings enclosed with letters and keep with letters. Keep originals separately, if still needed.

**PROTECT:** Store in archival-quality file folders or paper sleeves, which can then be stored flat in archival storage

boxes or upright in hanging folders (don't allow papers to slump). Label each folder with the date and the name of the family or individuals associated with its document. Consider first scanning each document to enable easier sharing.

TIP: *To make items easier to find, number the folders and keep a list of the contents in each one.*

## PHOTOS

**PRESERVE:** Organize by family, date, subject, event, place, photographer (e.g., photos Mom took), or size or type of image. Store in close-fitting individual photo storage envelopes or sleeves inside an archival box.

**PROTECT:** Keep prints in snug-fitting sleeves or envelopes (to prevent slid-

ing and scratching) made of archival-grade paper or clear plastic and stacked carefully in boxes. Store rare prints vertically in boxed sleeves. Faded color prints can be scanned and digitally restored before being kept in a cool, dry place.

TIP: *The cooler your photos are kept, the longer they will last, but don't refrigerate them or put them in the basement, as humidity is harmful. An interior closet shelf is best; check the collection regularly for pests.*

## MAKE HOMES FOR HEIRLOOMS

Be sure to take precautions against pests and extreme temperatures and humidity. Always wash your hands before touching items and remove rings and bracelets to avoid nicking or snagging them. Here's how to store various artifacts ...

• **ART:** Rotate displays of valuable pieces (6 months out, 6 months stored) to prevent overexposure to light, dust, and other environmental elements.

• **CHINA AND COLLECTIBLES:** Wrap in acid-free, lignin-free tissue, not newsprint. Keep breakables in sturdy, crush-resistant archival boxes.

• **FURNITURE:** Use a clean, slightly damp cloth instead of furniture polish and keep pieces out of direct sunlight.

---

## CATALOG YOUR KEEPSAKES

Keep an inventory of your family artifacts, including details such as ...

• how it came into your possession
• who owned it originally
• when it was made
• any family stories associated with it

Make at least two copies of your inventory and any pictures of heirlooms, one each for your genealogical files and to keep with your important papers.

TIP: *You may also want to catalog missing heirlooms and/or ones that aren't in your possession. To download a free Heirloom Inventory and History form, go to Familytreemagazine.com/heirloom_history.* -Sharon DeBartolo Carmack

• **MUSICAL INSTRUMENTS:** Use a soft cloth to remove dust and, if possible, regularly play an instrument to best monitor its function and repair needs.

• **QUILTS AND SAMPLERS:** Cushion and protect the surface(s) of large fabric items with archival tissue and roll them around an archival tube to avoid creases. Then roll a slightly wider piece of clean, washed muslin one and a half times around the artifact to form a protective outer layer and tuck the ends of the muslin into the ends of the tube. Gently tie cotton twill tape or muslin strips around the roll to secure.

• **CLOTHING:** Store laundered or dry-cleaned items such as wedding dresses and military uniforms on wooden hangers wrapped in polyester quilt batting covered with a muslin sleeve. Stuff archival tissue into sleeves and legs for support and place the garment in a muslin (not plastic or vinyl) garment bag.

• **MILITARY INSIGNIA, SCOUTING MEMORABILIA:** Protect with unbleached muslin or acid-free tissue and store in archival boxes.

**TIP:** *Display out of direct sun and against a backing of cotton, not wool, which contains medal-damaging sulfur.*

Photo: PattieS/Getty Images

## VALUE JUDGMENTS

How much are your items worth? Here are some different types of value:

• **Monetary value:** This is the price that an item would bring on the open market, or its fair market value.

• **Artistic value:** In general, the artist, school of art, or subject matter must already be famous for an artwork to have artistic value.

• **Historical and cultural value:** This is determined by events, people, and places associated with an item, which may or may not lend it monetary value. Purchase of an item by a museum could establish a monetary value.

• **Intrinsic value:** This is often different from monetary value. To your family, Grandma's candy dish might be worth $200, but an appraiser might value it at only $50 (its fair market or insurance value, as well as the tax deduction amount that might be taken if it were donated to a qualified charity).

• **Sentimental value:** This can be "priceless." In this case, the memories associated with an item exceed its monetary value.

Family archives are a wonderful legacy to pass on to future generations. Spending time now to organize and preserve your keepsakes and collections will yield unforgettable returns both now and in the future. ■

Excerpted from the Almanac's sister publication, *Family Tree* magazine. For more about all things genealogical, go to Familytreemagazine.com.

## FOOD

*(continued from page 70)*

### KUTIA (WHEAT BERRY PUDDING)

*The wheat in this dish represents the staff of life; the honey represents the spirit of Christ.*

2 cups wheat berries, rinsed
1 cup melted honey, or less, to taste
1 cup ground poppy seeds
½ cup chopped walnuts, almonds, or pecans

In a bowl, cover the wheat berries with cool water and soak overnight.

Drain wheat berries and put into a saucepan with enough fresh water to cover. Bring to a boil and simmer for 3 to 4 hours, adding water if needed, until wheat is soft. Cool.

In a bowl, combine honey, ground poppy seeds, and walnuts. Add wheat berries and stir well to combine. Do not let the *kutia* stand too long before serving, or it will get watery.

Makes 15 servings.

### KOLACHI (BRAIDED BREAD RINGS)

*Note that this recipe makes three breads.*

1 tablespoon yeast
1 cup plus 1 teaspoon sugar, divided
5 cups lukewarm (105° to 115°F) water, divided
¾ cup (1½ sticks) butter, melted
1 teaspoon salt
6 eggs, beaten, divided
12 to 14 cups all-purpose flour

Grease three 9-inch round pans or pie plates.

In a small bowl, dissolve yeast and 1 teaspoon of sugar in 1 cup of lukewarm water. Let stand for 10 minutes.

In a separate bowl, dissolve 1 cup of sugar in remaining 4 cups of lukewarm water. Stir in butter, salt, five eggs, and yeast mixture. Add flour gradually

Photos, from top: Koval Nadiya/Getty Images; Samantha Jones/Quinn Brein Communications

and knead until smooth and elastic. The dough should be just a little stiffer than bread dough. Cover and let rise in a warm place until doubled in bulk. Punch down and let rise again.

Divide dough into three equal pieces. Take one of these pieces and divide it into six equal pieces. Roll two pieces to a length of about 30 inches. Put the two lengths side by side. Entwine the two pieces of dough, forming a ropelike twist. Place entwined dough in a circle along the edge of one of the prepared pans, with ends of the dough meeting.

Repeat the process and make two more twists about 24 inches long from the remaining four pieces of dough. Take these two twists and entwine them in the opposite direction, making a double twist. Form the double twist into a circle. Cut ends at an angle and join neatly by pinching the ends together. Place inside the circle of dough already in the pan. There will be a small, empty round space in the middle of the pan; if necessary, put a greased canning jar in the middle to "hold the spot."

Repeat the process to make two more round *kolachi* with remaining two pieces of dough, placing each in one of the prepared pans. Let rise to almost double in bulk. (Be careful not to let the loaves rise too long, or the braiding will lose its definition.)

Preheat oven to 350°F.

Brush *kolachi* with remaining egg and bake for 45 minutes to 1 hour, or until *kolachi* sound hollow when tapped on the bottom. Cool on wire racks.

**Makes 3 rings.**

Photo: Maryna Voronova/Getty Images

## BORSCH (BEET SOUP)

*Serve with sour rye bread and kolachi.*

6 medium beets, peeled and cut into thin strips
1 carrot, peeled and sliced
2 tablespoons fresh lemon juice
½ cup dried white beans
3 tablespoons butter
1 large onion, sliced
1½ cups shredded cabbage
1½ cups tomato soup
2 tablespoons chopped fresh dill
sour cream, for topping (optional)

In a pot, combine beets, carrots, and 2 quarts of water; simmer for 20 minutes. Add lemon juice (this helps to keep the beets red) and stir. Add beans and simmer until tender.

In a separate pan, melt butter over medium heat. Add onions and cook until soft. Add cabbage and ½ cup of water to onions and simmer until cabbage is tender. Stir into beets. Add tomato soup and dill. Bring to a boil. Serve hot, topped with sour cream (if using).

**Makes about 10 cups.** *(continued)*

## VARENYKY (FILLED DUMPLINGS)

*When filled with prune, plum, or poppy seed, these can be served as part of the dessert course.*

3 tablespoons vegetable oil
1 egg
4½ cups all-purpose flour
1 teaspoon salt
½ cup (1 stick) butter, melted

In a bowl, combine oil, egg, and 1½ cups of water. Add flour and salt and mix to make a dough.

On a lightly floured surface, knead dough until smooth and soft. Put into a lightly oiled bowl and cover. Let dough rest for 20 minutes.

Again on a lightly floured surface, roll out dough until it is slightly thinner than a piecrust. Use a cookie cutter or glass to cut out 3-inch rounds.

Put about 1 teaspoon of filling *(recipes at right)* onto each round. Fold over to form a half-circle, then pinch edges together with your fingers to seal.

Bring a pot of water to a boil. Drop *varenyky* into the pot a few at a time. Stir with a wooden spoon to prevent them from sticking to the pot. (They'll float to the top when cooked, which can take from a few minutes up to 10 minutes.) Remove with a slotted spoon to a colander and drain thoroughly.

Place in a deep dish, sprinkle generously with melted butter, and toss gently to coat to prevent them from sticking together.

**Makes about 80 dumplings.**

### POTATO AND CHEESE FILLING

Cook 1 chopped onion in ¼ cup (½ stick) of butter. In a bowl, combine onions, ½ teaspoon salt, ¼ teaspoon freshly ground black pepper, 1 cup grated cheddar cheese, and 3 cups mashed potatoes and stir well to incorporate. Cool thoroughly before using.

### SAUERKRAUT FILLING

Cook 1 quart of sauerkraut for about 20 minutes, or until done. Drain, press out all water, and chop fine. Cook 1 chopped onion in ¼ cup of oil until golden. Add sauerkraut, ½ teaspoon salt, and ¼ teaspoon freshly ground black pepper and fry for 10 minutes. Cool thoroughly before using.

### PRUNE OR PLUM FILLING

Simmer 1 cup of fruit in ½ cup of water in a covered pot for 20 minutes. Drain and cool. Remove stones and chop fine. Add 2 tablespoons sugar, or to taste, and mix well before using.

### POPPY-SEED FILLING

In a pot over medium heat, combine 1 cup poppy seeds in enough milk to cover. Scald for 2 to 3 minutes. Drain off most of the milk. In a blender or food processor, purée poppy seeds and remaining milk. Add 1 egg yolk and 2 tablespoons sugar and blend well. Cool thoroughly before using. ■

# PRODUCE WEIGHTS AND MEASURES

## VEGETABLES

**ASPARAGUS:** 1 pound = 3 cups chopped

**BEANS (STRING):** 1 pound = 4 cups chopped

**BEETS:** 1 pound (5 medium) = 2½ cups chopped

**BROCCOLI:** 1 pound = 6 cups chopped

**CABBAGE:** 1 pound = 4½ cups shredded

**CARROTS:** 1 pound = 3½ cups sliced or grated

**CELERY:** 1 pound = 4 cups chopped

**CUCUMBERS:** 1 pound (2 medium) = 4 cups sliced

**EGGPLANT:** 1 pound = 4 cups chopped = 2 cups cooked

**GARLIC:** 1 clove = 1 teaspoon chopped

**LEEKS:** 1 pound = 4 cups chopped = 2 cups cooked

**MUSHROOMS:** 1 pound = 5 to 6 cups sliced = 2 cups cooked

**ONIONS:** 1 pound = 4 cups sliced = 2 cups cooked

**PARSNIPS:** 1 pound = 1½ cups cooked, puréed

**PEAS:** 1 pound whole = 1 to 1½ cups shelled

**POTATOES:** 1 pound (3 medium) sliced = 2 cups mashed

**PUMPKIN:** 1 pound = 4 cups chopped = 2 cups cooked and drained

**SPINACH:** 1 pound = ¾ to 1 cup cooked

**SQUASHES (SUMMER):** 1 pound = 4 cups grated = 2 cups sliced and cooked

**SQUASHES (WINTER):** 2 pounds = 2½ cups cooked, puréed

**SWEET POTATOES:** 1 pound = 4 cups grated = 1 cup cooked, puréed

**SWISS CHARD:** 1 pound = 5 to 6 cups packed leaves = 1 to 1½ cups cooked

**TOMATOES:** 1 pound (3 or 4 medium) = 1½ cups seeded pulp

**TURNIPS:** 1 pound = 4 cups chopped = 2 cups cooked, mashed

## FRUIT

**APPLES:** 1 pound (3 or 4 medium) = 3 cups sliced

**BANANAS:** 1 pound (3 or 4 medium) = 1¾ cups mashed

**BERRIES:** 1 quart = 3½ cups

**DATES:** 1 pound = 2½ cups pitted

**LEMON:** 1 whole = 1 to 3 tablespoons juice; 1 to 1½ teaspoons grated zest

**LIME:** 1 whole = 1½ to 2 tablespoons juice

**ORANGE:** 1 medium = 6 to 8 tablespoons juice; 2 to 3 tablespoons grated zest

**PEACHES:** 1 pound (4 medium) = 3 cups sliced

**PEARS:** 1 pound (4 medium) = 2 cups sliced

**RHUBARB:** 1 pound = 2 cups cooked

**STRAWBERRIES:** 1 quart = 4 cups sliced

# HOW WE PREDICT THE WEATHER

We derive our weather forecasts from a secret formula that was devised by the founder of this Almanac, Robert B. Thomas, in 1792. Thomas believed that weather on Earth was influenced by sunspots, which are magnetic storms on the surface of the Sun.

Over the years, we have refined and enhanced this formula with state-of-the-art technology and modern scientific calculations. We employ three scientific disciplines to make our long-range predictions: solar science, the study of sunspots and other solar activity; climatology, the study of prevailing weather patterns; and meteorology, the study of the atmosphere. We predict weather trends and events by comparing solar patterns and historical weather conditions with current solar activity.

Our forecasts emphasize temperature and precipitation deviations from averages, or normals. These are based on 30-year statistical averages prepared by government meteorological agencies and updated every 10 years. Our forecasts are based on the tabulations that span the period 1991 through 2020.

The borders of the 16 weather regions of the contiguous states **(page 205)** are based primarily on climatology and the movement of weather systems. For example, while the average weather in Richmond, Virginia, and Boston, Massachusetts, is very different (although both are in Region 2), both areas tend to be affected by the same storms and high-pressure centers and have weather deviations from normal that are similar.

We believe that nothing in the universe happens haphazardly, that there is a cause-and-effect pattern to all phenomena. However, although neither we nor any other forecasters have as yet gained sufficient insight into the mysteries of the universe to predict the weather with total accuracy, our results are almost always very close to our traditional claim of 80%.

# WEATHER PHOBIAS

| FEAR OF | PHOBIA |
|---|---|
| Clouds | Nephophobia |
| Cold | Cheimatophobia<br>Frigophobia<br>Psychrophobia |
| Dampness, moisture | Hygrophobia |
| Daylight, sunshine | Heliophobia<br>Phengophobia |
| Extreme cold, frost, ice | Cryophobia<br>Pagophobia |
| Floods | Antlophobia |
| Fog | Homichlophobia<br>Nebulaphobia |
| Heat | Thermophobia |
| Hurricanes, tornadoes | Lilapsophobia |
| Lightning, thunder | Astraphobia<br>Brontophobia<br>Keraunophobia |
| Northern lights, southern lights | Auroraphobia |
| Rain | Ombrophobia<br>Pluviophobia |
| Snow | Chionophobia |
| Thunder | Ceraunophobia<br>Tonitrophobia |
| Wind | Ancraophobia<br>Anemophobia |

# HOW ACCURATE WAS OUR FORECAST LAST WINTER?

Our overall accuracy rate in forecasting the direction of precipitation departure for a representative city in each region was 94.4%, as we were correct in 17 of the 18 regions. In Region 14, the Desert Southwest, we forecasted near-normal precipitation and the winter ended up being below normal. Even though we're tempted to take half credit, we'll chalk this up as a miss, given the widespread below-normal precipitation throughout the region.

Looking at temperatures, our forecasted departures from normal were largely correct from the High Plains to the West Coast. We were also correct in New England, but other areas near the East Coast ended up warmer than we expected. Overall, our accuracy rate in forecasting the direction of temperature departure for a representative city in each region was only about 50%. This makes our total accuracy rate 72.2%, slightly below our traditional average rate of 80%.

Our forecast for near- to below-normal snowfall across New England and portions of the Atlantic Corridor was correct in most areas, as was our forecast for near-normal snowfall across the Southeast. Our above-normal snowfall forecast in parts of the Deep South, in places like Nashville and Little Rock, was also correct. Our forecast of near- to above-normal snowfall in the Lower Lakes was largely correct, while much of the Ohio Valley saw less snow than we expected. Snowfall also underperformed our forecast across the High Plains, while our Intermountain West forecast of below-normal snowfall turned out to be largely correct. Much of Alaska, especially in northern and eastern areas, saw above-normal snowfall, which matched our forecast.

The table below shows our forecasted average precipitation vs. the actual result for one city in each region. On average, the actual values differed from our forecasts by 1.02 inches.

| REGION/ CITY | Nov.-Mar. Monthly Precip. Change vs. Normal (in.) PREDICTED | ACTUAL | REGION/ CITY | Nov.-Mar. Monthly Precip. Change vs. Normal (in.) PREDICTED | ACTUAL |
|---|---|---|---|---|---|
| 1. Caribou, ME | 0.2 | 0.6 | 10. Des Moines, IA | –0.7 | –0.9 |
| 2. Hartford, CT | –0.6 | –3.3 | 11. Houston, TX | 0.4 | 1.4 |
| 3. Scranton, PA | –0.3 | –1.2 | 12. Cheyenne, WY | 0.0 | 0.0 |
| 4. Atlanta, GA | 0.2 | 2.0 | 13. Spokane, WA | –0.6 | –1.1 |
| 5. Tampa, FL | –0.3 | –2.6 | 14. El Paso, TX | 0.0 | –0.6 |
| 6. Syracuse, NY | –0.6 | –0.4 | 15. Eugene, OR | –2.2 | –4.1 |
| 7. Cincinnati, OH | –0.5 | –1.4 | 16. Los Angeles, CA | –0.8 | –1.1 |
| 8. Nashville, TN | 0.7 | 2.9 | 17. Nome, AK | 0.4 | 0.6 |
| 9. Duluth, MN | 0.1 | 0.9 | 18. Kahului, HI | –2.2 | –3.6 |

WEATHER

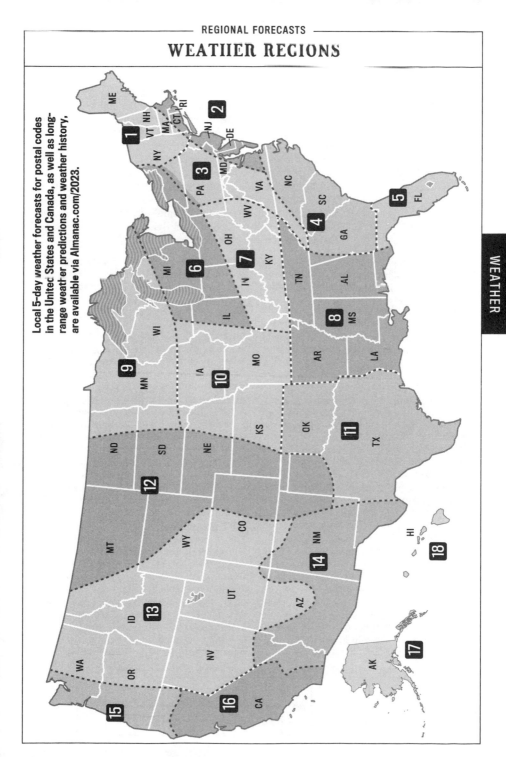

Local 5-day weather forecasts for postal codes in the United States and Canada, as well as long-range weather predictions and weather history, are available via Almanac.com/2023.

WEATHER

# NORTHEAST

Caribou

Burlington  Augusta

Concord

Albany

**SUMMARY: Winter** temperatures will be above normal in the north and below normal in the south. The coldest periods will be in early and late January and late February. Precipitation will be above normal. Snowfall will be below normal in the north and above normal in the south, with the snowiest periods in early to mid-December and the first half of January. **April** will be cooler and drier than normal, while **May** will be warmer and drier. **Summer** temperatures will be above normal, with rainfall slightly above normal. The hottest periods will be in early to mid-July and early August. **September** will be cooler and drier than normal, while **October** will be warmer and drier.

**NOV. 2022:** Temp. 42° (3° above avg.); precip. 4" (avg. north, 2" above south). 1–4 Rainy periods, warm. 5–11 Snow, then sunny, warmer. 12–18 Rain and snow showers, cool. 19–23 Snow showers, then flurries, cold. 24–27 Rain and snow showers, mild. 28–30 Snow, cold.

**DEC. 2022:** Temp. 29° (1° below avg.); precip. 3.5" (avg.). 1–7 Snow north, flurries south; very cold. 8–12 Sunny, cool. 13–18 Periods of snow and rain, mild. 19–25 Snow showers, chilly. 26–31 Flurries, cold.

**JAN. 2023:** Temp. 25.5° (2° above avg. north, 1° below south); precip. 6.5" (3" above avg.). 1–3 Snow to rain, mild. 4–14 Snowstorms, cold. 15–17 Flurries, chilly. 18–20 Snow to rain, mild. 21–25 Flurries, cold. 26–29 Sunny, very cold. 30–31 Snow, chilly.

**FEB. 2023:** Temp. 21.5° (1° above avg. north, 3.5° below south); precip. 0.5" (2" below avg.). 1–4 Sunny, cold. 5–12 Flurries, cold. 13–23 Sunny; mild north, cold south. 24–25 Snow showers, very cold. 26–28 Sunny, cold.

**MAR. 2023:** Temp. 33° (1° below avg.); precip. 4" (1" above avg.). 1–4 Sunny, cold. 5–8 Rain, mild. 9–13 Snow showers, cold. 14–21 Periods of snow, cold. 22–24 Flurries, chilly. 25–31 Periods of rain and snow, cold.

**APR. 2023:** Temp. 43° (2° below avg.); precip. 1" (2" below avg.). 1–3 Flurries, chilly. 4–8 Showers, warm. 9–11 Sunny, cool. 12–14 Snow north, rain south; cool. 15–22 Sunny, mild. 23–25 Showers, cool. 26–30 Sunny, cool.

**MAY 2023:** Temp. 61° (4° above avg.); precip. 2.5" (1" below avg.). 1–3 Showers, warm. 4–7 Sunny, warm. 8–15 Periods of rain, mild. 16–20 Sunny, warm. 21–24 T-storms north, sunny south; very warm. 25–31 T-storms, mild.

**JUNE 2023:** Temp. 66° (avg.); precip. 5" (1" above avg.). 1–8 A few t-storms, cool. 9–11 Sunny, cool. 12–16 A few t-storms, mild. 17–24 T-storms north, sunny south; warm. 25–30 A few showers, cool.

**JULY 2023:** Temp. 72° (2° above avg.); precip. 6" (2" above avg.). 1–4 A few t-storms, warm. 5–7 Sunny, warm. 8–12 Showers, mild. 13–16 A few t-storms, hot. 17–25 Showers, cool. 26–31 A few t-storms, warm.

**AUG. 2023:** Temp. 69° (2° above avg.); precip. 2" (2" below avg.). 1–7 A few t-storms, warm. 8–9 Sunny, hot. 10–15 A few t-storms, warm. 16–22 A few showers, cool. 23–24 Sunny, mild. 25–31 A few t-storms; cool north, warm south.

**SEPT. 2023:** Temp. 59° (2° below avg.); precip. 2.5" (1" below avg.). 1–4 Sunny, chilly. 5–9 A few showers, cool. 10–13 Sunny north, showers south; cool. 14–15 Showers, cool. 16–20 Sunny, cool. 21–27 A few showers, cool. 28–30 Showers, mild.

**OCT. 2023:** Temp. 50° (1° above avg.); precip. 2.5" (1" below avg.). 1–5 Sunny, cool. 6–8 Rain, mild. 9–14 Sunny, cool. 15–21 A few showers, mild. 22–25 Sunny, cool. 26–31 Sunny, warm.

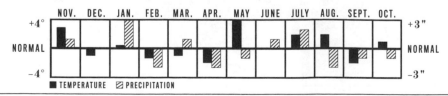

# ATLANTIC CORRIDOR

**SUMMARY: Winter** temperatures will be below normal, while precipitation and snowfall will be above normal. The coldest periods will be in early December, early and late January, and most of February. The snowiest periods will be in early to mid-January, late January, and late February. **April** will be cooler and drier than normal, while **May** will be warmer and rainier. **Summer** will be warmer than normal, with above-normal precipitation. The hottest periods will be in mid-July and early to mid-August. **September** and **October** will be cooler, on average, and drier than normal.

**WEATHER**

**NOV. 2022:** Temp. 46° (1° below avg.); precip. 4" (1" above avg.). 1–3 Rainy periods, mild. 4–8 Sunny, cold. 9–13 A few showers, mild. 14–19 Rain, mild. 20–27 Rain and snow showers, chilly. 28–30 Rain and snow showers north; turning cold.

**DEC. 2022:** Temp. 40° (1° below avg.); precip. 4.5" (1" above avg.). 1–5 Rain and snow showers, turning very cold. 6–14 Rainy periods, turning mild. 15–22 Sunny, turning cold. 23–26 Rain and snow, chilly. 27–31 Sunny, turning mild.

**JAN. 2023:** Temp. 34° (3° below avg.); precip. 7.5" (4" above avg.). 1–5 Rain and snow, turning cold. 6–13 Snowy periods north, rain and snow south; cool. 14–16 Sunny, cold. 17–22 Rainy, mild, then flurries, cold. 23–28 Sunny north, snow showers south; cold. 29–31 Snowstorm, cold.

**FEB. 2023:** Temp. 30° (5° below avg.); precip. 1" (2" below avg.). 1–4 Sunny, cold. 5–11 Snow showers, cold. 12–20 Sunny, cold. 21–24 Periods of snow, cold. 25–28 Sunny, cold.

**MAR. 2023:** Temp. 44° (avg.); precip. 4" (avg.). 1–3 Sunny north, rain and snow south; cold. 4–7 Showers, mild. 8–12 Rain to snow, then sunny; cold. 13–17 Showers, warmer. 18–20 Heavy rain, chilly. 21–25 Sunny, warm. 26–31 A few showers; mild north, warm south.

**APR. 2023:** Temp. 51° (2° below avg.); precip. 2.5" (1" below avg.). 1–6 A few showers, turning warm. 7–15 Rainy periods, cool. 16–25 Sunny north, showers south; cool. 26–30

Rainy periods, chilly.

**MAY 2023:** Temp. 65° (2° above avg.); precip. 5.5" (2" above avg.). 1–6 Rain, then sunny, mild. 7–9 Heavy rain north, showers south; cool. 10–15 A few showers, warm. 16–20 Heavy rain, turning cool. 21–26 Isolated showers, warm. 27–31 T-storms, mild.

**JUNE 2023:** Temp. 71° (1° below avg.); precip. 5" (1" above avg.). 1–6 A few showers, warm. 7–10 Sunny, cool. 11–14 T-storms, warm. 15–20 Sunny, cool. 21–23 T-storms, hot. 24–27 Heavy rain, cool. 28–30 Sunny, warm.

**JULY 2023:** Temp. 77° (avg.); precip. 5" (1" above avg.). 1–7 Sunny, mild. 8–10 T-storms, cool. 11–16 Sunny, turning hot. 17–21 A few showers, cool. 22–31 T-storms; cool north, warm south.

**AUG. 2023:** Temp. 78° (3° above avg.); precip. 3" (1" below avg.). 1–7 A few t-storms, warm. 8–11 Sunny, hot. 12–16 Sunny, mild. 17–25 A few t-storms; mild north, hot south. 26–31 Sunny, warm.

**SEPT. 2023:** Temp. 68° (1° below avg.); precip. 3" (1" below avg.). 1–3 Sunny; cool north, warm south. 4–12 Showers, cool north; sunny, turning hot south. 13–16 Showers, warm. 17–23 Sunny, cool. 24–30 A few showers, cool.

**OCT. 2023:** Temp. 57° (avg.); precip. 3" (1" below avg.). 1–6 Sunny, turning warm. 7–12 A few showers, cool. 13–20 A few showers, mild. 21–27 Sunny, mild. 28–31 A few showers, warm.

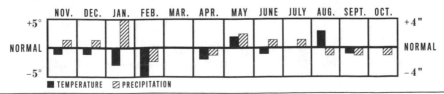

# APPALACHIANS

Elmira
Scranton •
Harrisburg •
Frederick •
Roanoke •
Asheville •

**SUMMARY: Winter** will be colder than normal, with near-normal precipitation and above-normal snowfall. The coldest periods will be early December, late January, and mid- to late February. The snowiest periods will be in early and late January and in February in the south. **April** will be colder than normal, while **May** will be warmer. Both April and May will have above-normal precipitation. **Summer** temperatures will be above normal, on average, while precipitation will be below normal. The hottest period will be in mid-July. **September** and **October** will be slightly cooler, on average, and drier than normal.

**NOV. 2022:** Temp. 43° (1° below avg.); precip. 4" (1" above avg.). 1–3 Rain north, dry south; mild. 4–8 Flurries, cold. 9–17 Scattered showers, mild. 18–23 Snow, then flurries, cold. 24–30 Rain and snow showers; mild, then turning cold.

**DEC. 2022:** Temp. 37° (1° below avg.); precip. 2.5" (1" below avg.). 1–5 Flurries north, very cold. 6–18 Periods of rain, snow showers north; mild. 19–22 Flurries, cold. 23–26 Rain and snow showers, chilly. 27–31 Isolated showers, mild.

**JAN. 2023:** Temp. 26° (5° below avg.); precip. 6.5" (3" above avg.). 1–4 Rain to snow, turning cold. 5–13 Periods of snow, cold. 14–17 Sunny, cold. 18–23 Rain, then flurries; mild, then cold. 24–31 Snow, very cold.

**FEB. 2023:** Temp. 23° (7° below avg.); precip. 0.5" (1" below avg.). 1–5 Sunny, cold. 6–11 Snow showers, cold. 12–24 Flurries north, occasional snow south; very cold. 25–28 Sunny, cold.

**MAR. 2023:** Temp. 40° (avg.); precip. 4" (1" above avg.). 1–3 Snow showers, cold. 4–6 Sunny, mild. 7–11 Rain, then flurries, turning cold. 12–19 Sunny, then heavy rain, mild. 20–25 Sunny, cool. 26–31 Scattered showers, mild.

**APR. 2023:** Temp. 49° (2° below avg.); precip. 5.5" (1.5" above avg.). 1–6 Sunny, mild. 7–15 Showers, cool. 16–20 Dry north, heavy rain south; chilly. 21–26 Sunny, then turning chilly. 27–30 Periods of rain, cool.

**MAY 2023:** Temp. 62° (1° above avg.); precip. 5" (1" above avg.). 1–11 Periods of rain, cool. 12–15 Sunny, mild. 16–21 Showers, cool, then turning warm. 22–26 Scattered t-storms, very warm. 27–31 A few showers, cool.

**JUNE 2023:** Temp. 67.5° (1.5° below avg.); precip. 3.5" (1" below avg.). 1–6 Scattered t-storms, cool. 7–10 Sunny, cool. 11–19 Isolated t-storms, mild. 20–24 Sunny, very warm. 25–27 Rainy, cool. 28–30 Sunny, cool.

**JULY 2023:** Temp. 75° (1° above avg.); precip. 4.5" (1" above avg.). 1–6 Isolated t-storms, mild. 7–10 Showers and t-storms, cool. 11–16 Sunny, turning hot. 17–19 Isolated t-storms, cool. 20–31 T-storms; cool north, mild south.

**AUG. 2023:** Temp. 74° (2° above avg.); precip. 1.5" (2" below avg.). 1–6 Scattered t-storms, mild. 7–11 Sunny, warm. 12–19 Sunny; cool north, warm south. 20–25 Scattered t-storms, warm. 26–31 Sunny, cool.

**SEPT. 2023:** Temp. 65° (avg.); precip. 3" (1" below avg.). 1–7 Scattered showers; cool north, mild south. 8–15 Showers north, dry south; cool north, hot south. 16–26 Sunny, cool. 27–30 Rain north, dry south; cool.

**OCT. 2023:** Temp. 53° (1° below avg.); precip. 1.5" (2" below avg.). 1–4 Sunny, cool. 5–9 Scattered showers, cool. 10–20 Occasional showers north, dry south; mild. 21–26 Sunny, cool. 27–31 Sunny, mild.

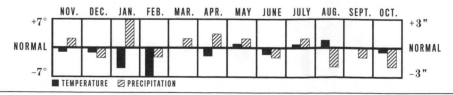

# SOUTHEAST

**SUMMARY: Winter** temperatures will be below normal, with the coldest periods in early December, early and late January, and mid-February. Precipitation will be below normal. Snowfall will be above normal in the east and below normal in the west, with the best chances for snow in early and late January and mid-February. **April** and **May** temperatures will be near normal, on average, with above-normal precipitation. **Summer** temperatures will be slightly above normal, with the hottest periods in mid- to late June and early July. Rainfall will be below normal. **September** and **October** will be warmer, on average, and drier than normal.

*Raleigh*

*Columbia*

*•Atlanta*

*Savannah*

**NOV. 2022:** Temp. 56° (avg.); precip. 2" (1" below avg.). 1–7 Sunny, turning cold. 8–10 A few showers north, sunny south; warm. 11–13 Sunny, cool. 14–18 Showers, turning warm. 19–24 Showers, mild. 25–27 Sunny, mild. 28–30 Rain, colder.

**DEC. 2022:** Temp. 47° (2° below avg.); precip. 5" (1" above avg.). 1–5 A few showers, then sunny; very cold. 6–11 Rainy periods, warm. 12–16 A few showers, colder. 17–18 Showers, mild. 19–21 Sunny, cold. 22–25 Rain, chilly. 26–28 Sunny, cool. 29–31 Rain, mild.

**JAN. 2023:** Temp. 42° (5° below avg.); precip. 6.5" (2" above avg.). 1–4 Rain, then sunny; very cold. 5–9 Rain and snow showers, frigid. 10–19 Rainy periods, chilly. 20–24 Sunny, very cold. 25–27 Rain and snow, cold. 28–31 Sunny, very cold.

**FEB. 2023:** Temp. 42° (5° below avg.); precip. 2" (2" below avg.). 1–5 Sunny, cold. 6–12 Rainy periods, chilly. 13–15 Snow showers, frigid. 16–20 Sunny, cold. 21–24 Rain and snow, very cold. 25–28 Sunny, cold.

**MAR. 2023:** Temp. 59° (3° above avg.); precip. 2.5" (2" below avg.). 1–3 Rain, cold. 4–8 A few showers, warm. 9–11 Sunny, chilly. 12–17 Sunny, warm. 18–20 Rain, colder. 21–31 Sunny, very warm.

**APR. 2023:** Temp. 63° (1° below avg.); precip. 6.5" (3" above avg.). 1–3 Sunny, warm. 4–6 Showers, mild. 7–12 Sunny, then rain; colder. 13–16 Sunny, cool. 17–23 Rain, then sunny; colder. 24–30 Showers, cool.

**MAY 2023:** Temp. 73° (1° above avg.); precip. 5" (1" above avg.). 1–7 T-storms, mild. 8–11 A few showers, cool. 12–17 Sunny, warm. 18–22 T-storms, mild. 23–25 Sunny, very warm. 26–31 T-storms, warm.

**JUNE 2023:** Temp. 79° (avg.); precip. 2.5" (2" below avg.). 1–13 T-storms, warm, then sunny, mild. 14–24 T-storms, warm, then sunny, hot. 25–30 T-storms, warm, then sunny, mild.

**JULY 2023:** Temp. 83° (avg.); precip. 5.5" (1" above avg.). 1–3 Sunny north, t-storms south; hot. 4–11 T-storms, mild. 12–14 Sunny, warm. 15–20 T-storms, warm. 21–23 Sunny, warm. 24–31 Rainy periods, mild.

**AUG. 2023.** Temp. 82° (1° above avg.); precip. 3.5" (1" below avg.). 1–6 T-storms, mild. 7–13 A few t-storms, warm. 14–19 Sunny, warm. 20–27 A few t-storms, warm. 28–31 Sunny north, t-storms south; mild.

**SEPT. 2023:** Temp. 77° (2° above avg.); precip. 3" (2" below avg.). 1–9 A few t-storms, warm. 10–15 Sunny, very warm. 16–17 A few showers, mild. 18–21 Sunny, mild. 22–27 A few t-storms, mild. 28–30 Sunny, mild.

**OCT. 2023:** Temp. 65° (avg.); precip. 1" (2" below avg.). 1–6 Sunny N, showers S; warm. 7–14 Sunny, cool. 15–21 Showers E, sunny W; warm. 22–31 Sunny, then showers; warm.

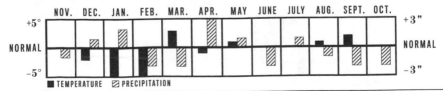

# FLORIDA

Jacksonville
Orlando
Tampa
Miami

**SUMMARY: Winter** will be colder and rainier than normal, with the coldest temperatures in early and late January and mid-February. **April** and **May** will be slightly warmer than normal, with rainfall above normal in the north and normal in the south. **Summer** will bring slightly above-normal temperatures, with below-normal rainfall. The hottest periods will be in early and mid-June and mid-August. **September** and **October** temperatures will be near normal, on average, with rainfall below normal.

**NOV. 2022:** Temp. 68° (1° below avg.); precip. 3.5" (1" above avg.). 1–3 Sunny, warm. 4–9 Sunny, chilly. 10–13 Sunny, mild. 14–18 Rain, heavy south; warm. 19–21 Sunny, cool. 22–25 Showers, warm. 26–30 Rain, turning chilly.

**DEC. 2022:** Temp. 64° (1° below avg.); precip. 3.5" (1" above avg.). 1–6 Sunny, cold north; showers, mild south. 7–11 Rainy periods, warm. 12–22 A few showers, cold. 23–27 Showers, cool. 28–31 Sunny, warm.

**JAN. 2023:** Temp. 58° (3° below avg.); precip. 3.5" (1" above avg.). 1–10 Showers, cold. 11–13 Rain, mild. 14–15 Sunny, cold. 16–18 A few showers, warm. 19–24 Sunny, very cold. 25–29 Showers, chilly. 30–31 Sunny, very cold.

**FEB. 2023:** Temp. 58° (4° below avg.); precip. 4.5" (2" above avg.). 1–9 Rainy periods, cold. 10–14 A few showers north, rain south; cold. 15–17 Sunny, very cold. 18–25 Rainy periods, chilly. 26–28 Sunny, warmer.

**MAR. 2023:** Temp. 67° (1° below avg.); precip. 1.5" (1" below avg.). 1–2 Rainy, cool. 3–9 Showers, warmer. 10–17 Sunny; cold, then mild. 18–21 Showers, colder. 22–31 Sunny, turning warmer.

**APR. 2023:** Temp. 74° (1° above avg.); precip. 3.5" (2" above avg. north, avg. south). 1–5 Sunny, warm. 6–12 T-storms, mild. 13–23 Sunny north, showers south; cool. 24–27 Rain, heavy north; mild. 28–30 Sunny, warm.

**MAY 2023:** Temp. 79° (1° above avg.); precip. 4.5" (avg.). 1–6 A few showers, mild. 7–13 A few t-storms, cool. 14–17 Sunny, warm. 18–25 Scattered t-storms, turning warm. 26–31 T-storms, warm.

**JUNE 2023:** Temp. 84° (1° above avg.); precip. 6" (1" below avg.). 1–4 Scattered t-storms, hot. 5–10 Isolated t-storms, mild. 11–18 A few t-storms, warm. 19–26 Sunny, hot north; t-storms, warm south. 27–30 A few t-storms, warm.

**JULY 2023:** Temp. 84° (avg.); precip. 6" (1" below avg.). 1–11 Scattered t-storms, warm. 12–18 Isolated t-storms, warm. 19–25 Scattered t-storms, mild. 26–31 A few t-storms, warm.

**AUG. 2023:** Temp. 83° (avg.); precip. 6" (2" below avg.). 1–8 A few t-storms, warm. 9–19 Scattered t-storms, hot. 20–26 Isolated t-storms, warm. 27–31 T-storms, cooler.

**SEPT. 2023:** Temp. 82° (1° above avg.); precip. 5.5" (2" below avg.). 1–8 A few t-storms, warm. 9–16 Scattered showers, warm. 17–24 A few t-storms, warm. 25–30 Sunny north, t-storms south; warm.

**OCT. 2023:** Temp. 75° (1° below avg.); precip. 3.5" (1" below avg.). 1–8 T-storms, mild. 9–14 A few showers; cool north, warm south. 15–24 Isolated showers north, t-storms south; warm. 25–31 Sunny, mild.

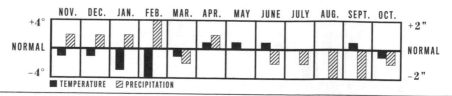

WEATHER

# LOWER LAKES

**SUMMARY: Winter** will be colder than normal, with the coldest temperatures in early December and late January to mid-February. Both precipitation and snowfall will be above normal. The snowiest periods will be in late November to early December and early to mid-January. **April** will be cooler than normal, while **May** will be warmer. Precipitation will be normal. **Summer** will be warmer than normal. Rainfall will be below normal in the east and near normal in the west. The hottest periods will be in mid-July and early and late August. **September** and **October** will be warmer and rainier than normal, on average.

**WEATHER**

**NOV. 2022:** Temp. 39° (1° below avg. east, 3° below west); precip. 3.5" (1" above avg.). 1–7 Rain and snow, then sunny; chilly. 8–16 Showers, cool. 17–22 Snow, cold. 23–25 Rain, mild. 26–30 Snow, very cold.

**DEC. 2022:** Temp. 33° (1° below avg.); precip. 4" (1" above avg.). 1–5 Snow, very cold. 6–13 Rainy periods, mild. 14–17 Rain and snow, cool. 18–22 Lake snows east, flurries west; cold. 23–28 Snow showers, cold. 29–31 Sunny, chilly.

**JAN. 2023:** Temp. 23° (5° below avg.); precip. 5" (3" above avg. east, 1" above west.). 1–10 Periods of snow, cold. 11–19 Periods of heavy snow, cold. 20–31 Lake snows east, flurries west; very cold.

**FEB. 2023:** Temp. 21° (7° below avg.); precip. 0.5" (1.5" below avg.). 1–3 Sunny, cold. 4–10 Snow showers and lake snows, very cold. 11–13 Sunny, cold. 14–25 Lake snows east, flurries west; cold. 26–28 Sunny, cold.

**MAR. 2023:** Temp. 37° (1° below avg.); precip. 3" (avg.). 1–4 Sunny, cold. 5–21 Periods of rain and snow, chilly. 22–27 Isolated showers, mild. 28–31 Rainy periods; cool east, warm west.

**APR. 2023:** Temp. 46° (3° below avg.); precip. 4" (avg.). 1–7 Scattered showers, mild. 8–10 Sunny, chilly. 11–14 Rain and snow, cold. 15–18 Sunny east, rain west; cold. 19–26 Sunny; warm, then turning cold. 27–30 Scattered showers, chilly.

**MAY 2023:** Temp. 61° (2° above avg.); precip. 4" (avg.). 1–7 Rainy periods, mild. 8–14 A few showers, turning warm. 15–24 Sunny east, isolated showers west; warm. 25–29 Sunny, cool. 30–31 T-storms, mild.

**JUNE 2023:** Temp. 67° (avg.); precip. 4.5" (1" below avg. east, 2" above west). 1–5 Scattered t-storms, cool. 6–8 Sunny, cool. 9–14 A few t-storms east, heavy rain west; warm. 15–25 Sunny east, heavy t-storms west; warm. 26–30 Sunny, mild.

**JULY 2023:** Temp. 72° (avg.); precip. 3.5" (avg.). 1–6 Isolated t-storms, cool. 7–15 Sunny east, t-storms west; turning hot. 16–24 Scattered t-storms; warm, then turning cool. 25–31 Isolated t-storms, cool.

**AUG. 2023:** Temp. 72° (2° above avg.); precip. 2" (2" below avg.). 1–5 A few t-storms, warm. 6–12 A few t-storms, hot. 13–16 Sunny, mild. 17–23 Isolated t-storms, warm. 24–31 Sunny; mild, then turning hot.

**SEPT. 2023:** Temp. 64° (1° above avg.); precip. 4" (1" above avg.). 1–3 Showers, cool east; sunny, hot west. 4–10 Rainy periods, warm. 11–14 A few showers, warm. 15–18 Sunny, cool. 19–22 Isolated showers, cool. 23–30 Showers, cool.

**OCT. 2023:** Temp. 54° (1° above avg.); precip. 4" (1" above avg.). 1–3 Sunny, mild. 4–12 Rainy periods, cool. 13–15 A few showers, warm. 16–23 Showers, then sunny; cool. 24–29 Sunny, warm. 30–31 Showers, mild.

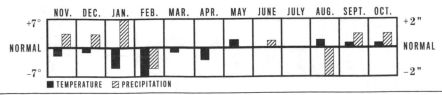

# OHIO VALLEY

Pittsburgh •
Cincinnati •
Louisville •  Charleston •

**SUMMARY: Winter** will be colder than normal, with below-normal precipitation but above-normal snowfall. The coldest periods will occur in early and mid-December, early and late January, and much of February, with the snowiest periods throughout January and in late February and early March. **April** will be cooler and drier than normal, while **May** will be warmer than normal with near-normal precipitation. **Summer** will be warmer and wetter than normal. The hottest periods will be in late June and mid- to late July. **September** and **October** will be warmer than normal, with near-normal precipitation.

**NOV. 2022:** Temp. 44° (1° below avg.); precip. 4" (1" above avg.). 1–3 Showers, warm. 4–7 Snow showers, cold. 8–14 Showers, mild. 15–17 A few showers, cool. 18–22 Rain and snow showers, cold. 23–28 Rainy periods, mild. 29–30 Snow, very cold.

**DEC. 2022:** Temp. 38° (1° below avg.); precip. 1.5" (1.5" below avg.). 1–5 Flurries, frigid. 6–13 A few showers, mild. 14–18 Rain and snow showers, mild. 19–21 Flurries, frigid. 22–24 Showers, mild. 25–28 Flurries, cold. 29–31 Rain, mild.

**JAN. 2023:** Temp. 27° (7° below avg.); precip. 5.5" (2" above avg.). 1–9 Snowy periods, very cold. 10–16 Snowstorm, then sunny; cold. 17–19 Rain and snow showers, mild. 20–31 Snow showers, very cold.

**FEB. 2023:** Temp. 27° (8° below avg.); precip. 1.5" (2" below avg.). 1–5 Sunny, bitter cold. 6–10 Snow showers, cold. 11–17 Flurries, frigid. 18–28 Snowy periods, very cold.

**MAR. 2023:** Temp. 48° (3° above avg.); precip. 3.5" (1" below avg.). 1–5 Sunny, chilly. 6–11 Rain and snow showers, colder. 12–16 A few showers, warm. 17–25 Showers, then sunny; mild. 26–31 Rainy periods, warm.

**APR. 2023:** Temp. 55° (1° below avg.); precip. 3" (1" below avg.). 1–10 Sunny; warm, then turning colder. 11–16 Rainy periods, cool. 17–19 A few showers, mild. 20–23 Sunny, cool. 24–30 Showers, chilly.

**MAY 2023:** Temp. 66° (2° above avg.); precip. 4" (avg.). 1–10 Rainy periods, cool. 11–15 Sunny, turning warmer. 16–25 Showers, then sunny; very warm. 26–31 A few showers, cool.

**JUNE 2023:** Temp. 73° (1° above avg.); precip. 5.5" (avg. east, 2" above west). 1–5 Rainy, mild. 6–8 Sunny, cool. 9–14 Scattered t-storms, warm. 15–18 Sunny, cool. 19–26 A few t-storms, hot. 27–30 Sunny, warm.

**JULY 2023:** Temp. 77° (1° above avg.); precip. 6" (2" above avg.). 1–3 Scattered t-storms, warm. 4–9 A few t-storms, cool. 10–15 Sunny, hot. 16–20 Scattered t-storms, warm. 21–28 A few t-storms, warm. 29–31 T-storms, cool.

**AUG. 2023:** Temp. 76° (2° above avg.); precip. 3.5" (avg.). 1–5 A few showers, mild. 6–12 Sunny, then scattered t-storms; warm. 13–16 Sunny, cool. 17–20 Scattered t-storms, warm. 21–24 Showers, cool. 25–31 Sunny, turning warmer.

**SEPT. 2023:** Temp. 72° (4° above avg.); precip. 2" (1" below avg.). 1–9 Sunny west, a few t-storms east; warm. 10–14 Sunny, very warm. 15–22 Sunny, cool. 23–30 A few showers, turning cooler.

**OCT. 2023:** Temp. 58° (avg.); precip. 3.5" (1" above avg.). 1–3 Sunny, cool. 4–9 Rainy periods; warm, then turning cooler. 10–15 Sunny, cool. 16–19 Rainy periods, mild. 20–30 Sunny, mild. 31 Showers, cool.

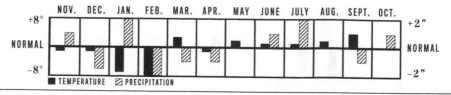

# DEEP SOUTH

**SUMMARY: Winter** will be colder than normal, with the coldest periods in early December and early and late January. Precipitation will be below normal, with above-normal snowfall in the north. The best chances for snow in the north will be in early to mid-January and mid-February. On average, **April** and **May** will be slightly warmer than normal, with above-normal rainfall. **Summer** will be warmer and wetter than normal, with the hottest periods in mid- to late June and mid- to late July. Watch for a tropical storm in mid-August. **September** and **October** will be slightly warmer and drier than normal, on average.

**NOV. 2022:** Temp. 54° (avg.); precip. 4.5" (avg.). 1–2 A few showers, warm. 3–7 Sunny, cool. 8–16 Rainy periods, mild. 17–19 Sunny, colder. 20–26 Rain, warmer. 27–30 Rain, turning cold.

**DEC. 2022:** Temp. 50° (avg.); precip. 4" (1" below avg.). 1–4 Flurries north, sunny south; very cold. 5–10 Rainy periods, warm. 11–13 Sunny, mild. 14–16 A few flurries north, sunny south; cold. 17–23 A few showers, cold. 24–28 Sunny, cold. 29–31 Rain, warm.

**JAN. 2023:** Temp. 40° (7° below avg.); precip. 9.5" (4" above avg.). 1–3 Rain, then sunny; very cold. 4–10 Snowy periods north, heavy rain south; cold. 11–18 Snow at times heavy north, rain south; cold. 19–24 Sunny north, showers south; cold. 25–27 Flurries north, rain south; cold. 28–31 Sunny, very cold.

**FEB. 2023:** Temp. 42° (6° below avg.); precip. 4.5" (1" below avg.). 1–4 Sunny, cold. 5–9 Flurries north, showers south; cold. 10–16 Periods of snow north, sunny south; cold. 17–19 Sunny, cold. 20–24 Rainy periods, cold. 25–28 Sunny, cold.

**MAR. 2023:** Temp. 59° (2° above avg.); precip. 3" (3" below avg.). 1–3 Showers, chilly. 4–8 A few showers, warm. 9–11 Sunny, chilly. 12–16 A few showers, warm. 17–20 Isolated showers, cool. 21–31 Sunny, warm.

**APR. 2023:** Temp. 64° (avg.); precip. 8.5" (3" above avg.). 1–6 A few t-storms, turning cool. 7–10 Sunny, mild. 11–15 Rainy periods, chilly. 16–20 Showers north, sunny south; mild. 21–30 Periods of rain, heavy south; cool.

**MAY 2023:** Temp. 74° (2° above avg.); precip. 5" (avg.). 1–3 T-storms, warm. 4–10 Scattered showers, cool. 11–17 Isolated showers, warm. 18–20 Sunny, warm. 21–22 Rain, heavy north; warm. 23–31 A few t-storms, warm.

**JUNE 2023:** Temp. 81° (2° above avg.); precip. 6.5" (1" below avg. north, 3" above south). 1–9 A few t-storms, warm. 10–19 A few t-storms north, sunny south; hot. 20–30 A few t-storms, warm.

**JULY 2023:** Temp. 82° (avg.); precip. 6" (1" above avg.). 1–8 Scattered t-storms, warm. 9–15 Sunny north, t-storms south; warm. 16–20 Scattered t-storms, warm. 21–26 Sunny north, a few t-storms south; hot. 27–31 T-storms; cool north, warm south.

**AUG. 2023:** Temp. 82° (1° above avg.); precip. 8" (1" above avg. east, 5" above west). 1–7 Scattered t-storms, mild. 8–14 Isolated t-storms, hot. 15–20 Sunny, hot north. 21–23 T-storms east, tropical storm threat west; warm. 24–31 Sunny, warm.

**SEPT. 2023:** Temp. 79° (2° above avg.); precip. 5.5" (1" above avg.). 1–8 A few t-storms east, heavy rain west; warm. 9–13 A few t-storms, warm. 14–23 Sunny north, t-storms south; warm. 24–30 A few showers and cool north, sunny and warm south.

**OCT. 2023:** Temp. 66° (avg.); precip. 1" (2" below avg.). 1–7 A few t-storms north, sunny south; warm. 8–11 Sunny, cool. 12–17 Sunny; warm north, cool south. 18–20 A few showers north, sunny south; mild. 21–29 Sunny, warm north, cool south. 30–31 Showers, turning chilly.

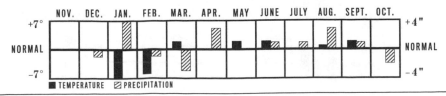

# UPPER MIDWEST

**SUMMARY: Winter** temperatures will be below normal, with the coldest periods in late November, early December, early and late January, and mid-February. Precipitation and snowfall will be below normal in the east and above normal in the west. The snowiest periods will be in late November, early and late December, and early and late March. On average, **April** and **May** temperatures will be near normal, with rainfall slightly above normal. **Summer** will be warmer and rainier than normal, with the hottest periods in late June and early and late August. **September** and **October** will have above-normal temperatures and near-normal precipitation, on average.

**NOV. 2022:** Temp. 27.5° (avg. east, 5° below west); precip. 3" (avg. east, 2" above west). 1–5 Rain to snow, cold. 6–9 Sunny east, showers west; mild. 10–14 Snow, cold. 15–20 Snow east, flurries west; very cold. 21–27 Snow showers, cold. 28–30 Snow, heavy east; very cold.

**DEC. 2022:** Temp. 18° (1° below avg.); precip. 2" (1" above avg.). 1–4 Heavy snow east, flurries west; frigid. 5–8 A few flurries, cold. 9–14 Rain and snow, chilly. 15–20 Lake snow east, sunny west; cold. 21–31 Snowy periods, cold.

**JAN. 2023:** Temp. 8.5° (2° below avg. east, 7° below west); precip. 1" (avg.). 1–4 Lake snow east, sunny west; frigid. 5–13 Snow east, sunny west; very cold. 14–17 Sunny, cold. 18–23 Snow east, flurries west; cold. 24–31 Snow showers, frigid.

**FEB. 2023:** Temp. 5° (7° below avg.); precip. 0.5" (0.5° below avg.). 1–7 Snow showers, cold. 8–12 Sunny, very cold. 13–20 Snow showers, chilly. 21–24 Periods of snow, very cold. 25–28 Sunny, cold.

**MAR. 2023:** Temp. 28° (avg.); precip. 0.5" (1" below avg.). 1–5 Sunny, mild. 6–9 Flurries east, snow west; chilly. 10–15 Flurries east, sunny west; chilly. 16–24 Sunny; cold, then turning mild. 25–27 Snow, chilly. 28–31 A few showers, mild.

**APR. 2023:** Temp. 40° (1° below avg.); precip. 2" (avg.). 1–6 Showers, mild. 7–9 Sunny, mild. 10–13 Rain and snow, cold. 14–17 Sunny east, rain west; mild. 18–25 Sunny; warm, then turning cold. 26–30 Sunny, warm.

**MAY 2023:** Temp. 55° (1° above avg.); precip. 4.5" (1" above avg.). 1–7 Showers, heavy east; warm. 8–10 Sunny, mild. 11–17 A few showers, warm. 18–22 T-storms, warm. 23–31 A few showers, warm.

**JUNE 2023:** Temp. 65° (1° above avg.); precip. 6.5" (2" above avg.). 1–5 A few showers, mild. 6–18 Scattered t-storms, heavy rain west; mild. 19–27 Sunny east, t-storms west; warm. 28–30 T-storms, warm.

**JULY 2023:** Temp. 67° (2° below avg.); precip. 3.5" (avg.). 1–4 Showers, cool. 5–10 Isolated showers, mild. 11–12 T-storms, warm. 13–15 A few t-storms, cool. 16–26 A few t-storms east, sunny west; mild. 27–31 Sunny, cool.

**AUG. 2023:** Temp. 69° (3° above avg.); precip. 5.5" (2" above avg.). 1–3 Sunny, cool. 4–7 Sunny, hot. 8–12 T-storms, mild. 13–22 T-storms, warm. 23–31 Isolated t-storms east, sunny west; very warm.

**SEPT. 2023:** Temp. 60° (1° above avg.); precip. 4" (2" above avg. east, avg. west). 1–7 Heavy rain east, showers west; warm. 8–13 Isolated showers, cool. 14–18 Sunny, warm. 19–24 T-storms east, sunny west; cool. 25–30 Showers, cool.

**OCT. 2023:** Temp. 50° (3° above avg.); precip. 0.5" (2" below avg.). 1–4 Isolated showers, warm. 5–11 A few showers, chilly. 12–14 Sunny, warm. 15–21 Isolated showers, mild. 22–31 Sunny, warm.

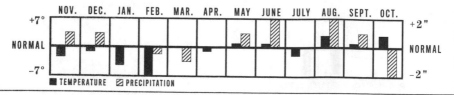

WEATHER

# HEARTLAND

**SUMMARY: Winter** will be colder than normal, on average, with the coldest periods in late November, early December, early to mid-January, and mid- to late February. Precipitation and snowfall will be above average in the east and below average in the west. The snowiest periods will be in late November, early to mid-January, and February. On average, **April** and **May** will feature near-normal temperatures and precipitation. **Summer** will be hotter and drier than normal, with the hottest periods in mid- to late June, mid-July, and early and late August. **September** and **October** will be warm, with near-normal rainfall, on average.

**NOV. 2022:** Temp. 42° (1° below avg.); precip. 2" (avg.). 1–3 Showers, warm. 4–6 Sunny, chilly. 7–9 Rainy periods, mild. 10–17 Showers, then sunny, turning colder. 18–22 Snowy periods, very cold. 23–30 Rain and snow showers, mild, then snow, frigid.

**DEC. 2022:** Temp. 36° (1° above avg.); precip. 1" (0.5" below avg.). 1–4 Snow showers, very cold. 5–12 A few showers, warm. 13–15 Snow showers, cold. 16–25 Sunny, mild, then snow showers, colder. 26–31 Sunny, turning milder.

**JAN. 2023:** Temp. 22° (8° below avg.); precip. 1" (avg.). 1–8 Flurries, frigid. 9–15 Snowstorm, then sunny; bitter cold. 16–18 Snowy periods, chilly. 19–22 Sunny, cold. 23–31 Flurries, frigid.

**FEB. 2023:** Temp. 23° (9° below avg.); precip. 2.5" (0.5" above avg.). 1–4 Sunny, very cold. 5–7 Snowstorm, cold. 8–17 Sunny, then snow showers; frigid. 18–22 Flurries, cold. 23–28 Snowy periods, very cold.

**MAR. 2023:** Temp. 46° (2° above avg.); precip. 2.5" (1" above avg. east, 1" below west). 1–5 Snow showers, then sunny; chilly. 6–10 Snow showers, cold. 11–17 Sunny west, rainy periods east; milder. 18–25 Rain and snow showers, then sunny; milder. 26–31 A few t-storms, warm.

**APR. 2023:** Temp. 53° (2° below avg.); precip. 4.5" (1" above avg.). 1–7 Scattered t-storms; warm, then cooler. 8–15 Rainy periods, chilly. 16–20 Sunny, mild. 21–30 Showers, cool.

**MAY 2023:** Temp. 66° (2° above avg.); precip. 4" (1" below avg.). 1–7 Rainy periods, cool. 8–11 Sunny, mild. 12–18 T-storms, warm. 19–24 Sunny, very warm. 25–31 A few t-storms, warm.

**JUNE 2023:** Temp. 75° (2° above avg.); precip. 3.5" (1.5" below avg.). 1–7 Sunny, warm. 8–16 Scattered t-storms; hot, then cooler. 17–25 Isolated t-storms, hot. 26–30 Sunny, hot.

**JULY 2023:** Temp. 77° (1° below avg.); precip. 5" (1" above avg.). 1–7 A few t-storms; cool north, hot south. 8–15 Scattered t-storms, hot. 16–26 Isolated t-storms, warm. 27–31 Sunny north, a few t-storms south; cool.

**AUG. 2023:** Temp. 78° (3° above avg.); precip. 2" (1.5" below avg.). 1–9 A few t-storms, hot. 10–18 Isolated t-storms, warm. 19–23 T-storms, then sunny; cooler. 24–31 Sunny, turning hot.

**SEPT. 2023:** Temp. 71° (3° above avg.); precip. 4.5" (1" above avg.). 1–6 Isolated t-storms, hot. 7–14 T-storms, very warm. 15–22 Sunny, mild. 23–30 Scattered showers, cool.

**OCT. 2023:** Temp. 59° (2° above avg.); precip. 2" (1" below avg.). 1–5 Rainy periods; cool, then warmer. 6–14 Sunny, chilly. 15–19 A few showers, cool. 20–29 Sunny, warm. 30–31 A few showers, chilly.

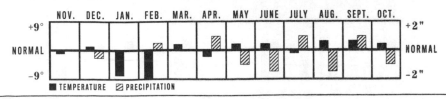

# TEXAS–OKLAHOMA

**SUMMARY: Winter** will be colder than normal, with the coldest periods in early to mid-January and early to mid-February. Precipitation will be below average, but snowfall will be above average in the north, with the best chances for snow in mid- to late January and early February. **April** and **May** will be warmer than average, with rainfall above normal in the north and normal in the south, on average. **Summer** will be hotter and drier than normal, with the hottest periods in late June, early to mid-July, and early August. Watch for tropical storms in late July and mid-August. **September** and **October** will be warmer than normal, with below-normal rainfall in the north and near-normal rainfall in the south, on average.

**NOV. 2022:** Temp. 60° (3° above avg.); precip. 3" (1" below avg. north, 1" above south). 1–6 Rain, then sunny, chilly. 7–13 Sunny north, showers south; warm. 14–22 Sunny, cool north; rainy periods, warm south. 23–30 Sunny; warm, then colder.

**DEC. 2022:** Temp. 53° (2° above avg.); precip. 1.5" (1" below avg.). 1–5 Sunny, very cold. 6–12 Isolated showers, warm. 13–20 Sunny, mild. 21–27 Rain and snow showers, cold. 28–31 Sunny, warm.

**JAN. 2023:** Temp. 43° (7° below avg.); precip. 3.5" (1" above avg.). 1–3 Sunny, very cold. 4–9 Rain and snow showers north, rainy periods south; cold. 10–14 Snowy periods north, rain and snow south; very cold. 15–25 Flurries OK, a few showers TX; cold. 26–29 Sunny, mild. 30–31 Snow north, rain south; cold.

**FEB. 2023:** Temp. 45° (8° below avg. north, 4° below south); precip. 2" (1.5" above avg. north, 0.5" below south). 1–10 Periods of rain and snow north, showers south; very cold. 11–19 Sunny; very cold, then warmer. 20–28 Rain and snow showers, cold.

**MAR. 2023:** Temp. 63° (3° above avg.); precip. 1" (1.5" above avg.). 1–5 Sunny, chilly. 6–14 Sunny, mild. 15–24 T-storms, then sunny, milder. 25–31 Isolated t-storms, warm.

**APR. 2023:** Temp. 68° (1° above avg.); precip. 3" (avg.). 1–5 A few t-storms, turning cooler. 6–11 Sunny, warm. 12–19 Isolated t-storms, cool. 20–24 A few t-storms north, sunny south; warm. 25–30 Rainy, cool north; isolated t-storms, turning warm south.

**MAY 2023:** Temp. 78° (4° above avg.); precip. 6" (2" above avg. north, avg. south). 1–9 Sunny, warm. 10–14 T-storms north, sunny south; warm. 15–18 Sunny, hot. 19–23 T-storms, warm. 24–31 Scattered t-storms; cool OK, hot TX.

**JUNE 2023:** Temp. 83° (3° above avg.); precip. 1.5" (2" below avg.). 1–9 Sunny, warm. 10–15 Isolated t-storms, warm. 16–23 Sunny, hot. 24–30 Isolated t-storms, hot.

**JULY 2023:** Temp. 84° (2° above avg.); precip. 3" (avg.). 1–8 Isolated t-storms, hot. 9–14 Sunny, hot. 15–23 Scattered t-storms, warm. 24–26 Tropical storm threat. 27–31 Isolated t-storms, warm.

**AUG. 2023:** Temp. 85° (3° above avg.); precip. 2.5" (1" below avg. north, 1" above south). 1–10 Sunny north, isolated t-storms south; hot. 11–20 Isolated t-storms, warm. 21–23 Tropical storm threat. 24–31 Sunny north, a few t-storms south; hot.

**SEPT. 2023:** Temp. 79° (2° above avg.); precip. 3.5" (2" below avg. north, 2" above south). 1–6 T-storms, warm. 7–12 Sunny, hot. 13–21 Scattered t-storms, cool. 22–30 Sunny north, t-storms south TX; warm.

**OCT. 2023:** Temp. 69° (1° above avg.); precip. 1.5" (2" below avg.). 1–5 Showers, then sunny, warm. 6–14 Sunny; cool, then warm. 15–21 A few showers, cool. 22–28 Sunny, warm. 29–31 Rainy periods, cool.

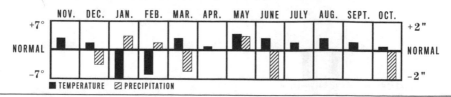

# HIGH PLAINS

**SUMMARY: Winter** will be colder than normal, with the coldest periods in late November, early December, early and late January, and early and late February. Precipitation and snowfall will be above normal in the north and below normal in the south. The snowiest periods will be in mid- to late November, mid- to late January, and early February. **April** and **May** will be warmer than normal, on average, with above-normal precipitation. **Summer** will be hotter and drier than normal, with the hottest periods in mid-June, early July, and early and late August. On average, **September** and **October** will be warmer and slightly wetter than normal.

**NOV. 2022:** Temp. 38° (4° below avg. north, 4° above south); precip. 1.3" (1" above avg. north, 0.5" below south). 1–10 Rain and snow showers, then sunny, cold. 11–16 Snowstorm north, then flurries, frigid; sunny, mild south. 17–24 Snow showers, chilly. 25–30 Snowy periods, cold north; sunny, mild south.

**DEC. 2022:** Temp. 30° (2° below avg. north, 4° above south); precip. 0.3" (0.2" below avg.). 1–9 Flurries; cold, then turning milder. 10–16 Snow showers, cold north; sunny, mild south. 17–22 Sunny, chilly. 23–31 Flurries; cold north, turning milder south.

**JAN. 2023:** Temp. 20° (8° below avg.); precip. 0.5" (avg.). 1–4 Snowy periods, very cold. 5–11 Snow showers, cold. 12–15 Sunny, turning milder. 16–25 A few snow showers, cold. 26–31 Flurries, cold.

**FEB. 2023:** Temp. 19° (9° below avg.); precip. 0.7" (0.2" above avg.). 1–9 Snowy periods, frigid. 10–16 Flurries, turning milder. 17–28 Snow showers, bitter cold.

**MAR. 2023:** Temp. 46° (7° above avg.); precip. 0.5" (0.5" below avg.). 1–5 Flurries, mild. 6–14 Snow showers, cold, then sunny, milder. 15–18 Snowy periods east, sunny west; chilly. 19–31 Sunny, warm.

**APR. 2023:** Temp. 49° (avg.); precip. 2.5" (1" above avg.). 1–11 Periods of rain and snow, chilly. 12–18 A few showers north, sunny south; cool. 19–24 Rainy periods, mild. 25–30 Showers, mild north; snowy periods, cold south.

**MAY 2023:** Temp. 59° (1° above avg.); precip. 4" (1.5" above avg.). 1–4 Showers, mild. 5–8 Sunny, turning hot. 9–15 Rainy, cool. 16–21 A few t-storms, warm. 22–31 Rainy periods; cool, then turning warmer.

**JUNE 2023:** Temp. 70° (2° above avg.); precip. 2" (0.5" below avg.). 1–5 Isolated t-storms, turning cooler. 6–17 T-storms; cool north, hot south. 18–30 Scattered t-storms, warm.

**JULY 2023:** Temp. 73° (2° below avg. north, 2° above south); precip. 1.5" (0.5" below avg.). 1–9 A few t-storms; cool, then turning hot. 10–15 Rainy periods, cool. 16–24 Sunny, hot. 25–31 A few showers, turning cooler.

**AUG. 2023:** Temp. 74° (3° above avg.); precip. 1" (1" below avg.). 1–5 Sunny north, a few t-storms south; warm. 6–9 Scattered t-storms, cool. 10–14 Sunny; cool, then turning warm. 15–22 Isolated t-storms, warm. 23–31 Sunny, turning hot.

**SEPT. 2023:** Temp. 63° (avg.); precip. 2.5" (1" above avg.). 1–9 Rainy periods, cool north; sunny, warm south. 10–13 Rainy, cool. 14–24 Sunny, turning warmer. 25–30 A few showers, cool.

**OCT. 2023:** Temp. 53° (4° above avg.); precip. 0.5" (0.5" below avg.). 1–9 Sunny, turning cooler. 10–16 Rain and snow showers east, sunny west; turning cooler. 17–22 Isolated showers, mild. 23–31 Sunny, warm.

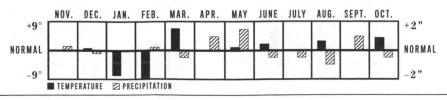

# INTERMOUNTAIN

Spokane
Pendleton
Boise
Reno
Salt Lake City
Grand Junction
Flagstaff

**SUMMARY: Winter** will be warmer than normal, with the coldest periods in mid-November and early February. Precipitation will be above normal, with above-average snowfall in the far north and far south. The snowiest periods will be in mid-November, late December, early to mid-January, and early February. **April** and **May** will be cooler than normal, with above-normal precipitation, on average. **Summer** will be slightly cooler than normal, with rainfall above average in the north and below normal in the south. The hottest periods will be in mid- to late July and early August. **September** and **October** will be cooler and drier than normal, on average.

**NOV. 2022:** Temp. 43° (2° above avg.); precip. 1" (avg.). 1–11 Periods of rain and snow north, sunny south; chilly. 12–16 Snowy periods, cold. 17–22 Showers north, sunny south; mild. 23–30 Rain and snow north, sunny south; mild.

**DEC. 2022:** Temp. 37° (4° above avg.); precip. 2.5" (1" above avg.). 1–4 Rain and snow north, sunny south; mild. 5–9 Rain and snow, mild. 10–12 Snowy periods, chilly. 13–21 Rain and snow showers; cold north, mild south. 22–31 Snowy periods; cold, then milder.

**JAN. 2023:** Temp. 40° (6° above avg.); precip. 2.5" (1" above avg.). 1–15 Rain and snow, mild. 16–19 Flurries north, snowstorm south; cold. 20–31 Periods of rain and snow, warm.

**FEB. 2023:** Temp. 36° (1° above avg.); precip. 3" (avg. north, 2" above south). 1–9 Snowy periods, cold. 10–17 Sunny, mild. 18–28 Rain and snow, mild.

**MAR. 2023:** Temp. 49° (5° above avg.); precip. 2" (0.5" above avg.). 1–7 Rain and snow showers, chilly. 8–14 Sunny, warm. 15–18 A few showers, mild. 19–23 Sunny, warm. 24–31 Periods of rain and snow, cool.

**APR. 2023:** Temp. 48° (2° below avg.); precip. 2" (1" above avg.). 1–3 Sunny north, rain and snow south; chilly. 4–7 Sunny, cool. 8–16 Rain and snow showers, chilly. 17–24 Showers; warm, then turning cooler. 25–30 A few rain and snow showers, chilly.

**MAY 2023:** Temp. 57° (1° below avg.); precip. 1.0" (avg.). 1–9 Rainy periods north, sunny south; mild. 10–20 A few showers, chilly. 21–31 Isolated t-storms, mild.

**JUNE 2023:** Temp. 66° (1° below avg.); precip. 0.5" (0.5" above avg. north, 0.5" below south). 1–5 Rainy periods north, sunny south; cool. 6–10 Sunny, warm. 11–20 Isolated t-storms, warm. 21–30 Scattered t-storms, turning cool.

**JULY 2023:** Temp. 76° (2° above avg.); precip. 0.2" (0.3" below avg.). 1–11 Isolated t-storms, warm. 12–26 Sunny north, t-storms south; hot. 27–31 Sunny, hot.

**AUG. 2023:** Temp. 71° (2° below avg.); precip. 1.5" (0.5" above avg.). 1–4 Sunny, hot. 5–9 T-storms, cool. 10–15 Scattered t-storms, cool. 16–27 Sunny, turning warm. 28–31 T-storms, cool.

**SEPT. 2023:** Temp. 62° (2° below avg.); precip. 0.5" (0.5" below avg.). 1–4 Showers north, sunny south; cool. 5–14 Sunny north, a few showers south; chilly. 15–30 Sunny; warm, then turning cooler.

**OCT. 2023:** Temp. 53° (1° above avg.); precip. 0.5" (0.5" below avg.). 1–12 Sunny, warm. 13–17 Sunny north, a few showers south; cool. 18–27 Rain and snow showers, cool. 28–31 Sunny; cool north, warm south.

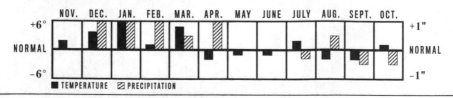

NOV. DEC. JAN. FEB. MAR. APR. MAY JUNE JULY AUG. SEPT. OCT.

+6° / NORMAL / –6°     +1" / NORMAL / –1"

■ TEMPERATURE ▨ PRECIPITATION

WEATHER

# DESERT SOUTHWEST

**SUMMARY: Winter** will be warmer than normal, with above-normal precipitation. The coldest periods will be in late November, mid- and late December, and mid-January. Snowfall will be below normal in most areas that normally receive snow, with the snowiest periods in early to mid-January and early February. On aver-

age, **April** and **May** will feature near-normal temperatures and slightly above-normal precipitation. **Summer** will be hotter than normal, with slightly above-normal rainfall. The hottest periods will occur in early and mid-June and early and late July. On average, **September** and **October** will be warmer than normal, with slightly above-normal rainfall.

WEATHER

**NOV. 2022:** Temp. 61° (4° above avg.); precip. 0.1" (0.4" below avg.). 1–12 Isolated showers, then sunny; chilly, then turning warmer. 13–30 Sunny; cool, then warmer.

**DEC. 2022:** Temp. 53° (5° above avg.); precip. 0.3" (0.2" below avg.). 1–10 Sunny, warm. 11–15 Isolated showers, cool. 16–22 Rainy periods, mild. 23–31 Flurries east, a few showers west; mild.

**JAN. 2023:** Temp. 51° (2° above avg.); precip. 1.1" (0.6" above avg.). 1–9 Rainy periods, mild. 10–17 Rain and snow showers east, a few showers west; cold. 18–21 Sunny, turning milder. 22–31 A few rain and snow showers east, showers west; mild.

**FEB. 2023:** Temp. 51° (1° below avg.); precip. 1" (0.5" above avg.). 1–6 Rainy, turning cool. 7–10 Rain and snow showers east, sunny west; cold. 11–18 Sunny, turning milder. 19–25 Rainy periods, mild. 26–28 Sunny, cool.

**MAR. 2023:** Temp. 63° (3° above avg.); precip. 0.5" (avg.). 1–6 Flurries east, a few showers west; chilly. 7–13 Sunny, turning warmer. 14–17 Isolated showers, mild. 18–22 Sunny, warm. 23–26 A few showers, mild. 27–31 Sunny, turning cooler.

**APR. 2023:** Temp. 65° (1° below avg.); precip. 0.7" (0.2" above avg.). 1–2 Scattered showers, chilly. 3–15 Sunny; warm, then turning cooler. 16–21 Sunny, warm. 22–30 A few showers, cool.

**MAY 2023:** Temp. 75° (1° above avg.); precip. 0.4" (0.1" below avg.). 1–10 Sunny, hot. 11–21 A few t-storms east, sunny west; cool. 22–31 Sunny, warm.

**JUNE 2023:** Temp. 87° (2° above avg.); precip. 0.5" (0.4" above avg. east, 0.4" below west). 1–6 Sunny, hot. 7–18 Sunny, warm, then turning hot. 19–24 A few t-storms, cool east; sunny, warm west. 25–30 Sunny, turning hot.

**JULY 2023:** Temp. 91° (3° above avg.); precip. 1.3" (0.8" below avg. east, 0.5" above west). 1–3 Isolated t-storms, hot. 4–12 Sunny, hot. 13–17 A few t-storms, hot. 18–31 Scattered t-storms; warm, then hot.

**AUG. 2023:** Temp. 87° (avg.); precip. 2" (1" above avg. east, 0.5" below west). 1–5 Scattered t-storms, warm. 6–11 Sunny, hot. 12–18 T-storms, warm. 19–31 Scattered t-storms, warm east; sunny, hot west.

**SEPT. 2023:** Temp. 79° (1° below avg.); precip. 1" (0.3" above avg. east, 0.3" below west). 1–6 Sunny, warm. 7–11 Isolated t-storms, cool. 12–18 Scattered t-storms east, sunny west; cool. 19–30 Sunny, hot.

**OCT. 2023:** Temp. 72° (3° above avg.); precip. 1.5" (0.5" above avg.). 1–11 Sunny, warm. 12–19 Showers, cool. 20–23 Sunny, warm. 24–31 Showers east, sunny west; warm.

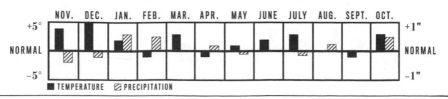

# PACIFIC NORTHWEST

Seattle
Portland
Eugene
Eureka

**SUMMARY: Winter** temperatures will be milder than normal, with slightly below-normal precipitation and snowfall. The coldest periods will be in mid-November and early and late December. The snowiest period will be in mid-November. **April** and **May** will be warmer and slightly wetter than normal, on average. **Summer** will be warmer and wetter than normal. The hottest periods will be in mid- to late July and early August. **September** and **October** will be slightly cooler and drier than normal, on average.

**NOV. 2022:** Temp. 48° (avg.); precip. 7" (1" above avg.). 1–9 Rainy, mild. 10–16 Periods of snow and rain, very cold. 17–26 Rainy periods, mild. 27–30 Showers, cool.

**DEC. 2022:** Temp. 46° (2° above avg.); precip. 9.5" (2.5" above avg.). 1–2 Rain and snow showers, cold. 3–9 Periods of heavy rain, warm. 10–14 Showers, then sunny, mild. 15–20 Sunny north, showers south; cool. 21–31 Periods of rain and snow; cold, then mild.

**JAN. 2023:** Temp. 49° (5° above avg.); precip. 6" (avg.). 1–14 Rainy periods, mild. 15–17 Sunny, cool. 18–25 Showers, cool. 26–31 Occasional rain, warm.

**FEB. 2023:** Temp. 46° (2° above avg.); precip. 2.5" (2" below avg.). 1–2 Showers, turning colder. 3–11 Sunny, then a few showers; cool. 12–19 Sunny, then scattered showers; mild. 20–23 Sunny, chilly. 24–28 Showers, mild.

**MAR. 2023:** Temp. 51° (4° above avg.); precip. 2" (2" below avg.). 1–7 Sunny, then a few showers; cool. 8–15 Sunny, warm. 16–18 Showers, mild. 19–27 A few showers, mild. 28–31 Rainy periods, chilly.

**APR. 2023:** Temp. 51° (avg.); precip. 4.5" (1" above avg.). 1–5 Sunny; warm, then cooler. 6–15 Rainy periods, chilly. 16–21 Sunny, then showers; mild. 22–27 A few showers, cool. 28–30 Sunny, mild.

**MAY 2023:** Temp. 58° (2° above avg.); precip. 2" (avg.). 1–8 Sunny, then rainy periods; cool. 9–13 Sunny, turning warm. 14–21 Scattered showers, chilly. 22–31 Sunny, turning hot.

**JUNE 2023:** Temp. 62° (1° above avg.); precip. 1" (0.5" below avg.). 1–7 Scattered showers, cool. 8–13 Sunny, turning warm. 14–18 Isolated showers, cool. 19–30 Sunny, isolated showers south; very warm, then cool.

**JULY 2023:** Temp. 69° (3° above avg.); precip. 0.8" (0.3" above avg.). 1–4 A few showers, cool. 5–7 Sunny, hot. 8–18 Showers, cool, then turning sunny, hot. 19–26 Isolated t-storms, then sunny; cooler. 27–31 Sunny, turning hot.

**AUG. 2023:** Temp. 66° (1° below avg.); precip. 2.5" (1.5" above avg.). 1–9 Sunny, hot, then showers, cool. 10–18 Scattered showers, cool. 19–23 Sunny, warm. 24–31 Rainy periods, cool.

**SEPT. 2023:** Temp. 61° (1° below avg.); precip. 2.5" (1" above avg.). 1–10 Rainy periods, cool. 11–16 Rainy north, sunny south; cool. 17–23 A few showers, warm. 24–30 Sunny, mild.

**OCT. 2023:** Temp. 55° (avg.); precip. 1.5" (2" below avg.). 1–12 Sunny, mild. 13–17 A few showers, cool. 18–20 Sunny, chilly. 21–25 Showers, then sunny, cool. 26–31 Rainy periods, cool.

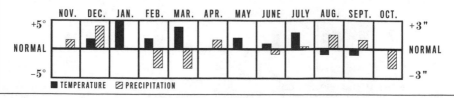

# PACIFIC SOUTHWEST

**SUMMARY: Winter** will be warmer and wetter than normal, with above-normal mountain snows. The coldest temperatures will occur in mid-November, mid-January, and early February. The stormiest periods will be in mid- to late December, early and late January, early and late February, and late March. **April** and **May** will be slightly warmer than normal, with rainfall near normal in the north and below normal in the south. **Summer** temperatures will be slightly below normal along the coast and hotter than normal inland. Rainfall will be near normal in the north and above normal in the south. The hottest periods will be in mid-June and early and late July. **September** and **October** will be warmer and drier than normal.

San Francisco

• Fresno

Los Angeles

San Diego•

**NOV. 2022:** Temp. 63° (4° above avg.); precip. 0.2" (0.8" below avg.). 1–12 Sunny, mild. 13–15 Rainy periods north, sunny south; cool. 16–24 Sunny, turning warm. 25–30 Isolated showers, mild.

**DEC. 2022:** Temp. 61° (6° above avg.); precip. 4.5" (2.5" above avg.). 1–9 Scattered showers north, sunny south; mild. 10–22 Rainy periods, warm. 23–26 A few showers, mild. 27–31 Periods of rain, mild.

**JAN. 2023:** Temp. 60° (4° above avg.); precip. 6" (3" above avg.). 1–12 Rainy periods, some heavy; mild. 13–27 Sunny; cool, then warm. 28–31 Rainy periods, mild.

**FEB. 2023:** Temp. 58° (2° above avg.); precip. 6" (3" above avg.). 1–7 Rainy periods, chilly. 8–18 Sunny, mild. 19–26 Rainy periods, some heavy; mild. 27–28 Sunny, mild.

**MAR. 2023:** Temp. 62° (4° above avg.); precip. 4" (1.5" above avg.). 1–5 Rainy periods, chilly. 6–13 Sunny, turning very warm. 14–16 Showers, mild. 17–21 Sunny, warm. 22–31 Rainy periods, cool.

**APR. 2023:** Temp. 60° (1° below avg.); precip. 1.5" (1" above avg. north, avg. south). 1–5 Sunny; warm north, cool south. 6–9 Rainy periods, chilly. 10–16 Isolated showers, cool. 17–24 Rainy periods north, isolated showers south; cool. 25–30 Sunny, mild.

**MAY 2023:** Temp. 67° (3° above avg.); precip.

0.2" (0.3" below avg.). 1–12 Sunny, warm. 13–19 A.M. sprinkles, P.M. sun; cool. 20–31 Sunny; hot inland, warm coast.

**JUNE 2023:** Temp. 70° (1° below avg. north, 3° above south); precip. 0.1" (avg.). 1–7 Sunny, mild. 8–18 A.M. clouds coast, P.M. sun; cool north, very warm south. 19–30 A.M. drizzle coast, sunny elsewhere; cool.

**JULY 2023:** Temp. 74° (avg. coast, 4° above inland); precip. 0" (avg.). 1–5 A.M. drizzle coast, sunny elsewhere; cool. 6–10 Sunny, very warm. 11–18 Clouds, cool coast; sunny, hot inland. 19–31 Sunny; mild coast, hot inland.

**AUG. 2023:** Temp. 73° (1° above avg.); precip. 0.4" (avg. north, 0.8" above south). 1–7 Sunny, warm. 8–20 Sunny inland; A.M. clouds, P.M. sun coast; cool. 21–27 A.M. sprinkles coast, sunny elsewhere; warm. 28–31 Sunny north, rainy periods south; cool.

**SEPT. 2023:** Temp. 75° (3° above avg.); precip. 0.1" (avg.). 1–8 Isolated showers, cool. 9–11 Sunny; mild coast, cool inland. 12–19 Sunny, turning hot. 20–30 Sunny, warm.

**OCT. 2023:** Temp. 68° (2° above avg.); precip. 0.1" (0.4" below avg.). 1–3 Sunny, mild. 4–7 Sunny; hot north, warm south. 8–16 Sunny north, isolated showers south; warm. 17–31 A few sprinkles, mild.

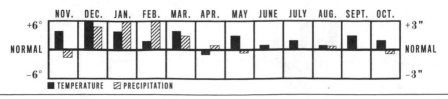

# ALASKA

**SUMMARY: Winter** temperatures will be much milder than normal, with the coldest periods in mid- to late November, early December, and late January. Precipitation and snowfall will be below normal, on average, with the snowiest periods in early November, mid-December, late January, and early February. **April** and **May** will be warmer than normal, with near-normal precipitation. **Summer**, on average, will be warmer than normal, with above-normal precipitation. The hottest periods will be in early and late July. On average, **September** and **October** will be milder than normal, with precipitation above normal N and below normal S.

**Key:** north (N), central (C), south (S), panhandle (P), elsewhere (EW).

**NOV. 2022:** Temp. 3° N, 32° S (1° below avg. N, 5° below S); precip. 0.2" N, 3" S (0.2" below avg. N, 2" below S). 1–5 Flurries, cold. 6–12 Snowy periods; turning mild N, cold EW. 13–19 Mainly dry; mild N, cold EW. 20–30 Snow showers, cold.

**DEC. 2022:** Temp. 2° N, 31° S (7° above avg. N, 1° below S); precip. 0.5" N, 3" S (0.3" above avg. N, 2" below S). 1–5 Flurries, very cold. 6–12 Rainy periods, mild P; flurries, cold EW. 13–21 A few snow showers, cold P; snowy periods, mild EW. 22–31 Flurries; mild N, turning cold EW.

**JAN. 2023:** Temp. 0° N, 39° S (10° above avg.); precip. 0.2" N, 5" S (avg.). 1–7 Rainy periods P, snow showers EW; mild. 8–16 Snow showers; cold P, mild EW. 17–26 Showers P, flurries EW; mild. 27–31 Flurries, cold N+C; snowy, cold S; rainy, mild P.

**FEB. 2023:** Temp. –1° N, 41° S (10° above avg.); precip. 0.2" N, 3" S (avg. N, 1" below S). 1–5 Snow showers, turning mild. 6–12 Clear, mild. 13–19 Snow showers N, showers S; mild. 20–28 Rain and snow showers P, flurries EW; mild.

**MAR. 2023:** Temp. –7° N, 38° S (4° above avg.); precip. 0.5" N, 5" S (avg.). 1–8 Snow showers N, rain and snow showers S; mild. 9–21 Flurries, cold N; showers, mild P; snowy, then clear, mild S. 22–31 A few snow showers, cold N; mainly dry, mild EW.

**APR. 2023:** Temp. 10° N, 47° S (6° above avg.); precip. 0.7" N, 3" S (avg.). 1–5 Flurries, cold N; sunny, mild EW. 6–18 Snow showers, mild N+C; showers, chilly P; sunny, mild S. 19–30 Showers P, mostly dry EW; mild.

**MAY 2023:** Temp. 24.5° N, 49° EW (2° above avg.); precip. 0.6" N, 3" S (avg.). 1–8 Flurries, cold N; a few showers, mild EW. 9–16 Rain and snow showers, cold N+C; showers, mild P; sunny, mild S. 17–27 Flurries, cold N; a few showers, warm EW. 28–31 Rainy, chilly P; a few showers, mild EW.

**JUNE 2023:** Temp. 35° N, 54.5° EW (1° below avg.); precip. 1.7" N, 4.5" S (1" above avg.). 1–5 Sprinkles N, a few showers S; mild. 6–19 Flurries N, rainy periods EW; cool. 20–30 Showers, warm N+C; rainy periods, cool S.

**JULY 2023:** Temp. 43.5° N, 58.5° EW (1° above avg.); precip. 1.7" N, 5.0" S (0.5" above avg.). 1–7 Showers; cool N+S, warm C. 8–15 Rainy periods, cool S; mainly dry, mild EW. 16–20 Rainy, cool P; a few showers, warm EW. 21–31 Sunny S, rainy periods EW; warm.

**AUG. 2023:** Temp. 45.5° N, 61° EW (4° above avg.); precip. 0.7" N, 5" S (0.5" below avg.). 1–9 A few showers; cool N, warm EW. 10–16 Rainy periods, cool N+C; a few showers, warm S. 17–21 Rain and snow showers, cool N; showers, cool C; sunny, mild S. 22–31 Rainy periods, mild.

**SEPT. 2023:** Temp. 37.5° N, 58° EW (3° above avg.); precip. 1.4" N, 6.5" S (0.3" above avg. N, 1" below S). 1–11 Showers, mild. 12–16 Snowy N, showers C+S, rainy P; cool. 17–24 Snow showers N, rainy periods C+P, a few showers S; turning cool. 25–30 Flurries, cool N+C; rainy periods, mild S.

**OCT. 2023:** Temp. 19° N, 42° S (1° below avg.); precip. 0.3" N, 6.8" S (0.2" below avg.). 1–12 Snow showers, cold N+C; rainy periods, mild S. 13–22 Snow showers, cold N+C; periods of rain and snow, mild S. 23–31 Flurries N, snowy periods C+S; cold.

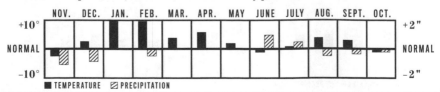

# HAWAII

**SUMMARY: Winter** temperatures will be warmer than normal, with the coolest periods in mid-November and mid- to late February. Rainfall will be below normal, with the stormiest periods in early and late November and early March. **April** will be warmer and drier than normal, while **May** will be warmer and rainier than normal. **Summer** will be slightly warmer than normal, with the hottest periods in late July and early and late August. Rainfall will be above normal. **September** and **October** temperatures will be near normal, on average, with the hottest periods in early and late September. Rainfall will be below normal in September and well above normal in October.

**KEY:** east (E), central (C), west (W). Note: Temperature and precipitation are substantially based upon topography. The detailed forecast focuses on the Honolulu–Waikiki area and provides general trends elsewhere.

**NOV. 2022:** Temp. 78.5° (1° above avg.); precip. 1.5" (4" below avg. E+W, 1" below C). 1–10 Rainy periods E+W, a few showers C; warm. 11–17 Sunny E, a few showers C+W; cool. 18–26 Daily showers E+C, rainy periods W; mild. 27–30 A few showers, mild.

**DEC. 2022:** Temp. 75° (avg.); precip. 1.3" (4" below avg. E+W, 2" below C). 1–6 Sunny E, a few showers C+W; warm. 7–15 Rainy periods E+W, a few showers C; warm. 16–21 A few showers, mild. 22–31 Rainy periods E+W, isolated showers C; mild.

**JAN. 2023:** Temp. 74° (1° above avg.); precip. 1.5" (4" below avg. E+W, 1" below C). 1–11 Sunny E, isolated showers C+W; warm. 12–19 Rainy periods E, sunny C, a few showers W; warm. 20–26 Isolated showers E+W, sunny C; warm. 27–31 Sunny, mild.

**FEB. 2023:** Temp. 74° (1° above avg.); precip. 1" (4" below avg. E+W, 1" below C). 1–4 A few showers, mild. 5–10 Rainy periods E, a few showers C+W; warm. 11–16 A few showers, cool. 17–19 Sunny, mild. 20–22 Showers, cool. 23–28 Sunny E, a few showers C+W; mild.

**MAR. 2023:** Temp. 75.5° (1.5° above avg.); precip. 2" (avg. E+C, 2" below W). 1–9 Rain, some heavy E; showers C+W; warm. 10–18 Showers E+W, isolated showers C; mild. 19–31 Rainy periods E, a few showers C+W; warm.

**APR. 2023:** Temp. 77° (2° above avg. E, 1° above W); precip. 1.7" (4" below avg. E, 1" above C+W). 1–9 Rainy periods E+W, showers C; mild. 10–11 A few showers E, sunny C+W; warm. 12–13 Sunny E, rain C+W; mild. 14–19 A

few showers, mild. 20–30 Rainy periods E+W, a few showers C; warm.

**MAY 2023:** Temp. 77.5° (1° above avg. E, avg. W); precip. 2.7" (1" above avg. E, 2" above C+W). 1–9 Rain E+W, sunny C; warm. 10–16 Rain and t-storms, some heavy; warm. 17–23 Rainy periods E+W, a few showers C; mild. 24–31 A few showers E+C, rainy periods W; mild.

**JUNE 2023:** Temp. 80° (1° above avg. E, avg. W); precip. 1.9" (5" above avg. E, 1.5" above C+W). 1–7 Rainy periods E, sunny C+W; mild. 8–12 Heavy rain E, a few showers C+W; mild. 13–22 Showers, mild. 23–30 Rain E, a few showers C+W; warm.

**JULY 2023:** Temp. 81° (1° above avg. E, 1° below W); precip. 0.5" (1" below avg. E, avg. C, 2" above W). 1–9 Rainy periods E+W, sunny C; mild. 10–21 Showers E+W, isolated showers C; mild. 22–31 Showers, warm.

**AUG. 2023:** Temp. 81.5° (avg.); precip. 1.1" (0.5" above avg.). 1–8 Showers E, a few showers C+W; hot. 9–14 Rain E, heavy at times; a few showers C+W; warm. 15–25 Showers E, isolated showers C+W; warm. 26–31 Showers E+W, sunny C; warm.

**SEPT. 2023:** Temp. 82.5° (1° above avg.); precip. 0.3" (0.5" below avg.). 1–5 Showers E+W, sunny C; warm. 6–17 Showers E+W+C; mild. 18–22 Showers E+W, sunny C; warm. 23–30 Rain E, isolated showers C+W; warm.

**OCT. 2023:** Temp. 79° (avg. E, 2° below W); precip. 8" (3" above avg. E, 6" above C+W). 1–7 Showers, warm. 8–12 Rain E+C; mild. 13–21 Showers E+W, sunny C; warm. 22–31 Rain, cool.

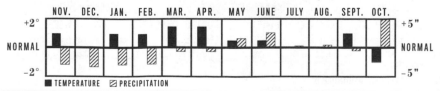

| | NOV. | DEC. | JAN. | FEB. | MAR. | APR. | MAY | JUNE | JULY | AUG. | SEPT. | OCT. | |
|---|---|---|---|---|---|---|---|---|---|---|---|---|---|
| +2° | | | | | | | | | | | | | +5" |
| NORMAL | | | | | | | | | | | | | NORMAL |
| -2° | | | | | | | | | | | | | -5" |

■ TEMPERATURE  ▨ PRECIPITATION

WEATHER

# SECRETS OF THE ZODIAC

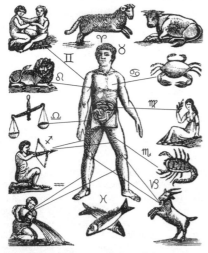

## The Man of the Signs

Ancient astrologers believed that each astrological sign influenced a specific part of the body. The first sign of the zodiac—Aries—was attributed to the head, with the rest of the signs moving down the body, ending with Pisces at the feet.

| | | |
|---|---|---|
| ♈ Aries, head | **ARI** | *Mar. 21–Apr. 20* |
| ♉ Taurus, neck | **TAU** | *Apr. 21–May 20* |
| ♊ Gemini, arms | **GEM** | *May 21–June 20* |
| ♋ Cancer, breast | **CAN** | *June 21–July 22* |
| ♌ Leo, heart | **LEO** | *July 23–Aug. 22* |
| ♍ Virgo, belly | **VIR** | *Aug. 23–Sept. 22* |
| ♎ Libra, reins | **LIB** | *Sept. 23–Oct. 22* |
| ♏ Scorpio, secrets | **SCO** | *Oct. 23–Nov. 22* |
| ♐ Sagittarius, thighs | **SAG** | *Nov. 23–Dec. 21* |
| ♑ Capricorn, knees | **CAP** | *Dec. 22–Jan. 19* |
| ♒ Aquarius, legs | **AQU** | *Jan. 20–Feb. 19* |
| ♓ Pisces, feet | **PSC** | *Feb. 20–Mar. 20* |

## ASTROLOGY VS. ASTRONOMY

**Astrology** is a tool we use to plan events according to the placements of the Sun, the Moon, and the planets in the 12 signs of the zodiac. In astrology, the planetary movements do not cause events; rather, they explain the path, or "flow," that events tend to follow. *The Moon's astrological place is given on the next page.* **Astronomy** is the study of the actual placement of the known planets and constellations. The Moon's astronomical place is given in the **Left-Hand Calendar Pages, 120–146.** *(The placement of the planets in the signs of the zodiac is not the same astrologically and astronomically.)*

The dates in the **Best Days** table, **pages 226–227,** are based on the astrological passage of the Moon.

### WHEN MERCURY IS RETROGRADE

Sometimes the other planets appear to be traveling backward through the zodiac; this is an illusion. We call this illusion *retrograde motion.*

Mercury's retrograde periods can cause our plans to go awry. However, intuition is high during these periods and coincidences can be extraordinary.

When Mercury is retrograde, stay flexible, allow more time for travel, and don't sign contracts. Review projects and plans but wait until Mercury is direct again to make final decisions.

In 2023, Mercury will be retrograde during January 1–18, April 21–May 14, August 23–September 14, and December 13–(January 1, 2024).

*–Celeste Longacre*

## GARDENING BY THE MOON'S SIGN

USE CHART ON NEXT PAGE TO FIND THE BEST DATES FOR THE FOLLOWING GARDEN TASKS . . .

**PLANT, TRANSPLANT, AND GRAFT:** Cancer, Scorpio, Pisces, or Taurus

**HARVEST:** Aries, Leo, Sagittarius, Gemini, or Aquarius

**BUILD/FIX FENCES OR GARDEN BEDS:** Capricorn

**CONTROL INSECT PESTS, PLOW, AND WEED:** Aries, Gemini, Leo, Sagittarius, or Aquarius

**PRUNE:** Aries, Leo, or Sagittarius. During a waxing Moon, pruning encourages growth; during a waning Moon, it discourages it.

# SETTING EGGS BY THE MOON'S SIGN

Chicks take about 21 days to hatch. Those born under a waxing Moon in Cancer, Scorpio, or Pisces are healthier and mature faster. To ensure that chicks are born during these times, "set eggs" (place eggs in an incubator or under a hen) 21 days before the desired hatching dates.

**EXAMPLE:**
The Moon is new on March 21 and full on April 6 (EDT). Between these dates, the Moon is in the sign of Cancer on March 28 through 30. To have chicks born on March 28, count back 21 days; set eggs on March 7.

*Below are the best days to set eggs in 2023, using only the fruitful dates between the new and full Moons and counting back 21 days:*

| | | | |
|---|---|---|---|
| **JAN.:** 3, 4, 12, 13, 30, 31 | **APR.:** 4, 5, 13, 14 | **JULY:** 4–6 | **OCT.:** 3, 4, 23, 30, 31 |
| **FEB.:** 8, 9 | **MAY:** 1, 2, 11, 12, 28–30 | **AUG.:** 1, 2, 9, 28, 29 | **NOV.:** 1, 27, 28 |
| **MAR.:** 7–9 | **JUNE:** 7, 8, 26 | **SEPT.:** 6, 7, 24–26 | **DEC.:** 5, 24, 25 |

## The Moon's Astrological Place, 2022–23

| | NOV. | DEC. | JAN. | FEB. | MAR. | APR. | MAY | JUNE | JULY | AUG. | SEPT. | OCT. | NOV. | DEC. |
|---|---|---|---|---|---|---|---|---|---|---|---|---|---|---|
| 1 | AQU | PSC | TAU | GEM | CAN | LEO | VIR | SCO | SAG | AQU | ARI | TAU | GEM | LEO |
| 2 | AQU | ARI | TAU | CAN | CAN | VIR | LIB | SCO | SAG | AQU | ARI | TAU | CAN | LEO |
| 3 | PSC | ARI | GEM | CAN | LEO | VIR | LIB | SAG | CAP | PSC | TAU | GEM | CAN | LEO |
| 4 | PSC | TAU | GEM | LEO | LEO | VIR | SCO | SAG | CAP | PSC | TAU | GEM | LEO | VIR |
| 5 | ARI | TAU | CAN | LEO | LEO | LIB | SCO | CAP | AQU | ARI | TAU | CAN | LEO | VIR |
| 6 | ARI | TAU | CAN | LEO | VIR | LIB | SCO | CAP | AQU | ARI | ARI | CAN | LEO | LIB |
| 7 | TAU | GEM | CAN | VIR | VIR | SCO | SAG | AQU | PSC | TAU | GEM | CAN | VIR | LIB |
| 8 | TAU | GEM | LEO | VIR | LIB | SCO | SAG | AQU | PSC | TAU | CAN | LEO | VIR | LIB |
| 9 | GEM | CAN | LEO | LIB | LIB | SAG | CAP | PSC | ARI | GEM | CAN | LEO | LIB | SCO |
| 10 | GEM | CAN | VIR | LIB | LIB | SAG | CAP | PSC | ARI | GEM | LEO | VIR | LIB | SCO |
| 11 | GEM | CAN | VIR | LIB | SCO | SAG | AQU | ARI | TAU | GEM | LEO | VIR | LIB | SAG |
| 12 | CAN | LEO | VIR | SCO | SCO | CAP | AQU | ARI | TAU | CAN | LEO | VIR | SCO | SAG |
| 13 | CAN | LEO | LIB | SCO | SAG | CAP | PSC | ARI | GEM | CAN | VIR | LIB | SCO | CAP |
| 14 | LEO | VIR | LIB | SAG | SAG | AQU | PSC | TAU | GEM | LEO | VIR | LIB | SAG | CAP |
| 15 | LEO | VIR | SCO | SAG | CAP | AQU | ARI | TAU | CAN | LEO | LIB | SCO | SAG | CAP |
| 16 | LEO | VIR | SCO | CAP | CAP | PSC | ARI | GEM | CAN | LEO | LIB | SCO | CAP | AQU |
| 17 | VIR | LIB | SCO | CAP | AQU | PSC | TAU | GEM | CAN | VIR | LIB | SCO | CAP | AQU |
| 18 | VIR | LIB | SAG | AQU | AQU | ARI | TAU | CAN | LEO | VIR | SCO | SAG | AQU | PSC |
| 19 | LIB | SCO | SAG | AQU | PSC | ARI | TAU | CAN | LEO | LIB | SCO | SAG | AQU | PSC |
| 20 | LIB | SCO | CAP | PSC | PSC | TAU | GEM | CAN | VIR | LIB | SAG | CAP | PSC | ARI |
| 21 | LIB | SAG | CAP | PSC | ARI | TAU | GEM | LEO | VIR | LIB | SAG | CAP | PSC | ARI |
| 22 | SCO | SAG | AQU | ARI | ARI | GEM | CAN | LEO | VIR | SCO | SAG | AQU | PSC | TAU |
| 23 | SCO | CAP | AQU | ARI | ARI | GEM | CAN | VIR | LIB | SCO | CAP | AQU | ARI | TAU |
| 24 | SAG | CAP | PSC | TAU | TAU | GEM | LEO | VIR | LIB | SAG | CAP | PSC | ARI | GEM |
| 25 | SAG | AQU | PSC | TAU | TAU | CAN | LEO | VIR | SCO | SAG | AQU | PSC | TAU | GEM |
| 26 | CAP | AQU | ARI | GEM | GEM | CAN | LEO | LIB | SCO | CAP | AQU | ARI | TAU | CAN |
| 27 | CAP | PSC | ARI | GEM | GEM | LEO | VIR | LIB | SCO | CAP | PSC | ARI | GEM | CAN |
| 28 | AQU | PSC | TAU | GEM | CAN | LEO | VIR | SCO | SAG | AQU | PSC | TAU | GEM | CAN |
| 29 | AQU | ARI | TAU | — | CAN | LEO | LIB | SCO | SAG | AQU | ARI | TAU | CAN | LEO |
| 30 | PSC | ARI | GEM | — | CAN | VIR | LIB | SAG | CAP | PSC | ARI | GEM | CAN | LEO |
| 31 | — | TAU | GEM | — | LEO | — | LIB | — | CAP | PSC | — | GEM | — | VIR |

# BEST DAYS FOR 2023

This chart is based on the Moon's sign and shows the best days
each month for certain activities. –*Celeste Longacre*

| | JAN. | FEB. | MAR. | APR. | MAY | JUNE | JULY | AUG. | SEPT. | OCT. | NOV. | DEC. |
|---|---|---|---|---|---|---|---|---|---|---|---|---|
| Quit smoking | 7, 17 | 8, 13 | 8, 12 | 9, 17 | 6, 15 | 11, 15 | 8, 13 | 4, 9 | 1, 5 | 2, 12 | 9, 12 | 6, 11 |
| Bake | 5–7 | 2, 3 | 1, 2, 28–30 | 25, 26 | 22, 23 | 18–20 | 15–17 | 12, 13 | 8, 9 | 5–7 | 2, 3, 29, 30 | 26–28 |
| Brew | 15–17 | 12, 13 | 11, 12 | 7, 8 | 4–6 | 1, 2, 28, 29 | 25–27 | 22, 23 | 18, 19 | 15–17 | 12, 13 | 9, 10 |
| Dry fruit, vegetables, or meat | 8, 9, 18, 19 | 14, 15 | 13, 14 | 9–11 | 15, 16 | 11–13 | 9, 10 | 5, 6 | 10–12 | 8, 9 | 4–6 | 1–3 |
| Make jams or jellies | 24, 25 | 20, 21 | 19, 20 | 16, 17 | 13, 14 | 9, 10 | 7, 8 | 3, 4, 30, 31 | 27, 28 | 24, 25 | 20–22 | 18, 19 |
| Can, pickle, or make sauerkraut | 15–17 | 12, 13 | 11, 12, 19, 20 | 16, 17 | 13, 14 | 9, 10 | 7, 8 | 12, 13 | 8, 9 | 5–7 | 2, 3 | 9, 10 |
| Begin diet to lose weight | 7, 17 | 8, 13 | 8, 12 | 9, 17 | 6, 15 | 11, 15 | 8, 13 | 4, 9 | 1, 5 | 2, 12 | 9, 12 | 6, 11 |
| Begin diet to gain weight | 2, 25 | 22, 26 | 25, 30 | 4, 21 | 2, 29 | 3, 25 | 22, 27 | 18, 23 | 20, 28 | 17, 25 | 22, 26 | 19, 24 |
| Cut hair to encourage growth | 1, 2, 28, 29 | 24, 25 | 24, 25 | 5, 21 | 2, 3, 29–31 | 26, 27 | 23, 24 | 19–21 | 15–17 | 24, 25 | 25, 26 | 22, 23 |
| Cut hair to discourage growth | 13, 14 | 9–11 | 8–10 | 16, 17 | 17, 18 | 14, 15 | 11, 12 | 7, 8 | 3–5 | 1, 2 | 9–11 | 6–8 |
| Perm hair | 22, 23 | 18, 19 | 17, 18 | 14, 15 | 11, 12 | 7, 8 | 5, 6 | 1, 2, 28, 29 | 25, 26 | 22, 23 | 18, 19 | 16, 17 |
| Color hair | 1, 2, 28, 29 | 24, 25 | 24, 25 | 20, 21 | 17–19 | 14, 15 | 11, 12 | 7, 8 | 3–5 | 1, 2, 28, 29 | 25, 26 | 22, 23 |
| Straighten hair | 18, 19 | 14, 15 | 13, 14 | 9–11 | 7, 8 | 3, 4, 30 | 1, 2, 28, 29 | 24, 25 | 20–22 | 18, 19 | 14, 15 | 11, 12 |
| Have dental care | 10–12 | 7, 8 | 6, 7 | 2–4, 30 | 1, 27, 28 | 23–25 | 20–22 | 17, 18 | 13, 14 | 10–12 | 7, 8 | 4, 5, 31 |
| Start projects | 22 | 21 | 22 | 21 | 20 | 19 | 18 | 17 | 15 | 15 | 14 | 13 |
| End projects | 5 | 4 | 6 | 5 | 4 | 2 | 2, 31 | 29 | 28 | 27 | 26 | 25 |
| Demolish | 15–17 | 12, 13 | 11, 12 | 7, 8 | 4–6 | 1, 2, 28, 29 | 25–27 | 22, 23 | 18, 19 | 15–17 | 12, 13 | 9, 10 |
| Lay shingles | 8, 9 | 4–6 | 3–5 | 1, 27–29 | 24–26 | 21, 22 | 18, 19 | 14–16 | 10–12 | 8, 9 | 4–6 | 1–3, 29, 30 |
| Paint | 1, 2, 28, 29 | 9–11 | 8–10 | 5, 6, 20, 21 | 2, 3, 29–31 | 26, 27 | 23, 24 | 19–21 | 15–17 | 13, 14 | 9–11 | 6–8 |
| Wash windows | 26, 27 | 22, 23 | 21–23 | 18, 19 | 15, 16 | 11–13 | 9, 10 | 5, 6 | 1, 2, 29, 30 | 26, 27 | 23, 24 | 20, 21 |
| Wash floors | 24, 25 | 20, 21 | 19, 20 | 16, 17 | 13, 14 | 9, 10 | 7, 8 | 3, 4, 30, 31 | 27, 28 | 24, 25 | 20–22 | 18, 19 |
| Go camping | 18, 19 | 14, 15 | 13, 14 | 9–11 | 7, 8 | 3, 4, 30 | 1, 2, 28, 29 | 24, 25 | 20–22 | 18, 19 | 14, 15 | 11, 12 |

See what to do when via Almanac.com/2023.

| | JAN. | FEB. | MAR. | APR. | MAY | JUNE | JULY | AUG. | SEPT. | OCT. | NOV. | DEC. |
|---|---|---|---|---|---|---|---|---|---|---|---|---|
| Entertain | 8, 9 | 4–6 | 3–5 | 1, 27–29 | 24–26 | 21, 22 | 18, 19 | 14–16 | 10–12 | 8, 9 | 4–6 | 1–3, 29, 30 |
| Travel for pleasure | 8, 9 | 4–6 | 3–5 | 1, 27–29 | 24–26 | 21, 22 | 18, 19 | 14–16 | 10–12 | 8, 9 | 4–6 | 1–3, 29, 30 |
| Get married | 13, 14 | 9–11 | 8–10 | 5, 6 | 2, 3, 29–31 | 26, 27 | 23, 24 | 19–21 | 15–17 | 13, 14 | 9–11 | 6–8 |
| Ask for a loan | 15–17 | 12, 13 | 11, 12 | 7, 8 | 17, 18 | 14, 15 | 11, 12 | 7, 8 | 3–5 | 1, 2 | 12, 13 | 9, 10 |
| Buy a home | 1, 2, 28, 29 | 24, 25 | 24, 25 | 21, 25, 26 | 4, 24–26 | 28, 29 | 25–27 | 22, 23 | 18, 19 | 15–17 | 25, 26 | 22, 23 |
| Move (house/household) | 3, 4, 30, 31 | 1, 26–28 | 26, 27 | 22–24 | 20, 21 | 16, 17 | 13, 14 | 9–11 | 6, 7 | 3, 4, 30, 31 | 1, 27, 28 | 24, 25 |
| Advertise to sell | 1, 2, 28, 29 | 24, 25 | 24, 25 | 1, 27–29 | 4, 24–26 | 1, 2, 28, 29 | 25–27 | 22, 23 | 18, 19 | 15–17 | 25, 26 | 22, 23 |
| Mow to promote growth | 24, 25 | 2, 3, 21 | 1, 2, 28–30 | 25, 26 | 4, 22, 23 | 1, 2, 28, 29 | 25–27 | 22, 23 | 18, 19 | 15–17 | 20–22 | 18, 19 |
| Mow to slow growth | 15–17 | 12, 13 | 11, 12 | 7, 8 | 6, 17, 18 | 14, 15 | 11, 12 | 7, 8 | 8, 9 | 1, 2 | 4–6 | 1–3 |
| Plant aboveground crops | 5, 24, 25 | 2, 3, 21 | 1, 2, 28–30 | 25, 26 | 4, 22, 23 | 1, 2, 28, 29 | 25–27 | 22, 23 | 18, 19 | 15–17 | 20–22 | 18, 19 |
| Plant belowground crops | 15–17 | 12, 13 | 11, 12 | 7, 8, 16, 17 | 13, 14 | 9, 10 | 7, 8 | 12, 13 | 3–5 | 5–7 | 2, 3 | 9, 10 |
| Destroy pests and weeds | 26, 27 | 22, 23 | 21–23 | 18, 19 | 15, 16 | 11–13 | 9, 10 | 5, 6 | 1, 2, 29, 30 | 26, 27 | 23, 24 | 20, 21 |
| Graft or pollinate | 5–7 | 2, 3 | 1, 2, 28–30 | 25, 26 | 22, 23 | 18–20 | 15–17 | 12, 13 | 8, 9 | 5–7 | 2, 3, 29, 30 | 26–28 |
| Prune to encourage growth | 26, 27 | 4, 22, 23 | 3–5, 31 | 1, 27–29 | 24–26 | 3, 21, 22 | 1, 2, 28, 29 | 24, 25 | 20–22 | 26, 27 | 23, 24 | 20, 21 |
| Prune to discourage growth | 8, 9, 18, 19 | 14, 15 | 13, 14 | 9–11 | 15, 16 | 11–13 | 9, 10 | 5, 6 | 10–12 | 8, 9 | 4–6 | 1–3 |
| Pick fruit | 10–12 | 7, 8 | 6, 7 | 2–4, 30 | 1, 27, 28 | 23–25 | 20–22 | 17, 18 | 13, 14 | 10–12 | 7, 8 | 4, 5, 31 |
| Harvest aboveground crops | 1, 2, 28, 29 | 24, 25 | 6, 24, 25 | 2–4, 30 | 27, 28 | 23–25 | 20–22 | 26, 27 | 23, 24 | 20, 21 | 25, 26 | 22, 23 |
| Harvest belowground crops | 10–12 | 7, 8 | 15, 16 | 12, 13 | 17, 18 | 14, 15 | 11, 12 | 7, 8 | 3–5 | 10–12 | 7, 8 | 4, 5 |
| Cut hay | 26, 27 | 22, 23 | 21–23 | 18, 19 | 15, 16 | 11–13 | 9, 10 | 5, 6 | 1, 2, 29, 30 | 26, 27 | 23, 24 | 20, 21 |
| Begin logging, set posts, pour concrete | 20, 21 | 16, 17 | 15, 16 | 12, 13 | 9, 10 | 5, 6 | 3, 4, 30, 31 | 26, 27 | 23, 24 | 20, 21 | 16, 17 | 13–15 |
| Purchase animals | 5–7 | 2, 3 | 1, 2, 28–30 | 25, 26 | 22, 23 | 18–20 | 15–17 | 12, 13 | 8, 9 | 5–7 | 2, 3, 29, 30 | 26–28 |
| Breed animals | 15–17 | 12, 13 | 11, 12 | 7, 8 | 4–6 | 1, 2, 28, 29 | 25–27 | 22, 23 | 18, 19 | 15–17 | 12, 13 | 9, 10 |
| Wean | 7, 17 | 8, 13 | 8, 12 | 9, 17 | 6, 15 | 11, 15 | 8, 13 | 4, 9 | 1, 5 | 2, 12 | 9, 12 | 6, 11 |
| Castrate animals | 22, 23 | 18, 19 | 17, 18 | 14, 15 | 11, 12 | 7, 8 | 5, 6 | 1, 2, 28, 29 | 25, 26 | 22, 23 | 18, 19 | 16, 17 |
| Slaughter livestock | 15–17 | 12, 13 | 11, 12 | 7, 8 | 4–6 | 1, 2, 28, 29 | 25–27 | 22, 23 | 18, 19 | 15–17 | 12, 13 | 9, 10 |

# BEST FISHING DAYS AND TIMES

The best times to fish are when the fish are naturally most active. The Sun, Moon, tides, and weather all influence fish activity. For example, fish tend to feed more at sunrise and sunset, and also during a full Moon (when tides are higher than average). However, most of us go fishing simply when we can get the time off. But there are best times, according to fishing lore:

■ One hour before and one hour after high tides, and one hour before and one hour after low tides. The times of high tides for Boston are given on **pages 120–146;** also see **pages 236–237.** (Inland, the times for high tides correspond with the times when the Moon is due south. Low tides are halfway between high tides.)

**GET TIDE TIMES AND HEIGHTS NEAREST TO YOUR LOCATION VIA ALMANAC.COM/2023.**

■ During the "morning rise" (after sunup for a spell) and the "evening rise" (just before sundown and the hour or so after).

■ During the rise and set of the Moon.

■ When the barometer is steady or on the rise. (But even during stormy periods, the fish aren't going to give up feeding. The clever angler will find just the right bait.)

■ When there is a hatch of flies—caddis flies or mayflies, commonly.

■ When the breeze is from a westerly quarter, rather than from the north or east.

■ When the water is still or slightly rippled, rather than during a wind.

## THE BEST FISHING DAYS FOR 2023, WHEN THE MOON IS BETWEEN NEW AND FULL

January 1–6
January 21–February 5
February 20–March 7
March 21–April 6
April 20–May 5
May 19–June 3
June 18–July 3
July 17–August 1
August 16–30
September 14–29
October 14–28
November 13–27
December 12–26

*Dates based on Eastern Time.*

## HOW TO ESTIMATE THE WEIGHT OF A FISH

Measure the fish from the tip of its nose to the tip of its tail. Then measure its girth at the thickest portion of its midsection.

The weight of a fat-bodied fish (bass, salmon) =
(length x girth x girth)/800

**SALMON**

The weight of a slender fish (trout, northern pike) =
(length x girth x girth)/900

**EXAMPLE:** If a trout is 20 inches long and has a 12-inch girth, its estimated weight is
(20 x 12 x 12)/900 =
2,880/900 = 3.2 pounds

**TROUT**

**CATFISH**

# GESTATION AND MATING TABLES

| | PROPER AGE OR WEIGHT FOR FIRST MATING | PERIOD OF FERTILITY (YRS.) | NUMBER OF FEMALES FOR ONE MALE | PERIOD OF GESTATION (DAYS) AVERAGE | RANGE |
|---|---|---|---|---|---|
| **CATTLE: Cow** | 15–18 mos.[1] | 10–14 | | 283 | 279–290[2] 262–300[3] |
| **Bull** | 1 yr., well matured | 10–12 | 50[4] / thousands[5] | | |
| **GOAT: Doe** | 10 mos. or 85–90 lbs. | 6 | | 150 | 145–155 |
| **Buck** | well matured | 5 | 30 | | |
| **HORSE: Mare** | 3 yrs. | 10–12 | | 336 | 310–370 |
| **Stallion** | 3 yrs. | 12–15 | 40–45[4] / record 252[5] | | |
| **PIG: Sow** | 5–6 mos. or 250 lbs. | 6 | | 115 | 110–120 |
| **Boar** | 250–300 lbs. | 6 | 50[6] / 35–40[7] | | |
| **RABBIT: Doe** | 6 mos. | 5–6 | | 31 | 30–32 |
| **Buck** | 6 mos. | 5–6 | 30 | | |
| **SHEEP: Ewe** | 1 yr. or 90 lbs. | 6 | | 147 / 151[8] | 142–154 |
| **Ram** | 12–14 mos., well matured | 7 | 50–75[6] / 35–40[7] | | |
| **CAT: Queen** | 12 mos. | 6 | | 63 | 60–68 |
| **Tom** | 12 mos. | 6 | 6–8 | | |
| **DOG: Bitch** | 16–18 mos. | 8 | | 63 | 58–67 |
| **Male** | 12–16 mos. | 8 | 8–10 | | |

[1]Holstein and beef: 750 lbs.; Jersey: 500 lbs. [2]Beef; 8–10 days shorter for Angus. [3]Dairy. [4]Natural. [5]Artificial. [6]Hand-mated. [7]Pasture. [8]For fine wool breeds.

## INCUBATION PERIOD OF POULTRY (DAYS)

| | |
|---|---|
| Chicken | 21 |
| Duck | 26–32 |
| Goose | 30–34 |
| Guinea | 26–28 |
| Turkey | 28 |

## AVERAGE LIFE SPAN OF ANIMALS IN CAPTIVITY (YEARS)

| | | | |
|---|---|---|---|
| Cat (domestic) | 14 | Goose (domestic) | 20 |
| Chicken (domestic) | 8 | Horse | 22 |
| Dog (domestic) | 13 | Pig | 12 |
| Duck (domestic) | 10 | Rabbit | 6 |
| Goat (domestic) | 14 | Turkey (domestic) | 10 |

| | ESTRAL/ESTROUS CYCLE (INCLUDING HEAT PERIOD) AVERAGE | RANGE | LENGTH OF ESTRUS (HEAT) AVERAGE | RANGE | USUAL TIME OF OVULATION | WHEN CYCLE RECURS IF NOT BRED |
|---|---|---|---|---|---|---|
| **Cow** | 21 days | 18–24 days | 18 hours | 10–24 hours | 10–12 hours after end of estrus | 21 days |
| **Doe goat** | 21 days | 18–24 days | 2–3 days | 1–4 days | Near end of estrus | 21 days |
| **Mare** | 21 days | 10–37 days | 5–6 days | 2–11 days | 24–48 hours before end of estrus | 21 days |
| **Sow** | 21 days | 18–24 days | 2–3 days | 1–5 days | 30–36 hours after start of estrus | 21 days |
| **Ewe** | 16½ days | 14–19 days | 30 hours | 24–32 hours | 12–24 hours before end of estrus | 16½ days |
| **Queen cat** | | 15–21 days | 3–4 days, if mated | 9–10 days, in absence of male | 24–56 hours after coitus | Pseudo-pregnancy |
| **Bitch** | 24 days | 16–30 days | 7 days | 5–9 days | 1–3 days after first acceptance | Pseudo-pregnancy |

# PLANTING BY THE MOON'S PHASE

## ACCORDING TO THIS AGE-OLD PRACTICE, CYCLES OF THE MOON AFFECT PLANT GROWTH.

Plant annual flowers and vegetables that bear crops above ground during the light, or waxing, of the Moon: from the day the Moon is new to the day it is full.

Plant flowering bulbs, biennial and perennial flowers, and vegetables that bear crops below ground during the dark, or waning, of the Moon: from the day after it is full to the day before it is new again.

The Planting Dates columns give the safe periods for planting in areas that receive frost. (See **page 232** for frost dates in your area.) The Moon Favorable columns give the best planting days within the Planting Dates based on the Moon's phases for 2023. (See **pages 120–146** for the exact days of the new and full Moons.)

*The dates listed in this table are meant as general guidelines only. For seed-sowing dates based on frost dates in your local area, go to* **Almanac.com/2023.**

---

Aboveground crops are marked *.
(E) means early;  (L) means late.

---

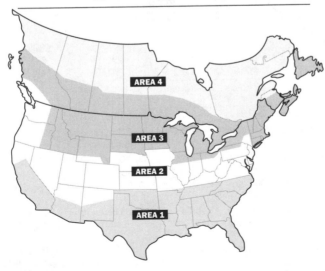

AREA 4

AREA 3

AREA 2

AREA 1

| | |
|---|---|
| * Barley | |
| * Beans | (E) |
| | (L) |
| Beets | (E) |
| | (L) |
| * Broccoli plants | (E) |
| | (L) |
| * Brussels sprouts | |
| * Cabbage plants | |
| Carrots | (E) |
| | (L) |
| * Cauliflower plants | (E) |
| | (L) |
| * Celery plants | (E) |
| | (L) |
| * Collards | (E) |
| | (L) |
| * Corn, sweet | (E) |
| | (L) |
| * Cucumbers | |
| * Eggplant plants | |
| * Endive | (E) |
| | (L) |
| * Kale | (E) |
| | (L) |
| Leek plants | |
| * Lettuce | |
| * Muskmelons | |
| * Okra | |
| Onion sets | |
| * Parsley | |
| Parsnips | |
| * Peas | (E) |
| | (L) |
| * Pepper plants | |
| Potatoes | |
| * Pumpkins | |
| Radishes | (E) |
| | (L) |
| * Spinach | (E) |
| | (L) |
| * Squashes | |
| Sweet potatoes | |
| * Swiss chard | |
| * Tomato plants | |
| Turnips | (E) |
| | (L) |
| * Watermelons | |
| * Wheat, spring | |
| * Wheat, winter | |

| AREA 1 | | AREA 2 | | AREA 3 | | AREA 4 | |
| PLANTING DATES | MOON FAVORABLE | PLANTING DATES | MOON FAVORABLE | PLANTING DATES | MOON FAVORABLE | PLANTING DATES | MOON FAVORABLE |
| --- | --- | --- | --- | --- | --- | --- | --- |
| 2/15-3/7 | 2/20-3/7 | 3/15-4/7 | 3/21-4/6 | 5/15-6/21 | 5/19-6/3, 6/18-21 | 6/1-30 | 6/1-3, 6/18-30 |
| 3/15-4/7 | 3/21-4/6 | 4/15-30 | 4/20-30 | 5/7-6/21 | 5/19-6/3, 6/18-21 | 5/30-6/15 | 5/30-6/3 |
| 8/7-31 | 8/16-30 | 7/1-31 | 7/1-3, 7/17-21 | 6/15-7/15 | 6/18-7/3 | — | — |
| 2/7-28 | 2/7-19 | 3/15-4/3 | 3/15-20 | 4/25-5/15 | 5/6-15 | 5/25-6/10 | 6/4-10 |
| 9/1-30 | 9/1-13, 9/30 | 8/15-31 | 8/15, 8/31 | 7/15-8/15 | 7/15-16, 8/2-15 | 6/15-7/8 | 6/15-17, 7/4-8 |
| 2/15-3/15 | 2/20-3/7 | 3/7-31 | 3/7, 3/21-31 | 5/15-31 | 5/19-31 | 6/1-25 | 6/1-3, 6/18-25 |
| 9/7-30 | 9/14-29 | 8/1-20 | 8/1, 8/16-20 | 6/15-7/7 | 6/18-7/3 | — | — |
| 2/11-3/20 | 2/20-3/7 | 3/7-4/15 | 3/7, 3/21-4/6 | 5/15-31 | 5/19-31 | 6/1-25 | 6/1-3, 6/18-25 |
| 2/11-3/20 | 2/20-3/7 | 3/7-4/15 | 3/7, 3/21-4/6 | 5/15-31 | 5/19-31 | 6/1-25 | 6/1-3, 6/18-25 |
| 2/15-3/7 | 2/15-19 | 3/7-31 | 3/8-20 | 5/15-31 | 5/15-18 | 5/25-6/10 | 6/4-10 |
| 8/1-9/7 | 8/2-15, 8/31-9/7 | 7/7-31 | 7/7-16 | 6/15-7/21 | 6/15-17, 7/4-16 | 6/15-7/8 | 6/15-17, 7/4-8 |
| 2/15-3/7 | 2/20-3/7 | 3/15-4/7 | 3/21-4/6 | 5/15-31 | 5/19-31 | 6/1-25 | 6/1-3, 6/18-25 |
| 8/7-31 | 8/16-30 | 7/1-8/7 | 7/1-3, 7/17-8/1 | 6/15-7/21 | 6/18-7/3, 7/17-21 | — | — |
| 2/15-28 | 2/20-28 | 3/7-31 | 3/7, 3/21-31 | 5/15-6/30 | 5/19-6/3, 6/18-30 | 6/1-30 | 6/1-3, 6/18-30 |
| 9/15-30 | 9/15-29 | 8/15-9/7 | 8/16-30 | 7/15-8/15 | 7/17-8/1 | — | — |
| 2/11-3/20 | 2/20-3/7 | 3/7-4/7 | 3/7, 3/21-4/6 | 5/15-31 | 5/19-31 | 6/1-25 | 6/1-3, 6/18-25 |
| 9/7-30 | 9/14-29 | 8/15-31 | 8/16-30 | 7/1-8/7 | 7/1-3, 7/17-8/1 | — | — |
| 3/15-31 | 3/21-31 | 4/1-17 | 4/1-6 | 5/10-6/15 | 5/19-6/3 | 5/30-6/20 | 5/30-6/3, 6/18-20 |
| 8/7-31 | 8/16-30 | 7/7-21 | 7/17-21 | 6/15-30 | 6/18-30 | — | — |
| 3/7-4/15 | 3/7, 3/21-4/6 | 4/7-5/15 | 4/20-5/5 | 5/7-6/20 | 5/19-6/3, 6/18-20 | 5/30-6/15 | 5/30-6/3 |
| 3/7-4/15 | 3/7, 3/21-4/6 | 4/7-5/15 | 4/20-5/5 | 6/1-30 | 6/1-3, 6/18-30 | 6/15-30 | 6/18-30 |
| 2/15-3/20 | 2/20-3/7 | 4/7-5/15 | 4/20-5/5 | 5/15-31 | 5/19-31 | 6/1-25 | 6/1-3, 6/18-25 |
| 8/15-9/7 | 8/16-30 | 7/15-8/15 | 7/17-8/1 | 6/7-30 | 8/18-30 | — | — |
| 2/11-3/20 | 2/20-3/7 | 3/7-4/7 | 3/7, 3/21-4/6 | 5/15-31 | 5/19-31 | 6/1-15 | 6/1-3 |
| 9/7-30 | 9/14-29 | 8/15-31 | 8/16-30 | 7/1-8/7 | 7/1-3, 7/17-8/1 | 6/25-7/15 | 6/25-7/3 |
| 2/15-4/15 | 2/15-19, 3/8-20, 4/7-15 | 3/7-4/7 | 3/8-20, 4/7 | 5/15-31 | 5/15-18 | 6/1-25 | 6/4-17 |
| 2/15-3/7 | 2/20-3/7 | 3/1-31 | 3/1-7, 3/21-31 | 5/15-6/30 | 5/19-6/3, 6/18-30 | 6/1-30 | 6/1-3, 6/18-30 |
| 3/15-4/7 | 3/21-4/6 | 4/15-5/7 | 4/20-5/5 | 5/15-6/30 | 5/19-6/3, 6/18-30 | 6/1-30 | 6/1-3, 6/18-30 |
| 4/15-6/1 | 4/20-5/5, 5/19-6/1 | 5/25-6/15 | 5/25-6/3 | 6/15-7/10 | 6/18-7/3 | 6/15-7/7 | 6/18-7/3 |
| 2/1-28 | 2/6-19 | 3/1-31 | 3/8-20 | 5/15-6/7 | 5/15-18, 6/4-7 | 6/1-25 | 6/4-17 |
| 2/20-3/15 | 2/20-3/7 | 3/1-31 | 3/1-7, 3/21-31 | 5/15-31 | 5/19-31 | 6/1-15 | 6/1-3 |
| 1/15-2/4 | 1/15-20 | 3/7-31 | 3/8-20 | 4/1-30 | 4/7-19 | 5/10-31 | 5/10-18 |
| 1/15-2/7 | 1/21-2/5 | 3/7-31 | 3/7, 3/21-31 | 4/15-5/7 | 4/20-5/5 | 5/15-31 | 5/19-31 |
| 9/15-30 | 9/15-29 | 8/7-31 | 8/16-30 | 7/15-31 | 7/17-31 | 7/10-25 | 7/17-25 |
| 3/1-20 | 3/1-7 | 4/1-30 | 4/1-6, 4/20-30 | 5/15-6/30 | 5/19-6/3, 6/18-30 | 6/1-30 | 6/1-3, 6/18-30 |
| 2/10-28 | 2/10-19 | 4/1-30 | 4/7-19 | 5/1-31 | 5/6-18 | 6/1-25 | 6/4-17 |
| 3/7-20 | 3/7 | 4/23-5/15 | 4/23-5/5 | 5/15-31 | 5/19-31 | 6/1-30 | 6/1-3, 6/18-30 |
| 1/21-3/1 | 2/6-19 | 3/7-31 | 3/8-20 | 4/15-30 | 4/15-19 | 5/15-6/5 | 5/15-18, 6/4-5 |
| 10/1-21 | 10/1-13 | 9/7-30 | 9/7-13, 9/30 | 8/15-31 | 8/15, 8/31 | 7/10-31 | 7/10-16 |
| 2/7-3/15 | 2/20-3/7 | 3/15-4/20 | 3/21-4/6, 4/20 | 5/15-31 | 5/19-31 | 6/1-25 | 6/1-3, 6/18-25 |
| 10/1-21 | 10/14-21 | 8/1-9/15 | 8/1, 8/16-30, 9/14-15 | 7/17-9/7 | 7/17-8/1, 8/16-30 | 7/20-8/5 | 7/20-8/1 |
| 3/15-4/15 | 3/21-4/6 | 4/15-30 | 4/20-30 | 5/15-6/15 | 5/19-6/3 | 6/1-30 | 6/1-3, 6/18-30 |
| 3/23-4/7 | 4/7 | 4/21-5/9 | 5/6-9 | 5/15-6/15 | 5/15-18, 6/4-15 | 6/1-30 | 6/4-17 |
| 2/7-3/15 | 2/20-3/7 | 3/15-4/15 | 3/21-4/6 | 5/1-31 | 5/1-5, 5/19-31 | 5/15-31 | 5/19-31 |
| 3/7-21 | 3/7, 3/21 | 4/7-30 | 4/20-30 | 5/15-31 | 5/19-31 | 6/1-15 | 6/1-3 |
| 1/20-2/15 | 1/20, 2/6-15 | 3/15-31 | 3/15-20 | 4/7-30 | 4/7-19 | 5/10-31 | 5/10-18 |
| 9/1-10/15 | 9/1-13, 9/30-10/13 | 8/1-20 | 8/2-15 | 7/1-8/15 | 7/4-16, 8/2-15 | — | — |
| 3/15-4/7 | 3/21-4/6 | 4/15-5/7 | 4/20-5/5 | 5/15-6/30 | 5/19-6/3, 6/18-30 | 6/1-30 | 6/1-3, 6/18-30 |
| 2/15-28 | 2/20-28 | 3/1-20 | 3/1-7 | 4/7-30 | 4/20-30 | 5/15-6/10 | 5/19-6/3 |
| 10/15-12/7 | 10/15-28, 11/13-27 | 9/15-10/20 | 9/15-29, 10/14-20 | 8/11-9/15 | 8/16-30, 9/14-15 | 8/5-30 | 8/16-30 |

# FROSTS AND GROWING SEASONS

Dates given are normal averages (from 1991–2020) for a light freeze; local weather and topography may cause variations. The possibility of frost occurring after the spring dates and before the fall dates is 30 percent. The classification of freeze temperatures is usually based on their effect on plants. **Light freeze:** 29° to 32°F—tender plants killed. **Moderate freeze:** 25° to 28°F—widely destructive to most plants. **Severe freeze:** 24°F and colder—heavy damage to most plants.

*–dates courtesy of National Centers for Environmental Information*

| STATE | CITY | GROWING SEASON (DAYS) | LAST SPRING FROST | FIRST FALL FROST | STATE | CITY | GROWING SEASON (DAYS) | LAST SPRING FROST | FIRST FALL FROST |
|---|---|---|---|---|---|---|---|---|---|
| AK | Juneau | 171 | Apr. 26 | Oct. 15 | NC | Fayetteville | 212 | Apr. 5 | Nov. 4 |
| AL | Mobile | 269 | Mar. 3 | Nov. 28 | ND | Bismarck | 126 | May 19 | Sept. 23 |
| AR | Pine Bluff | 230 | Mar. 22 | Nov. 8 | NE | Omaha | 174 | Apr. 23 | Oct. 15 |
| AZ | Phoenix | 354* | Jan. 9 | Dec. 30 | NE | North Platte | 131 | May 16 | Sept. 25 |
| AZ | Tucson | 309* | Feb. 2 | Dec. 9 | NH | Concord | 136 | May 15 | Sept. 29 |
| CA | Eureka | 268 | Mar. 4 | Nov. 28 | NJ | Newark | 211 | Apr. 6 | Nov. 4 |
| CA | Sacramento | 281* | Feb. 17 | Nov. 26 | NM | Carlsbad | 223 | Mar. 27 | Nov. 6 |
| CO | Denver | 154 | May 4 | Oct. 6 | NM | Los Alamos | 149 | May 9 | Oct. 6 |
| CO | Grand Junction | 159 | May 3 | Oct. 10 | NV | Las Vegas | 292* | Feb. 11 | Dec. 1 |
| CT | Hartford | 165 | Apr. 27 | Oct. 10 | NY | Albany | 159 | May 2 | Oct. 9 |
| DE | Wilmington | 199 | Apr. 13 | Oct. 30 | NY | Syracuse | 158 | May 5 | Oct. 11 |
| FL | Orlando | 337* | Jan. 30 | Jan. 3** | OH | Akron | 174 | Apr. 30 | Oct. 22 |
| FL | Tallahassee | 238 | Mar. 19 | Nov. 13 | OH | Cincinnati | 179 | Apr. 23 | Oct. 20 |
| GA | Athens | 217 | Mar. 31 | Nov. 4 | OK | Lawton | 206 | Apr. 7 | Oct. 31 |
| GA | Savannah | 253 | Mar. 12 | Nov. 21 | OK | Tulsa | 207 | Apr. 5 | Oct. 30 |
| IA | Atlantic | 142 | May 6 | Sept. 26 | OR | Pendleton | 155 | Apr. 30 | Oct. 3 |
| IA | Cedar Rapids | 155 | May 4 | Oct. 7 | OR | Portland | 260 | Mar. 6 | Nov. 22 |
| ID | Boise | 166 | Apr. 30 | Oct. 14 | PA | Franklin | 160 | May 9 | Oct. 17 |
| IL | Chicago | 193 | Apr. 17 | Oct. 28 | PA | Williamsport | 167 | May 1 | Oct. 16 |
| IL | Springfield | 177 | Apr. 20 | Oct. 15 | RI | Kingston | 148 | May 8 | Oct. 4 |
| IN | Indianapolis | 172 | Apr. 26 | Oct. 16 | SC | Charleston | 305* | Feb. 17 | Dec. 20 |
| IN | South Bend | 159 | May 7 | Oct. 14 | SC | Columbia | 235 | Mar. 21 | Nov. 12 |
| KS | Topeka | 182 | Apr. 19 | Oct. 19 | SD | Rapid City | 144 | May 9 | Oct. 1 |
| KY | Lexington | 185 | Apr. 20 | Oct. 23 | TN | Memphis | 229 | Mar. 24 | Nov. 9 |
| LA | Monroe | 238 | Mar. 14 | Nov. 8 | TN | Nashville | 206 | Apr. 6 | Oct. 30 |
| LA | New Orleans | 311* | Feb. 8 | Dec. 17 | TX | Amarillo | 184 | Apr. 20 | Oct. 22 |
| MA | Boston | 208 | Apr. 8 | Nov. 3 | TX | Denton | 235 | Mar. 21 | Nov. 12 |
| MA | Worcester | 167 | Apr. 29 | Oct. 14 | TX | San Antonio | 267 | Mar. 2 | Nov. 25 |
| MD | Baltimore | 192 | Apr. 16 | Oct. 26 | UT | Cedar City | 119 | May 31 | Sept. 28 |
| ME | Portland | 160 | May 1 | Oct. 9 | UT | Spanish Fork | 162 | May 2 | Oct. 12 |
| MI | Lansing | 151 | May 7 | Oct. 6 | VA | Norfolk | 239 | Mar. 23 | Nov. 18 |
| MI | Marquette | 152 | May 15 | Oct. 15 | VA | Richmond | 204 | Apr. 9 | Oct. 31 |
| MN | Duluth | 129 | May 19 | Sept. 26 | VT | Burlington | 158 | May 3 | Oct. 9 |
| MN | Willmar | 149 | May 4 | Oct. 1 | WA | Seattle | 246 | Mar. 12 | Nov. 14 |
| MO | Jefferson City | 193 | Apr. 14 | Oct. 25 | WA | Spokane | 158 | May 1 | Oct. 7 |
| MS | Columbia | 243 | Mar. 13 | Nov. 12 | WI | Green Bay | 148 | May 7 | Oct. 3 |
| MS | Tupelo | 218 | Mar. 30 | Nov. 4 | WI | Sparta | 133 | May 15 | Sept. 26 |
| MT | Fort Peck | 135 | May 13 | Sept. 26 | WV | Parkersburg | 186 | Apr. 20 | Oct. 24 |
| MT | Helena | 132 | May 15 | Sept. 25 | WY | Casper | 105 | June 1 | Sept. 15 |

*In leap years, add 1 day   **In following year*

Find more frost dates via Almanac.com/2023.

# PHENOLOGY: NATURE'S CALENDAR

*Study nature, love nature, stay close to nature. It will never fail you.*
–Frank Lloyd Wright, American architect (1867–1959)

For centuries, farmers and gardeners have looked to events in nature to tell them when to plant vegetables and flowers and when to expect insects. Making such observations is called "phenology," the study of phenomena. Specifically, this refers to the life cycles of plants and animals as they correlate to weather and temperature, or nature's calendar.

## VEGETABLES

- Plant peas when forsythias bloom.
- Plant potatoes when the first dandelion blooms.
- Plant beets, carrots, cole crops (broccoli, brussels sprouts, collards), lettuce, and spinach when lilacs are in first leaf or dandelions are in full bloom.
- Plant corn when oak leaves are the size of a squirrel's ear (about ½ inch in diameter). Or, plant corn when apple blossoms fade and fall.
- Plant bean, cucumber, and squash seeds when lilacs are in full bloom.
- Plant tomatoes when lilies-of-the-valley are in full bloom.
- Transplant eggplants and peppers when bearded irises bloom.
- Plant onions when red maples bloom.

## FLOWERS

- Plant morning glories when maple trees have full-size leaves.
- Plant zinnias and marigolds when black locusts are in full bloom.
- Plant pansies, snapdragons, and other hardy annuals when aspens and chokecherries have leafed out.

## INSECTS

- When purple lilacs bloom, grasshopper eggs hatch.
- When chicory blooms, beware of squash vine borers.
- When Canada thistles bloom, protect susceptible fruit; apple maggot flies are at peak.
- When foxglove flowers open, expect Mexican beetle larvae.
- When crabapple trees are in bud, eastern tent caterpillars are hatching.
- When morning glory vines begin to climb, Japanese beetles appear.
- When wild rocket blooms, cabbage root maggots appear.

If the signal plants are not growing in your area, notice other coincident events; record them and watch for them in ensuing seasons.

# TABLE OF MEASURES

## LINEAR
1 hand = 4 inches
1 link = 7.92 inches
1 span = 9 inches
1 foot = 12 inches
1 yard = 3 feet
1 rod = 5½ yards
1 mile = 320 rods = 1,760 yards = 5,280 feet
1 international nautical mile = 6,076.1155 feet
1 knot = 1 nautical mile per hour
1 fathom = 2 yards = 6 feet
1 furlong = ⅛ mile = 660 feet = 220 yards
1 league = 3 miles = 24 furlongs
1 chain = 100 links = 22 yards

## SQUARE
1 square foot = 144 square inches
1 square yard = 9 square feet
1 square rod = 30¼ square yards = 272¼ square feet = 625 square links
1 square chain = 16 square rods
1 acre = 10 square chains = 160 square rods = 43,560 square feet
1 square mile = 640 acres = 102,400 square rods

## CUBIC
1 cubic foot = 1,728 cubic inches
1 cubic yard = 27 cubic feet
1 cord = 128 cubic feet
1 U.S. liquid gallon = 4 quarts = 231 cubic inches
1 imperial gallon = 1.20 U.S. gallons = 0.16 cubic foot
1 board foot = 144 cubic inches

## DRY
2 pints = 1 quart
4 quarts = 1 gallon
2 gallons = 1 peck
4 pecks = 1 bushel

## LIQUID
4 gills = 1 pint
63 gallons = 1 hogshead
2 hogsheads = 1 pipe or butt
2 pipes = 1 tun

## KITCHEN
3 teaspoons = 1 tablespoon
16 tablespoons = 1 cup
1 cup = 8 ounces
2 cups = 1 pint
2 pints = 1 quart
4 quarts = 1 gallon

## AVOIRDUPOIS
(for general use)
1 ounce = 16 drams
1 pound = 16 ounces
1 short hundredweight = 100 pounds
1 ton = 2,000 pounds
1 long ton = 2,240 pounds

## APOTHECARIES'
(for pharmaceutical use)
1 scruple = 20 grains
1 dram = 3 scruples
1 ounce = 8 drams
1 pound = 12 ounces

# METRIC CONVERSIONS

## LINEAR
1 inch = 2.54 centimeters
1 centimeter = 0.39 inch
1 meter = 39.37 inches
1 yard = 0.914 meter
1 mile = 1.61 kilometers
1 kilometer = 0.62 mile

## SQUARE
1 square inch = 6.45 square centimeters
1 square yard = 0.84 square meter
1 square mile = 2.59 square kilometers

1 square kilometer = 0.386 square mile
1 acre = 0.40 hectare
1 hectare = 2.47 acres

## CUBIC
1 cubic yard = 0.76 cubic meter
1 cubic meter = 1.31 cubic yards

## HOUSEHOLD
½ teaspoon = 2.46 mL
1 teaspoon = 4.93 mL
1 tablespoon = 14.79 mL
¼ cup = 59.15 mL

⅓ cup = 78.86 mL
½ cup = 118.29 mL
¾ cup = 177.44 mL
1 cup = 236.59 mL
1 liter = 1.057 U.S. liquid quarts
1 U.S. liquid quart = 0.946 liter
1 U.S. liquid gallon = 3.78 liters
1 gram = 0.035 ounce
1 ounce = 28.349 grams
1 kilogram = 2.2 pounds
1 pound = 0.45 kilogram

**TO CONVERT CELSIUS AND FAHRENHEIT: °C = (°F − 32)/1.8; °F = (°C × 1.8) + 32**

There's more of everything at Almanac.com.

# TIDAL GLOSSARY

**APOGEAN TIDE:** A monthly tide of decreased range that occurs when the Moon is at apogee (farthest from Earth).

**CURRENT:** Generally, a horizontal movement of water. Currents may be classified as tidal and nontidal. Tidal currents are caused by gravitational interactions between the Sun, Moon, and Earth and are part of the same general movement of the sea that is manifested in the vertical rise and fall, called tide. Nontidal currents include the permanent currents in the general circulatory systems of the sea as well as temporary currents arising from more pronounced meteorological variability.

**DIURNAL TIDE:** A tide with one high water and one low water in a tidal day of approximately 24 hours.

**MEAN LOWER LOW WATER:** The arithmetic mean of the lesser of a daily pair of low waters, observed over a specific 19-year cycle called the National Tidal Datum Epoch.

**NEAP TIDE:** A tide of decreased range that occurs twice a month, when the Moon is in quadrature (during its first and last quarters, when the Sun and the Moon are at right angles to each other relative to Earth).

**PERIGEAN TIDE:** A monthly tide of increased range that occurs when the Moon is at perigee (closest to Earth).

**RED TIDE:** Toxic algal blooms caused by several genera of dinoflagellates that usually turn the sea red or brown. These pose a serious threat to marine life and may be harmful to humans.

**RIP CURRENT:** A potentially dangerous, narrow, intense, surf-zone current flowing outward from shore.

**SEMIDIURNAL TIDE:** A tide with one high water and one low water every half-day. East Coast tides, for example, are semidiurnal, with two highs and two lows during a tidal day of approximately 24 hours.

**SLACK WATER (SLACK):** The state of a tidal current when its speed is near zero, especially the moment when a reversing current changes direction and its speed is zero.

**SPRING TIDE:** A tide of increased range that occurs at times of syzygy each month. Named not for the season of spring but from the German *springen* ("to leap up"), a spring tide also brings a lower low water.

**STORM SURGE:** The local change in the elevation of the ocean along a shore due to a storm, measured by subtracting the astronomic tidal elevation from the total elevation. It typically has a duration of a few hours and is potentially catastrophic, especially on low-lying coasts with gently sloping offshore topography.

**SYZYGY:** The nearly straight-line configuration that occurs twice a month, when the Sun and the Moon are in conjunction (on the same side of Earth, at the new Moon) and when they are in opposition (on opposite sides of Earth, at the full Moon). In both cases, the gravitational effects of the Sun and the Moon reinforce each other, and tidal range is increased.

**TIDAL BORE:** A tide-induced wave that propagates up a relatively shallow and sloping estuary or river with a steep wave front.

**TSUNAMI:** Commonly called a tidal wave, a tsunami is a series of long-period waves caused by an underwater earthquake or volcanic eruption. In open ocean, the waves are small and travel at high speed; as they near shore, some may build to more than 30 feet high, becoming a threat to life and property.

**VANISHING TIDE:** A mixed tide of considerable inequality in the two highs and two lows, so that the lower high (or higher low) may appear to vanish. ■

# TIDE CORRECTIONS

Many factors affect tides, including the shoreline, time of the Moon's southing (crossing the meridian), and the Moon's phase. The High Tide Times column on the **Left-Hand Calendar Pages, 120–146,** lists the times of high tide at Commonwealth Pier in Boston (MA) Harbor. The heights of some of these tides, reckoned from Mean Lower Low Water, are given on the **Right-Hand Calendar Pages, 121–147.** Use the table below to calculate the approximate times and heights of high tide at the places shown. Apply the time difference to the times of high tide at Boston and the height difference to the heights at Boston. A more detailed and accurate tide calculator for the United States and Canada can be found via **Almanac.com/2023.**

**EXAMPLE:**

The conversion of the times and heights of the tides at Boston to those at Cape Fear, North Carolina, is given below:

| | |
|---|---|
| High tide at Boston | 11:45 A.M. |
| Correction for Cape Fear | – 3 55 |
| High tide at Cape Fear | 7:50 A.M. |
| | |
| Tide height at Boston | 11.6 ft. |
| Correction for Cape Fear | – 5.0 ft. |
| Tide height at Cape Fear | 6.6 ft. |

Estimations derived from this table are *not* meant to be used for navigation. *The Old Farmer's Almanac* accepts no responsibility for errors or any consequences ensuing from the use of this table.

| TIDAL SITE | TIME (H. M.) | HEIGHT (FT.) | TIDAL SITE | TIME (H. M.) | HEIGHT (FT.) |
|---|---|---|---|---|---|
| **CANADA** | | | Cape Cod Canal | | |
| Alberton, PE | *–5 45 | –7.5 | East Entrance | –0 01 | –0.8 |
| Charlottetown, PE | *–0 45 | –3.5 | West Entrance | –2 16 | –5.9 |
| Halifax, NS | –3 23 | –4.5 | Chatham Outer Coast | +0 30 | –2.8 |
| North Sydney, NS | –3 15 | –6.5 | Inside | +1 54 | **0.4 |
| Saint John, NB | +0 30 | +15.0 | Cohasset | +0 02 | –0.07 |
| St. John's, NL | –4 00 | –6.5 | Cotuit Highlands | +1 15 | **0.3 |
| Yarmouth, NS | –0 40 | +3.0 | Dennis Port | +1 01 | **0.4 |
| **MAINE** | | | Duxbury–Gurnet Point | +0 02 | –0.3 |
| Bar Harbor | –0 34 | +0.9 | Fall River | –3 03 | –5.0 |
| Belfast | –0 20 | +0.4 | Gloucester | –0 03 | –0.8 |
| Boothbay Harbor | –0 18 | –0.8 | Hingham | +0 07 | 0.0 |
| Chebeague Island | –0 16 | –0.6 | Hull | +0 03 | –0.2 |
| Eastport | –0 28 | +8.4 | Hyannis Port | +1 01 | **0.3 |
| Kennebunkport | +0 04 | –1.0 | Magnolia–Manchester | –0 02 | –0.7 |
| Machias | –0 28 | +2.8 | Marblehead | –0 02 | –0.4 |
| Monhegan Island | –0 25 | –0.8 | Marion | –3 22 | –5.4 |
| Old Orchard Beach | 0 00 | –0.8 | Monument Beach | –3 08 | –5.4 |
| Portland | –0 12 | –0.6 | Nahant | –0 01 | –0.5 |
| Rockland | –0 28 | +0.1 | Nantasket | +0 04 | –0.1 |
| Stonington | –0 30 | +0.1 | Nantucket | +0 56 | **0.3 |
| York | –0 09 | –1.0 | Nauset Beach | +0 30 | **0.6 |
| **NEW HAMPSHIRE** | | | New Bedford | –3 24 | –5.7 |
| Hampton | +0 02 | –1.3 | Newburyport | +0 19 | –1.8 |
| Portsmouth | +0 11 | –1.5 | Oak Bluffs | +0 30 | **0.2 |
| Rye Beach | –0 09 | –0.9 | Onset–R.R. Bridge | –2 16 | –5.9 |
| **MASSACHUSETTS** | | | Plymouth | +0 05 | 0.0 |
| Annisquam | –0 02 | –1.1 | Provincetown | +0 14 | –0.4 |
| Beverly Farms | 0 00 | –0.5 | Revere Beach | –0 01 | –0.3 |

| TIDAL SITE | TIME (H. M.) | HEIGHT (FT.) | TIDAL SITE | TIME (H. M.) | HEIGHT (FT.) |
|---|---|---|---|---|---|
| Rockport | –0 08 | –1.0 | **PENNSYLVANIA** | | |
| Salem | 0 00 | –0.5 | Philadelphia | +2 40 | –3.5 |
| Scituate | –0 05 | –0.7 | **DELAWARE** | | |
| Wareham | –3 09 | –5.3 | Cape Henlopen | –2 48 | –5.3 |
| Wellfleet | +0 12 | +0.5 | Rehoboth Beach | –3 37 | –5.7 |
| West Falmouth | –3 10 | –5.4 | Wilmington | +1 56 | –3.8 |
| Westport Harbor | –3 22 | –6.4 | **MARYLAND** | | |
| Woods Hole | | | Annapolis | +6 23 | –8.5 |
| Little Harbor | –2 50 | **0.2 | Baltimore | +7 59 | –8.3 |
| Oceanographic | | | Cambridge | +5 05 | –7.8 |
| Institute | –3 07 | **0.2 | Havre de Grace | +11 21 | –7.7 |
| **RHODE ISLAND** | | | Point No Point | +2 28 | –8.1 |
| Bristol | –3 24 | –5.3 | Prince Frederick– | | |
| Narragansett Pier | –3 42 | –6.2 | Plum Point | +4 25 | –8.5 |
| Newport | –3 34 | –5.9 | **VIRGINIA** | | |
| Point Judith | –3 41 | –6.3 | Cape Charles | –2 20 | –7.0 |
| Providence | –3 20 | –4.8 | Hampton Roads | –2 02 | –6.9 |
| Sakonnet | –3 44 | –5.6 | Norfolk | –2 06 | –6.6 |
| Watch Hill | –2 50 | –6.8 | Virginia Beach | –4 00 | –6.0 |
| **CONNECTICUT** | | | Yorktown | –2 13 | –7.0 |
| Bridgeport | +0 01 | –2.6 | **NORTH CAROLINA** | | |
| Madison | –0 22 | –2.3 | Cape Fear | –3 55 | –5.0 |
| New Haven | –0 11 | –3.2 | Cape Lookout | –4 28 | –5.7 |
| New London | –1 54 | –6.7 | Currituck | –4 10 | –5.8 |
| Norwalk | +0 01 | –2.2 | Hatteras | | |
| Old Lyme– | | | Inlet | –4 03 | –7.4 |
| Highway Bridge | –0 30 | –6.2 | Kitty Hawk | –4 14 | –6.2 |
| Stamford | +0 01 | –2.2 | Ocean | –4 26 | –6.0 |
| Stonington | –2 27 | –6.6 | **SOUTH CAROLINA** | | |
| **NEW YORK** | | | Charleston | –3 22 | –4.3 |
| Coney Island | –3 33 | –4.9 | Georgetown | –1 48 | **0.36 |
| Fire Island Light | –2 43 | **0.1 | Hilton Head | –3 22 | –2.9 |
| Long Beach | –3 11 | –5.7 | Myrtle Beach | –3 49 | –4.4 |
| Montauk Harbor | –2 19 | –7.4 | St. Helena– | | |
| New York City–Battery | –2 43 | –5.0 | Harbor Entrance | –3 15 | –3.4 |
| Oyster Bay | +0 04 | –1.8 | **GEORGIA** | | |
| Port Chester | –0 09 | –2.2 | Jekyll Island | –3 46 | –2.9 |
| Port Washington | –0 01 | –2.1 | St. Simon's Island | –2 50 | –2.9 |
| Sag Harbor | –0 55 | –6.8 | Savannah Beach | | |
| Southampton– | | | River Entrance | –3 14 | –5.5 |
| Shinnecock Inlet | –4 20 | **0.2 | Tybee Light | –3 22 | –2.7 |
| Willets Point | 0 00 | –2.3 | **FLORIDA** | | |
| **NEW JERSEY** | | | Cape Canaveral | –3 59 | –6.0 |
| Asbury Park | –4 04 | –5.3 | Daytona Beach | –3 28 | –5.3 |
| Atlantic City | –3 56 | –5.5 | Fort Lauderdale | –2 50 | –7.2 |
| Bay Head–Sea Girt | –4 04 | –5.3 | Fort Pierce Inlet | –3 32 | –6.9 |
| Beach Haven | –1 43 | **0.24 | Jacksonville– | | |
| Cape May | –3 28 | –5.3 | Railroad Bridge | –6 55 | **0.1 |
| Ocean City | –3 06 | –5.9 | Miami Harbor Entrance | –3 18 | –7.0 |
| Sandy Hook | –3 30 | –5.0 | St. Augustine | –2 55 | –4.9 |
| Seaside Park | –4 03 | –5.4 | | | |

*VARIES WIDELY; ACCURATE ONLY TO WITHIN 1½ HOURS. CONSULT LOCAL TIDE TABLES FOR PRECISE TIMES AND HEIGHTS.
**WHERE THE DIFFERENCE IN THE HEIGHT COLUMN IS SO MARKED, THE HEIGHT AT BOSTON SHOULD BE MULTIPLIED BY THIS RATIO.

# TIME CORRECTIONS

Astronomical data for Boston (42°22' N, 71°3' W) is given on **pages 104, 106, 108–109,** and **120–146.** Use the Key Letters shown on those pages with this table to find the number of minutes that you must add to or subtract from Boston time to get the correct time for your city. (Times are approximate.) For more information on the use of Key Letters, see **How to Use This Almanac, page 116.**

**GET TIMES SIMPLY AND SPECIFICALLY:** Download astronomical times calculated for your zip code and presented as Left-Hand Calendar Pages via **Almanac.com/2023.**

**TIME ZONES CODES** represent standard time. Atlantic is –1, Eastern is 0, Central is 1, Mountain is 2, Pacific is 3, Alaska is 4, and Hawaii-Aleutian is 5.

| STATE | CITY | NORTH LATITUDE ° | NORTH LATITUDE ' | WEST LONGITUDE ° | WEST LONGITUDE ' | TIME ZONE CODE | A | B | C | D | E |
|---|---|---|---|---|---|---|---|---|---|---|---|
| AK | Anchorage | 61 | 10 | 149 | 59 | 4 | –46 | +27 | +71 | +122 | +171 |
| AK | Cordova | 60 | 33 | 145 | 45 | 4 | –55 | +13 | +55 | +103 | +149 |
| AK | Fairbanks | 64 | 48 | 147 | 51 | 4 | –127 | +2 | +61 | +131 | +205 |
| AK | Juneau | 58 | 18 | 134 | 25 | 4 | –76 | –23 | +10 | +49 | +86 |
| AK | Ketchikan | 55 | 21 | 131 | 39 | 4 | –62 | –25 | 0 | +29 | +56 |
| AK | Kodiak | 57 | 47 | 152 | 24 | 4 | 0 | +49 | +82 | +120 | +154 |
| AL | Birmingham | 33 | 31 | 86 | 49 | 1 | +30 | +15 | +3 | –10 | –20 |
| AL | Decatur | 34 | 36 | 86 | 59 | 1 | +27 | +14 | +4 | –7 | –17 |
| AL | Mobile | 30 | 42 | 88 | 3 | 1 | +42 | +23 | +8 | –8 | –22 |
| AL | Montgomery | 32 | 23 | 86 | 19 | 1 | +31 | +14 | +1 | –13 | –25 |
| AR | Fort Smith | 35 | 23 | 94 | 25 | 1 | +55 | +43 | +33 | +22 | +14 |
| AR | Little Rock | 34 | 45 | 92 | 17 | 1 | +48 | +35 | +25 | +13 | +4 |
| AR | Texarkana | 33 | 26 | 94 | 3 | 1 | +59 | +44 | +32 | +18 | +8 |
| AZ | Flagstaff | 35 | 12 | 111 | 39 | 2 | +64 | +52 | +42 | +31 | +22 |
| AZ | Phoenix | 33 | 27 | 112 | 4 | 2 | +71 | +56 | +44 | +30 | +20 |
| AZ | Tucson | 32 | 13 | 110 | 58 | 2 | +70 | +53 | +40 | +24 | +12 |
| AZ | Yuma | 32 | 43 | 114 | 37 | 2 | +83 | +67 | +54 | +40 | +28 |
| CA | Bakersfield | 35 | 23 | 119 | 1 | 3 | +33 | +21 | +12 | +1 | –7 |
| CA | Barstow | 34 | 54 | 117 | 1 | 3 | +27 | +14 | +4 | –7 | –16 |
| CA | Fresno | 36 | 44 | 119 | 47 | 3 | +32 | +22 | +15 | +6 | 0 |
| CA | Los Angeles-Pasadena-Santa Monica | 34 | 3 | 118 | 14 | 3 | +34 | +20 | +9 | –3 | –13 |
| CA | Palm Springs | 33 | 49 | 116 | 32 | 3 | +28 | +13 | +1 | –12 | –22 |
| CA | Redding | 40 | 35 | 122 | 24 | 3 | +31 | +27 | +25 | +22 | +19 |
| CA | Sacramento | 38 | 35 | 121 | 30 | 3 | +34 | +27 | +21 | +15 | +10 |
| CA | San Diego | 32 | 43 | 117 | 9 | 3 | +33 | +17 | +4 | –9 | –21 |
| CA | San Francisco-Oakland-San Jose | 37 | 47 | 122 | 25 | 3 | +40 | +31 | +25 | +18 | +12 |
| CO | Craig | 40 | 31 | 107 | 33 | 2 | +32 | +28 | +25 | +22 | +20 |
| CO | Denver-Boulder | 39 | 44 | 104 | 59 | 2 | +24 | +19 | +15 | +11 | +7 |
| CO | Grand Junction | 39 | 4 | 108 | 33 | 2 | +40 | +34 | +29 | +24 | +20 |
| CO | Pueblo | 38 | 16 | 104 | 37 | 2 | +27 | +20 | +14 | +7 | +2 |
| CO | Trinidad | 37 | 10 | 104 | 31 | 2 | +30 | +21 | +13 | +5 | 0 |
| CT | Bridgeport | 41 | 11 | 73 | 11 | 0 | +12 | +10 | +8 | +6 | +4 |
| CT | Hartford-New Britain | 41 | 46 | 72 | 41 | 0 | +8 | +7 | +6 | +5 | +4 |
| CT | New Haven | 41 | 18 | 72 | 56 | 0 | +11 | +8 | +7 | +5 | +4 |
| CT | New London | 41 | 22 | 72 | 6 | 0 | +7 | +5 | +4 | +2 | +1 |
| CT | Norwalk-Stamford | 41 | 7 | 73 | 22 | 0 | +13 | +10 | +9 | +7 | +5 |
| CT | Waterbury-Meriden | 41 | 33 | 73 | 3 | 0 | +10 | +9 | +7 | +6 | +5 |
| DC | Washington | 38 | 54 | 77 | 1 | 0 | +35 | +28 | +23 | +18 | +13 |
| DE | Wilmington | 39 | 45 | 75 | 33 | 0 | +26 | +21 | +18 | +13 | +10 |

| STATE | CITY | NORTH LATITUDE ° | NORTH LATITUDE ' | WEST LONGITUDE ° | WEST LONGITUDE ' | TIME ZONE CODE | A | B | C | D | E |
|---|---|---|---|---|---|---|---|---|---|---|---|
| FL | Fort Myers | 26 | 38 | 81 | 52 | 0 | +87 | +63 | +44 | +21 | +4 |
| FL | Jacksonville | 30 | 20 | 81 | 40 | 0 | +77 | +58 | +43 | +25 | +11 |
| FL | Miami | 25 | 47 | 80 | 12 | 0 | +88 | +57 | +37 | +14 | −3 |
| FL | Orlando | 28 | 32 | 81 | 22 | 0 | +80 | +59 | +42 | +22 | +6 |
| FL | Pensacola | 30 | 25 | 87 | 13 | 1 | +39 | +20 | +5 | −12 | −26 |
| FL | St. Petersburg | 27 | 46 | 82 | 39 | 0 | +87 | +65 | +47 | +26 | +10 |
| FL | Tallahassee | 30 | 27 | 84 | 17 | 0 | +87 | +68 | +53 | +35 | +22 |
| FL | Tampa | 27 | 57 | 82 | 27 | 0 | +86 | +64 | +46 | +25 | +9 |
| FL | West Palm Beach | 26 | 43 | 80 | 3 | 0 | +79 | +55 | +36 | +14 | −2 |
| GA | Atlanta | 33 | 45 | 84 | 24 | 0 | +79 | +65 | +53 | +40 | +30 |
| GA | Augusta | 33 | 28 | 81 | 58 | 0 | +70 | +55 | +44 | +30 | +19 |
| GA | Macon | 32 | 50 | 83 | 38 | 0 | +79 | +63 | +50 | +36 | +24 |
| GA | Savannah | 32 | 5 | 81 | 6 | 0 | +70 | +54 | +40 | +25 | +13 |
| HI | Hilo | 19 | 44 | 155 | 5 | 5 | +94 | +62 | +37 | +7 | −15 |
| HI | Honolulu | 21 | 18 | 157 | 52 | 5 | +102 | +72 | +48 | +19 | −1 |
| HI | Lanai City | 20 | 50 | 156 | 55 | 5 | +99 | +69 | +44 | +15 | −6 |
| HI | Lihue | 21 | 59 | 159 | 23 | 5 | +107 | +77 | +54 | +26 | +5 |
| IA | Davenport | 41 | 32 | 90 | 35 | 1 | +20 | +19 | +17 | +16 | +15 |
| IA | Des Moines | 41 | 35 | 93 | 37 | 1 | +32 | +31 | +30 | +28 | +27 |
| IA | Dubuque | 42 | 30 | 90 | 41 | 1 | +17 | +18 | +18 | +18 | +18 |
| IA | Waterloo | 42 | 30 | 92 | 20 | 1 | +24 | +24 | +24 | +25 | +25 |
| ID | Boise | 43 | 37 | 116 | 12 | 2 | +55 | +58 | +60 | +62 | +64 |
| ID | Lewiston | 46 | 25 | 117 | 1 | 3 | −12 | −3 | +2 | +10 | +17 |
| ID | Pocatello | 42 | 52 | 112 | 27 | 2 | +43 | +44 | +45 | +46 | +46 |
| IL | Cairo | 37 | 0 | 89 | 11 | 1 | +29 | +20 | +12 | +4 | −2 |
| IL | Chicago-Oak Park | 41 | 52 | 87 | 38 | 1 | +7 | +6 | +6 | +5 | +4 |
| IL | Danville | 40 | 8 | 87 | 37 | 1 | +13 | +9 | +6 | +2 | 0 |
| IL | Decatur | 39 | 51 | 88 | 57 | 1 | +19 | +15 | +11 | +7 | +4 |
| IL | Peoria | 40 | 42 | 89 | 36 | 1 | +19 | +16 | +14 | +11 | +9 |
| IL | Springfield | 39 | 48 | 89 | 39 | 1 | +22 | +18 | +14 | +10 | +6 |
| IN | Fort Wayne | 41 | 4 | 85 | 9 | 0 | +60 | +58 | +56 | +54 | +52 |
| IN | Gary | 41 | 36 | 87 | 20 | 1 | +7 | +6 | +4 | +3 | +2 |
| IN | Indianapolis | 39 | 46 | 86 | 10 | 0 | +69 | +64 | +60 | +56 | +52 |
| IN | Muncie | 40 | 12 | 85 | 23 | 0 | +64 | +60 | +57 | +53 | +50 |
| IN | South Bend | 41 | 41 | 86 | 15 | 0 | +62 | +61 | +60 | +59 | +58 |
| IN | Terre Haute | 39 | 28 | 87 | 24 | 0 | +74 | +69 | +65 | +60 | +56 |
| KS | Fort Scott | 37 | 50 | 94 | 42 | 1 | +49 | +41 | +34 | +27 | +21 |
| KS | Liberal | 37 | 3 | 100 | 55 | 1 | +76 | +66 | +59 | +51 | +44 |
| KS | Oakley | 39 | 8 | 100 | 51 | 1 | +69 | +63 | +59 | +53 | +49 |
| KS | Salina | 38 | 50 | 97 | 37 | 1 | +57 | +51 | +46 | +40 | +35 |
| KS | Topeka | 39 | 3 | 95 | 40 | 1 | +49 | +43 | +38 | +32 | +28 |
| KS | Wichita | 37 | 42 | 97 | 20 | 1 | +60 | +51 | +45 | +37 | +31 |
| KY | Lexington-Frankfort | 38 | 3 | 84 | 30 | 0 | +67 | +59 | +53 | +46 | +41 |
| KY | Louisville | 38 | 15 | 85 | 46 | 0 | +72 | +64 | +58 | +52 | +46 |
| LA | Alexandria | 31 | 18 | 92 | 27 | 1 | +58 | +40 | +26 | +9 | −3 |
| LA | Baton Rouge | 30 | 27 | 91 | 11 | 1 | +55 | +36 | +21 | +3 | −10 |
| LA | Lake Charles | 30 | 14 | 93 | 13 | 1 | +64 | +44 | +29 | +11 | −2 |
| LA | Monroe | 32 | 30 | 92 | 7 | 1 | +53 | +37 | +24 | +9 | −1 |
| LA | New Orleans | 29 | 57 | 90 | 4 | 1 | +52 | +32 | +16 | −1 | −15 |
| LA | Shreveport | 32 | 31 | 93 | 45 | 1 | +60 | +44 | +31 | +16 | +4 |
| MA | Brockton | 42 | 5 | 71 | 1 | 0 | 0 | 0 | 0 | 0 | −1 |
| MA | Fall River-New Bedford | 41 | 42 | 71 | 9 | 0 | +2 | +1 | 0 | 0 | −1 |
| MA | Lawrence-Lowell | 42 | 42 | 71 | 10 | 0 | 0 | 0 | 0 | 0 | +1 |
| MA | Pittsfield | 42 | 27 | 73 | 15 | 0 | +8 | +8 | +8 | +8 | +8 |
| MA | Springfield-Holyoke | 42 | 6 | 72 | 36 | 0 | +6 | +6 | +6 | +5 | +5 |
| MA | Worcester | 42 | 16 | 71 | 48 | 0 | +3 | +2 | +2 | +2 | +2 |

| STATE | CITY | NORTH LATITUDE | | WEST LONGITUDE | | TIME ZONE CODE | KEY LETTERS (MINUTES) | | | | |
|---|---|---|---|---|---|---|---|---|---|---|---|
| | | ° | ' | ° | ' | | A | B | C | D | E |
| MD | Baltimore | 39 | 17 | 76 | 37 | 0 | +32 | +26 | +22 | +17 | +13 |
| MD | Hagerstown | 39 | 39 | 77 | 43 | 0 | +35 | +30 | +26 | +22 | +18 |
| MD | Salisbury | 38 | 22 | 75 | 36 | 0 | +31 | +23 | +18 | +11 | +6 |
| ME | Augusta | 44 | 19 | 69 | 46 | 0 | −12 | −8 | −5 | −1 | 0 |
| ME | Bangor | 44 | 48 | 68 | 46 | 0 | −18 | −13 | −9 | −5 | −1 |
| ME | Eastport | 44 | 54 | 67 | 0 | 0 | −26 | −20 | −16 | −11 | −8 |
| ME | Ellsworth | 44 | 33 | 68 | 25 | 0 | −18 | −14 | −10 | −6 | −3 |
| ME | Portland | 43 | 40 | 70 | 15 | 0 | −8 | −5 | −3 | −1 | 0 |
| ME | Presque Isle | 46 | 41 | 68 | 1 | 0 | −29 | −19 | −12 | −4 | +2 |
| MI | Cheboygan | 45 | 39 | 84 | 29 | 0 | +40 | +47 | +53 | +59 | +64 |
| MI | Detroit-Dearborn | 42 | 20 | 83 | 3 | 0 | +47 | +47 | +47 | +47 | +47 |
| MI | Flint | 43 | 1 | 83 | 41 | 0 | +47 | +49 | +50 | +51 | +52 |
| MI | Ironwood | 46 | 27 | 90 | 9 | 1 | 0 | +9 | +15 | +23 | +29 |
| MI | Jackson | 42 | 15 | 84 | 24 | 0 | +53 | +53 | +53 | +52 | +52 |
| MI | Kalamazoo | 42 | 17 | 85 | 35 | 0 | +58 | +57 | +57 | +57 | +57 |
| MI | Lansing | 42 | 44 | 84 | 33 | 0 | +52 | +53 | +53 | +54 | +54 |
| MI | St. Joseph | 42 | 5 | 86 | 26 | 0 | +61 | +61 | +60 | +60 | +59 |
| MI | Traverse City | 44 | 46 | 85 | 38 | 0 | +49 | +54 | +57 | +62 | +65 |
| MN | Albert Lea | 43 | 39 | 93 | 22 | 1 | +24 | +26 | +28 | +31 | +33 |
| MN | Bemidji | 47 | 28 | 94 | 53 | 1 | +14 | +26 | +34 | +44 | +52 |
| MN | Duluth | 46 | 47 | 92 | 6 | 1 | +6 | +16 | +23 | +31 | +38 |
| MN | Minneapolis-St. Paul | 44 | 59 | 93 | 16 | 1 | +18 | +24 | +28 | +33 | +37 |
| MN | Ortonville | 45 | 19 | 96 | 27 | 1 | +30 | +36 | +40 | +46 | +51 |
| MO | Jefferson City | 38 | 34 | 92 | 10 | 1 | +36 | +29 | +24 | +18 | +13 |
| MO | Joplin | 37 | 6 | 94 | 30 | 1 | +50 | +41 | +33 | +25 | +18 |
| MO | Kansas City | 39 | 1 | 94 | 20 | 1 | +44 | +37 | +33 | +27 | +23 |
| MO | Poplar Bluff | 36 | 46 | 90 | 24 | 1 | +35 | +25 | +17 | +8 | +1 |
| MO | St. Joseph | 39 | 46 | 94 | 50 | 1 | +43 | +38 | +35 | +30 | +27 |
| MO | St. Louis | 38 | 37 | 90 | 12 | 1 | +28 | +21 | +16 | +10 | +5 |
| MO | Springfield | 37 | 13 | 93 | 18 | 1 | +45 | +36 | +29 | +20 | +14 |
| MS | Biloxi | 30 | 24 | 88 | 53 | 1 | +46 | +27 | +11 | −5 | −19 |
| MS | Jackson | 32 | 18 | 90 | 11 | 1 | +46 | +30 | +17 | +1 | −10 |
| MS | Meridian | 32 | 22 | 88 | 42 | 1 | +40 | +24 | +11 | −4 | −15 |
| MS | Tupelo | 34 | 16 | 88 | 34 | 1 | +35 | +21 | +10 | −2 | −11 |
| MT | Billings | 45 | 47 | 108 | 30 | 2 | +16 | +23 | +29 | +35 | +40 |
| MT | Butte | 46 | 1 | 112 | 32 | 2 | +31 | +39 | +45 | +52 | +57 |
| MT | Glasgow | 48 | 12 | 106 | 38 | 2 | −1 | +11 | +21 | +32 | +42 |
| MT | Great Falls | 47 | 30 | 111 | 17 | 2 | +20 | +31 | +39 | +49 | +58 |
| MT | Helena | 46 | 36 | 112 | 2 | 2 | +27 | +36 | +43 | +51 | +57 |
| MT | Miles City | 46 | 25 | 105 | 51 | 2 | +3 | +11 | +18 | +26 | +32 |
| NC | Asheville | 35 | 36 | 82 | 33 | 0 | +67 | +55 | +46 | +35 | +27 |
| NC | Charlotte | 35 | 14 | 80 | 51 | 0 | +61 | +49 | +39 | +28 | +19 |
| NC | Durham | 36 | 0 | 78 | 55 | 0 | +51 | +40 | +31 | +21 | +13 |
| NC | Greensboro | 36 | 4 | 79 | 47 | 0 | +54 | +43 | +35 | +25 | +17 |
| NC | Raleigh | 35 | 47 | 78 | 38 | 0 | +51 | +39 | +30 | +20 | +12 |
| NC | Wilmington | 34 | 14 | 77 | 55 | 0 | +52 | +38 | +27 | +15 | +5 |
| ND | Bismarck | 46 | 48 | 100 | 47 | 1 | +41 | +50 | +58 | +66 | +73 |
| ND | Fargo | 46 | 53 | 96 | 47 | 1 | +24 | +34 | +42 | +50 | +57 |
| ND | Grand Forks | 47 | 55 | 97 | 3 | 1 | +21 | +33 | +43 | +53 | +62 |
| ND | Minot | 48 | 14 | 101 | 18 | 1 | +36 | +50 | +59 | +71 | +81 |
| ND | Williston | 48 | 9 | 103 | 37 | 1 | +46 | +59 | +69 | +80 | +90 |
| NE | Grand Island | 40 | 55 | 98 | 21 | 1 | +53 | +51 | +49 | +46 | +44 |
| NE | Lincoln | 40 | 49 | 96 | 41 | 1 | +47 | +44 | +42 | +39 | +37 |
| NE | North Platte | 41 | 8 | 100 | 46 | 1 | +62 | +60 | +58 | +56 | +54 |
| NE | Omaha | 41 | 16 | 95 | 56 | 1 | +43 | +40 | +39 | +37 | +36 |
| NH | Berlin | 44 | 28 | 71 | 11 | 0 | −7 | −3 | 0 | +3 | +7 |
| NH | Keene | 42 | 56 | 72 | 17 | 0 | +2 | +3 | +4 | +5 | +6 |

| STATE | CITY | NORTH LATITUDE ° | NORTH LATITUDE ′ | WEST LONGITUDE ° | WEST LONGITUDE ′ | TIME ZONE CODE | KEY LETTERS (MINUTES) A | B | C | D | E |
|---|---|---|---|---|---|---|---|---|---|---|---|
| NH | Manchester-Concord | 42 | 59 | 71 | 28 | 0 | 0 | 0 | +1 | +2 | +3 |
| NH | Portsmouth | 43 | 5 | 70 | 45 | 0 | −4 | −2 | −1 | 0 | 0 |
| NJ | Atlantic City | 39 | 22 | 74 | 26 | 0 | +23 | +17 | +13 | +8 | +4 |
| NJ | Camden | 39 | 57 | 75 | 7 | 0 | +24 | +19 | +16 | +12 | +9 |
| NJ | Cape May | 38 | 56 | 74 | 56 | 0 | +26 | +20 | +15 | +9 | +5 |
| NJ | Newark-East Orange | 40 | 44 | 74 | 10 | 0 | +17 | +14 | +12 | +9 | +7 |
| NJ | Paterson | 40 | 55 | 74 | 10 | 0 | +17 | +14 | +12 | +9 | +7 |
| NJ | Trenton | 40 | 13 | 74 | 46 | 0 | +21 | +17 | +14 | +11 | +8 |
| NM | Albuquerque | 35 | 5 | 106 | 39 | 2 | +45 | +32 | +22 | +11 | +2 |
| NM | Gallup | 35 | 32 | 108 | 45 | 2 | +52 | +40 | +31 | +20 | +11 |
| NM | Las Cruces | 32 | 19 | 106 | 47 | 2 | +53 | +36 | +23 | +8 | −3 |
| NM | Roswell | 33 | 24 | 104 | 32 | 2 | +41 | +26 | +14 | 0 | −10 |
| NM | Santa Fe | 35 | 41 | 105 | 56 | 2 | +40 | +28 | +19 | +9 | 0 |
| NV | Carson City-Reno | 39 | 10 | 119 | 46 | 3 | +25 | +19 | +14 | +9 | +5 |
| NV | Elko | 40 | 50 | 115 | 46 | 3 | +3 | 0 | −1 | −3 | −5 |
| NV | Las Vegas | 36 | 10 | 115 | 9 | 3 | +16 | +4 | −3 | −13 | −20 |
| NY | Albany | 42 | 39 | 73 | 45 | 0 | +9 | +10 | +10 | +11 | +11 |
| NY | Binghamton | 42 | 6 | 75 | 55 | 0 | +20 | +19 | +19 | +18 | +18 |
| NY | Buffalo | 42 | 53 | 78 | 52 | 0 | +29 | +30 | +30 | +31 | +32 |
| NY | New York | 40 | 45 | 74 | 0 | 0 | +17 | +14 | +11 | +9 | +6 |
| NY | Ogdensburg | 44 | 42 | 75 | 30 | 0 | +8 | +13 | +17 | +21 | +25 |
| NY | Syracuse | 43 | 3 | 76 | 9 | 0 | +17 | +19 | +20 | +21 | +22 |
| OH | Akron | 41 | 5 | 81 | 31 | 0 | +46 | +43 | +41 | +39 | +37 |
| OH | Canton | 40 | 48 | 81 | 23 | 0 | +46 | +43 | +41 | +38 | +36 |
| OH | Cincinnati-Hamilton | 39 | 6 | 84 | 31 | 0 | +64 | +58 | +53 | +48 | +44 |
| OH | Cleveland-Lakewood | 41 | 30 | 81 | 42 | 0 | +45 | +43 | +42 | +40 | +39 |
| OH | Columbus | 39 | 57 | 83 | 1 | 0 | +55 | +51 | +47 | +43 | +40 |
| OH | Dayton | 39 | 45 | 84 | 10 | 0 | +61 | +56 | +52 | +48 | +44 |
| OH | Toledo | 41 | 39 | 83 | 33 | 0 | +52 | +50 | +49 | +48 | +47 |
| OH | Youngstown | 41 | 6 | 80 | 39 | 0 | +42 | +40 | +38 | +36 | +34 |
| OK | Oklahoma City | 35 | 28 | 97 | 31 | 1 | +67 | +55 | +46 | +35 | +26 |
| OK | Tulsa | 36 | 9 | 95 | 60 | 1 | +59 | +48 | +40 | +30 | +22 |
| OR | Eugene | 44 | 3 | 123 | 6 | 3 | +21 | +24 | +27 | +30 | +33 |
| OR | Pendleton | 45 | 40 | 118 | 47 | 3 | −1 | +4 | +10 | +16 | +21 |
| OR | Portland | 45 | 31 | 122 | 41 | 3 | +14 | +20 | +25 | +31 | +36 |
| OR | Salem | 44 | 57 | 123 | 1 | 3 | +17 | +23 | +27 | +31 | +35 |
| PA | Allentown-Bethlehem | 40 | 36 | 75 | 28 | 0 | +23 | +20 | +17 | +14 | +12 |
| PA | Erie | 42 | 7 | 80 | 5 | 0 | +36 | +36 | +35 | +35 | +35 |
| PA | Harrisburg | 40 | 16 | 76 | 53 | 0 | +30 | +26 | +23 | +19 | +16 |
| PA | Lancaster | 40 | 2 | 76 | 18 | 0 | +28 | +24 | +20 | +17 | +13 |
| PA | Philadelphia-Chester | 39 | 57 | 75 | 9 | 0 | +24 | +19 | +16 | +12 | +9 |
| PA | Pittsburgh-McKeesport | 40 | 26 | 80 | 0 | 0 | +42 | +38 | +35 | +32 | +29 |
| PA | Reading | 40 | 20 | 75 | 56 | 0 | +26 | +22 | +19 | +16 | +13 |
| PA | Scranton-Wilkes-Barre | 41 | 25 | 75 | 40 | 0 | +21 | +19 | +18 | +16 | +15 |
| PA | York | 39 | 58 | 76 | 43 | 0 | +30 | +26 | +22 | +18 | +15 |
| RI | Providence | 41 | 50 | 71 | 25 | 0 | +3 | +2 | +1 | 0 | 0 |
| SC | Charleston | 32 | 47 | 79 | 56 | 0 | +64 | +48 | +36 | +21 | +10 |
| SC | Columbia | 34 | 0 | 81 | 2 | 0 | +65 | +51 | +40 | +27 | +17 |
| SC | Spartanburg | 34 | 56 | 81 | 57 | 0 | +66 | +53 | +43 | +32 | +23 |
| SD | Aberdeen | 45 | 28 | 98 | 29 | 1 | +37 | +44 | +49 | +54 | +59 |
| SD | Pierre | 44 | 22 | 100 | 21 | 1 | +49 | +53 | +56 | +60 | +63 |
| SD | Rapid City | 44 | 5 | 103 | 14 | 2 | +2 | +5 | +8 | +11 | +13 |
| SD | Sioux Falls | 43 | 33 | 96 | 44 | 1 | +38 | +40 | +42 | +44 | +46 |
| TN | Chattanooga | 35 | 3 | 85 | 19 | 0 | +79 | +67 | +57 | +45 | +36 |
| TN | Knoxville | 35 | 58 | 83 | 55 | 0 | +71 | +60 | +51 | +41 | +33 |
| TN | Memphis | 35 | 9 | 90 | 3 | 1 | +38 | +26 | +16 | +5 | −3 |
| TN | Nashville | 36 | 10 | 86 | 47 | 1 | +22 | +11 | +3 | −6 | −14 |

| STATE/PROVINCE | CITY | NORTH LATITUDE ° | NORTH LATITUDE ′ | WEST LONGITUDE ° | WEST LONGITUDE ′ | TIME ZONE CODE | KEY LETTERS (MINUTES) A | B | C | D | E |
|---|---|---|---|---|---|---|---|---|---|---|---|
| TX | Amarillo | 35 | 12 | 101 | 50 | 1 | +85 | +73 | +63 | +52 | +43 |
| TX | Austin | 30 | 16 | 97 | 45 | 1 | +82 | +62 | +47 | +29 | +15 |
| TX | Beaumont | 30 | 5 | 94 | 6 | 1 | +67 | +48 | +32 | +14 | 0 |
| TX | Brownsville | 25 | 54 | 97 | 30 | 1 | +91 | +66 | +46 | +23 | +5 |
| TX | Corpus Christi | 27 | 48 | 97 | 24 | 1 | +86 | +64 | +46 | +25 | +9 |
| TX | Dallas-Fort Worth | 32 | 47 | 96 | 48 | 1 | +71 | +55 | +43 | +28 | +17 |
| TX | El Paso | 31 | 45 | 106 | 29 | 2 | +53 | +35 | +22 | +6 | −6 |
| TX | Galveston | 29 | 18 | 94 | 48 | 1 | +72 | +52 | +35 | +16 | +1 |
| TX | Houston | 29 | 45 | 95 | 22 | 1 | +73 | +53 | +37 | +19 | +5 |
| TX | McAllen | 26 | 12 | 98 | 14 | 1 | +93 | +69 | +49 | +26 | +9 |
| TX | San Antonio | 29 | 25 | 98 | 30 | 1 | +87 | +66 | +50 | +31 | +16 |
| UT | Kanab | 37 | 3 | 112 | 32 | 2 | +62 | +53 | +46 | +37 | +30 |
| UT | Moab | 38 | 35 | 109 | 33 | 2 | +46 | +39 | +33 | +27 | +22 |
| UT | Ogden | 41 | 13 | 111 | 58 | 2 | +47 | +45 | +43 | +41 | +40 |
| UT | Salt Lake City | 40 | 45 | 111 | 53 | 2 | +48 | +45 | +43 | +40 | +38 |
| UT | Vernal | 40 | 27 | 109 | 32 | 2 | +40 | +36 | +33 | +30 | +28 |
| VA | Charlottesville | 38 | 2 | 78 | 30 | 0 | +43 | +35 | +29 | +22 | +17 |
| VA | Danville | 36 | 36 | 79 | 23 | 0 | +51 | +41 | +33 | +24 | +17 |
| VA | Norfolk | 36 | 51 | 76 | 17 | 0 | +38 | +28 | +21 | +12 | +5 |
| VA | Richmond | 37 | 32 | 77 | 26 | 0 | +41 | +32 | +25 | +17 | +11 |
| VA | Roanoke | 37 | 16 | 79 | 57 | 0 | +51 | +42 | +35 | +27 | +21 |
| VA | Winchester | 39 | 11 | 78 | 10 | 0 | +38 | +33 | +28 | +23 | +19 |
| VT | Brattleboro | 42 | 51 | 72 | 34 | 0 | +4 | +5 | +5 | +6 | +7 |
| VT | Burlington | 44 | 29 | 73 | 13 | 0 | 0 | +4 | +8 | +12 | +15 |
| VT | Rutland | 43 | 37 | 72 | 58 | 0 | +2 | +5 | +7 | +9 | +11 |
| VT | St. Johnsbury | 44 | 25 | 72 | 1 | 0 | −4 | 0 | +3 | +7 | +10 |
| WA | Bellingham | 48 | 45 | 122 | 29 | 3 | 0 | +13 | +24 | +37 | +47 |
| WA | Seattle-Tacoma-Olympia | 47 | 37 | 122 | 20 | 3 | +3 | +15 | +24 | +34 | +42 |
| WA | Spokane | 47 | 40 | 117 | 24 | 3 | −16 | −4 | +4 | +14 | +23 |
| WA | Walla Walla | 46 | 4 | 118 | 20 | 3 | −5 | +2 | +8 | +15 | +21 |
| WI | Eau Claire | 44 | 49 | 91 | 30 | 1 | +12 | +17 | +21 | +25 | +29 |
| WI | Green Bay | 44 | 31 | 88 | 0 | 1 | 0 | +3 | +7 | +11 | +14 |
| WI | La Crosse | 43 | 48 | 91 | 15 | 1 | +15 | +18 | +20 | +22 | +25 |
| WI | Madison | 43 | 4 | 89 | 23 | 1 | +10 | +11 | +12 | +14 | +15 |
| WI | Milwaukee | 43 | 2 | 87 | 54 | 1 | +4 | +6 | +7 | +8 | +9 |
| WI | Oshkosh | 44 | 1 | 88 | 33 | 1 | +3 | +6 | +9 | +12 | +15 |
| WI | Wausau | 44 | 58 | 89 | 38 | 1 | +4 | +9 | +13 | +18 | +22 |
| WV | Charleston | 38 | 21 | 81 | 38 | 0 | +55 | +48 | +42 | +35 | +30 |
| WV | Parkersburg | 39 | 16 | 81 | 34 | 0 | +52 | +46 | +42 | +36 | +32 |
| WY | Casper | 42 | 51 | 106 | 19 | 2 | +19 | +19 | +20 | +21 | +22 |
| WY | Cheyenne | 41 | 8 | 104 | 49 | 2 | +19 | +16 | +14 | +12 | +11 |
| WY | Sheridan | 44 | 48 | 106 | 58 | 2 | +14 | +19 | +23 | +27 | +31 |

### CANADA

| STATE/PROVINCE | CITY | NORTH LATITUDE ° | NORTH LATITUDE ′ | WEST LONGITUDE ° | WEST LONGITUDE ′ | TIME ZONE CODE | A | B | C | D | E |
|---|---|---|---|---|---|---|---|---|---|---|---|
| AB | Calgary | 51 | 5 | 114 | 5 | 2 | +13 | +35 | +50 | +68 | +84 |
| AB | Edmonton | 53 | 34 | 113 | 25 | 2 | −3 | +26 | +47 | +72 | +93 |
| BC | Vancouver | 49 | 13 | 123 | 6 | 3 | 0 | +15 | +26 | +40 | +52 |
| MB | Winnipeg | 49 | 53 | 97 | 10 | 1 | +12 | +30 | +43 | +58 | +71 |
| NB | Saint John | 45 | 16 | 66 | 3 | −1 | +28 | +34 | +39 | +44 | +49 |
| NS | Halifax | 44 | 38 | 63 | 35 | −1 | +21 | +26 | +29 | +33 | +37 |
| NS | Sydney | 46 | 10 | 60 | 10 | −1 | +1 | +9 | +15 | +23 | +28 |
| ON | Ottawa | 45 | 25 | 75 | 43 | 0 | +6 | +13 | +18 | +23 | +28 |
| ON | Peterborough | 44 | 18 | 78 | 19 | 0 | +21 | +25 | +28 | +32 | +35 |
| ON | Thunder Bay | 48 | 27 | 89 | 12 | 0 | +47 | +61 | +71 | +83 | +93 |
| ON | Toronto | 43 | 39 | 79 | 23 | 0 | +28 | +30 | +32 | +35 | +37 |
| QC | Montreal | 45 | 28 | 73 | 39 | 0 | −1 | +4 | +9 | +15 | +20 |
| SK | Saskatoon | 52 | 10 | 106 | 40 | 1 | +37 | +63 | +80 | +101 | +119 |

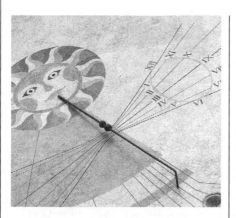

**ATOMIC TIME (TA) SCALE:** A time scale based on atomic or molecular resonance phenomena. Elapsed time is measured by counting cycles of a frequency locked to an atomic or molecular transition.

**DATE:** A unique instant defined in a specified time scale. NOTE: The date can be conventionally expressed in years, months, days, hours, minutes and seconds, and fractions thereof.

**GREENWICH MEAN TIME (GMT):** A 24-hour system based on mean solar time plus 12 hours at Greenwich, England. Greenwich Mean Time can be considered approximately equivalent to Coordinated Universal Time (UTC), which is broadcast from all standard time-and-frequency radio stations. However, GMT is now obsolete and has been replaced by UTC.

**INTERNATIONAL ATOMIC TIME (TAI):** An atomic time scale based on data from a worldwide set of atomic clocks. It is the internationally agreed-upon time reference conforming to the definition of the second, the fundamental unit of atomic time in the International System of Units (SI).

**LEAP SECOND:** A second used to adjust UTC to be within 0.9 sec of UT1 (a time scale based on Earth's varying rotation rate). An inserted "positive" second or omitted "negative" second may be applied at the end of June or December of each year.

**MEAN SOLAR TIME:** Apparent solar time corrected for the effects of orbital eccentricity and the tilt of Earth's axis relative to the ecliptic plane; in other words, corrected by the equation of time, which is defined as the hour angle of the true Sun minus the hour angle of the mean Sun.

**SECOND:** The basic unit of time or time interval in the International System of Units (SI), which is equal to 9,192,631,770 periods of radiation corresponding to the transition between the two hyperfine levels of the ground state of cesium-133 as defined at the 1967 Conférence Générale des Poids et Mesures.

**SIDEREAL TIME:** The measure of time defined by the apparent diurnal motion of the vernal equinox; hence, a measure of the rotation of Earth with respect to the reference frame that is related to the stars rather than the Sun. A mean solar day is about 4 minutes longer than a sidereal day.

*–(U.S.) National Institute of Standards and Technology (NIST)*

# GENERAL STORE CLASSIFIEDS

---

*The Old Farmer's Almanac* has no liability whatsoever for any third-party claims arising in connection with such advertisements or any products or services mentioned therein.

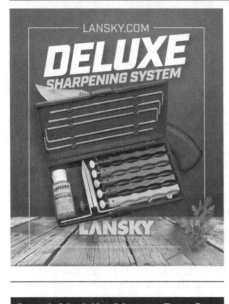

# 2022 ESSAY CONTEST WINNERS
## *"My Most Memorable Wildlife Experience"*

We received hundreds of wonderfully wild tales! Thank you to everyone who took the time to share your experience.

## First Prize: $300

Our trip to Galveston Island, Texas, to camp for Spring Break a bust, our vanload of friends began the trek back to campus in Wisconsin. The Sun had long set by the time we reached Big Thicket National Preserve north of Beaumont. We drove in after-hours to find the gate open with a sign instructing us to find an empty site and pay in the morning. As we wound through the bayou, we noticed warning signs along the drive: "Beware of Alligators," "Alligators in Area," "Watch for Alligators." This seemed ominous. The Spanish moss hung from the trees while ground fog rose as we pulled into an empty site. While friends were setting up tents, I set up the camp kitchen, preparing a late-night dinner in the damp, late-winter chill. Then I heard it. The leaves rustled. Sticks moved. There was the distinct sound of tent nylon being tested, and I jumped on top of the picnic table with a shout of "Alligator!" Everyone paused, ready to run, and as I turned toward the tent that my boyfriend had set up, I saw a very startled armadillo looking back at me.

*–Sarah Wilde, Arena, Wisconsin*

## Second Prize: $200

My dad died in 2016. I was crushed; he was one of my best friends, my confidant, my fixer-of-all. His loss affected me immensely. I found myself talking to any blue jay that happened upon my yard, believing that my dad was visiting for a chat. Fast-forward to 2021 . . . I lost my Mom in January; her 90-year-old body couldn't recover from COVID. I began talking to her through any cardinal visiting my yard. Then, in October, I lost my cherished husband, Jim, after 42 years together. During a particularly good cry the day after his funeral, a bright blue jay hopped onto the patio chair and looked at me through the kitchen window. "Hi, Dad!" I exclaimed. "Are you checking on me today? Or is that you, Jim?" No sooner had I uttered these words than another jay hopped up next to the first. "There you are, Jim! But where's Mom?" And with that, a beautiful cardinal joined the jays on the chair. An avid birdwatcher, I know that these birds do not travel together! I'm convinced that my loved ones were telling me they are at peace and watching over me.

*–Susan Felts, Bel Air, Maryland*

# Third Prize: $100

I was one of five civilian guests of the U.S. Air Force attending an Arctic survival training course. On Day 4, a C-130 transport outfitted with skis touched down on the polar ice cap above northeast Greenland. With the temp at –55°F, Sgt. Jesse instructed us to immediately dig a shelter. My survival partner and I struggled to dig into an 8-foot-high wall of bulletproof snow and ice. As we labored, I thought of the rare white Beluga whales that I hoped to see. I had whales, whales, whales on my mind. During that night, I dreamt that I heard whale vocal-izations, lots of whales "singing" to one another. I woke up excited and shared my dream at breakfast. I quickly learned that nearly everyone had heard the whales. We realized that a pod of whales had swum beneath our survival camp during the night. For me, this had been more thrilling than seeing a Beluga whale. Our survival shelter was an acoustical chamber constructed with ice. As the whales swam beneath us, the clarity of their songs reverberated within the void—songs that replay in my memory to this day.

*–Peter Benoit, Queensbury, New York*

# Honorable Mention

As a child living on the coast of Maine, I grew up with a cove full of wildlife. One afternoon, I heard crying from the ocean. Down on the beach, I found a baby doll-size harbor seal pup lying on rocky seaweed. She was drying out and very small. My heart almost stopped. We called Marine Rescue, which advised us to wait for her mother to return. I heard her mournful crying all night. In the morning, Marine Rescue took her to a facility, wrapped in a towel. Our family donated money for medical treatment and food for "Sugar Baby." We got a special tour of the marine facility and saw her happily swimming in a tank with other rescued seals. Months later, we attended her ocean beach release. Sugar Baby (now 50 pounds!) flopped toward the ocean but turned around, seemingly scared of the freedom and waves. Finally, she swam along the shore and out to sea. Though happy, I cried with sadness; she was leaving. The next summer, my dad excitedly yelled, "Sugar Baby's swimming out front!" She was back to say hello and thank us! I helped to save this wild baby creature's life. I still love you, Sugar.

*–Linda Butler, Yarmouth, Maine* ■

## ANNOUNCING THE 2023 ESSAY CONTEST TOPIC:
## A FUNNY THING THAT HAPPENED TO ME
SEE CONTEST RULES ON PAGE 251.

# MADDENING MIND-MANGLERS

## Are You as Smart as a 200- or 100-Year-Old?

The TV show may have asked *Are You Smarter Than a Fifth Grader?*,
but how will you do with these puzzles from centuries past?
No "problem," right? *Good luck!*

### From the 1823 Old Farmer's Almanac:

**1.** My farm contains 312 acres and is in the form of a right-angled parallelogram. The sum of the length and breadth and a diameter line from corner to corner is 832 rods. What are the length and breadth of my farm?

**2.** A man has a ewe sheep that has a ewe lamb in the first year and two in each year after. If each of these breeds in a like manner, how many sheep will the farmer have in 10 years?

**3.**
Like man, primeval form'd at natur's birth,
I first originated from the earth.
Strange adverse properties in me unite,
I'm sometimes heavy, and I'm sometimes light.
I'm hollow, solid, oval, round, and square.
I'm limpid and opaque, I'm foul and fair.
I'm crooked, straight, broad, narrow, smooth, and rough.
I'm sometimes tender, and I'm sometimes tough.
Sometimes I'm musical, and at others, mute.
Sometimes I sadden and sometimes I suit.
I'm fragile, flexile, concave, and convex.
Sometimes I please, and at others, I perplex.
I'm colorless as snow without a stain,
Yet of all colors found in Flora's train.
I've frighten'd thousands—thousands I've decoy'd,
Millions preserv'd, and millions I've destroy'd.
At the same instant, I am new and old—
Am worthless, yet am worth my weight in gold.
Sometimes I lie at rest on a downy pillow;
I'm at others roaming on the raging billow.
Sometimes I'm passing to and fro through town,
Turning each thing I meet with upside down:
A thousand antic capers I display,
Yet I am lifeless as a lump of clay.
I'm seen at theatre, church, ball, and fair,
Where lads and lasses often at me stare:
*What am I, critic? Construe and declare.*

*From the 1923* **Old Farmer's Almanac:**

**4.**

Often we are covered in wisdom and wit,
And oft with a cloth where the dinner
  guests sit.
In beauty around you, and over your
  head,
We are countless, though numbered
  when bound to be read.
*What are we?*

---

*Do you have a favorite puzzler for "Maddening Mind-Manglers" that you'd like to share? Send it to us at Mind-Manglers, The Old Farmer's Almanac, P.O. Box 520, Dublin, NH 03444, or via Almanac.com/Contact, Subject: Mind-Manglers.*

---

### ANSWERS

**1.** 312 acres multiplied by 160 is equal to 49,920 square rods. This divided by 832 is equal to 60. Then 832 divided by 2 is equal to 416, which less 60 is equal to 356, the length of the diagonal. 416 added to 60 is equal to 476, the sum of the sides. The diagonal squared is equal to 126,736. The area, 49,920, multiplied by 2 is equal to 99,840. Then 126,736 less 99,840 is equal to 26,896, the square root of which is equal to 164, the difference in the sides. Now the sum of the sides, 476, divided by 2, is equal to 238. The difference in the sides, 164, divided by 2 is equal to 82. Thus 238 plus 82 is equal to 320, the length, and 238 less 82 is equal to 156, the breadth. **2.** Rule: Doubling the old stock of any year and adding it to the increase will give the increase in the following year. Example: Year 1—old stock 1, increase 1, aggregate 2; Year 2—old stock 2, increase 3, aggregate 5; Year 3—old stock 5, increase 7, aggregate 12; Year 4—old stock 12, increase 17, aggregate 29. Answer: 5,741. **3.** "Glass" (submitted by one reader). Three others submitted "water," which was also given consideration because "when congealed, it is quite analogous to glass." **4.** "Leaves."

# ESSAY AND RECIPE CONTEST RULES

Cash prizes (first, $300; second, $200; third, $100) will be awarded for the best essays in 200 or fewer words on the subject "A Funny Thing That Happened to Me" and the best recipes using ginger. Entries must be yours, original, and unpublished. Amateur cooks only, please. One recipe per person. All entries become the property of Yankee Publishing, which reserves all rights to the material. The deadline for entries is Friday, January 27, 2023. Enter at Almanac.com/EssayContest or at Almanac.com/RecipeContest or label "Essay Contest" or "Recipe Contest" and mail to The Old Farmer's Almanac, P.O. Box 520, Dublin, NH 03444. Include your name, mailing address, and email address. Winners will appear in *The 2024 Old Farmer's Almanac* and on Almanac.com. ∎

# ANECDOTES & PLEASANTRIES

*A sampling from the thousands of letters, clippings, articles, and emails sent to us during the past year by our Almanac family in the United States and Canada.*

ILLUSTRATIONS BY TIM ROBINSON

## How to Unstick the Suez Ship

When the container ship *Ever Given* got stuck crosswise in the Suez Canal in 2021, it took 6 days to figure out how to get it loose. Maybe we should have just asked the kids. Or not.

**5-YEAR-OLD:** "Just push it back and it will float away. I've seen things like this in my life, like sticks in the creek."

**5yo:** "Get a crane and a rope and a ramp and a car. The car will run on the ramp and cut the rope and land on the boat with a crash. This will bump the boat back into the sea. If this doesn't work, just add another car. Double the force."

**6yo:** "Just cut it." *[Cut what?]* "Cut off the corner of the boat."

**7yo:** "Blow up the land that the boat is stuck on without hurting the boat. Little explosions. Get a bunch of helicopters with winches on the bottom. Attach the helicopters to the front and back of the boat, then they fly in opposite directions—just a little—until the boat turns free."

**8yo:** "Push it." *[How?]* "I don't know. Get a giant hunk of metal and a bunch of pistons."

**12yo:** "Everyone in Egypt brings their own rope. They tie all the ropes along the side of the boat and everyone pulls as hard as they can. If we get all the people in Egypt, the weight will turn it and then they can steer it."

**14yo:** "Force everyone on the boat to undergo intense, rigorous training until one of them develops psychic powers from the stress. Then they would snap and levitate the boat out. I can't think of any possible way that this wouldn't work."

–*J. R., Oakville, Ontario*

# HOW TO TURN YOUR HAND OVER WITHOUT TURNING YOUR HAND OVER

1. Keeping your elbow in, extend one forearm out in front of you with the *palm up.*
2. Bring the palm up to the same shoulder.
3. Keeping the same position, bring the hand down in front of your stomach, as though you were doing a slow karate chop.
4. Push your hand away from your stomach until it is back to position #1, as though you were pushing something off to the side with the back of your hand. Your hand will now be on edge, not palm up.
5. Bring the thumb side of your hand up to your shoulder.
6. Bring your hand down in front of your stomach, as though you were pushing something down.
7. Move your hand back to position #1, as though you were pushing open a door with the heel edge of your hand—which is now *palm down.*

–*T. D., West Farmington, Ohio*

---

## RIDDLES

### KNOW YOUR PLACE
If I'm in second place and you pass me, what place are you in?
–*R. M., Tahoe City, California*

### ON TOP OF YOUR GAME?
What sport is played all over the world, has four letters in its name, and starts with a t?
–*A. C., West Haven, Connecticut*

### COOKING TIP
How do you keep pieces of Canadian bacon from curling in the skillet?
–*B. D., Robertsville, Missouri*

## The Pitcher Who Bit His Own Backside

Clarence Waldo "Climax" Blethen (1893–1973), pride of Dover-Foxcroft, Maine, was a professional baseball pitcher who patched together a nearly two-decade career remarkably unnoteworthy except for one thing: perhaps the weirdest sports injury of all time.

On June 6, 1933, while playing for the Knoxville (Tenn.) Smokies of the American Association, Blethen had occasion to slide into second base. This was all well and good, except that when he hit the dirt, the false teeth that he had taken out and put into his back pocket for safekeeping took a chunk out of one of his cheeks. The injury bothered him for the rest of the game, but the real "bottom" line is that it secured his place in baseball history.

–*G. S., Memphis, Tennessee*

*(continued)*

## PRAIRIE ANGELS

*When coyotes are crying in the morning,*
*You'd do well to listen to what they know.*
*The north wind will be blowing inward,*
*And it could bring lots of snow.*

*When coyotes wail before dusk,*
*They're foretelling changing skies.*
*They are the Prairie Angels,*
*Melodic in their harmony, with a song*
   *that never lies.*

*Coyotes sing to me in the evening,*
*A lullaby that rocks me to sleep.*
*Coyotes are heaven's messengers,*
*If you but pay heed to the lonesome songs*
   *that they keep.*

*They call out in symphony with the earth,*
*Celebrating the coming of spring's rebirth.*
*And yip with joy their chaotic praise,*
*Predictions of warmer days.*

*They synchronize their prophetic song*
*With scarlet-blazed skies of dawn,*
*And carols content in midnight's glow,*
*A serenade that only the Sun and the*
   *Moon and the Maker know.*

*—Jean Bonin, Millet, Alberta*

# News You Can ~~Use~~ Lose

**IN BRIEF(S):** Somebody has invented self-cleaning underwear. Made of beechwood, eucalyptus, bamboo, and copper fibers, it supposedly can last for weeks or even months without washing, although you're supposed to let it dry out for a few hours every night. *Yes. Please do.*

*—E. K., Milton, Florida*

**WHY WITCHES WEAR POINTY HATS:** In England back in the Middle Ages, women did most of the beer brewing, both at home and to pick up a little extra cash at market stalls. They wore conical hats to attract customers, stirred their brews in cauldrons, and kept cats around to control the mice attracted to the brewing grains. With the arrival of the Reformation in the early 16th century came finger-pointing at "witches" who cast curses. Seeing an opportunity to cut down on their competition, male brewers began accusing their female peers of being on the dark side, which forevermore linked witches to pointy hats, cauldrons, and black cats.

*—R. S., Goffstown, New Hampshire*

**FRENCH BORDER GETS STONED:** Apparently with nothing better to do than create an international incident, a Belgian farmer decided to move an in-the-way rock about 7½ feet—not realizing that it was a border marker dating to 1819 and he was stealing a quarter-acre from France. *Sacre bleu!*

*—H. G., Regina, Saskatchewan*

**GNAWING NIGHTMARE:** Minnesota recently named as its state fossil the bones of *Castoroides ohioensis,* a giant, 200-lb., bear-size beaver, which, as far as we're concerned, could have done anything it dam well pleased.

*–G. G., Thief River Falls, Minnesota*

**CREEPY CASTOR:** An irate beaver greeted an elderly "trespasser" in its remote Massachusetts pond with head lacerations, a torn hand tendon, puncture wounds, and significant blood loss. "It was like *Jaws,*" the man reportedly said.

*–A. N., Newton, Massachusetts*

**RESEARCH DOLLARS (WELL, EUROS) AT WORK:** A study based in Germany has determined that baby bats babble just like human babies, joining the only other nonhumans to do this, male songbirds. This must be important somehow.

*–T. S., Kamloops, British Columbia*

**AVALANCHE OF NUTS:** In a winter panic if there ever was one, a red squirrel in Fargo, North Dakota, filled every nook and cranny of a Chevy Avalanche pickup with 42 gallons of stored black walnuts.

*–B. N., Dickinson, North Dakota*

**BLIND JUSTICE:** Also in Massachusetts, Brad Day came to the aid of his wife, Laurie Rose, who was attacked by a rabid raccoon while trying to corral their chicken, Alice. Day whacked the raccoon four or five times with a frying pan to get it to cease and desist—which was no mean feat inasmuch as he is blind. Laurie, we might surmise, is probably lucky to have survived both of them.

*–H. R., Durham, North Carolina*

## This Year's Cringers

(Feel free to leave the room.)

- What do you call a pig with laryngitis? Disgruntled.
- Why do bees stay in their hives during winter? Swarm.
- Why is "dark" spelled with a k and not c? Because you can't see in the dark.
- Why is it unwise to share your secrets with a clock? Well, time will tell.
- When I told my contractor that I didn't want carpeted steps, she gave me a blank stare.

Send your contribution for *The 2024 Old Farmer's Almanac* by January 27, 2023, to "A & P," The Old Farmer's Almanac, P.O. Box 520, Dublin, NH 03444, or via Almanac.com/Contact.

# Takes 10 Years Off Your Face in Just 10 Minutes

## Women are raving about the life-changing effects of this powerful, natural formula.

Women are raving about the life-changing effects of this powerful, natural formula.

Known as advanced liposome technology, this powerful distribution system ensures that vital nutrients are delivered exactly where your skin needs them the most, providing your skin with the appearance of "maximum plump."

### New Age-Defying Cream in High Demand

Al Sears, MD, of Palm Beach, Florida, released an anti-aging cream that adapts breakthrough medical technology into the realm of skincare, and he's struggling to keep up with consumer demand.

Dr. Sears is South Florida's leading anti-aging pioneer. He has authored over 500 reports, scientific papers, and books on anti-aging. A frequent lecturer at global anti-aging conferences, Dr. Sears spoke at a Palm Beach Health & Wellness Festival featuring Dr. Oz, along with special guest, Suzanne Somers. Thousands of people were in attendance as Dr. Sears discussed his latest anti-aging breakthroughs.

This powerful cream, known as **Restore**, keeps selling out faster than it's produced — and people are raving about the effect it's having on their skin.

"Within a few minutes of applying the cream, the under-eye area looks nice and smooth as well as those annoying lines between the nose and lips that deepen as we age. I definitely feel I look younger whenever I use it," said Amy B., of Montville, New Jersey.

"The lines around my mouth and eyes have a smooth appearance. I love having younger-looking skin, so I will continue using **Restore**," raves Cathy C., of Florida.

### Powerful New Delivery System

"All of **Restore's** powerful ingredients are encapsulated in a liposome shell — an organic container that carries the nutrients so they are better able to beautify the appearance of your skin," explained Dr. Sears.

When you apply liposome cream to your face, the liposomes release their contents in a way that gives aging skin a more youthful appearance. Regular skin creams don't have this capability.

> **"Advanced liposome technology ensures that vital nutrients are delivered exactly where your skin needs them the most."**

### Take 10 Years off Your Face in Just 10 Minutes

Once on your skin, **Restore** releases a unique blend of botanicals, vitamins and essential oils that reduce the appearance of fine lines and wrinkles, and gives skin the appearance of a plump, and more even tone.

**Restore's** first beautifying agent is Madonna lily leaf stem cell extract. It helps produce the appearance of an even-toned complexion. This powerful formula also features guarana seed extract, coenzyme Q10, and avocado oil. Japanese researchers discovered coenzyme Q10 has an attractive appearance on your skin, and French studies have shown that avocado oil enhances the appearance of skin thickness.

### Where To Get Restore

Right now the only way to get this powerful age-defying delivery technology is through Dr. Sears.

To get life-changing results like Amy and Cathy, buyers should contact the Sears Health Hotline at **1-800-690-1935**. "We simply don't have enough supply to get **Restore** shipped directly to stores," said Dr. Sears. "The hotline allows us to ship the product directly to the customer – the one who really wants it."

Dr. Sears feels so strongly about this product, he offers a 100% money-back guarantee on every order. "Just send back the bottle and any unused product within 90 days, and I'll send you your money back, less shipping and handling." said Dr. Sears.

# A Reference Compendium

**REFERENCE**

REFERENCE

## PHASES OF THE MOON

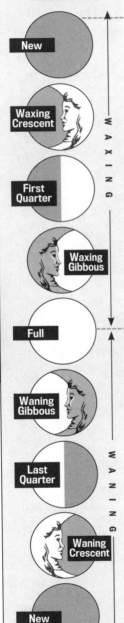

New

Waxing Crescent

First Quarter

Waxing Gibbous

Full

Waning Gibbous

Last Quarter

Waning Crescent

New

WAXING

WANING

# WHEN WILL THE MOON RISE?

Use the following saying to remember the time of moonrise on a day when a Moon phase occurs. Keep in mind that the phase itself may happen earlier or later that day, depending on location.

**The new Moon always rises near sunrise;**

**The first quarter, near noon;**

**The full Moon always rises near sunset;**

**The last quarter, near midnight.**

Moonrise occurs about 50 minutes later each day.

## FULL MOON NAMES

| NAME | MONTH | VARIATIONS |
|------|-------|------------|
| Full Wolf Moon | JANUARY | Full Greetings Moon |
| Full Snow Moon | FEBRUARY | Full Hungry Moon |
| Full Worm Moon | MARCH | Full Eagle Moon<br>Full Sore Eye Moon<br>Full Sugar Moon<br>Full Wind Strong Moon |
| Full Pink Moon | APRIL | Full Budding Moon<br>Moon When the Geese Lay Eggs |
| Full Flower Moon | MAY | Full Frog Moon<br>Full Planting Moon |
| Full Strawberry Moon | JUNE | Full Hoer Moon<br>Full Hot Moon |
| Full Buck Moon | JULY | Full Raspberry Moon<br>Full Salmon Moon |
| Full Sturgeon Moon | AUGUST | Full Black Cherries Moon<br>Full Flying Up Moon |
| Full Harvest Moon* | SEPTEMBER | Full Corn Moon<br>Full Yellow Leaf Moon |
| Full Hunter's Moon | OCTOBER | Full Falling Leaves Moon<br>Full Migrating Moon |
| Full Beaver Moon | NOVEMBER | Full Frost Moon |
| Full Cold Moon | DECEMBER | Full Long Night Moon |

*The Harvest Moon is always the full Moon closest to the autumnal equinox. If the Harvest Moon occurs in October, the September full Moon is usually called the Corn Moon.

# THE ORIGIN OF FULL MOON NAMES

Historically, some Native Americans who lived in the area that is now the United States kept track of the seasons by giving a distinctive name to each recurring full Moon. (This name was applied to the entire lunar month in which it occurred.) The names were used by various tribes and/or by colonial Americans, who also brought their own traditions.

## Meanings of Full Moon Names

**JANUARY'S** full Moon was called the **Wolf Moon** because wolves were more often heard at this time.

**FEBRUARY'S** full Moon was called the **Snow Moon** because it was a time of heavy snow. It was also called the **Hungry Moon** because hunting was difficult and hunger often resulted.

**MARCH'S** full Moon was called the **Worm Moon** because, as the weather warmed, wormlike insect larvae emerged from winter homes such as the bark of trees.

**APRIL'S** full Moon was called the **Pink Moon** because it heralded the appearance of the moss pink, or wild ground phlox—one of the first spring flowers.

**MAY'S** full Moon was called the **Flower Moon** because blossoms were abundant everywhere at this time.

**JUNE'S** full Moon was called the **Strawberry Moon** because it appeared when the strawberry harvest took place.

**JULY'S** full Moon was called the **Buck Moon;** it arrived when a male deer's antlers were in full growth mode.

**AUGUST'S** full Moon was called the **Sturgeon Moon** because this large fish, which is found in the Great Lakes and Lake Champlain, was caught easily at this time.

**SEPTEMBER'S** full Moon was called the **Corn Moon** because this was the time to harvest corn.

The **Harvest Moon** is the full Moon that occurs closest to the autumnal equinox. It can occur in either September or October. Around this time, the Moon rises only about 30 minutes later each night, providing extra light after sunset for harvesting.

**OCTOBER'S** full Moon was called the **Hunter's Moon** because this was the time to hunt in preparation for winter.

**NOVEMBER'S** full Moon was called the **Beaver Moon** because it was the time when beavers finished preparations for winter and retreated to their lodges.

**DECEMBER'S** full Moon was called the **Cold Moon.** It was also called the **Long Night Moon** because nights at this time of year were the longest.

REFERENCE

## THE ORIGIN OF MONTH NAMES

**JANUARY.** For the Roman god Janus, protector of gates and doorways. Janus is depicted with two faces, one looking into the past, the other into the future.

**FEBRUARY.** From the Latin *februa,* "to cleanse." The Roman Februalia was a festival of purification and atonement that took place during this time of year.

**MARCH.** For the Roman god of war, Mars. This was the time of year to resume military campaigns that had been interrupted by winter.

**APRIL.** From the Latin *aperio,* "to open (bud)," because plants begin to grow now.

**MAY.** For the Roman goddess Maia, who oversaw the growth of plants. Also from the Latin *maiores,* "elders," who were celebrated now.

**JUNE.** For the Roman goddess Juno, patroness of marriage and the well-being of women. Also from the Latin *juvenis,* "young people."

**JULY.** To honor Roman dictator Julius Caesar (100 B.C.–44 B.C.). In 46 B.C., with the help of Sosigenes, he developed the Julian calendar.

**AUGUST.** To honor the first Roman emperor (and grandnephew of Julius Caesar), Augustus Caesar (63 B.C.–A.D. 14).

**SEPTEMBER.** From the Latin *septem,* "seven," because this was the seventh month of the early Roman calendar.

**OCTOBER.** From the Latin *octo,* "eight," because this was the eighth month of the early Roman calendar.

**NOVEMBER.** From the Latin *novem,* "nine," because this was the ninth month of the early Roman calendar.

**DECEMBER.** From the Latin *decem,* "ten," because this was the tenth month of the early Roman calendar.

---

## Easter Dates (2023–26)

Christian churches that follow the Gregorian calendar celebrate Easter on the first Sunday after the paschal full Moon on or just after the vernal equinox.

| YEAR | EASTER |
| --- | --- |
| 2023 | April 9 |
| 2024 | March 31 |
| 2025 | April 20 |
| 2026 | April 5 |

The Julian calendar is used by some churches, including many Eastern Orthodox. The dates below are Julian calendar dates for Easter converted to Gregorian dates.

| YEAR | EASTER |
| --- | --- |
| 2023 | April 16 |
| 2024 | May 5 |
| 2025 | April 20 |
| 2026 | April 12 |

## FRIGGATRISKAIDEKAPHOBIA TRIVIA

*Here are a few facts about Friday the 13th:*

In the 14 possible configurations for the annual calendar (see any perpetual calendar), the occurrence of Friday the 13th is this:

**6 of 14 years have one Friday the 13th.**
**6 of 14 years have two Fridays the 13th.**
**2 of 14 years have three Fridays the 13th.**

No year is without one Friday the 13th, and no year has more than three.

Months that have a Friday the 13th begin on a Sunday.

2023 has a Friday the 13th in January and October.

REFERENCE

# THE ORIGIN OF DAY NAMES

The days of the week were named by ancient Romans with the Latin words for the Sun, the Moon, and the five known planets. These names have survived in European languages, but English names also reflect Anglo-Saxon and Norse influences.

| ENGLISH | LATIN | FRENCH | ITALIAN | SPANISH | ANGLO-SAXON AND NORSE |
|---------|-------|--------|---------|---------|------------------------|
| SUNDAY | dies Solis (Sol's day) | dimanche | domenica | domingo | Sunnandaeg (Sun's day) |
| | | *from the Latin for "Lord's day"* | | | |
| MONDAY | dies Lunae (Luna's day) | lundi | lunedì | lunes | Monandaeg (Moon's day) |
| TUESDAY | dies Martis (Mars's day) | mardi | martedì | martes | Tiwesdaeg (Tiw's day) |
| WEDNESDAY | dies Mercurii (Mercury's day) | mercredi | mercoledì | miércoles | Wodnesdaeg (Woden's day) |
| THURSDAY | dies Jovis (Jupiter's day) | jeudi | giovedì | jueves | Thursdaeg (Thor's day) |
| FRIDAY | dies Veneris (Venus's day) | vendredi | venerdì | viernes | Frigedaeg (Frigga's day) |
| SATURDAY | dies Saturni (Saturn's day) | samedi | sabato | sábado | Saeterndaeg (Saturn's day) |
| | | *from the Latin for "Sabbath"* | | | |

# How to Find the Day of the Week for Any Given Date

*To compute the day of the week for any given date as far back as the mid-18th century, proceed as follows:*

Add the last two digits of the year to one-quarter of the last two digits (discard any remainder), the day of the month, and the month key from the key box below. Divide the sum by 7; the remainder is the day of the week (1 is Sunday, 2 is Monday, and so on). If there is no remainder, the day is Saturday. If you're searching for a weekday prior to 1900, add 2 to the sum before dividing; prior to 1800, add 4. The formula doesn't work for days prior to 1753. From 2000 through 2099, subtract 1 from the sum before dividing.

*Example:*

**THE DAYTON FLOOD WAS ON MARCH 25, 1913.**

Last two digits of year: . . . . . . . . . . . . 13
One-quarter of these two digits: . . . . . . 3
Given day of month: . . . . . . . . . . . . . . 25
Key number for March: . . . . . . . . . . . . 4
　　　　　　　　　　　　　　　　Sum: 45

*45 ÷ 7 = 6, with a remainder of 3. The flood took place on Tuesday, the third day of the week.*

### KEY

JANUARY . . . . . . . . . . . 1
　LEAP YEAR . . . . . . . . 0
FEBRUARY . . . . . . . . . . 4
　LEAP YEAR . . . . . . . . 3
MARCH . . . . . . . . . . . . 4
APRIL . . . . . . . . . . . . . 0
MAY . . . . . . . . . . . . . . 2
JUNE . . . . . . . . . . . . . 5
JULY . . . . . . . . . . . . . 0
AUGUST . . . . . . . . . . . 3
SEPTEMBER . . . . . . . . . 6
OCTOBER . . . . . . . . . . 1
NOVEMBER . . . . . . . . . 4
DECEMBER . . . . . . . . . 6

# ANIMAL SIGNS OF THE CHINESE ZODIAC

The animal designations of the Chinese zodiac follow a 12-year cycle and are always used in the same sequence. The Chinese year of 354 days begins 3 to 7 weeks into the western 365-day year, so the animal designation changes at that time, rather than on January 1. This year, the Lunar New Year in China starts on January 22.

## RAT

Ambitious and sincere, you can be generous with your money. Compatible with the dragon and the monkey. Your opposite is the horse.

| | | |
|---|---|---|
| 1924 | 1936 | 1948 |
| 1960 | 1972 | 1984 |
| 1996 | 2008 | 2020 |

## OX OR BUFFALO

A leader, you are bright, patient, and cheerful. Compatible with the snake and the rooster. Your opposite is the sheep.

| | | |
|---|---|---|
| 1925 | 1937 | 1949 |
| 1961 | 1973 | 1985 |
| 1997 | 2009 | 2021 |

## TIGER

Forthright and sensitive, you possess great courage. Compatible with the horse and the dog. Your opposite is the monkey.

| | | |
|---|---|---|
| 1926 | 1938 | 1950 |
| 1962 | 1974 | 1986 |
| 1998 | 2010 | 2022 |

## RABBIT OR HARE

Talented and affectionate, you are a seeker of tranquility. Compatible with the sheep and the pig. Your opposite is the rooster.

| | | |
|---|---|---|
| 1927 | 1939 | 1951 |
| 1963 | 1975 | 1987 |
| 1999 | 2011 | 2023 |

## DRAGON

Robust and passionate, your life is filled with complexity. Compatible with the monkey and the rat. Your opposite is the dog.

| | | |
|---|---|---|
| 1928 | 1940 | 1952 |
| 1964 | 1976 | 1988 |
| 2000 | 2012 | 2024 |

## SNAKE

Strong-willed and intense, you display great wisdom. Compatible with the rooster and the ox. Your opposite is the pig.

| | | |
|---|---|---|
| 1929 | 1941 | 1953 |
| 1965 | 1977 | 1989 |
| 2001 | 2013 | 2025 |

## HORSE

Physically attractive and popular, you like the company of others. Compatible with the tiger and the dog. Your opposite is the rat.

| | | |
|---|---|---|
| 1930 | 1942 | 1954 |
| 1966 | 1978 | 1990 |
| 2002 | 2014 | 2026 |

## SHEEP OR GOAT

Aesthetic and stylish, you enjoy being a private person. Compatible with the pig and the rabbit. Your opposite is the ox.

| | | |
|---|---|---|
| 1931 | 1943 | 1955 |
| 1967 | 1979 | 1991 |
| 2003 | 2015 | 2027 |

## MONKEY

Persuasive, skillful, and intelligent, you strive to excel. Compatible with the dragon and the rat. Your opposite is the tiger.

| | | |
|---|---|---|
| 1932 | 1944 | 1956 |
| 1968 | 1980 | 1992 |
| 2004 | 2016 | 2028 |

## ROOSTER OR COCK

Seeking wisdom and truth, you have a pioneering spirit. Compatible with the snake and the ox. Your opposite is the rabbit.

| | | |
|---|---|---|
| 1933 | 1945 | 1957 |
| 1969 | 1981 | 1993 |
| 2005 | 2017 | 2029 |

## DOG

Generous and loyal, you have the ability to work well with others. Compatible with the horse and the tiger. Your opposite is the dragon.

| | | |
|---|---|---|
| 1934 | 1946 | 1958 |
| 1970 | 1982 | 1994 |
| 2006 | 2018 | 2030 |

## PIG OR BOAR

Gallant and noble, your friends will remain at your side. Compatible with the rabbit and the sheep. Your opposite is the snake.

| | | |
|---|---|---|
| 1935 | 1947 | 1959 |
| 1971 | 1983 | 1995 |
| 2007 | 2019 | 2031 |

REFERENCE

# A Table Foretelling the Weather Through All the Lunations of Each Year, or Forever

This table is the result of many years of actual observation and shows what sort of weather will probably follow the Moon's entrance into any of its quarters. For example, the table shows that the week following January 14, 2023, will be fair and frosty if the wind is north or northeast or have rain or snow if the wind is south or southwest, because the Moon enters the last quarter on that day at 9:10 P.M. EST. (See the **Left-Hand Calendar Pages, 120–146,** for Moon phases.)

EDITOR'S NOTE: Although the data in this table is taken into consideration in the year-long process of compiling the annual long-range weather forecasts for *The Old Farmer's Almanac,* we rely far more on our projections of solar activity.

| TIME OF CHANGE | SUMMER | WINTER |
|---|---|---|
| Midnight to 2 A.M. | Fair | Hard frost, unless wind is south or west |
| 2 A.M. to 4 A.M. | Cold, with frequent showers | Snow and stormy |
| 4 A.M. to 6 A.M. | Rain | Rain |
| 6 A.M. to 8 A.M. | Wind and rain | Stormy |
| 8 A.M. to 10 A.M. | Changeable | Cold rain if wind is west; snow, if east |
| 10 A.M. to noon | Frequent showers | Cold with high winds |
| Noon to 2 P.M. | Very rainy | Snow or rain |
| 2 P.M. to 4 P.M. | Changeable | Fair and mild |
| 4 P.M. to 6 P.M. | Fair | Fair |
| 6 P.M. to 10 P.M. | Fair if wind is northwest; rain if wind is south or southwest | Fair and frosty if wind is north or northeast; rain or snow if wind is south or southwest |
| 10 P.M. to midnight | Fair | Fair and frosty |

*This table was created more than 180 years ago by Dr. Herschell for the* Boston Courier; *it first appeared in* The Old Farmer's Almanac *in 1834.*

## SAFE ICE THICKNESS*

| ICE THICKNESS | PERMISSIBLE LOAD |
|---|---|
| 3 inches | Single person on foot |
| 4 inches | Group in single file |
| 7½ inches | Passenger car (2-ton gross) |
| 8 inches | Light truck (2½-ton gross) |
| 10 inches | Medium truck (3½-ton gross) |

| ICE THICKNESS | PERMISSIBLE LOAD |
|---|---|
| 12 inches | Heavy truck (8-ton gross) |
| 15 inches | 10 tons |
| 20 inches | 25 tons |
| 30 inches | 70 tons |
| 36 inches | 110 tons |

**\*Solid, clear, blue/black pond and lake ice**

*The strength value of river ice is 15 percent less. Slush ice has only half the strength of blue ice.*

REFERENCE

## HEAT INDEX °F (°C)

| TEMP. °F (°C) | RELATIVE HUMIDITY (%) | | | | | | | | |
|---|---|---|---|---|---|---|---|---|---|
| | 40 | 45 | 50 | 55 | 60 | 65 | 70 | 75 | 80 |
| 100 (38) | 109 (43) | 114 (46) | 118 (48) | 124 (51) | 129 (54) | 136 (58) | | | |
| 98 (37) | 105 (41) | 109 (43) | 113 (45) | 117 (47) | 123 (51) | 128 (53) | 134 (57) | | |
| 96 (36) | 101 (38) | 104 (40) | 108 (42) | 112 (44) | 116 (47) | 121 (49) | 126 (52) | 132 (56) | |
| 94 (34) | 97 (36) | 100 (38) | 103 (39) | 106 (41) | 110 (43) | 114 (46) | 119 (48) | 124 (51) | 129 (54) |
| 92 (33) | 94 (34) | 96 (36) | 99 (37) | 101 (38) | 105 (41) | 108 (42) | 112 (44) | 116 (47) | 121 (49) |
| 90 (32) | 91 (33) | 93 (34) | 95 (35) | 97 (36) | 100 (38) | 103 (39) | 105 (41) | 109 (43) | 113 (45) |
| 88 (31) | 88 (31) | 89 (32) | 91 (33) | 93 (34) | 95 (35) | 98 (37) | 100 (38) | 103 (39) | 106 (41) |
| 86 (30) | 85 (29) | 87 (31) | 88 (31) | 89 (32) | 91 (33) | 93 (34) | 95 (35) | 97 (36) | 100 (38) |
| 84 (29) | 83 (28) | 84 (29) | 85 (29) | 86 (30) | 88 (31) | 89 (32) | 90 (32) | 92 (33) | 94 (34) |
| 82 (28) | 81 (27) | 82 (28) | 83 (28) | 84 (29) | 84 (29) | 85 (29) | 86 (30) | 88 (31) | 89 (32) |
| 80 (27) | 80 (27) | 80 (27) | 81 (27) | 81 (27) | 82 (28) | 82 (28) | 83 (28) | 84 (29) | 84 (29) |

**RISK LEVEL FOR HEAT DISORDERS:**  CAUTION  EXTREME CAUTION  DANGER

**EXAMPLE:** *When the temperature is 88°F (31°C) and the relative humidity is 60 percent, the heat index, or how hot it feels, is 95°F (35°C).*

## THE UV INDEX FOR MEASURING ULTRAVIOLET RADIATION RISK

*The U.S. National Weather Service's daily forecasts of ultraviolet levels use these numbers for various exposure levels:*

| UV INDEX NUMBER | EXPOSURE LEVEL | ACTIONS TO TAKE |
|---|---|---|
| 0, 1, 2 | Low | Wear UV-blocking sunglasses on bright days. In winter, reflection off snow can nearly double UV strength. If you burn easily, cover up and apply SPF 30+ sunscreen. |
| 3, 4, 5 | Moderate | Apply SPF 30+ sunscreen; wear a hat and sunglasses. Stay in shade when sun is strongest. |
| 6, 7 | High | Apply SPF 30+ sunscreen; wear a hat, sunglasses, and protective clothing; limit midday exposure. |
| 8, 9, 10 | Very High | Apply SPF 30+ sunscreen; wear a hat, sunglasses, and protective clothing; limit midday exposure. Seek shade. Unprotected skin will be damaged and can burn quickly. |
| 11 or higher | Extreme | Apply SPF 30+ sunscreen; wear a hat, sunglasses, and protective clothing; avoid midday exposure; seek shade. Unprotected skin can burn in minutes. |

REFERENCE

| 85 | 90 | 95 | 100 |
|---|---|---|---|
| 135 (57) | | | |
| 126 (52) | 131 (55) | | |
| 117 (47) | 122 (50) | 127 (53) | 132 (56) |
| 110 (43) | 113 (45) | 117 (47) | 121 (49) |
| 102 (39) | 105 (41) | 108 (42) | 112 (44) |
| 96 (36) | 98 (37) | 100 (38) | 103 (39) |
| 90 (32) | 91 (33) | 93 (34) | 95 (35) |
| 85 (29) | 86 (30) | 86 (30) | 87 (31) |

# What Are Cooling/Heating Degree Days?

In an attempt to measure the need for air-conditioning, each degree of a day's mean temperature that is above a base temperature, such as 65°F (U.S.) or 18°C (Canada), is considered one cooling degree day. If the daily mean temperature is 75°F, for example, that's 10 cooling degree days.

Similarly, to measure the need for heating fuel consumption, each degree of a day's mean temperature that is below 65°F (18°C) is considered one heating degree. For example, a day with a high of 60°F and low of 40°F results in a mean of 50°, or 15 degrees less than 65°. Hence, that day had 15 heating degree days.

# HOW TO MEASURE HAIL

The **TORRO HAILSTORM INTENSITY SCALE** was introduced by Jonathan Webb of Oxford, England, in 1986 as a means of categorizing hailstorms. The name derives from the private and mostly British research body named the TORnado and storm Research Organisation.

## INTENSITY/DESCRIPTION OF HAIL DAMAGE

H0  True hail of pea size causes no damage

H1  Leaves and flower petals are punctured and torn

H2  Leaves are stripped from trees and plants

H3  Panes of glass are broken; auto bodies are dented

H4  Some house windows are broken; small tree branches are broken off; birds are killed

H5  Many windows are smashed; small animals are injured; large tree branches are broken off

H6  Shingle roofs are breached; metal roofs are scored; wooden window frames are broken away

H7  Roofs are shattered to expose rafters; autos are seriously damaged

H8  Shingle and tile roofs are destroyed; small tree trunks are split; people are seriously injured

H9  Concrete roofs are broken; large tree trunks are split and knocked down; people are at risk of fatal injuries

H10  Brick houses are damaged; people are at risk of fatal injuries

## HOW TO MEASURE WIND SPEED

The **BEAUFORT WIND FORCE SCALE** is a common way of estimating wind speed. It was developed in 1805 by Admiral Sir Francis Beaufort of the British Navy to measure wind at sea. We can also use it to measure wind on land.

Admiral Beaufort arranged the numbers 0 to 12 to indicate the strength of the wind from calm, force 0, to hurricane, force 12. Here's a scale adapted to land.

*"Used Mostly at Sea but of Help to All Who Are Interested in the Weather"*

| BEAUFORT FORCE | DESCRIPTION | WHEN YOU SEE OR FEEL THIS EFFECT | WIND SPEED (mph) | (km/h) |
|---|---|---|---|---|
| 0 | CALM | Smoke goes straight up | less than 1 | less than 2 |
| 1 | LIGHT AIR | Wind direction is shown by smoke drift but not by wind vane | 1–3 | 2–5 |
| 2 | LIGHT BREEZE | Wind is felt on the face; leaves rustle; wind vanes move | 4–7 | 6–11 |
| 3 | GENTLE BREEZE | Leaves and small twigs move steadily; wind extends small flags straight out | 8–12 | 12–19 |
| 4 | MODERATE BREEZE | Wind raises dust and loose paper; small branches move | 13–18 | 20–29 |
| 5 | FRESH BREEZE | Small trees sway; waves form on lakes | 19–24 | 30–39 |
| 6 | STRONG BREEZE | Large branches move; wires whistle; umbrellas are difficult to use | 25–31 | 40–50 |
| 7 | NEAR GALE | Whole trees are in motion; walking against the wind is difficult | 32–38 | 51–61 |
| 8 | GALE | Twigs break from trees; walking against the wind is very difficult | 39–46 | 62–74 |
| 9 | STRONG GALE | Buildings suffer minimal damage; roof shingles are removed | 47–54 | 75–87 |
| 10 | STORM | Trees are uprooted | 55–63 | 88–101 |
| 11 | VIOLENT STORM | Widespread damage | 64–72 | 102–116 |
| 12 | HURRICANE | Widespread destruction | 73+ | 117+ |

## RETIRED ATLANTIC HURRICANE NAMES

*These storms have been some of the most destructive and costly.*

| NAME | YEAR | NAME | YEAR | NAME | YEAR | NAME | YEAR |
|---|---|---|---|---|---|---|---|
| Noel | 2007 | Irene | 2011 | Otto | 2016 | Michael | 2018 |
| Gustav | 2008 | Sandy | 2012 | Harvey | 2017 | Dorian | 2019 |
| Ike | 2008 | Ingrid | 2013 | Irma | 2017 | Eta | 2020 |
| Paloma | 2008 | Erika | 2015 | Maria | 2017 | Iota | 2020 |
| Igor | 2010 | Joaquin | 2015 | Nate | 2017 | Laura | 2020 |
| Tomas | 2010 | Matthew | 2016 | Florence | 2018 | Ida | 2021 |

REFERENCE

| ATLANTIC TROPICAL (AND SUBTROPICAL) STORM NAMES FOR 2023 | | | EASTERN NORTH-PACIFIC TROPICAL (AND SUBTROPICAL) STORM NAMES FOR 2023 | | |
|---|---|---|---|---|---|
| Arlene | Harold | Ophelia | Adrian | Irwin | Ramon |
| Bret | Idalia | Philippe | Beatriz | Jova | Selma |
| Cindy | Jose | Rina | Calvin | Kenneth | Todd |
| Don | Katia | Sean | Dora | Lidia | Veronica |
| Emily | Lee | Tammy | Eugene | Max | Wiley |
| Franklin | Margot | Vince | Fernanda | Norma | Xina |
| Gert | Nigel | Whitney | Greg | Otis | York |
| | | | Hilary | Pilar | Zelda |

The lists above are used in rotation and recycled every 6 years,
e.g., the 2023 list will be used again in 2029.

## How to Measure Hurricane Strength

The SAFFIR-SIMPSON HURRICANE WIND SCALE assigns a rating from 1 to 5 based on a hurricane's intensity. It is used to give an estimate of the potential property damage from a hurricane landfall. Wind speed is the determining factor in the scale, as storm surge values are highly dependent on the slope of the continental shelf in the landfall region. Wind speeds are measured at a height of 33 feet (10 meters) using a 1-minute average.

**CATEGORY ONE.** Average wind: 74–95 mph. Significant damage to mobile homes. Some damage to roofing and siding of well-built frame homes. Large tree branches snap and shallow-rooted trees may topple. Power outages may last a few to several days.

Frame homes may sustain major roof damage. Many trees snap or topple, blocking numerous roads. Electricity and water may be unavailable for several days to weeks.

**CATEGORY TWO.** Average wind: 96–110 mph. Mobile homes may be destroyed. Major roof and siding damage to frame homes. Many shallow-rooted trees snap or topple, blocking roads. Widespread power outages could last from several days to weeks. Potable water may be scarce.

**CATEGORY THREE.** Average wind: 111–129 mph. Most mobile homes destroyed.

**CATEGORY FOUR.** Average wind: 130–156 mph. Mobile homes destroyed. Frame homes severely damaged or destroyed. Windborne debris may penetrate protected windows. Most trees snap or topple. Residential areas isolated by fallen trees and power poles. Most of the area uninhabitable for weeks to months.

**CATEGORY FIVE.** Average wind: 157+ mph. Most homes destroyed. Nearly all windows blown out of high-rises. Most of the area uninhabitable for weeks to months.

REFERENCE

## HOW TO MEASURE A TORNADO

The original **FUJITA SCALE** (or F Scale) was developed by Dr. Theodore Fujita to classify tornadoes based on wind damage. All tornadoes, and other severe local windstorms, were assigned a number according to the most intense damage caused by the storm. An enhanced F (EF) scale was implemented in the United States on February 1, 2007. The EF scale uses 3-second gust estimates based on a more detailed system for assessing damage, taking into account different building materials.

| F SCALE | | EF SCALE (U.S.) |
|---|---|---|
| F0 · 40-72 mph (64-116 km/h) | LIGHT DAMAGE | EF0 · 65-85 mph (105-137 km/h) |
| F1 · 73-112 mph (117-180 km/h) | MODERATE DAMAGE | EF1 · 86-110 mph (138-178 km/h) |
| F2 · 113-157 mph (181-253 km/h) | CONSIDERABLE DAMAGE | EF2 · 111-135 mph (179-218 km/h) |
| F3 · 158-207 mph (254-332 km/h) | SEVERE DAMAGE | EF3 · 136-165 mph (219-266 km/h) |
| F4 · 208-260 mph (333-419 km/h) | DEVASTATING DAMAGE | EF4 · 166-200 mph (267-322 km/h) |
| F5 · 261-318 mph (420-512 km/h) | INCREDIBLE DAMAGE | EF5 · over 200 mph (over 322 km/h) |

## Wind/Barometer Table

| BAROMETER (REDUCED TO SEA LEVEL) | WIND DIRECTION | CHARACTER OF WEATHER INDICATED |
|---|---|---|
| 30.00 to 30.20, and steady | WESTERLY | Fair, with slight changes in temperature, for one to two days |
| 30.00 to 30.20, and rising rapidly | WESTERLY | Fair, followed within two days by warmer and rain |
| 30.00 to 30.20, and falling rapidly | SOUTH TO EAST | Warmer, and rain within 24 hours |
| 30.20 or above, and falling rapidly | SOUTH TO EAST | Warmer, and rain within 36 hours |
| 30.20 or above, and falling rapidly | WEST TO NORTH | Cold and clear, quickly followed by warmer and rain |
| 30.20 or above, and steady | VARIABLE | No early change |
| 30.00 or below, and falling slowly | SOUTH TO EAST | Rain within 18 hours that will continue a day or two |
| 30.00 or below, and falling rapidly | SOUTHEAST TO NORTHEAST | Rain, with high wind, followed within two days by clearing, colder |
| 30.00 or below, and rising | SOUTH TO WEST | Clearing and colder within 12 hours |
| 29.80 or below, and falling rapidly | SOUTH TO EAST | Severe storm of wind and rain imminent; in winter, snow or cold wave within 24 hours |
| 29.80 or below, and falling rapidly | EAST TO NORTH | Severe northeast gales and heavy rain or snow, followed in winter by cold wave |
| 29.80 or below, and rising rapidly | GOING TO WEST | Clearing and colder |

**NOTE:** *A barometer should be adjusted to show equivalent sea-level pressure for the altitude at which it is to be used. A change of 100 feet in elevation will cause a decrease of ¹⁄₁₀ inch in the reading.*

REFERENCE

## WINDCHILL TABLE

As wind speed increases, your body loses heat more rapidly, making the air feel colder than it really is. The combination of cold temperature and high wind can create a cooling effect so severe that exposed flesh can freeze.

| WIND SPEED (mph) | TEMPERATURE (°F) | | | | | | | | | | | | | | |
|---|---|---|---|---|---|---|---|---|---|---|---|---|---|---|---|
| **Calm** | **35** | **30** | **25** | **20** | **15** | **10** | **5** | **0** | **–5** | **–10** | **–15** | **–20** | **–25** | **–30** | **–35** |
| **5** | 31 | 25 | 19 | 13 | 7 | 1 | –5 | –11 | –16 | –22 | –28 | –34 | –40 | –46 | –52 |
| **10** | 27 | 21 | 15 | 9 | 3 | –4 | –10 | –16 | –22 | –28 | –35 | –41 | –47 | –53 | –59 |
| **15** | 25 | 19 | 13 | 6 | 0 | –7 | –13 | –19 | –26 | –32 | –39 | –45 | –51 | –58 | –64 |
| **20** | 24 | 17 | 11 | 4 | –2 | –9 | –15 | –22 | –29 | –35 | –42 | –48 | –55 | –61 | –68 |
| **25** | 23 | 16 | 9 | 3 | –4 | –11 | –17 | –24 | –31 | –37 | –44 | –51 | –58 | –64 | –71 |
| **30** | 22 | 15 | 8 | 1 | –5 | –12 | –19 | –26 | –33 | –39 | –46 | –53 | –60 | –67 | –73 |
| **35** | 21 | 14 | 7 | 0 | –7 | –14 | –21 | –27 | –34 | –41 | –48 | –55 | –62 | –69 | –76 |
| **40** | 20 | 13 | 6 | –1 | –8 | –15 | –22 | –29 | –36 | –43 | –50 | –57 | –64 | –71 | –78 |
| **45** | 19 | 12 | 5 | –2 | –9 | –16 | –23 | –30 | –37 | –44 | –51 | –58 | –65 | –72 | –79 |
| **50** | 19 | 12 | 4 | –3 | –10 | –17 | –24 | –31 | –38 | –45 | –52 | –60 | –67 | –74 | –81 |
| **55** | 18 | 11 | 4 | –3 | –11 | –18 | –25 | –32 | –39 | –46 | –54 | –61 | –68 | –75 | –82 |
| **60** | 17 | 10 | 3 | –4 | –11 | –19 | –26 | –33 | –40 | –48 | –55 | –62 | –69 | –76 | –84 |

FROSTBITE OCCURS IN 30 MINUTES 10 MINUTES 5 MINUTES

**EXAMPLE:** *When the temperature is 15°F and the wind speed is 30 miles per hour, the windchill, or how cold it feels, is –5°F. See a Celsius version of this table via Almanac.com/2023.*

–courtesy of National Weather Service

## HOW TO MEASURE EARTHQUAKES

In 1979, seismologists developed a measurement of earthquake size called **MOMENT MAGNITUDE.** It is more accurate than the previously used Richter scale, which is precise only for earthquakes of a certain size and at a certain distance from a seismometer. All earthquakes can now be compared on the same magnitude scale.

| MAGNITUDE | DESCRIPTION | EFFECT |
|---|---|---|
| LESS THAN 3 | MICRO | GENERALLY NOT FELT |
| 3–3.9 | MINOR | OFTEN FELT, LITTLE DAMAGE |
| 4–4.9 | LIGHT | SHAKING, SOME DAMAGE |
| 5–5.9 | MODERATE | SLIGHT TO MAJOR DAMAGE |
| 6–6.9 | STRONG | DESTRUCTIVE |
| 7–7.9 | MAJOR | SERIOUS DAMAGE |
| 8 OR MORE | GREAT | SEVERE DAMAGE |

## A GARDENER'S WORST PHOBIAS

| NAME OF FEAR | OBJECT FEARED |
|---|---|
| Alliumphobia | Garlic |
| Anthophobia | Flowers |
| Apiphobia | Bees |
| Arachnophobia | Spiders |
| Botanophobia | Plants |
| Bufonophobia | Toads |
| Dendrophobia | Trees |
| Entomophobia | Insects |
| Lachanophobia | Vegetables |
| Melissophobia | Bees |
| Mottephobia | Moths |
| Myrmecophobia | Ants |
| Ornithophobia | Birds |
| Ranidaphobia | Frogs |
| Rupophobia | Dirt |
| Scoleciphobia | Worms |
| Spheksophobia | Wasps |

## PLANTS FOR LAWNS

*Choose varieties that suit your soil and your climate. All of these can withstand mowing and considerable foot traffic.*

Ajuga or bugleweed *(Ajuga reptans)*
Corsican mint *(Mentha requienii)*
Dwarf cinquefoil *(Potentilla tabernaemontani)*
English pennyroyal *(Mentha pulegium)*
Green Irish moss *(Sagina subulata)*
Pearly everlasting *(Anaphalis margaritacea)*
Roman chamomile *(Chamaemelum nobile)*
Rupturewort *(Herniaria glabra)*
Speedwell *(Veronica officinalis)*
Stonecrop *(Sedum ternatum)*
Sweet violets *(Viola odorata* or *V. tricolor)*
Thyme *(Thymus serpyllum)*
White clover *(Trifolium repens)*
Wild strawberries *(Fragaria virginiana)*
Wintergreen or partridgeberry *(Mitchella repens)*

## Lawn-Growing Tips

• Test your soil: The pH balance should be 6.2 to 6.7; less than 6.0 puts your lawn at risk for fungal diseases. If the pH is too low, correct it with liming, best done in the fall.

• The best time to apply fertilizer is just before a light rain.

• If you put lime and fertilizer on your lawn, spread half of it as you walk north to south, the other half as you walk east to west to cut down on missed areas.

• Any feeding of lawns in the fall should be done with a low-nitrogen, slow-acting fertilizer.

• In areas of your lawn where tree roots compete with the grass, apply some extra fertilizer to benefit both.

• Moss and sorrel in lawns usually means poor soil, poor aeration or drainage, or excessive acidity.

• Control weeds by promoting healthy lawn growth with natural fertilizers in spring and early fall.

• Raise the level of your lawn-mower blades during the hot summer days. Taller grass resists drought better than short.

• You can reduce mowing time by redesigning your lawn, reducing sharp corners and adding sweeping curves.

• During a drought, let the grass grow longer between mowings and reduce fertilizer.

• Water your lawn early in the morning or in the evening.

# Flowers and Herbs That Attract Butterflies

Allium . . . . . . . . . . . . . . . . . . . . . . . *Allium*
Aster . . . . . . . . . . *Aster, Symphyotrichum*
Bee balm . . . . . . . . . . . . . . . . . . *Monarda*
Butterfly bush . . . . . . . . . . . . . . . *Buddleia*
Catmint . . . . . . . . . . . . . . . . . . . . . *Nepeta*
Clove pink . . . . . . . . . . . . . . . . . . *Dianthus*
Cornflower . . . . . . . . . . . . . . . . . *Centaurea*
Creeping thyme . . . . . . *Thymus serpyllum*
Daylily . . . . . . . . . . . . . . . . . . *Hemerocallis*
Dill . . . . . . . . . . . . . *Anethum graveolens*
False indigo . . . . . . . . . . . . . . . . *Baptisia*
Fleabane . . . . . . . . . . . . . . . . . . . *Erigeron*
Floss flower . . . . . . . . . . . . . . . . *Ageratum*
Globe thistle . . . . . . . . . . . . . . . *Echinops*
Goldenrod . . . . . . . . . . . . . . . . . . *Solidago*
Helen's flower . . . . . . . . . . . . . . *Helenium*
Hollyhock . . . . . . . . . . . . . . . . . . . . *Alcea*
Honeysuckle . . . . . . . . . . . . . . . . *Lonicera*
Lavender . . . . . . . . . . . . . . . . *Lavandula*
Lilac . . . . . . . . . . . . . . . . . . . . . . . *Syringa*
Lupine . . . . . . . . . . . . . . . . . . . . . *Lupinus*
Lychnis . . . . . . . . . . . . . . . . . . . . *Lychnis*

Mallow . . . . . . . . . . . . . . . . . . . . . . *Malva*
Mealycup sage . . . . . . . . *Salvia farinacea*
Milkweed . . . . . . . . . . . . . . . . . . *Asclepias*
Mint . . . . . . . . . . . . . . . . . . . . . . . *Mentha*
Oregano . . . . . . . . . . . . *Origanum vulgare*
Pansy . . . . . . . . . . . . . . . . . . . . . . . *Viola*
Parsley . . . . . . . . . . . . . . . *Petroselinum crispum*
Phlox . . . . . . . . . . . . . . . . . . . . . . . *Phlox*
Privet . . . . . . . . . . . . . . . . . . . . *Ligustrum*
Purple coneflower . . *Echinacea purpurea*
Rock cress . . . . . . . . . . . . . . . . . . . *Arabis*
Sea holly . . . . . . . . . . . . . . . . . . *Eryngium*
Shasta daisy . . . . . . . . . . . *Leucanthemum*
Snapdragon . . . . . . . . . . . . . *Antirrhinum*
Stonecrop . . . . . . . *Hylotelephium, Sedum*
Sweet alyssum . . . . . . . . . . . . . *Lobularia*
Sweet marjoram . . . . *Origanum majorana*
Sweet rocket . . . . . . . . . . . . . . . . *Hesperis*
Tickseed . . . . . . . . . . . . . . . . . . *Coreopsis*
Verbena . . . . . . . . . . . . . . . . . . . . *Verbena*
Zinnia . . . . . . . . . . . . . . . . . . . . . . *Zinnia*

# FLOWERS* THAT ATTRACT HUMMINGBIRDS

Beard tongue . . . . . . . . . . . . . . *Penstemon*
Bee balm . . . . . . . . . . . . . . . . . . *Monarda*
Butterfly bush . . . . . . . . . . . . . . . *Buddleia*
Catmint . . . . . . . . . . . . . . . . . . . . . *Nepeta*
Clove pink . . . . . . . . . . . . . . . . . . *Dianthus*
Columbine . . . . . . . . . . . . . . . . *Aquilegia*
Coral bells . . . . . . . . . . . . . . . . . *Heuchera*
Daylily . . . . . . . . . . . . . . . . . *Hemerocallis*
Desert candle . . . . . . . . . . . . . . . . . *Yucca*
Flag iris . . . . . . . . . . . . . . . . . . . . . . . *Iris*
Flowering tobacco . . . . . . *Nicotiana alata*
Foxglove . . . . . . . . . . . . . . . . . . . *Digitalis*
Larkspur . . . . . . . . . . . . . . . . *Delphinium*
Lily . . . . . . . . . . . . . . . . . . . . . . . . *Lilium*
Lupine . . . . . . . . . . . . . . . . . . . . . *Lupinus*
Petunia . . . . . . . . . . . . . . . . . . . . *Petunia*
Pincushion flower . . . . . . . . . . . *Scabiosa*
Red-hot poker . . . . . . . . . . . . . . *Kniphofia*
Scarlet sage . . . . . . . . . . . *Salvia splendens*

Soapwort . . . . . . . . . . . . . . . . . . *Saponaria*
Summer phlox . . . . . . . . *Phlox paniculata*
Trumpet honeysuckle . . . . . . . . *Lonicera sempervirens*
Verbena . . . . . . . . . . . . . . . . . . . . *Verbena*
Weigela . . . . . . . . . . . . . . . . . . . . *Weigela*

**\*NOTE:** *Choose varieties in red and orange shades, if available.*

# pH PREFERENCES OF TREES, SHRUBS, FLOWERS, AND VEGETABLES

An accurate soil test will indicate your soil pH and will specify the amount of lime or sulfur that is needed to bring it up or down to the appropriate level. A pH of 6.5 is just about right for most home gardens, since most plants thrive in the 6.0 to 7.0 (slightly acidic to neutral) range. Some plants (azaleas, blueberries) prefer more strongly acidic soil in the 4.0 to 6.0 range, while a few (asparagus, plums) do best in soil that is neutral to slightly alkaline. Acidic, or sour, soil (below 7.0) is counteracted by applying finely ground limestone, and alkaline, or sweet, soil (above 7.0) is treated with ground sulfur.

| COMMON NAME | OPTIMUM pH RANGE | COMMON NAME | OPTIMUM pH RANGE | COMMON NAME | OPTIMUM pH RANGE |
|---|---|---|---|---|---|
| **TREES AND SHRUBS** | | Bee balm | 6.0–7.5 | Snapdragon | 5.5–7.0 |
| Apple | 5.0–6.5 | Begonia | 5.5–7.0 | Sunflower | 6.0–7.5 |
| Azalea | 4.5–6.0 | Black-eyed Susan | 5.5–7.0 | Tulip | 6.0–7.0 |
| Beautybush | 6.0–7.5 | Bleeding heart | 6.0–7.5 | Zinnia | 5.5–7.0 |
| Birch | 5.0–6.5 | Canna | 6.0–8.0 | | |
| Blackberry | 5.0–6.0 | Carnation | 6.0–7.0 | **VEGETABLES** | |
| Blueberry | 4.0–5.0 | Chrysanthemum | 6.0–7.5 | Asparagus | 6.0–8.0 |
| Boxwood | 6.0–7.5 | Clematis | 5.5–7.0 | Bean | 6.0–7.5 |
| Cherry, sour | 6.0–7.0 | Coleus | 6.0–7.0 | Beet | 6.0–7.5 |
| Crab apple | 6.0–7.5 | Coneflower, purple | 5.0–7.5 | Broccoli | 6.0–7.0 |
| Dogwood | 5.0–7.0 | Cosmos | 5.0–8.0 | Brussels sprout | 6.0–7.5 |
| Fir, balsam | 5.0–6.0 | Crocus | 6.0–8.0 | Cabbage | 6.0–7.5 |
| Hemlock | 5.0–6.0 | Daffodil | 6.0–6.5 | Carrot | 5.5–7.0 |
| Hydrangea, blue-flowered | 4.5–5.5 | Dahlia | 6.0–7.5 | Cauliflower | 5.5–7.5 |
| Hydrangea, pink-flowered | 6.0–7.0 | Daisy, Shasta | 6.0–8.0 | Celery | 5.8–7.0 |
| Juniper | 5.0–6.0 | Daylily | 6.0–8.0 | Chive | 6.0–7.0 |
| Laurel, mountain | 4.5–6.0 | Delphinium | 6.0–7.5 | Collard | 6.5–7.5 |
| Lemon | 6.0–7.5 | Foxglove | 6.0–7.5 | Corn | 5.5–7.0 |
| Lilac | 6.0–7.0 | Geranium | 5.5–6.5 | Cucumber | 5.5–7.0 |
| Maple, sugar | 6.0–7.5 | Gladiolus | 5.0–7.0 | Eggplant | 6.0–7.0 |
| Oak, white | 5.0–6.5 | Hibiscus | 6.0–8.0 | Garlic | 5.5–8.0 |
| Orange | 6.0–7.5 | Hollyhock | 6.0–8.0 | Kale | 6.0–7.5 |
| Peach | 6.0–7.0 | Hyacinth | 6.5–7.5 | Leek | 6.0–8.0 |
| Pear | 6.0–7.5 | Iris, blue flag | 5.0–7.5 | Lettuce | 6.0–7.0 |
| Pecan | 6.4–8.0 | Lily-of-the-valley | 4.5–6.0 | Okra | 6.0–7.0 |
| Plum | 6.0–8.0 | Lupine | 5.0–6.5 | Onion | 6.0–7.0 |
| Raspberry, red | 5.5–7.0 | Marigold | 5.5–7.5 | Pea | 6.0–7.5 |
| Rhododendron | 4.5–6.0 | Morning glory | 6.0–7.5 | Pepper, sweet | 5.5–7.0 |
| Willow | 6.0–8.0 | Narcissus, trumpet | 5.5–6.5 | Potato | 4.8–6.5 |
| | | Nasturtium | 5.5–7.5 | Pumpkin | 5.5–7.5 |
| **FLOWERS** | | Pansy | 5.5–6.5 | Radish | 6.0–7.0 |
| Alyssum | 6.0–7.5 | Peony | 6.0–7.5 | Spinach | 6.0–7.5 |
| Aster, New England | 6.0–8.0 | Petunia | 6.0–7.5 | Squash, crookneck | 6.0–7.5 |
| Baby's breath | 6.0–7.0 | Phlox, summer | 6.0–8.0 | Squash, Hubbard | 5.5–7.0 |
| Bachelor's button | 6.0–7.5 | Poppy, oriental | 6.0–7.5 | Swiss chard | 6.0–7.0 |
| | | Rose, hybrid tea | 5.5–7.0 | Tomato | 5.5–7.5 |
| | | Rose, rugosa | 6.0–7.0 | Watermelon | 5.5–6.5 |

REFERENCE

# How to Rotate Crops

Crop rotation is the practice of planting annual vegetables with their botanical families. Each vegetable family rotates together; it is not necessary to grow every family or every plant in each family. The benefits of rotating crops include fewer pests and soil-borne diseases, improved soil nutrition, and better soil structure. Failure to rotate vegetable crops eventually results in plants that fail to thrive and decreased harvest.

Here's how crop rotation works: In a single-crop plot, legumes (pea family) are planted in year 1, nightshade plants (tomatoes, etc.) in year 2, and gourds in year 3. In year 4, the cycle begins again. Alternatively, these three crops could be planted in three separate plots in year 1 and moved to the next plot in ensuing years. Additional families can be added. A simple plot plan keeps track of what goes where.

## PLANT FAMILIES AND MEMBERS

Plants in the same family are genetically related and thus share similar characteristics (e.g., leaf appearance, tendrils for climbing).

**CARROT,** aka **PARSLEY** (Apiaceae, aka Umbelliferae): caraway, carrot*, celeriac, celery, chervil, coriander, dill, fennel, lovage, parsley, parsnip

**GOOSEFOOT,** aka **CHARD** (Chenopodiaceae): beet*, orache, quinoa, spinach, Swiss chard

**GOURD,** aka **SQUASH** (Cucurbitaceae): cucumber, gourd, melon, pumpkin, squash (summer and winter), watermelon

**GRASS** (Poaceae, aka Gramineae): sweet corn

**MALLOW** (Malvaceae): okra

**MINT** (Lamiaceae, aka Labiatae): anise hyssop, basil, Chinese artichoke, lavender, mint, oregano, rosemary, sage, savory (summer and winter), sweet marjoram, thyme

**MORNING GLORY** (Convolvulaceae): sweet potato

**MUSTARD** (Brassicaceae, aka Cruciferae): arugula, bok choy, broccoli, brussels sprouts, cabbage, cauliflower, collard, kale, kohlrabi, komatsuna, mizuna, mustard greens, radish*, rutabaga, turnip, watercress

**NIGHTSHADE** (Solanaceae): eggplant, pepper, potato, tomatillo, tomato

**ONION** (Amaryllidaceae*): chives, garlic, leek, onion, shallot

**PEA** (Fabaceae, aka Leguminosae): bush, kidney, lima, pole, and soy beans; lentil; pea; peanut

**SUNFLOWER** (Asteraceae, aka Compositae): artichoke (globe and Jerusalem), calendula, chamomile, endive, escarole, lettuce, radicchio, salsify, sunflower, tarragon

*These can be planted among any family.*

REFERENCE

## SOWING VEGETABLE SEEDS

| | |
|---|---|
| **SOW OR PLANT IN COOL WEATHER** | Beets, broccoli, brussels sprouts, cabbage, lettuce, onions, parsley, peas, radishes, spinach, Swiss chard, turnips |
| **SOW OR PLANT IN WARM WEATHER** | Beans, carrots, corn, cucumbers, eggplant, melons, okra, peppers, squashes, tomatoes |
| **SOW OR PLANT FOR ONE CROP PER SEASON** | Corn, eggplant, leeks, melons, peppers, potatoes, spinach (New Zealand), squashes, tomatoes |
| **RESOW FOR ADDITIONAL CROPS** | Beans, beets, cabbage, carrots, kohlrabi, lettuce, radishes, rutabagas, spinach, turnips |

## A Beginner's Vegetable Garden

The vegetables suggested below are common, easy-to-grow crops. Make 11 rows, 10 feet long, with at least 18 inches between them. Ideally, the rows should run north and south to take full advantage of the sun. This garden, planted as suggested, can feed a family of four for one summer, with a little extra for canning and freezing or giving away.

**ROW**
1. Zucchini (4 plants)
2. Tomatoes (5 plants, staked)
3. Peppers (6 plants)
4. Cabbage

**ROW**
5. Bush beans
6. Lettuce
7. Beets
8. Carrots
9. Swiss chard
10. Radishes
11. Marigolds
    (to discourage rabbits!)

## SOIL FIXES

If you have **sandy** soil, amend with compost; humus; aged manure; sawdust with extra nitrogen; heavy, clay-rich soil.

If your soil contains a lot of **silt**, amend with coarse sand (not beach sand) or gravel and compost, or aged horse manure mixed with fresh straw.

If your soil is dense with **clay**, amend with coarse sand (not beach sand) and compost.

### TO IMPROVE YOUR SOIL, ADD THE PROPER AMENDMENT(S) . . .

**bark, ground:** made from various tree barks; improves soil structure

**compost:** an excellent conditioner

**leaf mold:** decomposed leaves, which add nutrients and structure to soil

**lime:** raises the pH of acidic soil and helps to loosen clay soil.

**manure:** best if composted; never add fresh ("hot") manure; is a good conditioner

**coarse sand (not beach sand):** improves drainage in clay soil

**topsoil:** usually used with another amendment; replaces existing soil

REFERENCE

## IMPORTANT TIMES TO . . .

| | . . . FERTILIZE: | . . . WATER: |
|---|---|---|
| **BEANS** | After heavy bloom and set of pods | When flowers form and during pod-forming and picking |
| **BEETS** | At time of planting | Before soil gets bone dry |
| **BROCCOLI** | 3 weeks after transplanting | Continuously for 4 weeks after transplanting |
| **BRUSSELS SPROUTS** | 3 weeks after transplanting | Continuously for 4 weeks after transplanting |
| **CABBAGE** | 2 weeks after transplanting | Frequently in dry weather |
| **CARROTS** | 5 to 6 weeks after sowing | Before soil gets bone-dry |
| **CAULIFLOWER** | 3 to 4 weeks after transplanting | Frequently |
| **CELERY** | At time of transplanting, and after 2 months | Frequently |
| **CORN** | When 8 to 10 inches tall, and when first silk appears | When tassels form and when cobs swell |
| **CUCUMBERS** | 1 week after bloom, and every 3 weeks thereafter | Frequently |
| **LETTUCE** | 3 weeks after transplanting | Frequently |
| **MELONS** | 1 week after bloom, and again 3 weeks later | Once a week |
| **ONION SETS** | At time of planting, and then every 2 weeks until bulbing begins | In early stage to get plants going |
| **PARSNIPS** | 1 year before planting | Before soil gets bone-dry |
| **PEAS** | After heavy bloom and set of pods | When flowers form and during pod-forming and picking |
| **PEPPERS** | At time of planting, and after first fruit-set | Need a steady supply |
| **POTATO TUBERS** | At bloom time or time of second hilling | When the size of marbles |
| **PUMPKINS** | Just before vines start to run, when plants are about 1 foot tall | 1 inch of water per week; water deeply, especially during fruit set |
| **RADISHES** | Before spring planting | Need plentiful, consistent moisture |
| **SPINACH** | When plants are one-third grown | Frequently |
| **SQUASHES, SUMMER & WINTER** | When first blooms appear | Frequently |
| **TOMATOES** | When fruit are 1 inch in diameter, and then every 2 weeks | For 3 to 4 weeks after transplanting and when flowers and fruit form |

**REFERENCE**

## HOW TO GROW HERBS

| HERB | START SEEDS INDOORS (WEEKS BEFORE LAST SPRING FROST) | START SEEDS OUTDOORS (WEEKS BEFORE/AFTER LAST SPRING FROST) | HEIGHT/ SPREAD (INCHES) | SOIL | LIGHT** |
|---|---|---|---|---|---|
| BASIL* | 6–8 | Anytime after | 12–24/12 | Rich, moist | ○ |
| BORAGE* | Not recommended | Anytime after | 12–36/12 | Rich, well-drained, dry | ○ |
| CHERVIL | Not recommended | 3–4 before | 12–24/8 | Rich, moist | ◑ |
| CHIVES | 8–10 | 3–4 before | 12–18/18 | Rich, moist | ○ |
| CILANTRO/ CORIANDER | Not recommended | Anytime after | 12–36/6 | Light | ○◑ |
| DILL | Not recommended | 4–5 before | 36–48/12 | Rich | ○ |
| FENNEL | 4–6 | Anytime after | 48–80/18 | Rich | ○ |
| LAVENDER, ENGLISH* | 8–12 | 1–2 before | 18–36/24 | Moderately fertile, well-drained | ○ |
| LAVENDER, FRENCH | Not recommended | Not recommended | 18–36/24 | Moderately fertile, well-drained | ○ |
| LEMON BALM* | 6–10 | 2–3 before | 12–24/18 | Rich, well-drained | ○◑ |
| LOVAGE* | 6–8 | 2–3 before | 36–72/36 | Fertile, sandy | ○◑ |
| MINT | Not recommended | Not recommended | 12–24/18 | Rich, moist | ◑ |
| OREGANO* | 6–10 | Anytime after | 12–24/18 | Poor | ○ |
| PARSLEY* | 10–12 | 3–4 before | 18–24/6–8 | Medium-rich | ◑ |
| ROSEMARY* | 8–10 | Anytime after | 48–72/48 | Not too acidic | ○ |
| SAGE | 6–10 | 1–2 before | 12–48/30 | Well-drained | ○ |
| SORREL | 6–10 | 2–3 after | 20–48/12–14 | Rich, organic | ○ |
| SUMMER SAVORY | 4–6 | Anytime after | 4–15/6 | Medium-rich | ○ |
| SWEET CICELY | 6–8 | 2–3 after | 36–72/36 | Moderately fertile, well-drained | ○◑ |
| TARRAGON, FRENCH | Not recommended | Not recommended | 24–36/12 | Well-drained | ○◑ |
| THYME, COMMON* | 6–10 | 2–3 before | 2–12/7–12 | Fertile, well-drained | ○◑ |

*Recommend minimum soil temperature of 70°F to germinate

** ○ FULL SUN   ◑ PARTIAL SHADE

REFERENCE

Annual

Annual, biennial

Annual, biennial

Perennial

Annual

Annual

Annual

Perennial

Tender perennial

Perennial

Perennial

Perennial

Tender perennial

Biennial

Tender perennial

Perennial

Perennial

Annual

Perennial

Perennial

Perennial

# DRYING HERBS

Before drying, remove any dead or diseased leaves or stems. Wash under cool water, shake off excess water, and put on a towel to dry completely. Air drying preserves an herb's essential oils; use for sturdy herbs. A microwave dries herbs more quickly, so mold is less likely to develop; use for moist, tender herbs.

**HANGING METHOD:** Gather four to six stems of fresh herbs in a bunch and tie with string, leaving a loop for hanging. Or, use a rubber band with a paper clip attached to it. Hang the herbs in a warm, well-ventilated area, out of direct sunlight, until dry. For herbs that have full seed heads, such as dill or coriander, use a paper bag. Punch holes in the bag for ventilation, label it, and put the herb bunch into the bag before you tie a string around the top of the bag. The average drying time is 1 to 3 weeks.

**MICROWAVE METHOD:** This is better for small quantities, such as a cup or two at a time. Arrange a single layer of herbs between two paper towels and put them in the microwave for 1 to 2 minutes on high power. Let the leaves cool. If they are not dry, reheat for 30 seconds and check again. Repeat as needed. Let cool. Do not overcook, or the herbs will lose their flavor.

# STORING HERBS AND SPICES

**FRESH HERBS:** Dill and parsley will keep for about 2 weeks with stems immersed in a glass of water tented with a plastic bag. Most other fresh herbs (and greens) will keep for short periods unwashed and refrigerated in tightly sealed plastic bags with just enough moisture to prevent wilting. For longer storage, use moisture- and gas-permeable paper and cellophane. Plastic cuts off oxygen to the plants and promotes spoilage.

**SPICES AND DRIED HERBS:** Store in a cool, dry place.

# COOKING WITH HERBS

A **BOUQUET GARNI** is usually made with bay leaves, thyme, and parsley tied with string or wrapped in cheesecloth. Use to flavor casseroles and soups. Remove after cooking.

**FINES HERBES** use equal amounts of fresh parsley, tarragon, chives, and chervil chopped fine. Commonly used in French cooking, they make a fine omelet or add zest to soups and sauces. Add to salads and butter sauces or sprinkle on noodles, soups, and stews.

## HOW TO GROW BULBS

**REFERENCE**

| COMMON NAME | LATIN NAME | HARDINESS ZONE | SOIL | LIGHT* | SPACING (INCHES) |
|---|---|---|---|---|---|
| **SPRING-PLANTED BULBS** | | | | | |
| ALLIUM | *Allium* | 3–10 | Well-drained/moist | ○ | 12 |
| BEGONIA, TUBEROUS | *Begonia* | 10–11 | Well-drained/moist | ◑● | 12–15 |
| BLAZING STAR/ GAYFEATHER | *Liatris* | 7–10 | Well-drained | ○ | 6 |
| CALADIUM | *Caladium* | 10–11 | Well-drained/moist | ◑● | 8–12 |
| CALLA LILY | *Zantedeschia* | 8–10 | Well-drained/moist | ○◑ | 8–24 |
| CANNA | *Canna* | 8–11 | Well-drained/moist | ○ | 12–24 |
| CYCLAMEN | *Cyclamen* | 7–9 | Well-drained/moist | ◑ | 4 |
| DAHLIA | *Dahlia* | 9–11 | Well-drained/fertile | ○ | 12–36 |
| DAYLILY | *Hemerocallis* | 3–10 | Adaptable to most soils | ○◑ | 12–24 |
| FREESIA | *Freesia* | 9–11 | Well-drained/moist/sandy | ○◑ | 2–4 |
| GARDEN GLOXINIA | *Incarvillea* | 4–8 | Well-drained/moist | ○ | 12 |
| GLADIOLUS | *Gladiolus* | 4–11 | Well-drained/fertile | ○◑ | 4–9 |
| IRIS | *Iris* | 3–10 | Well-drained/sandy | ○ | 3–6 |
| LILY, ASIATIC/ORIENTAL | *Lilium* | 3–8 | Well-drained | ○◑ | 8–12 |
| PEACOCK FLOWER | *Tigridia* | 8–10 | Well-drained | ○ | 5–6 |
| SHAMROCK/SORREL | *Oxalis* | 5–9 | Well-drained | ○◑ | 4–6 |
| WINDFLOWER | *Anemone* | 3–9 | Well-drained/moist | ○◑ | 3–6 |
| **FALL-PLANTED BULBS** | | | | | |
| BLUEBELL | *Hyacinthoides* | 4–9 | Well-drained/fertile | ○◑ | 4 |
| CHRISTMAS ROSE/ HELLEBORE | *Helleborus* | 4–8 | Neutral–alkaline | ○◑ | 18 |
| CROCUS | *Crocus* | 3–8 | Well-drained/moist/fertile | ○◑ | 4 |
| DAFFODIL | *Narcissus* | 3–10 | Well-drained/moist/fertile | ○◑ | 6 |
| FRITILLARY | *Fritillaria* | 3–9 | Well-drained/sandy | ○◑ | 3 |
| GLORY OF THE SNOW | *Chionodoxa* | 3–9 | Well-drained/moist | ○◑ | 3 |
| GRAPE HYACINTH | *Muscari* | 4–10 | Well-drained/moist/fertile | ○◑ | 3–4 |
| IRIS, BEARDED | *Iris* | 3–9 | Well-drained | ○◑ | 4 |
| IRIS, SIBERIAN | *Iris* | 4–9 | Well-drained | ○◑ | 4 |
| ORNAMENTAL ONION | *Allium* | 3–10 | Well-drained/moist/fertile | ○ | 12 |
| SNOWDROP | *Galanthus* | 3–9 | Well-drained/moist/fertile | ○◑ | 3 |
| SNOWFLAKE | *Leucojum* | 5–9 | Well-drained/moist/sandy | ○◑ | 4 |
| SPRING STARFLOWER | *Ipheion uniflorum* | 6–9 | Well-drained loam | ○◑ | 3–6 |
| STAR OF BETHLEHEM | *Ornithogalum* | 5–10 | Well-drained/moist | ○◑ | 2–5 |
| STRIPED SQUILL | *Puschkinia scilloides* | 3–9 | Well-drained | ○◑ | 6 |
| TULIP | *Tulipa* | 4–8 | Well-drained/fertile | ○◑ | 3–6 |
| WINTER ACONITE | *Eranthis* | 4–9 | Well-drained/moist/fertile | ○◑ | 3 |

| DEPTH (INCHES) | BLOOMING SEASON | HEIGHT (INCHES) | NOTES |
|---|---|---|---|
| 3–4 | Spring to summer | 6–60 | Usually pest-free; a great cut flower |
| 1–2 | Summer to fall | 8–18 | North of Zone 10, lift in fall |
| 4 | Summer to fall | 8–20 | An excellent flower for drying; north of Zone 7, plant in spring, lift in fall |
| 2 | Summer | 8–24 | North of Zone 10, plant in spring, lift in fall |
| 1–4 | Summer | 24–36 | Fragrant; north of Zone 8, plant in spring, lift in fall |
| Level | Summer | 18–60 | North of Zone 8, plant in spring, lift in fall |
| 1–2 | Spring to fall | 3–12 | Naturalizes well in warm areas; north of Zone 7, lift in fall |
| 4–6 | Late summer | 12–60 | North of Zone 9, lift in fall |
| 2 | Summer | 12–36 | Mulch in winter in Zones 3 to 6 |
| 2 | Summer | 12–24 | Fragrant; can be grown outdoors in warm climates |
| 3–4 | Summer | 6–20 | Does well in woodland settings |
| 3–6 | Early summer to early fall | 12–80 | North of Zone 10, lift in fall |
| 4 | Spring to late summer | 3–72 | Divide and replant rhizomes every two to five years |
| 4–6 | Early summer | 36 | Fragrant; self-sows; requires excellent drainage |
| 4 | Summer | 18–24 | North of Zone 8, lift in fall |
| 2 | Summer | 2–12 | Plant in confined area to control |
| 2 | Early summer | 3–18 | North of Zone 6, lift in fall |
| 3–4 | Spring | 8–20 | Excellent for borders, rock gardens and naturalizing |
| 1–2 | Spring | 12 | Hardy, but requires shelter from strong, cold winds |
| 3 | Early spring | 5 | Naturalizes well in grass |
| 6 | Early spring | 14–24 | Plant under shrubs or in a border |
| 3 | Midspring | 6–30 | Different species can be planted in rock gardens, woodland gardens, or borders |
| 3 | Spring | 4–10 | Self-sows easily; plant in rock gardens, raised beds, or under shrubs |
| 2–3 | Late winter to spring | 6–12 | Use as a border plant or in wildflower and rock gardens; self-sows easily |
| 4 | Early spring to early summer | 3–48 | Naturalizes well; a good cut flower |
| 4 | Early spring to midsummer | 18–48 | An excellent cut flower |
| 3–4 | Late spring to early summer | 6–60 | Usually pest-free; a great cut flower |
| 3 | Spring | 6–12 | Best when clustered and planted in an area that will not dry out in summer |
| 4 | Spring | 6–18 | Naturalizes well |
| 3 | Spring | 4–6 | Fragrant; naturalizes easily |
| 4 | Spring to summer | 6–24 | North of Zone 5, plant in spring, lift in fall |
| 3 | Spring | 4–6 | Naturalizes easily; makes an attractive edging |
| 4–6 | Early to late spring | 8–30 | Excellent for borders, rock gardens, and naturalizing |
| 2–3 | Late winter to spring | 2–4 | Self-sows and naturalizes easily |

**REFERENCE**

# Substitutions for Common Ingredients

| ITEM | QUANTITY | SUBSTITUTION |
|---|---|---|
| BAKING POWDER | 1 teaspoon | ¼ teaspoon baking soda plus ¼ teaspoon cornstarch plus ½ teaspoon cream of tartar |
| BUTTERMILK | 1 cup | 1 tablespoon lemon juice or vinegar plus milk to equal 1 cup; or 1 cup plain yogurt |
| CHOCOLATE, UNSWEETENED | 1 ounce | 3 tablespoons cocoa plus 1 tablespoon unsalted butter, shortening, or vegetable oil |
| CRACKER CRUMBS | ¾ cup | 1 cup dry bread crumbs; or 1 tablespoon quick-cooking oats (for thickening) |
| CREAM, HEAVY | 1 cup | ¾ cup milk plus ⅓ cup melted unsalted butter (this will not whip) |
| CREAM, LIGHT | 1 cup | ⅞ cup milk plus 3 tablespoons melted, unsalted butter |
| CREAM, SOUR | 1 cup | ⅞ cup buttermilk or plain yogurt plus 3 tablespoons melted, unsalted butter |
| CREAM, WHIPPING | 1 cup | ⅔ cup well-chilled evaporated milk, whipped; or 1 cup nonfat dry milk powder whipped with 1 cup ice water |
| EGG | 1 whole | 2 yolks plus 1 tablespoon cold water; or 3 tablespoons vegetable oil plus 1 tablespoon water (for baking); or 2 to 3 tablespoons mayonnaise (for cakes) |
| EGG WHITE | 1 white | 2 teaspoons meringue powder plus 3 tablespoons water, combined |
| FLOUR, ALL-PURPOSE | 1 cup | 1 cup plus 3 tablespoons cake flour (not advised for cookies or quick breads); or 1 cup self-rising flour (omit baking powder and salt from recipe) |
| FLOUR, CAKE | 1 cup | 1 cup minus 3 tablespoons sifted all-purpose flour plus 3 tablespoons cornstarch |
| FLOUR, SELF-RISING | 1 cup | 1 cup all-purpose flour plus 1½ teaspoons baking powder plus ¼ teaspoon salt |
| HERBS, DRIED | 1 teaspoon | 1 tablespoon fresh, minced and packed |
| HONEY | 1 cup | 1¼ cups sugar plus ½ cup liquid called for in recipe (such as water or oil); or 1 cup pure maple syrup |
| KETCHUP | 1 cup | 1 cup tomato sauce plus ¼ cup sugar plus 3 tablespoons apple-cider vinegar plus ½ teaspoon salt plus pinch of ground cloves combined; or 1 cup chili sauce |
| LEMON JUICE | 1 teaspoon | ½ teaspoon vinegar |
| MAYONNAISE | 1 cup | 1 cup sour cream or plain yogurt; or 1 cup cottage cheese (puréed) |
| MILK, SKIM | 1 cup | ⅓ cup instant nonfat dry milk plus ¾ cup water |

REFERENCE

| ITEM | QUANTITY | SUBSTITUTION |
|------|----------|--------------|
| MILK, TO SOUR | 1 cup | 1 tablespoon vinegar or lemon juice plus milk to equal 1 cup. Stir and let stand 5 minutes. |
| MILK, WHOLE | 1 cup | ½ cup evaporated whole milk plus ½ cup water; or ¾ cup 2 percent milk plus ¼ cup half-and-half |
| MOLASSES | 1 cup | 1 cup honey or dark corn syrup |
| MUSTARD, DRY | 1 teaspoon | 1 tablespoon prepared mustard less 1 teaspoon liquid from recipe |
| OAT BRAN | 1 cup | 1 cup wheat bran or rice bran or wheat germ |
| OATS, OLD-FASHIONED | 1 cup | 1 cup steel-cut Irish or Scotch oats |
| QUINOA | 1 cup | 1 cup millet or couscous (whole wheat cooks faster) or bulgur |
| SUGAR, DARK-BROWN | 1 cup | 1 cup light-brown sugar, packed; or 1 cup granulated sugar plus 2 to 3 tablespoons molasses |
| SUGAR, GRANULATED | 1 cup | 1 cup firmly packed brown sugar; or 1¾ cups confectioners' sugar (makes baked goods less crisp); or 1 cup superfine sugar |
| SUGAR, LIGHT-BROWN | 1 cup | 1 cup granulated sugar plus 1 to 2 tablespoons molasses; or ½ cup dark-brown sugar plus ½ cup granulated sugar |
| SWEETENED CONDENSED MILK | 1 can (14 oz.) | 1 cup evaporated milk plus 1¼ cups granulated sugar. Combine and heat until sugar dissolves. |
| VANILLA BEAN | 1-inch bean | 1 teaspoon vanilla extract |
| VINEGAR, APPLE-CIDER | — | malt, white-wine, or rice vinegar |
| VINEGAR, BALSAMIC | 1 tablespoon | 1 tablespoon red- or white-wine vinegar plus ½ teaspoon sugar |
| VINEGAR, RED-WINE | — | white-wine, sherry, champagne, or balsamic vinegar |
| VINEGAR, RICE | — | apple-cider, champagne, or white-wine vinegar |
| VINEGAR, WHITE-WINE | — | apple-cider, champagne, fruit (raspberry), rice, or red-wine vinegar |
| YEAST | 1 cake (⅗ oz.) | 1 package (¼ ounce) or 1 scant tablespoon active dried yeast |
| YOGURT, PLAIN | 1 cup | 1 cup sour cream (thicker; less tart) or buttermilk (thinner; use in baking, dressings, sauces) |

REFERENCE

# Types of Fat

One way to minimize your total blood cholesterol is to manage the amount and types of fat in your diet. Aim for monounsaturated and polyunsaturated fats; avoid saturated and trans fats.

**MONOUNSATURATED FAT** lowers LDL (bad cholesterol) and may raise HDL (good cholesterol) or leave it unchanged; found in almonds, avocados, canola oil, cashews, olive oil, peanut oil, and peanuts.

**POLYUNSATURATED FAT** lowers LDL and may lower HDL; includes omega-3 and omega-6 fatty acids; found in corn oil, cottonseed oil, fish such as salmon and tuna, safflower oil, sesame seeds, soybeans, and sunflower oil.

**SATURATED FAT** raises both LDL and HDL; found in chocolate, cocoa butter, coconut oil, dairy products (milk, butter, cheese, ice cream), egg yolks, palm oil, and red meat.

**TRANS FAT** raises LDL and lowers HDL; a type of fat common in many processed foods, such as most margarines (especially stick), vegetable shortening, partially hydrogenated vegetable oil, many commercial fried foods (doughnuts, french fries), and commercial baked goods (cookies, crackers, cakes).

## FREEZER STORAGE TIME
*(freezer temperature 0°F or colder)*

| PRODUCT | MONTHS IN FREEZER |
|---|---|
| **FRESH MEAT** | |
| Beef | 6 to 12 |
| Lamb | 6 to 9 |
| Veal | 6 to 9 |
| Pork | 4 to 6 |
| Ground beef, veal, lamb, pork | 3 to 4 |
| Frankfurters | 1 to 2 |
| Sausage, fresh pork | 1 to 2 |
| Cold cuts | Not recommended |
| **FRESH POULTRY** | |
| Chicken, turkey (whole) | 12 |
| Chicken, turkey (pieces) | 6 to 9 |
| Cornish game hen, game birds | 6 to 9 |
| Giblets | 3 to 4 |
| **COOKED POULTRY** | |
| Breaded, fried | 4 |
| Pieces, plain | 4 |
| Pieces covered with broth, gravy | 6 |
| **FRESH FISH AND SEAFOOD** | |
| Clams, mussels, oysters, scallops, shrimp | 3 to 6 |
| Fatty fish (bluefish, mackerel, perch, salmon) | 2 to 3 |
| Lean fish (flounder, haddock, sole) | 6 |
| **FRESH FRUIT (PREPARED FOR FREEZING)** | |
| All except those listed next | 10 to 12 |

| PRODUCT | MONTHS IN FREEZER |
|---|---|
| Avocados, bananas, plantains | 3 |
| Lemons, limes, oranges | 4 to 6 |
| **FRESH VEGETABLES (PREPARED FOR FREEZING)** | |
| Beans, beets, bok choy, broccoli, brussels sprouts, cabbage, carrots, cauliflower, celery, corn, greens, kohlrabi, leeks, mushrooms, okra, onions, peas, peppers, soybeans, spinach, summer squashes | 10 to 12 |
| Asparagus, rutabagas, turnips | 8 to 10 |
| Artichokes, eggplant | 6 to 8 |
| Tomatoes (overripe or sliced) | 2 |
| Bamboo shoots, cucumbers, endive, lettuce, radishes, watercress | Not recommended |
| **CHEESE** (except those listed below) | 6 |
| Cottage cheese, cream cheese, feta, goat, fresh mozzarella, Neufchâtel, Parmesan, processed cheese (opened) | Not recommended |
| **DAIRY PRODUCTS** | |
| Margarine (not diet) | 12 |
| Butter | 6 to 9 |
| Cream, half-and-half | 4 |
| Milk | 3 |
| Ice cream | 1 to 2 |

REFERENCE

# WHEN TO REPLACE/CLEAN/RENEW COMMON HOUSEHOLD ITEMS

How long do commonly used food products stay viable or safe after opening or using? What are the recommended time frames for replacing or cleaning things—inside and outside the home? Here are some guidelines for items found around the house.

| ITEM | STATUS | STORAGE | DURATION | TIPS |
|---|---|---|---|---|
| Baking soda | Open | Pantry, cupboard | 6 months | Put a little in bowl, add lemon juice or vinegar. If it fizzes, it's still suitable for baking. |
| Butter | Open | Counter | 1 to 2 days | Can turn rancid; refrigeration will extend life. |
| | Open | Refrigerator | 1 to 2 months | |
| Jelly/jam | Open | Refrigerator | 6 to 12 months | Replace if smell or color changes; mold may occur. |
| Mayonnaise | Open | Refrigerator | 2 months | Throw away if discoloration or odor occurs. |
| Nut oils | Open | Pantry, cupboard | 3 to 8 months | Store in a cool, dry place; refrigeration may extend life. |
| Olive/ vegetable oil | Open | Pantry, cupboard | 3 to 5 months | Store in a cool, dry place; refrigeration may extend life. |
| Peanut butter | Open | Pantry, cupboard | 2 to 3 months | Replace if rancid taste or smell occurs. |
| | Open | Refrigerator | 6 to 9 months | |
| Red/white wine | Open | Refrigerator | 2 to 5 days | Use a stopper for a tight seal. |

| ITEM | USE | STORAGE | REPLACE | TIPS |
|---|---|---|---|---|
| 20-lb. propane tank | As needed | Outside | 10 to 12 years | Can not be refilled past date on tank; recertified tanks good for additional 5 years. |
| Bleach | As needed | Laundry area | 6 to 12 months | Will begin to break down after 6 months. |
| Fire extinguisher | As needed | Kitchen, other | 12 years | Check gauge monthly to ensure factory-recommended pressure level. |
| Gasoline for equipment | As needed | Shed, detached garage | 3 to 6 months | Store in tightly closed container, away from heat sources and light. |
| Smoke alarms | Ongoing | Bedrooms, hallways | 10 years | Test monthly to ensure proper function. |
| Sponges | Daily | Kitchen | 1 to 2 weeks | To clean between replacements, soak in 1:10 bleach/warm water solution for 1 minute, microwave damp (if nonmetallic) for 1 minute, or run through dishwasher cycle. |
| Toothbrushes | Daily | Bathroom | 3 to 4 months | Replace more often if bristles fray or when user(s) have been sick. |

| ITEM | USE | LOCATION | CLEAN | TIPS |
|---|---|---|---|---|
| Bird feeders | Daily | Outdoors | Twice a month | To avoid bacteria buildup, wash with soap and boiling water or diluted bleach solution; rinse and dry completely. |
| Chimney | Heating season | Furnace, fireplace | Once a year | Professional inspection will show if chimney sweep or maintenance is needed. |
| Dryer vent hose | Daily, weekly | Dryer to outdoor vent | Once a year | Clean lint trap after each use; if clothes do not dry properly, check/clean vent hose. |
| Gutters | During storms | Roofline | Twice a year | Leaves will be more prevalent during fall, so clean out more often. |

REFERENCE

## PLASTICS

In your quest to go green, use this guide to use and sort plastic. The number, usually found with a triangle symbol on a container, indicates the type of resin used to produce the plastic. Visit **EARTH911.COM** for recycling information in your state.

**PETE**

**NUMBER 1** · *PETE or PET (polyethylene terephthalate)*
IS USED IN . . . . . . . . . . . . microwavable food trays; salad dressing, soft drink, water, and juice bottles
STATUS . . . . . . . . . . . . . . . . hard to clean; absorbs bacteria and flavors; avoid reusing
IS RECYCLED TO MAKE. . . carpet, furniture, new containers, Polar fleece

**HDPE**

**NUMBER 2** · *HDPE (high-density polyethylene)*
IS USED IN . . . . . . . . . . . . household cleaner and shampoo bottles, milk jugs, yogurt tubs
STATUS . . . . . . . . . . . . . . transmits no known chemicals into food
IS RECYCLED TO MAKE. . . detergent bottles, fencing, floor tiles, pens

**V**

**NUMBER 3** · *V or PVC (vinyl)*
IS USED IN . . . . . . . . . . . . cooking oil bottles, clear food packaging, mouthwash bottles
STATUS . . . . . . . . . . . . . . . . is believed to contain phalates that interfere with hormonal development; avoid
IS RECYCLED TO MAKE. . . cables, mudflaps, paneling, roadway gutters

**LDPE**

**NUMBER 4** · *LDPE (low-density polyethylene)*
IS USED IN . . . . . . . . . . . . bread and shopping bags, carpet, clothing, furniture
STATUS . . . . . . . . . . . . . . transmits no known chemicals into food
IS RECYCLED TO MAKE. . . envelopes, floor tiles, lumber, trash-can liners

**PP**

**NUMBER 5** · *PP (polypropylene)*
IS USED IN . . . . . . . . . . . . .ketchup bottles, medicine and syrup bottles, drinking straws
STATUS . . . . . . . . . . . . . . transmits no known chemicals into food
IS RECYCLED TO MAKE. . . battery cables, brooms, ice scrapers, rakes

**PS**

**NUMBER 6** · *PS (polystyrene)*
IS USED IN . . . . . . . . . . . . disposable cups and plates, egg cartons, take-out containers
STATUS . . . . . . . . . . . . . . . .is believed to leach styrene, a possible human carcinogen, into food; avoid
IS RECYCLED TO MAKE. . . foam packaging, insulation, light switchplates, rulers

**OTHER**

**NUMBER 7** · *Other (miscellaneous)*
IS USED IN . . . . . . . . . . . . .3- and 5-gallon water jugs, nylon, some food containers
STATUS . . . . . . . . . . . . . . . contains bisphenol A, which has been linked to heart disease and obesity; avoid
IS RECYCLED TO MAKE. . . .custom-made products

# Metric Conversion

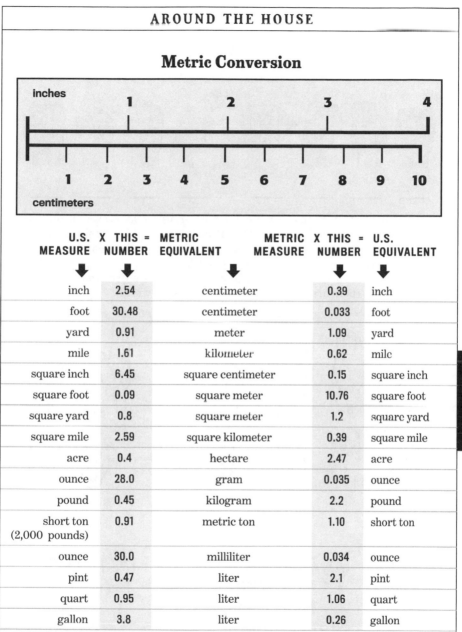

| U.S. MEASURE | X THIS = NUMBER | METRIC EQUIVALENT | METRIC MEASURE | X THIS = NUMBER | U.S. EQUIVALENT |
|---|---|---|---|---|---|
| inch | 2.54 | centimeter | | 0.39 | inch |
| foot | 30.48 | centimeter | | 0.033 | foot |
| yard | 0.91 | meter | | 1.09 | yard |
| mile | 1.61 | kilometer | | 0.62 | mile |
| square inch | 6.45 | square centimeter | | 0.15 | square inch |
| square foot | 0.09 | square meter | | 10.76 | square foot |
| square yard | 0.8 | square meter | | 1.2 | square yard |
| square mile | 2.59 | square kilometer | | 0.39 | square mile |
| acre | 0.4 | hectare | | 2.47 | acre |
| ounce | 28.0 | gram | | 0.035 | ounce |
| pound | 0.45 | kilogram | | 2.2 | pound |
| short ton (2,000 pounds) | 0.91 | metric ton | | 1.10 | short ton |
| ounce | 30.0 | milliliter | | 0.034 | ounce |
| pint | 0.47 | liter | | 2.1 | pint |
| quart | 0.95 | liter | | 1.06 | quart |
| gallon | 3.8 | liter | | 0.26 | gallon |

If you know the U.S. measurement and want to convert it to metric, multiply it by the number in the left shaded column (example: 1 inch equals 2.54 centimeters). If you know the metric measurement, multiply it by the number in the right shaded column (example: 2 meters equals 2.18 yards).

## SIGN LANGUAGE: WHAT'S THE TITLE?

*Use the alphabet below to decode.*

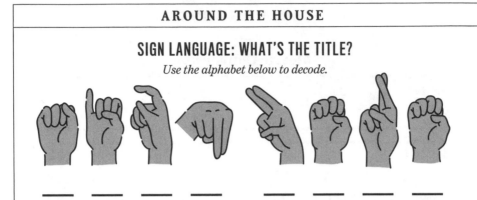

Sign language is a way to communicate without using your voice. It involves using your hands, body posture, and facial expressions. Although sign language is used mostly by people who are deaf or can't hear well, it can be used by anyone. There are even animals that use sign language. A gorilla named Koko learned more than 1,000 signs! In North America, we use American Sign Language, but there are different versions across the world.

*Using the alphabet below, spell your name.*

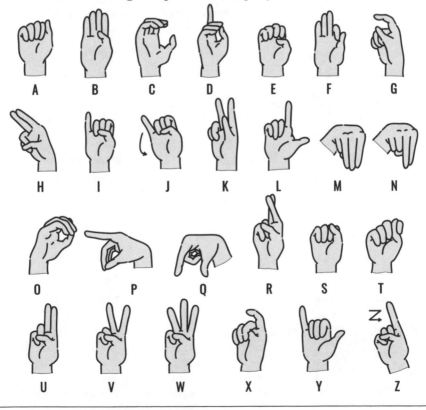

Illustrations: Antonov Maxim/Shutterstock

REFERENCE

Get further useful information at Almanac.com.

*Here are some common signs and phrases to get you started . . .*

**HELLO:** Open your hand with all of your fingers pointing up and your thumb crossed in front of your palm. Touch the side of your forehead, then quickly move your hand away from your head.

**GOOD-BYE:** Open your palm, fold down your fingers, then open your palm again. Repeat once or twice.

**YES:** Make an "S" sign and bend your wrist forward like you are nodding "yes."

**NO:** Open and close your index and middle finger over your thumb twice.

**FAMILY:** Make an "F" sign with each hand, palms facing out, with thumbs touching. Move your hands away from each other, making a circle in front of you. End with the backs of your hands facing out.

**SORRY:** Make an "S" sign and rub your chest in a circular motion toward your shoulder.

**I LOVE YOU:** With your palm facing out, hold up your thumb, index finger, and pinky.

**LOVE:** Make a fist with each hand and cross your arms over your chest.

**PLEASE:** Open your hand and rub your chest in a circular motion.

**THANK YOU:** Open your hand and touch your chin with your fingertips. Move the hand away from you.

REFERENCE

# Where Do You Fit in Your Family Tree?

Technically it's known as consanguinity; that is, the quality or state of being related by blood or descended from a common ancestor. These relationships are shown below for the genealogy of six generations of one family. *–family tree information courtesy of Frederick H. Rohles*

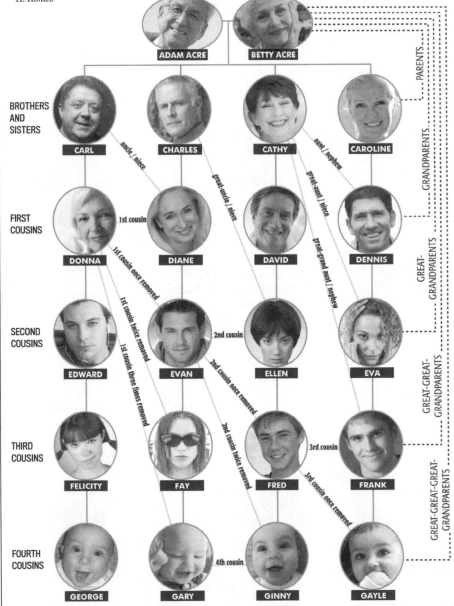